EXPLORING SIGNATURE PEDAGOGIES

EXPLORING SIGNATURE PEDAGOGIES

Approaches to Teaching Disciplinary Habits of Mind

Edited by
Regan A. R. Gurung, Nancy L. Chick, and Aeron Haynie

Foreword by
Anthony A. Ciccone

STERLING, VIRGINIA

Published by Stylus Publishing, LLC
22883 Quicksilver Drive
Sterling, Virginia 20166-2102

Library of Congress Cataloging-in-Publication-Data
Exploring signature pedagogies : approaches to teaching disciplinary habits of mind / edited by Regan A. R. Gurung, Nancy L. Chick, and Aeron Haynie ; foreward by Tony Ciccone. — 1st ed.
p. cm.
Includes bibliographical references and index.
ISBN 978-1-57922-306-9 (cloth : alk. paper) — ISBN 978-1-57922-307-6 (pbk. : alk. paper)
1. College teaching. 2. Universities and colleges—Curricula. 3. Interdisciplinary approach in education. I. Gurung, Regan A. R. II. Chick, Nancy L., 1968- III. Haynie, Aeron, 1964-
LB2331.E95 2009 378.1'25—dc22

2008031384

13-digit ISBN: 978-1-57922-306-9 (cloth)
13-digit ISBN: 978-1-57922-307-6 (paper)

Printed in the United States of America

All first editions printed on acid free paper that meets the American National Standards Institute Z39-48 Standard.

First Edition, 2009

10 9 8 7 6 5 4 3 2 1

DEDICATION

To the University of Wisconsin System's Office of Professional and Instructional Development for its work in developing and supporting outstanding teacher-scholars. The authors would like to express their particular appreciation for Lisa Kornetsky, Donna Silver, Tony Ciccone, and Jane Ewens.

CONTENTS

SECTION FOUR—NATURAL SCIENCES AND MATHEMATICS

ACKNOWLEDGMENTS

We extend our deepest gratitude to Lisa Kornetsky, Donna Silver, and their staff at the University of Wisconsin System's Office of Professional and Instructional Development (OPID) for working tirelessly to foster faculty development across the UW System and across the nation (as part of the Carnegie Leadership Cluster). We all thank Jane Ewens and Tony Ciccone for their advice and leadership as directors of the UW System Wisconsin Teaching Fellows and Scholars Programs (respectively), especially because the three editors of this book met when they were Wisconsin Teaching Fellows together. We would also like to thank the scholars who contributed their works to this text and who put up with our demanding schedule and editorial suggestions. Without their experience as educators, their passion for the topics, and their perseverance through the editorial and publishing process, we would not have this wonderful product to offer teachers across the disciplines. Special thanks go to John von Knorring, President and Publisher of Stylus Publishing, and his staff for making this project a reality, and to our spouses, families, and friends for helping us keep our sanity. They mostly succeeded.

FOREWORD

I first became aware of teaching as intellectual work in 1970. As one of 10 newly hired graduate teaching assistants in French at the State University of New York at Buffalo, I listened intently as the first-year course coordinator explained the mysterious workings of the textbook and the theory behind its methodology. The *practice,* however, seemed relatively straightforward—a variety of focused activities to be followed in a specific order, at a lively pace, with individual and choral response, and, we were told, with minimal grammatical explanation. And make sure you don't fall behind the other sections. And so, morning after morning, we dutifully marched students through the language of Molière and Voltaire, one irregular verb at a time. I was to learn later that we were using what was at the time, for better or worse, the *signature pedagogy* of beginning language instruction—that is, a pedagogy that reflected the belief that language could be acquired through focused attention to, and oral and written imitation of, patterns derived from structural linguistics, plus a behaviorist approach to mastery learning.

What a difference in the afternoon graduate seminars! There some of the best literary critical minds challenged us to understand and apply theories that they themselves were in the process of constructing. We needed to choose a focus for the semester within the course content in the first two weeks and were expected to present our work in progress at any time. Moreover, these presentations had to advance everyone's understanding of the important questions raised in the course. Similarly, we were expected to take advantage of the parts of the curriculum that would advance our own research, and ultimately lead us to and through the dissertation. If the beginning language class was a forced march through linguistic forms, the graduate seminar was more like a creative dance. Although both involved watching and listening to models, the former sought mastery through repetition whereas the latter encouraged understanding through elaboration. The *signature pedagogy* of my graduate apprenticeship in French literature and criticism—seminars, comprehensive exams, dissertation, and defense—bore little apparent resemblance to first-year language teaching.

Five years later, at the University of Wisconsin–Milwaukee, I found myself teaching second-year French and a graduate seminar on Molière in the same semester. I remember quite clearly wondering how these two teaching and learning experiences could possibly be on the same continuum. Did drill and practice of linguistic forms ultimately lead in some tortuous (and torturous) way to an understanding of 17th-century French literature? Put another way, was the study of French merely the completion of a *major,* that is, the collection of credit-bearing experiences, or the learning of a *discipline,* that is, a coherent set of knowledge, skills, and dispositions that help us make sense of, and participate meaningfully in, the human experience?

Although this rumination did not help me plan the next class session, it did force me to ask the larger questions that the authors of this much anticipated volume begin to answer: What does our pedagogy reveal, intentionally or otherwise, about the habits of head, hand, and heart we purport to foster through our disciplines? Is there, or should there be, a consistent connection between the way a discipline creates or discovers new knowledge and the way it apprentices new learners? Do the surface differences of a discipline's pedagogy, which are so clearly evident when we look at how the discipline is taught at various levels, resolve themselves at a deeper level into a set of guiding principles and assumptions?

Lee Shulman defines signature pedagogies as "the types of teaching that organize the fundamental ways in which future practitioners are educated for their new professions" (p. 52). In taking up his challenge to look for homologous signatures in disciplines outside the professions, Gurung, Chick, and Haynie have opened up fruitful paths of inquiry. The first question may be the most important one because it raises the crucial issue for the nonprofessional fields: If signature pedagogies are the fundamental ways in which future practitioners are educated for their new professions, for what "profession" do undergraduate majors in humanities, fine arts, social science, and natural science prepare students? If the chemistry student is not likely to become a practicing chemist, the history student an historian, the English major a literary critic, or the art student a practicing artist (the case may be less clear in the fine arts), what are we preparing students to "profess" in these fields? How do students educated in these broad areas think and act in the world? What do they value and how do they make that determination? Are there significant, *signature* differences between fields? These questions get to the heart of the undergraduate experience in higher education.

In thinking about signature pedagogies outside the professional fields, then, the authors confront the ultimate learning questions of their disciplines in a much broader way than is customary. Posing questions about ultimate outcomes and purposes necessarily moves all of us beyond what to cover in individual courses, to the scope and sequence of the entire curriculum. We begin to ask and answer an essential teaching question: What differences will this set of knowledge, skills, and dispositions make in the lives of our students?

If we are fortunate enough to get this far, and this book will certainly move us in the right direction, we are ready for the next important teaching question: What are the ways in which my discipline seeks to communicate and impart this set of knowledge, skills, and dispositions to its learners? Here the authors perform a much-needed service by cataloging (and ultimately critiquing) the conventional or generic ways their disciplines have been taught. Using their insights into the habits of mind that distinguish each discipline, each author carefully explains how his or her discipline's usual pedagogy may be at odds with, or at least unsupportive of, these desired habits. These pedagogies may be widespread within the discipline, but they are not for that reason *signature* in any way. In some cases, they are not unique; the lecture/discussion format is ubiquitous at large institutions no matter what the discipline. In other cases, they seem merely expedient; the "cookbook" lab comes to mind. In their review, the authors refuse to mistake the pedagogies of expediency or convenience for the signature pedagogy of the discipline, even where little else seems to meet the definition.

The authors make their unique contribution to signature pedagogies, however, when they examine the role that the scholarship of teaching and learning can play in the conversation. Signature pedagogies reflect the deep structures of the discipline or profession. They represent core values and thus evolve slowly and only when significant changes require it. Shulman points to changes in the signature pedagogy of the medical profession brought about by changes in objective conditions (fewer patients to "learn on" because of shortened hospital stays) and new technologies for teaching (p. 56). This is as it should be because signature pedagogies exist *because they have proved effective over time.* But in the absence of clear-cut signature pedagogies, as the authors ask here, how can we identify which of the prevailing, often surface-level, pedagogies make the best claim as new or legitimate signatures of the disciplines? Systematic inquiry into the student learning produced by these pedagogies can begin to provide some of the answers. For example, if the production of a fully formed critical reading, as historically associated with the pedagogy of English literature as medical rounds are with medical education, loses its luster in the harsh light of less-than-stellar effects on student learning, perhaps it's time for a change.

As legitimate scholarly inquiry into disciplinary pedagogy and the student learning it leads to, the lens of the scholarship of teaching and learning helps the discipline specialist first *describe* the prevailing practice, then *question* the relationship between practice and desired goals. Similarly, it helps the discipline specialist *describe* the learning actually achieved, then *design and test* pedagogy that may improve student results. Seen in this light, the scholarship of teaching and learning becomes an important bridge between the signature pedagogies of the past (where they exist) and the signature pedagogies of the future.

These authors have clearly shown the value in looking for the signature pedagogies of their disciplines. Nothing uncovers hidden assumptions about desired knowledge, skills, and dispositions better than a careful examination of our most cherished practices. In this sense, the authors inspire specialists in other disciplines to do the same. Furthermore, they invite other colleagues to explore whether relatively new, interdisciplinary fields such as women's studies and global studies have, or should have, a signature pedagogy consistent with their understanding of what it means to "apprentice" in these areas.

Shulman notes that "we can learn a great deal by examining the signature pedagogies of a variety of professions and asking how they might improve teaching and learning in professions in which they are not now signatures" (p. 56). This book supports this claim for the nonprofessional disciplines as well. Reading across these chapters, the discipline specialist encounters arguments for the value of pedagogies that rely on inductive reasoning: in physics, teaching from phenomena to principles; in math, beginning with real-world problems; in history, developing arguments from authentic artifacts; in geography, using personal experience to develop "spatial cognition." The importance of helping students handle complexity and ambiguity is also a consistent theme: in the study of texts, understanding and appreciating multiple meanings; in creative writing, questioning the received definitions of "good writing"; in theater, accepting the value of critique as pedagogy that is simultaneously formative and summative. Finally, by asking themselves what it means to "think like a . . .," the authors lay the foundation for profitable exchange within and between disciplines.

Signature pedagogy is one of those concepts that invite creative and thought-provoking elaboration. In Shulman's sense, signatures are defining characteristics that, when explicated, reveal the deepest beliefs and practices of professional apprenticeship. In another sense, however, when practitioners or discipline specialists use a signature pedagogy, they *sign on* to a tradition. Now, signing on to something can be done in many ways and for many reasons. We can sign on resignedly; "it's always been done this way." We can sign on casually, because we have more important things to think about. Or we can "read the fine print" first, understand deeply, commit to a course of action, and make it our own. This last type of "signing on" is, I believe, more consistent with the Shulman meaning. It is also what these authors have engaged in when they committed to understanding and evaluating prevailing practices and to "practice their signatures" as they lead us toward more effective pedagogies worthy of our own commitment. They have also helped us understand the value of what is gradually becoming the signature practice for investigating student learning—the scholarship of teaching and learning.

Back to the foreign language classroom. The current signature pedagogy of language instruction, what many call the "proficiency-oriented approach," is very different from the earlier structural linguistics/behavioral method. Learners are encouraged to produce personal meaning, to communicate in groups, to formulate sentences they haven't yet heard. This evolution took place because the profession paid attention to the research on second language acquisition, the less-than-stellar results it had been getting, and the changing reasons for studying a language. Systematic inquiry into student learning prompted and guided much of this evolution. Similar attention to research on the understanding of "texts" has brought about concomitant changes in the literature classroom. Learners now confront a wider variety of authentic cultural materials and move beyond surface understanding of the words to the deeper meanings of the human experience that language can express. Is there a signature pedagogy that unifies these learning experiences? Perhaps not yet, but one thread seems common: Language instruction throughout the curriculum must lead learners to understand how meaning is made and expressed in different cultures and how making sense of experience, and expressing that sense, lies at the core of the human experience.

I have had the pleasure of working closely with many of these authors through my involvement with the University of Wisconsin System Teaching Fellows and Scholars Program. Investigating the concept of signature pedagogies, as they have done, enables all of us to ask and begin to answer the important questions about learning in our disciplines, and ultimately about learning itself. Perhaps the desired harmony of purpose, practice, and results in teaching and learning lies in examining further the key signatures they have begun to uncover.

Anthony A. Ciccone

Senior Scholar and Director, Carnegie Academy for the Scholarship of Teaching and Learning

Reference

Shulman, L. (Summer 2005). Signature pedagogies in the professions, *Dædalus, 134,* 52–59.

PREFACE

This book builds on the scholarship of teaching and learning (SoTL) but takes this important work in a new direction: How does each discipline foster deep learning and help students think like disciplinary experts? With contributions from the sciences, humanities, and the arts, this book offers a critical evaluation of how to best foster student learning across the disciplines. The 14 chapters provide a summary of disciplinary SoTL work, examine and analyze traditional disciplinary pedagogies, and identify or propose signature pedagogies for the discipline.

The time is now ripe to reflect thoughtfully on the state of SoTL and, more importantly, to focus future pedagogical research and provide pragmatic ways to apply past research to the classroom across disciplines. This book takes us into the "second wave" of SoTL—a next generation of the movement—and moves beyond highlighting case studies, best practices, and individual scholars or institutions by focusing on the work itself, its methodologies, and its implications for the disciplines. This book presents the framework for a new synthesis that digs deep and aims to catalyze further pedagogical research.

Authors in each chapter in this collection first provide a description of the unique content and characteristic pedagogies in their disciplines. What pedagogies are most often used in the classrooms of the field? They then review and evaluate the pedagogical research related to their discipline, paying special attention to how faculty collect evidence of effective teaching and learning and highlighting what future pedagogical research is needed. What does the pedagogical literature of the discipline suggest are the optimal ways to teach material in that field—and verify that learning? Finally, authors assess how the common pedagogies within their disciplines reflect and engage students in the ways of knowing, the habits of mind, and the values shared by experts in the field. These chapters build on the works of Shulman (2005) and his paradigm shift to thinking about signature pedagogies in the academic disciplines, Lendol Calder on "historical mindedness" (2006), Huber and Morreale (2002) on disciplinary styles in SoTL, and Pace and Middendorf (2004) on the shift from generic to disciplinary learning, as well as others who have done significant work within their disciplines—on their disciplines. Chapters are not so much about the evolution of discourse *about* teaching and learning or how the disciplines influence the *design* of disciplinary-specific SoTL (cf. Huber & Morreale, 2002); instead they focus on how a discipline is *being taught* and what students *are learning* about the discipline.

This book takes a critical look at how instructors in different disciplines teach in ways that reflect how disciplinary practitioners think, know, and value. Shulman (2005) has pointed out that many of the professions have undertaken such "signature pedagogies" in their attempts to train future professionals, but many academic disciplines haven't yet explored how their pedagogies reflect their disciplinary perspectives—or don't. This book fills this void by offering contributions by SoTL scholars from the humanities, fine arts, social sciences, and mathematics and natural sciences who begin this exploration. They review the SoTL work from their disciplines, describe and evaluate the generic pedagogies in their field, and articulate elements of a signature pedagogy that will both improve teaching and learning *and* provide an agenda for future pedagogical research in the disciplines.

Correspondingly, this book is aimed both at faculty members who are interested in improving their own teaching and their students' learning, and at pedagogical researchers. We trust the book will provide readers with a template against which to measure their own pedagogies and provide a basis for comparison and improvement. By taking a closer, more systematic look at the pedagogies used within the disciplines and their impacts on student learning, our book moves away from generic teaching tips and classroom activities and toward the habits of mind within the disciplines themselves.

Readers will benefit not only from the chapters most relevant to their disciplines, however. As faculty members consider how their courses fit into the broader curriculum and relate to the other disciplines (a curricular perspective encouraged in Harvard's *General Education in a Free Society* in 1945 and even more strongly today by the American Association of Colleges and Universities [AAC&U]), it's useful to understand the "values, knowledge, and manner of thinking" of the other disciplines. Such an awareness allows faculty to more deliberately design learning activities and goals not only within the discipline but also within the broader objectives of liberal education. It also facilitates the cross-disciplinary understandings needed in developing the first-year seminars and other interdisciplinary projects that make up over half of the general education reforms of the last 13 years (Ratcliff, Johnson, La Nasa, & Gaff, 2001).

The editors and most of the authors of this volume are alumni of the University of Wisconsin System's Wisconsin Teaching Fellows or Scholars Programs. The only exception is when a Fellow recruited a colleague in the visual arts for the collaborative fine arts chapter, as well as the creative writing author, a campus-based Teaching Fellow whom the editors enlisted to make sure the book had sufficient consideration of the fine arts. Awarded the prestigious 2005 TIAA-CREF Theodore M. Hesburgh Certificate of Excellence, the Wisconsin Teaching Fellows (WTF) and Teaching Scholars (WTS) Programs have been in existence for over 20 years and are designed for pre-tenured faculty and staff (WTF) and mid- to late-career faculty and academic staff (WTS). One Scholar and one Fellow are selected each year from each of the UW System's 14 campuses and Extension. Throughout the program year, each Fellow designs a SoTL project aimed at understanding the effects of a "best practice" on student learning. Each Scholar—coming to the program with knowledge of and interest in SoTL, demonstrated success in implementing and disseminating teaching and learning innovations, and a record of campus leadership on issues of teaching and learning—undertakes a scholarly teaching project aimed at advancing the understanding of what works to improve student learning and of how SoTL work can be done most effectively. As an essential part of this process, Teaching Scholars are expected to serve as leaders and mentors in UW System SoTL work. At the end of the program year, Teaching Scholars and Fellows are expected to disseminate the results of their project in a public forum.

References

Calder, L. (2006). Uncoverage: Toward a signature pedagogy for the history survey. *Journal of American History 92,* 1358–1370.

Huber, M. T., & Morreale, S. (2002). *Disciplinary styles in the scholarship of teaching and learning.* Washington, DC: American Association for Higher Education and The Carnegie Foundation for the Advancement of Teaching.

Pace, D., & Middendorf, J. (2004). *Decoding the disciplines: Helping students learn disciplinary ways of thinking.* San Francisco: Jossey-Bass.

Ratcliff, J. L., Johnson, D. K., La Nasa, S. M., & Gaff, J. G. (2001). *The status of general education in the year 2000: Summary of a national survey.* Washington, DC: Association of American Colleges & Universities.

Shulman, L. S. (Summer 2005). Signature pedagogies in the professions. *Dædalus 134,* 52–59.

1

FROM GENERIC TO SIGNATURE PEDAGOGIES

Teaching Disciplinary Understandings

Nancy L. Chick, Aeron Haynie, and Regan A. R. Gurung

What are the best ways to teach students? This broad question has a number of answers ranging from "It depends" to "Anything involving active learning pedagogies," and beyond. Many of us who teach believe we do a wonderful job (and many of us assuredly do), but how we come to that conclusion varies. Some of us look at our students' high grades, some of us enjoy sky-high student evaluations, and still others just intuitively feel that our students are learning. Although many faculty find these indicators sufficient to establish teaching excellence, others look for answers in books on teaching (Brookfield, 2006; McKeachie & Svinicki, 2006; Palmer, 1998; Weimer, 2002) years of pedagogical research, the scholarship of teaching and learning (SoTL), or that are to be found in a wide variety of books on teaching (Brookfield, 2006; McKeachie & Svinicki, 2006; Palmer, 1998; Weimer, 2002).

What Does It Mean to Have Learned?

In addition to traditional questions about teaching—such as the generic, teacher-centered "What are the best ways to teach students?"—SoTL asks more content- and learning-centered questions such as "What are we teaching, and what are our students learning?" SoTL has been asking these questions for 20 years, finding its answers not through anecdotal evidence, student evaluations, or teaching awards but through systematically designed, peer-reviewed projects. Ultimately, to fulfill its goal of building a body of knowledge, SoTL projects are made public in a variety of forms, ranging from objective and measurable forms of evaluation to qualitative and quantitative studies (Weimer, 2006). Although much pedagogical research has focused on broadly applicable strategies such as active learning, increasing engagement in large classes, and the use of discussion (e.g., Gurung & Schwartz, 2009; Huba & Freed, 2000; Prince, 2004) that can be used across disciplines, much of this research is published in journals for particular disciplines (e.g., *Journal of Chemical Education, College English, Teaching Philosophy, The Journal of American History Journal of Economic Education*) and is read primarily by teachers within those disciplines (Weimer, 2008). SoTL as a formal field of study in its own right has primarily appeared in interdisciplinary venues (e.g., the journals *MountainRise, IJ-SoTL, inventio, The Journal of Excellence in College Teaching*; books from Jossey-Bass and Stylus; and conferences sponsored by individual campuses, the Carnegie Foundation for the Advancement of Teaching, and the International Society for the Scholarship of Teaching and Learning), and it is also making inroads into disciplinary outlets (e.g., *Teaching of Psychology).* Together these resources have given rise to a large body of best practices, wisdom, and guiding principles for effective teaching that lead to greater student learning.

Signature Pedagogies

Implicitly or explicitly, faculty want students to learn more than basic content; we want them to understand and practice disciplinary ways of thinking or habits of mind. But do the individual disciplines have unique pedagogies that foster these ways of thinking? Do psychologists teach in ways to make their students more likely to think like psychologists? Does the English professor teach her students to read literary texts as literary scholars do? Does the physicist employ strategies to ensure her student understands the world as physicists do? Similar questions have been directly asked of (and mostly answered in) the professional programs (Shulman, Summer 2005). This is not surprising. Business programs produce graduates who directly enter the world of business. Law programs and nursing programs likewise graduate and train lawyers and nurses who need explicit skills to wage courtroom battles and to save lives. In the nonprofessional programs, however, shaping pedagogies and practices that reflect the way experts in the discipline perform is not so pressing. Few of the thousands of English majors will end up as literary scholars. Even fewer history majors are employed as historians. As a result, disciplines in the liberal arts and sciences (LAS) pride themselves in training their students to be critical thinkers, strong writers, and adept in quantitative skills, essential, but generic skills that aren't unique to specific disciplines. Most LAS disciplines have core content areas they expect their students to master in addition to the aforementioned skills, so the primary focus of LAS programs is to convey such content and skills.

Yet, educating students to practice the intellectual moves and values of experts in the field has been a subtext of most disciplinary learning outcomes. Some faculty and departments are explicit about teaching their students to think more like disciplinary experts, whereas others focus on disciplinary content and related skills, with expert thinking an implicit goal. However, this goal requires specific pedagogical techniques that may be unique to that discipline—what is called a signature pedagogy. But, educators don't often systematically investigate whether "students have mastered each of the ways of thinking that are essential to a particular discipline" (Pace & Middendorf, 2004, p. 4). This assessment of disciplinary learning is a main mission of SoTL. By directly studying not only whether students are learning (i.e., the goal of standard SoTL), but also whether their learning reflects the ways of thinking and doing of disciplinary experts (i.e., a signature pedagogy), teachers and pedagogical researchers have new questions to answer.

The chapters in this book similarly assume that questions about good teaching extend beyond the generic. Even apart from content, disciplines vary in their ways of thinking, knowing, and doing, as well as in what they value (Huber & Hutchings, 2005; Wineburg, 2003). What it means to think, create, demonstrate, know, and evaluate in the biology classroom is different from the meaning of these activities in the creative writing classroom. Because of the differences in what we want students to learn, the pedagogies used to achieve that deep understanding of a discipline vary—or should. Such is the claim of signature pedagogies, which Shulman (2005, February) described as "elements of instruction and of socialization" that teach disciplinary novices "to think, to perform, and to act with integrity" to the discipline (Summer 2005, p. 52). As these pedagogies encourage students "to do, think, and value what practitioners in the field are doing, thinking, and valuing", they "disclose important information about the personality of a disciplinary field—its values, knowledge, and manner of thinking—almost, perhaps, its total world view" (Calder, 2006). Signature pedagogies invoke the core characteristics of a discipline to help students think like a biologist, a creative writer, or a sociologist, rather than simply expecting them to passively accept analysis or findings of an expert who already thinks like a biologist, a creative writer, or a sociologist.

The concept of signature pedagogies builds on widely accepted assumptions about what leads to significant learning. For example, Wiggins and McTighe (2005) and Fink (2003) propose a "backwards design" in which educators first identify significant and lasting learning goals, then design assessments by which students demonstrate evidence of this learning, and finally generate learning activities that guide students to develop and demonstrate this learning. This principle suggests that effective teaching results from core values and principles of our courses and of our disciplines, rather than from generic views of learning. In fact, Pace and Middendorf's *Decoding the Disciplines: Helping Students Learn Disciplinary Ways of Thinking* (2004) asserts that higher-level thinking is inhibited by such generic conceptions and lays the groundwork for questions about the central values, habits, and ways of thinking within their disciplines.

In addition to these disciplinary questions encouraged by Pace and Middendorf, signature pedagogies require faculty to look critically at the pedagogical research and ask: How well have conventional methods helped students develop deep, disciplinary understandings? What pedagogies would be more effective in achieving this goal? What roles have disciplinary experts and the disciplinary modes of inquiry played in this conversation (Huber & Morreale, 2002)? Ultimately, formulating a signature pedagogy for one's discipline not only guides personal pedagogical decisions but also provides a clear agenda for future SoTL.

As Shulman has illustrated in his work on signature pedagogy, some professions have practiced signature pedagogies for years: clinical rounds in medicine, on-the-spot questioning in law school, and design studios in engineering. However, it's been over 100 years since concerns for teaching disciplinary ways of knowing and doing have been part of broad conversations in higher education. In the late 19th century, many disciplines shifted away from recitations in which students were given the results of others' disciplinary work toward doing this work themselves. Scientists instituted laboratory teaching, so that students would practice thinking like scientists, and some social science classrooms integrated seminars focused on their own inquiry-based thinking (Huber & Hutchings, 2005). In the intervening century, which has seen many changes in higher education, this attention to discipline-specific pedagogy has been largely dormant. In fact, as indicated in the title of Shulman's 2004 ISSOTL Conference plenary "In Search of Signature Pedagogies" (2004), such pedagogies have been explicitly discussed and formulated in only a handful of academic disciplines (e.g., history, political science), most of which were responses to Shulman's (Summer 2005) call.

This book presents essays that examine what is known about disciplinary pedagogies—generic and signature—in the liberal arts and sciences. Each of the 14 chapters reviews the traditional ways of teaching within the discipline, analyzes what those pedagogies teach students about the discipline, reviews the pedagogical research underlying these practices, sketches out potential signature pedagogies that more effectively convey disciplinary ways of thinking and doing, and establishes an agenda for future research.

The Growth of the Scholarship of Teaching and Learning

Most of the debates about higher education in the United States have focused on the curriculum, or what is taught. Only in recent decades has *how* it's taught been the subject of scholarly inquiry, analysis, and evaluation (Huber & Hutchings, 2005). The SoTL movement has been documenting what works best in the classroom and what does not. Clearly, educators are beginning to notice the fruits of SoTL's labors, and a growing number of publications within the academy have drawn attention to the importance of taking a close look at how we teach and how students learn. Universities, colleges, and high schools nationwide are beginning not only to recognize and value educators who are interested in SoTL but also to require that teaching and learning be studied (O'Meara & Rice, 2005). As emphasized by both Seldin (2003) and Hatch (2006), faculty are being held accountable for the effectiveness of their teaching, and in turn are starting to engage in intellectual exchanges not only about their research agendas but also about how they teach their students. Huber and Hutchings (2005) call this type of intellectual exchange a "teaching commons." Unfortunately, the call for accountability can be interpreted (and used) as another attack on higher education, though a more optimistic appraisal is to see that it also represents an opportunity for faculty to take charge of the process. Put simply, the SoTL movement encourages educators to take a closer look at how they teach and how their students learn, to use the same methodologies that they would use for formal investigations in their disciplines, and to hold their research to the same standards, most notably peer review. Boyer's (1990) exploration of the diverse nature of scholarship raised awareness of pedagogical research, although SoTL in one form or the other (e.g., action research, teacher research) has been taking place from the beginnings of formal education (Rice, 2005). In the late 1980s, colleges and universities began to look more closely at faculty priorities; as a result assessment, active learning, cost containment, and accountability became buzzwords (Edgerton, 2005). More than just politically motivated fads, however, these initiatives invite faculty to give their teaching the same kind of careful, rigorous attention as their research.

Boyer's (1990) somewhat incendiary *Scholarship Reconsidered* used the phrase "scholarship of teaching" and was the first loud voice to suggest that "scholarship" be expanded to include the work done on teaching and learning. The results of his publication are staggering. For example, shortly after its publication, 62% of chief academic officers in colleges reported that *Scholarship Reconsidered* had influenced decisions regarding faculty reward (Glassick, Huber, & Maeroff, 1997). Other national studies confirmed the impact of Boyer's report on the reform of the faculty reward system and, in particular, on the recognition of scholarship on teaching (e.g., Braxton, Luckey, & Holland, 2002; Gurung, Kerns, Ansburg, Alexander, & Johnson, 2008). More recently, the American Association for Higher Education (now defunct), responding to the impetus of its annual Forum on Faculty Roles and Rewards conferences, launched a two-year project that surveyed chief academic officers to identify campus-wide best practices for encouraging the scholarship of teaching. The result, *Faculty Priorities Reconsidered: Rewarding Multiple Forms of Scholarship,* nicely illustrates how the scholarship of teaching and pedagogical research is being fostered nationwide (O'Meara & Rice, 2005).

It has been nearly 20 years since *Scholarship Reconsidered* was published, and today SoTL is a well-known and understood concept that is the driving principle behind such national and international organizations as the International Alliance for Teaching Scholars (IATS) and the International Society for the Scholarship of Teaching and Learning (ISSOTL). The scholarship of teaching and learning, by which faculty continuously evaluate the quality of their teaching and its effect on student learning, is now one of the most energizing areas of research in the field of higher education. Galvanized by the efforts of the Carnegie Academy for the Scholarship of Teaching and Learning (CASTL; cf. Shulman, Hutchings, Huber), the Lilly Foundation (cf. Richlin and the Preparing Future Faculty program), the Visible Knowledge Project, and the Peer Review of Teaching Project, the banner of SoTL has been taken up by academics from diverse fields.

A variety of methodologies has emerged from the disciplinary diversity of SoTL practioners, but contrary to one of the biggest misconceptions about SoTL, research does not have to be quantitative to be valid: both qualitative and quantitative approaches are valuable. This misconception has unfortunately turned away many humanities and fine arts educators, giving the false impression that only social scientists can do SoTL. In fact, some of the strongest advocates of SoTL have come from outside the social sciences (e.g., Bass, Hutchings). The chapters in this volume that represent practices in the humanities and fine arts are testimony to the validity and richness of non-quantitative approaches. These disciplines have too long been excluded (or at least have understandably felt excluded) from SoTL because of this bias.

Practicing Our Signatures

Many SoTL books present case studies that provide valuable illustrations of how faculty from a variety of disciplines modified their pedagogical approaches to fit their course goals and student learning goals. Hutchings's *Opening Lines* (2000), for example, poses the key questions to be asked in SoTL and offers case studies in which faculty from different disciplines answer the key questions. Huber and Morreale's *Disciplinary Styles in the Scholarship of Teaching and Learning* (2002) follows a stage-setting first chapter with subsequent chapters answering questions raised in the first. This format is the norm in most SoTL books. We take a somewhat different approach: chapters in this book throw a wide net over their entire disciplines. Authors do not focus on their classes, their universities, or their students, but instead on their disciplines as a whole, and how they have engaged with issues of teaching and learning.

The chapters that follow represent a rich variety of disciplines in the humanities, the fine arts, the social sciences, and the natural sciences. Each chapter explains the habits of mind that distinguish the discipline, presents the traditional or generic ways of teaching in the discipline, considers what they teach students about the discipline, and concludes by thoughtfully articulating a signature pedagogy that teaches students the distinctive practices and values of that discipline. Each chapter also documents the discipline's varying levels of engagement with SoTL. Some disciplines, such as biology and psychology, have a long tradition of SoTL, while others, like the fine arts, are still in the early stages. In addition to providing an overview of the issues relating to the reader's own discipline, each chapter offers a glimpse into the ways that other disciplines think, behave, and train potential experts.

The first disciplinary chapter builds on Calder's (2006) landmark article, which challenges the conventional "coverage" model of teaching history and urges historians to develop a consensus on what they do, suggesting the "participation in an evidence-based argumentative discourse about the human past" as a starting point. Building on this premise, Voelker and Sipress in chapter 2 delineate the gap between the type of historical work that historians engage in and usual methods of teaching lower-level surveys. It is the first of many in this book that illustrate the relevance of signature pedagogies to general education or introductory courses populated by majors and non-majors alike. Voelker and Sipress an argument found in many of these chapters, namely that introductory courses should teach non-majors the most important habits of the disciplines, not just a collection of facts.

Chapter 3 continues the conversation about how we expose students—most of whom will not become disciplinary professionals—to the defining values of the humanities. Chick draws extensively on recent work in literary studies to describe her discipline's default pedagogy, in which the professor presents fully formed readings of a literary work, noting this strategy's failure to teach students how to develop their own literary readings. Chick argues that a signature pedagogy for literature studies should instead 'unpack the discipline' by engaging students in the field's complex conversations about literary texts and the discipline itself and ask such questions as how do we read literature, engage contradictory meanings within a text, and argue for the importance of literature within society?

Chapter 4 documents the lack of scholarship on teaching creative writing and offers insights into why this field—and others in the fine arts—have resisted full SoTL involvement. Meacham describes the dominant ways of teaching creative writing, including teaching students to read as writers and participation in writers' workshops. In evaluating these pedagogies, Meacham calls for a "pedagogy of reflection" in which instructors make the processes of creative writing (composing, revising, responding to criticism, and publishing) more transparent. Similarly to Chick's call to teach the complex questions within and about literary studies, Meacham encourages creative writing teachers to let students in on the disciplinary question of what shapes standards of greatness and to open up their definition of "good writing" to include other, less traditionally valued genres.

Although each chapter's aim is to describe the unique methodologies and habits of a particular discipline, issues and even exercises sometimes overlap, especially in broad disciplinary groups. Meacham's analysis of the creative writing workshop and Kornetsky and Klebesadel's discussion of critique as a central method in both performing and visual arts pedagogy is one such connection. Just as Meacham cautions about the potential for power imbalance in writing workshops, Kornetsky and Klebesadel (chapter 6) explain how fine arts critiques are often teacher-centered and can demoralize students who are personally invested in their acting or art. These authors call for more systematic investigations of how critique produces disciplinary learning and values, and how it could be improved.

Chapter 5 demonstrates that a signature pedagogy may emerge from its disciplinary history. Don, Garvey, and Sadeghpour reach far back in the study of music to describe the tensions between the traditional European conservatory model and expectations of American students, who often view music theory as irrelevant to their interests. Through a detailed review of the SoTL literature in music theory and performance, the authors propose a pedagogy that integrates these two areas of study, focuses less on content coverage, allows more creativity in the classroom, and expands the canon beyond classical European composers.

Although the social sciences generally have a stronger history of engagement with SoTL than the arts, chapter 7 on geography illustrates that not all disciplines within the social sciences have applied their field's emphasis on research to the subject of teaching. In this chapter, Komoto identifies "spatial cognition" as a key way of thinking in geography and examines how a variety of teaching methods, such as using the Internet, journal writing, role playing, and incorporating students' personal experiences, might improve students' development of this habit.

Searching for signature pedagogies can raise larger questions about what constitutes a discipline. For example, according to Bartell and Vespia in chapter 8, the field of human development is interdisciplinary in nature, has no unifying professional organization, and has no one pedagogical model. The authors focus on six representative human development programs across the country, looking at how each attempts to teach students within the major, and they propose a developmental approach to teaching undergraduates.

In chapter 9, Peden and Wilson observe that the 2007 guidelines for learning outcomes in psychology suggest how to think like a psychologist, but do not articulate how to teach it. Noting that the lecture is still the default mode of instruction, they propose that instructors integrate critical-thinking skills with content material. Similarly to Komoto's chapter on geography, these authors stress the importance of connecting skills and ideas, something, they argue, that traditional lecture courses do not achieve.

Among the questions these chapters consider is whether and how introductory courses should engage students in the deep thinking of their discipline. A signature pedagogy's commitment to what it means to think like a disciplinary practitioner answers Shulman's call for professionalizing teaching, and fulfills the vision of teaching as a professional activity in which the classroom is a site where apprentices learn the ways of the profession. While some work on signature pedagogies has focused on doctorate programs that directly train disciplinary practitioners (Golde, 2007), the chapters in this book argue that starting with introductory courses is key. In such courses, the goal is often to cover enough material to introduce a discipline's key facts, concepts, texts, and theories. This approach may gloss over the discipline itself, assuming students will "get it" along the way or "connect the dots and see the larger figures that emerge from the units of our curriculum" (Bernstein, Marx, & Bender, 2005, p. 38). Several chapters in this volume argue instead that introductory courses should be intentional and explicit about their disciplinarity to help students correct misconceptions about the field, make more informed decisions about their majors, and situate each course within the wider contexts of the liberal arts and sciences.

In proposing a signature pedagogy for introductory sociology courses, Fujieda examines research that suggests that these courses often perpetuate misconceptions about sociology. Perhaps even more disturbing, commonly used teaching methods in these courses may contradict the discipline's goals of promoting diversity and social justice by rewarding students who are already equipped to do well and penalizing less privileged students. This research supports studies in other disciplines (e.g., biology, mathematics) that show how traditional pedagogies can disenfranchise members of underrepresented groups, such as women and minority students. Making the key assumptions and practices of our disciplines more transparent can open up opportunities for members of underrepresented groups who may not automatically see themselves as future practitioners. Fujieda proposes a signature pedagogy that integrates experiential learning and collaborative teaching while also honoring students' nonacademic ways of knowing.

The chapter on agricultural science (chapter 11) and the chapter on computer science (chapter 13) address the need to provide students with learning experiences that more authentically mirror the experiences of practitioners, especially as those experiences have changed over time. Sharing the music chapter's historical perspective, Wattiaux traces the educational roots of the agricultural sciences from early hands-on learning to a more lecture-based dispensing of scientific facts. He argues that the complex skills needed to negotiate modern agriculture are best achieved through a combination of scientific knowledge and hands-on, experiential learning and proposes capstone experiences that combine both. Similarly, Christie's chapter on computer science pedagogy argues for classes that more accurately mirror the collaborative, problem-solving workplace. She moreover focuses on the discrepancy between introductory courses that teach programming as an individual effort and upper-level courses that more appropriately train students in "object-oriented" tasks.

One of the disciplines with the strongest histories of SoTL is biology. In chapter 12, Bauer-Dantoin highlights how biologists have come to use the same rigorous scientific method in examining teaching and learning that they use in their research. She traces the development of "scientific teaching" that facilitates collaborative, experimental, evidence-based learning with open-ended inquiry labs as a central component. Lattery (chapter 15) offers a similar critique of "cookbook" labs that fail to develop students' conceptual understanding of physics. He cites Sokoloff's (Sokoloff & Thornton,1997) development of "real-time physics" labs that allow students to move from phenomena to principles, thus better training them to think inductively. This focus on inductive learning is echoed in Ernie, LeDocq, Serros, and Tong's chapter on teaching mathematics (chapter 14). They focus on popular misconceptions about math promoted by traditional, deductive approaches to learning. They note that traditional pedagogy does not encourage conceptual reasoning but instead fosters students' beliefs that math problems are unrelated to their lives and can be solved quickly by working alone to memorize a set of formulas.

As these chapters illustrate, signature pedagogies aren't based on extreme assumptions that the ways of thinking in one discipline are inapplicable to others. Indeed, reading the book as a whole should ease concerns that students' increased abilities to think disciplinarily will narrow their thinking abilities and habits of mind (see Nelson [1999] and Voelker & Sipress, this volume) or will defeat the broadening goals of the liberal arts and sciences. On the contrary, when students' varied undergraduate classes are taught with explicit attention to disciplinarity, they gain a "metadisciplinary awareness" that empowers them to see beyond discipline-specific or even course-specific silos neatly contained within different classrooms, different intellectual preferences, and different languages (Nowacek, 2007). As students gradually and metacognitively recognize the different yet overlapping ways of thinking, knowing, and doing within their different courses, they begin to see a conversation among their courses, allowing them to situate themselves within that conversation and shift from one perspective to another.

This metadisciplinary awareness is also valuable to faculty who teach in liberal arts and sciences institutions. This book will help them orient themselves within the different disciplines just down the hall or a few buildings over and facilitate the cross-pollinating conversations essential to the liberal arts and sciences. Being aware of the best pedagogical practices from the SoTL literature across the disciplines will help faculty better examine and assess their own teaching. In the process of editing this volume, each of us has gained valuable insights about our own pedagogical styles from learning more about the pedagogical practices of other disciplines—an experience that will be shared by readers who venture into disciplinary chapters beyond their own. Even wandering into chapters about disciplines similar to one's own can be revealing. For example, biology, psychology, and physics are all disciplines that pride themselves on using the scientific method. Whereas similar techniques are often used to train students to use the scientific method, there are also many differences in the way techniques are used and tips that can be borrowed and traded across disciplinary lines. There are major pragmatic benefits to be gained from crossing disciplinary lines. Seeing how different disciplines foster their habits of mind may give readers ideas for doing so in their own discipline. Reflecting on whether one's own teaching or the disciplinary application of SoTL helps students develop the characteristic skills used by experts in one's field provides a healthy challenge—one we hope that readers of our book will take up.

There are other challenges that these chapters raise for the educator in us all, providing a rich and fertile agenda for future scholarship on teaching and learning. We have posed but left partially unanswered a number of questions for subsequent exploration. For example, for which courses is the use of signature pedagogies most appropriate: courses designed for majors, upper-level courses, introductory courses, or all? To what extent or in what proportion should general education and introductory courses use traditional pedagogies and signature pedagogies? How do we also ensure that students don't lock themselves into their major's disciplinary habit of mind of and then fail to use interdisciplinary problem-solving strategies that may be more beneficial than disciplinary strategies alone? What might a model for multiple signature pedagogies within a discipline look like, as adapted to the varying levels or purposes of a course (e.g., introductory survey, upper-level elective, capstone, graduate seminar)? These questions and the others raised in the chapters ahead will help foster conversations within these disciplines, as well as disciplines that haven't yet entered the discussion.

In reading this book, faculty will learn more about their own disciplines, even through the chapters seemingly far from their own disciplinary comfort zones. As illustrated by the SoTL programs that brought together the authors of this volume, the ultimate values of such cross-disciplinary conversations about habits of mind, deep understanding, and enduring principles are manifold. Hall's *The Academic Self: An Owner's Manual* (2002) encourages all professors to write and share statements of professional identity, not only as "personal touchstone[s]" (p. 19) but also as ways to communicate with professors in other fields. We hope the chapters in this book have the same effects: not only to deepen the pedagogical and SoTL knowledge within one's own discipline but also to reach out across the disciplines to appreciate the professional differences—and similarities—within the academic community.

References

Bernstein, D. M., Marx, S., & Bender, H. (2005). Disciplining the minds of students. *Change, 37*(2), 36–43.

Braxton, J., Luckey, W., & Holland, P. (2002). *Institutionalizing a broader view of scholarship through Boyer's four domains.* ASHE-ERIC Higher Education Report, *29*(2). San Francisco: Jossey-Bass.

Brookfield, S. D. (2006). *The skillful teacher.* San Francisco: Jossey-Bass.

Boyer, E. L. (1990). *Scholarship reconsidered: Priorities of the professoriate.* San Francisco: Jossey-Bass.

Calder, L. (2006). Uncoverage: Toward a signature pedagogy for the history survey. *Journal of American History.* Retrieved March 7, 2007, from http://www.indiana.edu/~jah/textbooks/2006/calder/index.html

Edgerton, R. (2005). Foreword. In K. O'Meara & R. E. Rice (Eds.), *Faculty priorities reconsidered: Rewarding multiple forms of scholarship* (pp. xi–xvi). San Francisco: Jossey-Bass.

Fink, L. D. (2003). *Creating significant learning experiences: An integrated approach to designing college courses.* San Francisco: Jossey-Bass.

Glassick, C. E., Huber, M. T., & Maeroff, G. I. (1997). *Scholarship assessed: Evaluation of the professoriate.* San Francisco: Jossey-Bass.

Golde, C. M. (2007). Signature pedagogies in doctoral education: Are they adaptable for the preparation of education researchers? *Educational Researcher, 36*(6), 344–351.

Gurung, R. A. R., Kerns, N., Ansburg, P., Alexander, P., & Johnson, D. (2008). The scholarship of teaching and learning in psychology: A national perspective. *Teaching of Psychology.*

Gurung, R. A. R., & Schwartz, B. (2009). *Optimizing teaching and learning: Pedagogical research in practice.* Malden, MA: Blackwell.

Hall, D. H. (2002). *The academic self: An owner's manual.* Columbus: Ohio State University Press.

Hatch, T. (2006). *Into the classroom: Developing the scholarship of teaching and learning.* San Francisco: Jossey-Bass.

Huba, M. E., & Freed, J. E. (2000). *Learner-centered assessment on college campuses.* Needham Heights, MA: Allyn and Bacon.

Huber, M. T., & Hutchings, P. (2005). *The advancement of learning: Building the teaching commons.* San Francisco: Jossey-Bass.

Huber, M. T., & Morreale, S. (2002). *Disciplinary styles in the scholarship of teaching and learning.* Washington, DC: American Association for Higher Education and The Carnegie Foundation for the Advancement of Teaching.

Hutchings, P. (2000). *Opening lines: Approaches to the scholarship of teaching and learning.* Menlo Park, CA: The Carnegie Foundation for the Advancement of Teaching.

McKeachie, W. J., & Svinicki, M. (2006). *McKeachie's teaching tips: Strategies, research, and theory for college and university teachers* (12th ed.). Boston: Houghton Mifflin.

Nelson, C. (1999). On the persistence of unicorns: The trade-off between content and critical thinking revisited. In B. Pescosolido & R. Amizade (Eds.), *The social worlds of higher education: Handbook for teaching in a new century* (pp. 168–184). Boston: Pine Forge Press.

Nowacek, R. S. (2007). Toward a theory of interdisciplinary connections: a classroom study of talk and text. *Research in the Teaching of English, 41*(4), 368–401.

O'Meara, K., & Rice, R. E. (2005). *Faculty priorities reconsidered: Rewarding multiple forms of scholarship.* San Francisco, CA: Jossey-Bass.

Pace, D., & Middendorf, J. (2004). *Decoding the disciplines: Helping students learn disciplinary ways of thinking.* San Francisco: Jossey-Bass.

Palmer, P. J. (1998). *The courage to teach: Exploring the inner landscape of a teacher's life.* San Francisco: Jossey-Bass.

Prince, M. (2004). Does active learning work? A review of the research. *Journal of Engineering Education, 93,* 223–231.

Rice, R. E. (2005). "Scholarship Reconsidered": History and context. In K. O'Meara & R. E. Rice (Eds.) *Faculty priorities reconsidered: Rewarding multiple forms of scholarship* (pp. 17–31). San Francisco: Jossey-Bass.

Seldin, P. (2003). *The teaching portfolio: A practical guide to improved performance and promotion/tenure decisions.* Bolton, MA: Anker.

Shulman, L. S. (2004, October). *In search of signature pedagogies: Learning from lessons of practice.* Paper presented at the meeting of the International Society for the Scholarship of Teaching and Learning, Bloomington, IN.

Shulman, L. S. (2005, February). *The signature pedagogies of the professions of law, medicine, engineering, and the clergy: Potential lessons for the education of teachers.* Paper presented at the Math and Science Partnerships Workshop in "Teacher Education for Effective Teaching and Learning" hosted by the National Research Council's Center for Education, Irvine, CA. Retrieved January 5, 2007, from http://hub.mspnet.org/media/data/Shulman_Signature_Pedagogies.pdf?media_000000001297.pdf

Shulman, L. S. (Summer 2005). Signature pedagogies in the professions. *Dædalus, 134,* 52–59.

Sokoloff, D., & Thornton, R. (1997). Using interactive lecture demonstrations to create an active learning environment. *The Physics Teacher, 35,* 340–347.

Weimer, M. (2002). *Learner-centered teaching.* San Francisco: Jossey-Bass.

Weimer, M. (2006). *Enhancing scholarly work on teaching and learning: Professional literature that makes a difference.* San Francisco, CA: Jossey-Bass.

Weimer, M. (2008, January). Positioning scholarly work on teaching and learning. *International Journal for the Scholarship of Teaching and Learning, 2*(1). Retrieved February 10, 2008, from http://academics.georgiasouthern.edu/ijsotl/issue_v2n1.htm

Wiggins, G., & McTighe, J. (2005). *Understanding by design.* Upper Saddle River, NJ: Pearson.

Wineburg, S. (2003). Teaching the mind good habits. *The Chronicle of Higher Education, 49*(31), p. B20. Retrieved May 16, 2007, from http://chronicle.com/weekly/v49/i31/31b02001.htm

SECTION ONE

HUMANITIES

2

FROM LEARNING HISTORY TO DOING HISTORY

Beyond the Coverage Model

Joel M. Sipress and David J. Voelker

Bain (2000) writes of the odd experience of pursuing a graduate degree in history while simultaneously working as a high school history teacher: "During the evenings, I interacted with others who defined historical study as a way of thinking, a manner of conducting research, and a style of writing." History at the university was "a way of knowing the universe." In the high school, by contrast, "history was a subject students took and teachers taught, differing from other subjects only in the facts covered" (p. 331). This dichotomy between history as a "way of knowing" and history as a subject to be learned is not simply a phenomenon of high schools. On the contrary, it is often reproduced within the university classroom, particularly in introductory-level courses. The scholarly life of the historian is defined by participation in a contested academic discourse in which rival truth claims are subjected to rigorous scrutiny on the basis of evidence drawn from the human past. By contrast, the dominant approach to teaching the history "survey" (as the introductory course is revealingly called) has long been a "coverage" model that emphasizes the transmission of knowledge from professor and textbook to student. In some cases, the knowledge covered is little more than a body of factual information to be reproduced on objective

The authors would like to thank Todd Estes, Ruth Homrighaus, Nikki Mandell, and Brian Steele for their comments on a draft of this essay.

examinations. More often, it also includes a set of themes and concepts to be demonstrated in more analytically sophisticated exercises, such as papers and essay tests. In either case, the coverage model casts the professor in the role of producer of scholarly knowledge, with the students relegated to the status of consumers whose tasks are to absorb and reproduce expert knowledge. In the process, the contested discourse that defines historical scholarship is rendered invisible.

The reduction of students to mere consumers of historical knowledge stands at odds with the proclaimed values of the American historical profession, as well as the basic principles of liberal education. In a series of recent position papers designed to persuade both policy makers and the public at large of the value of the discipline, the Teaching Division of the American Historical Association (AHA) emphasizes the importance of historical scholarship and study to the development of globally aware citizens and leaders. According to this group, historical study trains students in "civic awareness and responsibility by engaging them in issues that transcend their immediate surroundings." The study of history helps students "develop their capacities to synthesize information, weigh evidence, evaluate points of view, and think analytically" (Manning, 2006, p. 24). The mere consumption of authorized historical knowledge, however, is unlikely to cultivate the habits of mind associated with active citizenship and liberal learning. An introductory course with a top priority (and organizing principle) of coverage will prevent most students from recognizing that their professors are not merely dispensing preexisting information, but are actually constructing knowledge by presenting arguments and evidence. Students will thus fail to understand the interpretative nature of historical study, which means that they will not possess the wherewithal or skills to critically evaluate historical claims they encounter in their lives beyond the classroom. If the study of history is to achieve the broader civic functions suggested by the AHA, then historical ways of knowing must be emphasized in the introductory course—the only history course that most undergraduate students will ever take.

Of course, some instructors have long encouraged introductory students to think like historians. Operating as individual practitioners within the confines of particular classrooms, however, these professors have had relatively little impact on the dominant pedagogical discourse within the discipline, particularly at larger universities, where large class sizes may create barriers to discussion and student writing. In recent years, however, a growing body of historians has begun to openly challenge the dominance of the coverage model by suggesting that all students, even at the introductory level, be asked to do history. Are we witnessing the emergence of a pedagogic counter-model—a new signature pedagogy in the making? Perhaps. But before this counter-model can take hold, we must make more explicit (to ourselves and to our students) that to "do history" is, at its most fundamental level, to enter an evidence-based argumentative discourse about the human past.

Traditional Historical Pedagogy

Historians have been talking seriously about teaching for many years—since the professionalization of the discipline more than a century ago, in fact. These discussions, however, have often focused on what to cover and how to cover it rather than on the purpose of the introductory course. Over the past few decades, for instance, historians have spent a great deal of time and energy assimilating postmodernism, multiculturalism, and social history (the study of the lives of ordinary people) into their approaches to teaching introductory history courses. All three of these intellectual movements raised questions about the "master narratives" often used to structure introductory courses on Western civilization, the United States, and even world history. Although few historians have entirely relinquished such master narratives, most deploy these overarching stories more self-consciously and with more sophistication than in earlier days. In part because of these sorts of discussions, instructors have enriched introductory history courses with a diversity of themes and supplementary readings, which can have the effect of encouraging historical thinking.

The traditional coverage model of teaching introductory history nevertheless remains dominant. For example, Kornblith and Lasser (2001) moderated a virtual round table on the U.S. history survey course, asking 11 historians (from public and private institutions, most of them larger universities) to describe how they teach this staple introductory course. The resulting discussion ran about 30 pages when an edited version was published in the *Journal of American History* (*JAH*) as an installment in the journal's annual section entitled "Textbooks and Teaching." The discussion revealed the diverse priorities that historians have for this course. A number of the participants expressed anxiety about student ignorance of basic American history, such as the significance of the post–Civil War Reconstruction period.

This anxiety was often paired with a sense of responsibility to ensure that their students, some of whom will go on to teach high school history, master these basics. After encountering survey data showing the historical ignorance of college seniors, for instance, one participant said that he "began thinking that some way of drilling content, content, content, into students' minds must be pursued" (Kornblith & Lasser, 2001, p. 1412). Although these historians' descriptions of their courses varied, they shared a sense that the survey "should give students a basic literacy in American political history" (p. 1421), with politics being construed broadly, while also raising students' awareness of the diversity of the American experience (in terms of race, class, ethnicity, sex, and so on).

As Calder (2006a) pointed out in his groundbreaking *Journal of American History* essay "Uncoverage: Toward a Signature Pedagogy for the History Survey," one striking aspect of this discussion is the lack of any references to "serious studies of cognition, learning, historical thinking, or course design" (p. 1362). Calder is correct that historians have been slow to pick up on the "cognitive revolution" that had emerged in educational theory by the 1980s. The editors of *Knowing, Teaching, & Learning History* explained this development:

> More than anything else, the cognitive revolution has problematized the 'copy model' of mind, in which learning was thought to be an unquestioned reflex of teaching, something that sprang forth automatically from a well-planned lecture or carefully crafted textbook narrative. (Stearns, Seixas, & Wineburg, 2000, p. 4)

It may be the case that historians' well-intentioned and productive debates about the proper content of introductory historical courses has led us to take student learning more or less for granted.

This problem is suggested by a second conspicuous absence in the round table discussion: the lack of attention to assignments and assessments. Apart from a couple of references to student papers, the question of assessment never came up in the round table. The unspoken assumption seems to have been that students simply learn whatever material they cover. In other words, there was little attention to *how* students make the leap from being exposed to material to actually learning something worthwhile, nor was there any discussion of how instructors would know if students were learning. To be fair, a number of the participants mentioned that they assigned historical monographs to supplement the textbook, but they did not discuss how the students were meant to read these books or what they were supposed to do with them. Likewise, several of the participants mentioned the importance of historical thinking, but none of them attempted to define it, and a couple expressed concern that placing too much emphasis on historical thinking might lead to confusion or to a lack of attention to factual evidence.

The round table participants by no means come across as careless or ineffective teachers, but the traditional mode of teaching reflected in their discussion, although it does encompass some diversity, rests upon a shared assumption that introductory students are learners who will absorb a body of knowledge presented to them through lectures and readings, and who will demonstrate learning by repeating it back to their instructors on exams. This approach seems widespread, but nobody has yet carried out a thorough qualitative survey of how historians teach introductory courses. Those limited surveys that do exist, however, suggest that the majority of instructors supplement the textbook with additional readings, regularly assign primary sources, and give written exams (Cohen, 2005; Townsend, 2005). These data reveal that most history instructors take pains to ensure that students analyze primary sources and are doing more than mere memorizing, but it does not suggest the demise of the coverage model. Neither written exams, nor primary source readings, nor even active learning exercises necessarily depart from the foundational assumption of the traditional model, where students are essentially absorbing and replicating a received body of knowledge. To be sure, introductory history courses today are often rich in content, but most continue to prioritize coverage.

The Emerging Model: Doing History

Over the past decade, the coverage model has been subjected to increasing challenge in the pages of some of the discipline's most influential and widely read professional publications. Central to this challenge is a changing conception of what it means for students to know and learn history. In 2002, Calder published a critique of the coverage model in *Perspectives*, the monthly newsmagazine of the American Historical Association. Calder argued that the coverage approach to historical knowledge "covers up the epistemological linchpins of our discipline." As an alternative, Calder suggested "uncoverage," a term and concept borrowed from Wiggins and McTighe (2005). By "uncoverage," Calder meant "a deliberate attempt to lay bare for students the central assumptions, forms of inquiry, and cognitive habits that transform data into knowledge for practitioners of our discipline" (p. 44). Calder was hardly the first instructor to step outside the coverage model. In fact, a course developed by Breihan that centered on historical argumentation was the subject of a 1990 published study (Walvoord & Breihan, 1990). That same year, Holt (1990) suggested that history students at all levels be presented with and asked to think creatively about the raw materials of history and of historical debate. Two years later, in the pages of *Perspectives*, Wineburg (1992) questioned whether content-oriented history education fosters habits of critical thought. Calder, however, moved beyond these earlier efforts. He did not simply offer "uncoverage" as an alternative to the traditional model. Instead, he challenged historians to systematically investigate the relative merits of the two approaches. On the basis of research into his own course, he posited that exercises that are specifically designed to uncover the "routines of historical thought" and recurring exercises that sharpen skills will help beginning students "get started with historical thinking" (2002, p. 45).

By 2006, Calder had moved beyond such tentative conclusions. Citing the work of cognitive psychologists, he argued that the coverage model with its "facts first" approach was "wrongheaded" and a failure even on its own terms. Factual knowledge, he argued, is not accumulated like furniture, but rather develops in the context of questions and problems. By emphasizing factual knowledge as an end in itself, the coverage model left students with neither an understanding of the discipline of history nor a base of historical knowledge. Calder thus concluded that "coverage-oriented surveys," which are "[b]uilt on wobbly, lay theories of human cognition," "must share in the blame for Americans' deplorable ignorance of history" (2006a, p. 1362). While Calder cited a number of other scholars, including Wineburg and Bain, about the shortcomings of the coverage model, he rested his alternative approach upon evidence that he gathered through thorough investigation of student learning in his own courses. He explicated his research methodology, which included surveys, examinations, and "think alouds," through an excellent companion website to his "Uncoverage" article (Calder, 2006b).

Calder is unusually direct in challenging pedagogical orthodoxy, but he is only one of a growing number of scholars exploring and advocating approaches to history education that move beyond the coverage model. This group of like-minded scholars, which also includes Walvoord, Breihan, Bain, and Wineburg, is part of an emerging "scholarship of teaching and learning" (SoTL) movement that, since the 1990s, has attempted to develop and test more rigorous pedagogies for higher education. SoTL distinguishes itself from general discussions of "good teaching" by focusing on gathering evidence of student learning—something that a number of historians have begun to do. Wineburg (2001a) sums up the thrust of much of this scholarship in the title of his influential work, *Historical Thinking and Other Unnatural Acts*. For Wineburg and others, it is *historical thinking* itself, rather than a particular body of historical knowledge, that should be the emphasis of history education. Along similar lines, British scholar Booth (2000) critiques the "transmission model" of learning, in which the transfer of factual knowledge from professor to student serves as the principal objective of history teaching. Instead, Booth calls for a history curriculum in which "students gain insight into their subject, themselves and the world around them by questioning established notions, considering diverse views, and building independent judgments" (2003, p. 5). Bain (2000) challenges historians and history teachers to break down the dichotomy between history as a disciplinary "way of thinking" and history as a subject matter to be mastered, and Jeffrey (2003) proposes that students in the survey class be asked to *do* history rather than simply learn it.

This outpouring of pedagogical and scholarly innovation leads Calder (2006a) to ask whether historians might be close to establishing a new signature pedagogy for the history survey. In the end, he leaves that question unanswered and suggests that, in a discipline renowned for its freewheeling intellectual diversity, it may not be possible (or desirable) to define a single distinctive approach to introductory courses. And indeed, though critics of the coverage model agree that students must be asked to "think historically," a common understanding of what exactly constitutes historical thinking, let alone how to promote it, has yet to emerge. Even among critics of the coverage model, definitions of "historical thinking" abound. Calder, for instance, organizes his introductory course around six "cognitive habits": questioning, connecting, sourcing, making inferences, considering alternative perspectives, and recognizing limits to one's own knowledge (2006a, p. 1364). Andrews and Burke (2007), by contrast, propose the "five C's" of historical thinking: change over time, context, causality, contingency, and complexity (p. 32). Booth and Hyland (2000) identify 10 characteristics of high-level learning in history, a list so long and detailed as to defy concise summary.

Absent a shared understanding of historical thinking and a set of learning goals that flow from that definition, a new signature pedagogy for the introductory course seems a distant prospect. Nevertheless, some common themes emerge out of this conversation. First, critics of the coverage model agree that the discipline of history is, in Bain's words, an "epistemic activity" characterized by distinctive ways of knowing (2000, p. 352). Central to this epistemic activity is the rendering of judgments—judgments that, while contested, must rest upon concrete evidence drawn from the human past. Second, for the habit of historical judgment to develop, students must directly engage opposing perspectives on significant issues. They must, as Booth suggests, explore "a variety of sources, historical approaches and interpretations, and dimensions of an issue" (2003, pp. 28–29). This exploration of conflicting perspectives must happen, Calder (2006a) emphasizes, even at the introductory level. Finally, it is insufficient for students to merely encounter and consume the historical judgments of others. Rather, for students to learn to think historically, they must *do* history by entering into a contested, evidence-based discourse regarding the human past.

Although critics of the coverage model ask students to do history in pedagogically diverse ways, the underlying epistemic activity is essentially the same: students directly enter a contested discourse in which they produce their own judgments and argue for them on the basis of historical evidence. Jeffrey (2003) and Musselman (2004), for instance, both ask students to draw conclusions on the basis of primary source documents provided to the class. Jeffrey requires that students make a case for their conclusions in a brief formal paper, and Musselman conducts a series of structured in-class debates. Calder (2006a) assigns primary-source-based papers as well, but he also asks students to argue in writing for the inclusion of either Howard Zinn's *A People's History of the United States* or Paul Johnson's *A History of the American People* in a hypothetical adult education course, thereby requiring them to think critically about the interpretations of two very different overviews of U.S. history. Breihan (Walvoord & Breihan, 1990) has students address meta-issues of modern history, such as the value of political stability, the meaning of economic growth, and the necessity of war, in both argumentative essays and in-class debates. Despite the superficial differences in teaching methods and materials, all of these instructors ask their students do history by having them argue about the human past.

A number of scholars have placed argument explicitly at the center of their analyses of historical thinking (Calder 2006a; Sipress, 2004; Spoehr & Spoehr, 1994; Walvoord & Breihan, 1990). Often, however, the theme of argument remains implicit. An important step toward a new signature pedagogy for the introductory course would therefore be to render visible, both to ourselves and our students, the centrality of argument to the practice of history. Estes provides a model for doing so. Like others, Estes declares his central teaching goal to be helping students learn to think like historians. To achieve this goal, he systematically introduces students to a "culture of argument." This acculturation process is woven into the course readings and assignments, but it begins with a section in his syllabus entitled "Why Historians Argue All the Time—And why YOU will be too, this semester" (Estes, 2007, p. 186).

Reorienting the introductory course away from coverage and toward doing history involves more than simply subtracting a bit of coverage to make room for some historical thinking. Rather, historical thinking needs to become the organizing principle of the course. In *Understanding by Design*, Wiggins and McTighe (2005) argue that instructors often put the cart before the horse by beginning course design with questions about which topics to cover, which books to assign, and what kinds of papers or exams to require. Instead, Wiggins and McTighe recommend a "backward design" process that asks instructors to start by carefully articulating the desired outcomes of the course. What should students know, understand, and be able to do, as a result of taking the course? After comprehensively defining course goals, the instructor then asks difficult questions: How will I know if each student has developed the specified knowledge and skills? What will each student do to demonstrate his or her understanding? If we truly wish our students to understand what it means to think historically, we must thus dispense with any lingering attachment to coverage and instead redesign the introductory course with this outcome in mind. If students are to learn how to argue about the past as historians do, the entire course design, from beginning until end, must advance this goal. Making this shift does not mean eliminating "content" from introductory courses or relegating such pedagogical tools as textbooks and lectures to the dustbin. It does, however, require us to dispense with the notion that content mastery is an end in itself, and instead to view historical content as simply the subject matter about which our students will learn to argue.

Proponents of the emerging model do not indulge the fantasy that they are preparing their introductory students for a life of slipping off to the archives during their office lunch breaks. But they are committed to helping students understand the nature of historical inquiry and interpretation. This understanding has at least two significant implications. First, students will approach the world with an eye to historical context and with an awareness of the deep roots of the present in the past. This awareness may often lead them to ask useful questions in the face of practical problems and challenges, whether personal, professional, or civic. Second, students will not take historical claims for granted. Upon encountering a historical claim—such as those that frequently arise in political discussions—novice historians will start asking important questions about context and evidence. In short, the emerging model might better prepare students to incorporate historical modes of thinking into their daily lives.

Challenges to Doing History in the Classroom

Recent scholarship suggests many possible ways to teach students to think historically, but it also points to several challenges that must be recognized and addressed. First and foremost, students bring to the college classroom deeply rooted preconceptions regarding history. These preconceptions can be a significant barrier to student learning in the introductory course. Historical thinking is, as Wineburg (2001a) puts it, an "unnatural act." Lee (2004) points out that when young people first encounter history, they bring with them the lessons that they have learned in daily life. In particular, they assume that the past is given—a useful assumption in everyday life, particularly in light of the strong moral distinction between "telling the truth" and "telling lies" (p. 134). In a study of children and adolescents, Lee found that when faced with conflicting historical accounts, all but a handful of students sought to resolve the conflict by reference to a given past (by declaring, for instance, that one or the other account must be mistaken). Only a small proportion of the students recognized that the accounts themselves were constructions. These findings led Lee to conclude that historical thinking is "counter-intuitive," not just for high school students but perhaps also for many adults. Wineburg (2001b) reached similar conclusions in a study that contrasted how high school students and professional historians approach historical documents. The professional historians began immediately to interrogate the texts by raising questions about author, audience, and context. The high school students, by contrast, saw the same documents as authoritative sources of information regarding a given past, much as they would a standard course textbook. Thus, instructors should not imagine students to be blank slates when they enter the classroom. Student beliefs and attitudes about history (and about learning generally) affect their ability to learn to do history (Simpson & Nist, 1997).

These findings are consistent with long-established research on the cognitive development of college students. In his classic study of cognitive development among undergraduates, Perry (1970) found that most students enter college with a "dualistic" understanding of knowledge that takes truth to be clear-cut and revealed by authority. To recognize history as a contested discourse, students must therefore embrace a new cognitive frame. Perry's research suggests that this initial cognitive shift may come quite easily. Relatively early in their college experiences, he found, most students abandon simple dualism in favor of a perspective that he labels "multiplicity," in which the individual accepts that knowledge is often subject to rival truth claims. For students to embrace the contested nature of history, then, little more may be necessary than to expose them to clashing views on controversial historical issues. Historical thinking, however, requires more than just the recognition that historians differ in their views of the past. Perry found that students who made the transition from dualism to multiplicity came to see some realms of knowledge as clear-cut and others as uncertain, but within the realm of uncertainty they viewed disagreement as a mere matter of opinion. For historians, it is not sufficient for conflicting historical claims to be perceived as simple matters of opinion. On the contrary, historical judgments must be justified on the basis of evidence.

To think historically thus requires a second shift in cognitive frame. Here, Perry's findings suggest that the challenge is more substantial. Although most students shifted relatively quickly from dualism to multiplicity, Perry found his subjects quite resistant to abandoning the view that contested truth claims are merely matters of opinion. In fact, Perry found that most of his sample (made of mostly male Harvard students) graduated from college comfortably ensconced in the cognitive frame of multiplicity. The most difficult challenge of the introductory course therefore appears not to be persuading students that history is a contested discourse, but rather teaching them to distinguish between unfounded opinions and well-supported conclusions. As one study has found, it is not sufficient to simply tell students that they must cite evidence, nor is it enough to merely explain how to do it (Sipress, 2004). Rather, instructors must foster a process of developmental change in which students themselves come to understand the nature of historical argument and the role of evidence within it. Nelson (1999) urges us not simply to make our disciplinary criteria of judgment (i.e., evidence) explicit, but also to require that students systematically apply these criteria when making judgments among rival positions. As Nelson suggests, students may initially view the process of making disciplinary judgments as little more than "Teachers' Games," but mastery of the disciplinary game seems to be an important step toward a deeper understanding of disciplinary ways of knowing.

Teaching for historical understanding also engenders at least a few substantial practical difficulties. Within history departments, some faculty may prefer to cleave to more traditional pedagogies, in part perhaps from inertia, but also for more principled reasons. Revising pedagogy—embracing what may constitute a paradigm shift—requires a considerable investment of time. Especially given that many history faculty already have difficulty balancing the demands of teaching, scholarship, and service, some will prefer to devote time instead to further developing their own historical expertise, which can also enhance their courses. Other historians continue to believe that students need to master a core body of basic knowledge before they are ready to think like historians. These traditionalists may well be persuaded to change their minds, however, given the evidence coming out of cognitive psychology and the scholarship of teaching and learning indicating that the traditional coverage-driven pedagogy is not in fact the most effective route to producing well-informed students.

The most substantial challenges facing history instructors who want to move beyond coverage may be logistical. At many institutions, introductory history courses are part of general education programs that serve large numbers of students. The economics of higher education these days virtually dictate that such courses enroll scores of students per section. These large classes can inhibit discussion and place practical limits on writing assignments. Such challenges can be met, but we sorely need instructors to document and share their strategies for guiding students to do history in large classrooms. Assessment of historical thinking poses another practical challenge. Within the coverage model, assessment seems fairly straightforward—a fact that helps explain the absence of attention to assessment in the round table discussion mentioned above. According to surveys, most history instructors already avoid multiple-choice exams, even for introductory courses, and instead use a variety of written exam formats. Not all written exam formats, however, can be said to effectively gauge historical understanding (as opposed to recitation of "covered" material). Many popular essay and identification questions seem to require mainly that students repeat back something they heard in lecture or read in the textbook. The challenge of bolstering assessment will be especially difficult for large introductory courses. One study suggests the effectiveness of asking students to evaluate historical statements by providing evidence both to support and refute the claim in question (Voelker, 2008). For the emerging model to come to fruition, historians will need to devise, test, and share new methods of requiring students to demonstrate historical thinking in ways that can be readily assessed.

Conclusion

Although we lack a comprehensive, qualitative study of how historians teach introductory college courses, there are numerous signs of growing professional interest in pedagogies that challenge the traditional coverage-driven model. The *Journal of American History's* "Textbooks and Teaching" section, initiated in 1992, has published increasingly sophisticated discussions of teaching. The March 2006 issue of the *JAH* urged American historians to begin "Taking Seriously the Scholarship of Teaching and Learning" (Kornblith & Lasser, 2006). Likewise, *The History Teacher* has begun publishing more articles that tie claims about effective teaching to evidence of student learning. The program of the 2008 annual meeting of the American Historical Association included a panel entitled "Teaching by Having Students Think Historically." The Teaching American History (TAH) program, funded by the U.S. Department of Education, has increased the quantity and quality of the dialogue between K–12 history teachers and college-level history educators. Historian Mandell, a veteran TAH director, went on to coauthor (with Malone) *Thinking Like a Historian: Rethinking History Instruction* (2007), a field-tested model for teaching and learning historical thinking. Mandell and Malone explicitly advocate that students of all ages learn history by doing history. In sum, the journals and institutions of the historical profession display mounting interest both in the scholarship of teaching and learning and in the revised pedagogies that it brings.

Nevertheless, in many ways both history SoTL and a potential new signature pedagogy informed by it remain in their infancy. The systematic investigation of student learning must begin with a clear definition of what we want our students to learn. The same may be said of a new signature pedagogy. Although SoTL scholars and pedagogical innovators in history wish to encourage the habits of historical thinking by asking students to do history, the issue of what it actually means to do history has heretofore received insufficient attention from scholars and teachers. We suggest that the essential element of historical practice is participation in an evidence-based argumentative discourse about the human past. This definition of historical practice is implicit in much of the work of the pedagogical innovators mentioned above. Rendering the theme of historical argument explicit would be an important step toward the development of both SoTL research and a new signature pedagogy in history. With a shared understanding of what it means to do history, historians will be able to engage in research and discuss how best to promote and assess student learning in the field, utilizing SoTL tools and methods.

A final thought: the defenders of pedagogical tradition may protest that to abandon coverage is to surrender the struggle for cultural literacy. How, they may ask, can we expect our students to think like historians when they know so little? And yet, as long as there have been surveys to gauge the historical knowledge of Americans, there has been a crisis of historical ignorance. As Wineburg (2004) put it: "A sober look at a century of history testing provides no evidence for the 'gradual disintegration of cultural memory' or a 'growing historical ignorance.' The only thing growing seems to be our amnesia of past ignorance" (pp. 1405–1406). Wineburg points out that traditional history pedagogy has been a demonstrable failure, even on its own terms. He concludes:

> Technology may have changed since 1917, but the capacity of the human mind to retain information has not. Students could master and retain the piles of information contained in 1917 or 1943 textbooks no better than they can retain what fills today's gargantuan tomes. Light rail excursions through mounds of factual information may be entertaining, but such dizzying tours leave few traces in memory. The mind demands pattern and form, and both are built up slowly and require repeated passes, with each pass going deeper and probing further. (p. 1413)

Proponents of the coverage model no doubt have good intentions, but over the past century, their preferred pedagogy has come up short again and again. If we truly wish our students to understand the past, it is not enough to ask them to simply consume our expert knowledge. Rather, we must invite them into our realm—the realm of historical discourse—and encourage them to construct historical knowledge for themselves. After all, isn't that how we, as historians, gained our own understanding of the past?

References

Andrews, T., & Burke, F. (2007). What does it mean to think historically? *Perspectives: The Newsmagazine of the American Historical Association 45*(1), 32–35.

Bain, R. (2000). Into the breach: using research and theory to shape history instruction. In P. Stearns, P. Seixas, & S. Wineburg (Eds.), *Knowing, teaching, & learning history: National and international perspectives* (pp. 331–352). New York: New York University Press.

Booth, A. (2000). Creating a context to enhance student learning in history. In A. Booth & P. Hyland (Eds.), *The practice of university history teaching* (pp. 31–46). Manchester, UK: Manchester University Press.

Booth, A. (2003). *Teaching history at university: Enhancing learning and understanding.* London: Routledge.

Booth, A., & Hyland, P. (2000). Developing scholarship in history teaching. In A. Booth & P. Hyland (Eds.), *The practice of university history teaching* (pp. 1–13). Manchester, UK: Manchester University Press.

Calder, L. (2002, March). Looking for learning in the history survey. *Perspectives: The Newsmagazine of the American Historical Association 40*(3), 43–45.

Calder, L. (2006a). Uncoverage: Toward a signature pedagogy for the history survey. *Journal of American History 92,* 1358–70.

Calder, L. (2006b). Uncoverage: Toward a signature pedagogy for the history survey. Retrieved on January 10, 2008 from http://www.indiana.edu/~jah/textbooks/2006/calder/index.html

Cohen, D. (2005). By the book: Assessing the place of textbooks in U.S. survey courses. *Journal of American History, 91,* 1405–1415.

Estes, T. (2007). Constructing the syllabus: Devising a framework for helping students learn to think like historians. *History Teacher, 40,* 183–201.

Filene, P. (2007). *Reframing the survey course.* Paper presented at the annual meeting of the Organization of American Historians, Minneapolis.

Grim, V., Pace, D., & Shopkow, L. (2004). Learning to use evidence in the study of history. In D. Pace & J. Middendorf (Eds.), *Decoding the disciplines: Helping students learn disciplinary ways of thinking* (pp. 57–65). San Francisco: Jossey-Bass.

Holt, T. (1990). *Thinking historically: Narrative, imagination, and understanding.* New York: College Entrance Exam Board.

Jeffrey, J. (2003, April). The survey, again. *OAH Magazine of History 17*(3), 52–54.

Kornblith, G., & Lasser, C. (Eds.). (2001). Teaching the American history survey at the opening of the twenty-first century: A round table discussion. *Journal of American History, 87,* 1409–1441.

Kornblith, G., & Lasser, C. (2006). Beyond best practices: Taking seriously the scholarship of teaching and learning. *Journal of American History 92,* 1356–57.

Lee, P. (2004). Understanding history. In P. Seixas (Ed.), *Theorizing historical consciousness* (pp. 129–164). Toronto: University of Toronto Press.

Manning, P. (2006, March). Presenting history to policy makers: Three position papers. *Perspectives: The Newsmagazine of the American Historical Association 44*(3), 22–24.

Musselman, E. (2004). Using structured debate to achieve autonomous students discussion. *The History Teacher 37*, 335–349.

Nelson, C. (1999). On the persistence of unicorns: The trade-off between content and critical thinking revisited. In B. Pescosolido & R. Amizade (Ed.), *The social worlds of higher education: Handbook for teaching in a new century* (pp. 168–184). Boston: Pine Forge Press.

Perry, W. (1970). *Forms of intellectual and ethical development in the college years: A scheme.* New York: Holt, Rinehart, and Winston.

Stearns, P., Seixas, P., & Wineburg, S. (Eds.). (2000). *Knowing, teaching, & learning history: National and international perspectives.* New York: New York University Press.

Simpson, M. L., & Nist, S. L. (1997). Perspectives on learning history: A case study. *Journal of Literacy Research 29*, 363–395.

Sipress, J. (2004). Why students don't get evidence and what we can do about it. *The History Teacher 37*, 351–363.

Spoehr, K., & Spoehr, L. (1994). Learning to think historically. *Educational Psychologist 29*, 71–77.

Townsend, R. B. (2005, August). College board examines survey course. *OAH Newsletter, 33,* 1, 8, 12.

Voelker, D. (2008, August). Assessing student understanding in introductory courses: A sample strategy. *History Teacher 41,* 505–518.

Walvoord, B., & Breihan, J. (1990). Arguing and debating: Breihan's history course. In B. Walvoord & L. McCarthy (Eds.), *Thinking and writing in college: A naturalistic study of students in four disciplines* (pp. 97–143). Urbana, IL: National Council of Teachers of English, 1990.

Wiggins, G., & McTighe, J. (2005). *Understanding by design* (2nd ed.). Upper Saddle River, NJ: Pearson.

Wineburg, S. (1992, March). Probing the depths of students' historical knowledge. [Electronic version] *Perspectives 30*(3). Retrieved from http://www.historians.org/perspectives/issues/1992/9203/9203TEC1.cfm

Wineburg, S. (2001a). *Historical thinking and other unnatural acts: Charting the future of teaching the past.* Philadelphia: Temple University Press.

Wineburg, S. (2001b). On the reading of historical texts: Notes on the breach between school and academy. In S. Wineburg, *Historical thinking and other unnatural acts: Charting the future of teaching the past* (pp. 63–88). Philadelphia: Temple University Press.

Wineburg, S. (2004, March). Crazy for history. *Journal of American History 90*, 1401–1414.

3

UNPACKING A SIGNATURE PEDAGOGY IN LITERARY STUDIES

Nancy L. Chick

Whatever our research interests, or our theoretical positions, teaching is our job; and applying our specific scholarly skills to the problems of doing it well could give us something to talk about that's really worthwhile.

—Elaine Showalter, "What Teaching Literature Should Really Mean"

"Why major in literature—what do we tell our students?" was the question posed to 12 literary scholars, from a community college to a variety of Ivy Leagues, in a 2002 symposium written for *PMLA,* the journal of the Modern Language Association (MLA, the primary professional organization of literary and language scholars).[1] The question is significantly different from "Why major in literature—how do we teach our students?" but the responses still offer literature teacher-scholars and students insight into the state of the discipline in the 21st century, its current changes and challenges, and its persistent values.

The symposium was a response to two specific problems confronting literary studies. The first is the declining number of literature majors and the resulting probability of declining institutional resources. Even as the numbers of students attending and graduating from college rose between 1970 and 2000, B.A.s in English fell by 20% (Miller, 2006). Increasingly, these literature majors also seek a second major, which they consider "their 'real' major" (Alonso, 2002). In these concerns, the symposium focuses on English majors as tomorrow's professionals and contributors to the field, because a future with fewer literary scholars and educators poses a serious threat to the health of the discipline. However, these diminishing numbers are also reflected in the rest of the student body: Unless required, fewer non-majors will take literature courses at all. The dip in literature majors is thus the canary in the coal mine, symbolic of American college students' waning interests in literature, literary reading, and our disciplinary values. Confirming what most of us have long suspected, the National Endowment of the Arts' "Reading at Risk" (NEA, 2004) and "To Read or Not to Read" (NEA, 2007) studies document a dramatic decline in the reading habits and abilities of teenagers and adults, including college graduates. For example, the average number of adults who had read a single work of literature (broadly defined) within the last year dropped by over 10% between 1982 and 2002, and the rates among 18- to 24-year-olds fell by 17%, making them the group least likely to read literature (NEA, 2004). In terms of reading proficiency, rates have remained steady or are dropping among all adults at all education levels, and college graduates' rates have fallen over 20% between 1992 and 2003 (NEA, 2007).

A second disciplinary change revolves around the place of literature itself in the discipline. In the 1970s, 1980s, and 1990s, literary theory began to share and sometimes vie for attention with and sometimes become more important than literature. The rise of cultural studies caused the literary canon to become more contested than ever before, with challenges to redraw and even dissolve its borders. As a result, for some, it was no longer clear what literature was being studied in literary studies, and many experienced this change with great anxiety. For example, according to Schwartz, "Literature's Year 2000 Problem" was the politicization of literature. His advice to theorists was to "study political science. . . . Move to Washington. Become an agent of change. Work for a nonprofit organization . . ., [but] please stop trying to twist literary study" (1999).[2] Alonso similarly describes this "crisis" by saying "there is no longer a consensus on the object of literary studies or on the justifications for pursuing this field as an intellectual project" (2002, p. 401), and Pope sounds the alarm about "dangerous signs, symptoms perhaps of the forgetting of literature" (2002, p. 505). Others, however, describe some of these changes more positively. Shirane describes how the field "has transformed itself" from being too "narrowly construed as the study of national literatures or of belles letters" to now teaching "new generations to have a better understanding of the world as a multiplicity of global, intertwined cultures" (2002, p. 513).

Despite the potential gravity of these current issues in the discipline, the essays in the *PMLA* symposium—and countless other publications—illustrate, even as they disagree, that there is common ground. There is a core to what we do, a reason why many of us were drawn to literary studies, a common purpose to what we do and will continue to do as scholars and teachers, and what we want our students to do, think, and feel in our classes. Graff (2006) contends that the attention to these disciplinary conflicts of the last 50 years has made it easy to forget that there is "more consensus . . . than we're used to acknowledging" (p. 371). For instance, in a succinct and often-cited list, Scholes (1985) identifies the fundamental, universal practices of the discipline, despite one's theoretical stance, area of specialization, or enrollment numbers: reading (comprehension of texts), interpretation (seeking subtextual meanings of texts), and criticism (determining the greater implications, significance, and value of texts with results most often presented in writing). Graff notes another universal practice of the discipline: With very few exceptions all literary scholars teach undergraduates, an observation that echoes Showalter's (2003) recommendation that this common practice of literary scholars "could give us something to talk about that's really worthwhile." This observation—from two major scholars in the field and the 1998 MLA president (Showalter) and the 2008 MLA president (Graff)—is significant because it locates the teaching of literature firmly within the discipline, rather than something literary scholars do on the side in order to support their disciplinary practices of reading, research, and writing.

When Showalter asserted that "applying our specific scholarly skills to the problems of [teaching] well" would lead to valuable disciplinary conversations, she was arguing for a scholarship of teaching and learning (SoTL) in literary studies presented "in a language that our [disciplinary] colleagues will understand." In addition to how such research is written, she was also referring to the "language" of research design, encouraging projects that don't conform to external pressures for experimental design or expectations for empirical data, but instead draw on our own disciplinary methodologies of research and analysis. Informed by this disciplinary SoTL, literary teeacher-scholars would more effectively "help students learn how literary scholars think, read, analyze, annotate, evaluate, and interpret texts." In other words, she was calling for a SoTL that reflects the disciplinary ways of knowing, doing, and valuing.

SoTL in the Discipline

The discipline we call English or English Studies is actually a collection of several disciplines, including literary studies, composition studies, creative writing, and linguistics, with the first two representing the majority. Literary studies revolves around the interpretation of literary texts and is often divided into areas of specialization according to one or more of the following categories: nationality or geography (e.g., American literature, British literature), chronology (e.g., Renaissance literature, Romanticism, Modernism), politics (e.g., postcolonial literature), and perspective or theory (e.g., feminist, Marxist, New Historicist, Jungian). Composition studies focuses on research on and postsecondary instruction of writing, rhetoric, and discourse analysis, with its attention to writing processes, student writing, and classroom practices.

The differences between literary studies and composition studies result in some general differences between the SoTL of the two fields. Logically, although there are of course exceptions, literary SoTL tends to focus on issues of reading, whereas composition SoTL focuses on writing. A review of the online archives of *Pedagogy*, the premier SoTL journal in literary studies, reveals some common themes in literary SoTL: teaching specific texts (multicultural texts, canonical texts, children's literature, theoretical texts, graphic novels, hypertexts, major literary anthologies, films [e.g., Kahn, 2004; Wilner, 2002]), teaching within specific contexts (overseas, rural or urban areas, culturally diverse or homogenous regions, working-class classrooms [e.g., Mack, 2006]), teaching with a specific classroom dynamic (an "out" lesbian or gay instructor, a white instructor teaching multicultural texts, an international instructor [e.g., Chatterjee, 2001]), teaching with technology (digital archives and other resources, student-generated hypertexts [e.g., DeVoss & Selfe, 2001; Jones, 2007]), teaching literature in conjunction with other goals (interdisciplinarity, service learning, environmentalism [e.g., Garrard, 2007]), and teaching literary reading practices (understanding complex texts, ambiguity, the challenges of poetry, responding to texts [e.g., Linkon, 2005]).

The broader field of English has been engaged in SoTL longer than others in the humanities, and composition leads literary studies in formally embracing SoTL in its most respected venues, with creative writing even less engaged (Whitman & Richlin, 2007; see Meacham in this book for an analysis of creative writing SoTL).[3] One explanation for composition's lead may be its closer ties to educational research and its methodologies, making traditional SoTL methodologies more familiar and meaningful to composition scholars than to literary scholars, as Showalter suggests.

Nevertheless, this lag is only relative. Literary teacher-scholars have a variety of firmly established SoTL resources and outlets. *Pedagogy*, which first appeared in 2001, publishes the most SoTL in literary studies, and some publications of the National Council of Teachers of English (NCTE) publish literary SoTL alongside other articles about teaching literature, particularly *College English*, *Teaching English in the Two-Year College*, and *Research in the Teaching of English*. Also in 2001, the annual MLA conference was the site of a symposium called "Understanding Teaching," which charged that literary scholars "don't talk about [teaching] in the same way we talk about our scholarship" (Showalter, 2003). That same year, the MLA International Bibliography was expanded to include more publications on teaching (Guillory, 2002).

Many of these publications, however, are what many SoTLers would call teacher narratives, first-person reflections or analyses of teaching practices and outcomes. Some are "teaching tips" based primarily on one's own teaching (Witman & Richlin, 2007, p. 4). These works probably form the basis for Guillory's claim that SoTL in literature is "less conceptually developed" (2002, p. 164), and for Witman and Richlin's claim that SoTL in the humanities hasn't yet fully applied the necessary "meta-conceptual concentration" (p. 13) because they often appear in strictly narrative or anecdotal form without drawing from relevant research in other fields, such as psychology, sociology, and education. Although these genres of narratives and teaching tips are valuable, and literary scholars certainly find great value in effective narratives, Whitman and Richlin note that these publications offer no way of verifying the relevance of such tips outside the context of the narrative, and Guillory says they fall short of the "measure of sophistication" of "competent scholarship on literature itself" (p. 165). The narratives are from the subjective and limited point of the view of the instructor, whereas evidence drawn from the classroom at least allows for comparison between that subjective experience and the students' own narratives or further evidence of their learning. He looks to disciplinary history for further explanation of the relatively undeveloped role of pedagogical research in literary studies. On one hand, teaching literature is central to the discipline's history, because some major schools of literary criticism (New Criticism, deconstruction) and the discipline's major practice of close reading—"the most fundamental methodological [and pedagogic] protocol of our profession"—began as conversations about how to teach literature more effectively (p. 168). On the other hand, as with the professionalization of other academic disciplines, pedagogy, craft, and practice were relegated to secondary teaching while content, knowledge, theory, and the research of discovery became the focus in higher education.

Salvatori (2002) looks more closely at the MLA symposium's claim that "the discourse of teaching among university teachers [has] not caught up with advances in other areas of research" (p. 297). She acknowledges a tradition of teaching anecdotes that may be considered problematic when viewed through a SoTL lens: they're primarily entertaining, teacher-centered, not meant to be published (according to the literal etymology of "anecdote"), unsystematic, and irreproducible.[4] As such, these specific narratives lack important elements of scholarship. However, Salvatori also notes more than 20 years of disciplinary pedagogical research with all the key elements of SoTL, claiming that these diminished characterizations of SoTL in English are "gesture[s] of misrecognition" (p. 298). Her work with Donahue (2002) articulates the main characteristics of SoTL in English, including highlighting and honoring "*student language* and the status of *student text*" (emphasis in original, pp. 70–71) through our "dominant styles of inquiry and methodologies," such as "textual interpretation and critique, discourse analysis, historical analysis, theoretical formulation" (p. 82). Indeed, literary SoTL is particularly strong in grounding learning problems within larger contexts (institutional, disciplinary, and even cultural) and theories (literary, pedagogical, and cultural). Further, Salvatori's description of "the most salient characteristics" of SoTL—"an unprecedented attentiveness to students' work, their cultural capital, and their learning as a litmus test for the theories that inform a teacher's approach" and "the classroom as a site where student voices are actually heard, where their knowledges are actually acknowledged and engaged" (p. 298)—implies that English scholars are uniquely positioned to employ them.

The Default Literary Pedagogy: Professorial Packing

Ultimately, most SoTL scholars would argue that a discipline isn't defined by its journals or other scholarly publications (Miller, 2006) or in its institutional history; instead, it's defined in classrooms, in the narrative arcs of departmental curricula and individual syllabi, and in the day-to-day routines of "doing literary studies."[5] Such a disciplinary vision begs the question of how the field is represented in these instances. Blau (2003) asserts that we have much to learn from composition pedagogy, which is based on process, learning, collaboration, and the learner—not only supported by current learning theory but also more likely to reflect and embody key disciplinary moves. The most common ways of teaching literature, on the other hand, are based on products, texts, competition, and the professor—neither in line with what we know about how students learn nor reflective of literary scholars' ways of thinking, doing, and valuing.

Bass (1999), not just a leading SoTL scholar but also a Ph.D. in American literature, illustrates this dominant pedagogical focus in literature classes when recalling that he "tended to replicate the pedagogies that worked best—quite frankly—on *me*" (p. 3). He describes the "unending self-deception" in teaching that allows us to assume that what worked for us should work for everyone (p. 4). This kind of pedagogical narcissism leads us to see ourselves when we look at our students, thus ignoring their separate identities, the differences between and among them, and the contexts for learning. As Bass suggests, we thus miss the key point that most of us were motivated, eager students who excelled in literature classrooms, not those who struggled, not those who were disengaged, and not those who didn't get it. Assuming that our best learning experiences would also be the best for our students also suggests a naïveté, a failure to empathize, and lack of understanding of novice learners, non-majors, learning preferences, socioeconomic impacts on education, and other factors that affect learning.[6] In fact, because it's simply "*naturalized*," pedagogical narcissism glosses over concerns for research, evidence, and any sense of audience other than oneself (emphasis in original; Bass, 1999, p. 4). Similarly, McKeown (2006) notes that our teaching is "still too often premised on anecdotal assumptions about how English should be taught" and on a "'common sense' factor" by which we "teach English the way we were taught," drawing more from our experiences in English classrooms from primary through graduate school than "what current research tells us" (4).[7] This approach is likely the source for the teacher-centered anecdotes described by Salvatori as entertaining narratives but not much more.

Perhaps the most common result of this approach to teaching is what may be called professorial packing, an inversion of the common metaphor for the essential disciplinary act of "unpacking" a literary text and its meanings. Unpacking a text connotes opening up something, sifting out what's inside, and exploring the contents. The process turns a singular entity (a text) into multiple elements. There's a sense of anticipation, delight, and wonder in the process. In contrast, professorial packing occurs when a professor presents his or her fully formed interpretations to students—in essence packing the text (and the students) with the professor's own interpretations, rather than teaching the students themselves to unpack texts. Blau explains that this traditional approach to teaching literature comes in a variety of forms, most often in lectures about a text, or pseudo-Socratic discussions in which we ask questions designed to elicit our interpretations from the students. It also appears when we present a text's historical or biographical contexts before the students read it, which may then too narrowly focus their interpretations to that information given by us, or, paradoxically, when we withhold basic but necessary information about a text, setting up students to give a faulty interpretation that's corrected when we finally reveal that necessary information. Even those small instances when we provide students with definitions of unfamiliar terms illustrate this practice because in each the professor is again packing the text and the students with the meanings, rather than helping the students discover the meanings themselves.

Graff (2006) notes that, in the 1960s and 1970s, graduate school training for new teaching assistants in English was limited to talking about interpretations of texts, "interesting things an instructor could say—or try to get students to say—about a literary work" with no discussion of their own or students' impressions of literature, reading, and interpretation (p. 375). These English professors of the 1970s, 1980s, 1990s, and today have been trained not to recognize students' literary preconceptions and expectations, not to discuss the discipline itself and its value, not to guide student practice of disciplinary ways of thinking, but to teach literature by presenting interpretations that interest the teachers. Given this context in which most English Ph.D.s are being trained solely in content knowledge and not pedagogy or even pedagogical content knowledge, it's understandable that they rely on their strengths—presenting interpretations—and begin teaching as they were taught. In this moment when a novice teacher and content expert faces a literature classroom for the first time, we see the beginnings of the relationship between pedagogical narcissism and professorial packing. We've all experienced professors who guided us toward their interpretations, and who rewarded us for mirroring them in class discussion and in our writing. Some of our fondest memories in the classroom even revolve around charismatic teachers and professors who dazzled us with the way they read texts, and the impulse to be like them is often why we got our Ph.D.s. And so, without thinking about the differences between us and many of our students, we emulate those professors who inspired us. In short, we rely on the default pedagogy of the discipline—packing texts, packing interpretations, packing the students—without thinking carefully about what students learn from it.

This conventional, literary pedagogy does not reflect the ways of knowing and doing in literary studies and, like many other disciplines, is typically focused on the goal of coverage of texts rather than deep disciplinary understanding. After lecturing about 10 George Herbert poems in one late-semester day because his Renaissance survey hadn't yet addressed this major poet, Blau (2003) later admitted that this strategy served the syllabus, the pressures of coverage, and his love of the poet. Like Blau, Gregory (2005) recalls teaching one of his favorite poems by presenting his meticulous analysis. Eventually, he also acknowledged that his students weren't learning much aside from "why some people—namely me or other strange persons like me—might find [the] poem *interesting*" (p. 96). Both Blau and Gregory had good intentions in the way they taught these beloved works, assuming that their own knowledge and enthusiasm would simply be transmitted to students, but as with any lecture—even a good lecture—students learn the information they're given. In these moments, the students were learning Blau's and Gregory's interpretations instead of how they arrived at the interpretations, or how the students might develop their own interpretations. As Blau later realized, the "experience of learning was mine, not theirs" (p. 2), because he was doing the disciplinary work the students should do, presenting only the results or products of this work and hiding or even hoarding the intellectual moves necessary to get there. This kind of professorial packing is in part the literary equivalent of teaching scientific facts rather than the nature of science or the process of scientific inquiry.

In these instances, the students also learn that the professor knows the text well, perhaps too well. If they don't see the process of reading and rereading, including what the professor was thinking when first reading a text and then in developing an interpretation, it's understandable why many students think of interpretation as "overanalyzing." From their perspectives, the professor is performing some sort of hocus-pocus, conjuring up meaning through mysterious spells, pulling an interpretation out of a hat. Blau also points out an ethical problem here. In these moments, we rarely admit to our prior contextual knowledge—knowledge the students don't have and don't realize we're using—that makes interpreting texts easier, we give the impression that the distance between our skills and theirs is insurmountable. By inadvertently inflating our interpretive skills rather than explaining that we're also drawing from knowledge they don't yet have (but can develop), we not only "misrepresent the gap" between ourselves and our students (Blau, 2003, p. 91); we also guard the gap between expert and novice, between disciplinary understanding and disciplinary misconceptions.

Aside from dazzling students with our brilliance (if we are that lucky), a consequence of professorial packing is "a culture of interpretive dependence" (Blau, 2003, p. 20). At some point, a cycle has been created: we accept or claim students' interpretive dependence as they expect us to give our interpretations to them (the consumers of these interpretations), which they then mirror back to us on exams and in essays. This cycle reinforces the "professor as puzzlemaster" misconception, as students grant us complete interpretive authority and envision their role as struggling to figure out our obscure interpretations (Chick, Hassel, & Rybak, 2008).[7] Some may argue that this practice provides novices with interpretive training wheels modeling expert interpretations, but under closer scrutiny it seems not only to provide these wheels but also to pedal the bike. Again, it models the product rather than the process, as the professor has done the disciplinary work without showing the students how to do that work themselves.

Ultimately, it raises questions about our conceptions of teaching and what is being taught. Professorial packing assumes that teaching means transferring information from professor to student and that what's being taught is the professor's interpretation—not the intellectual moves required to generate interpretations, regardless of text. We know from learning theory, however, that this unidirectional, product-oriented model of teaching and learning doesn't help novices learn (Bransford, Brown, & Cocking, 2000), and we know that learning literature means far more than just learning our own interpretations.

When seeking a more effective way to teach students to read, understand, remember, and value literature, Gregory (2005) jumped outside of the discipline to propose a "liberal arts pedagogy," rejecting what he saw as the only options for an "English pedagogy," which he describes as "stultifying"

(p. 98). His dismissal of the possibility for a meaningful literary pedagogy is telling, pointing not only to what some feel about the current state of disciplinary cohesiveness but more importantly to the need for articulating a pedagogy that does, in fact, reflect and pass on our practices and values.

Because of the discipline's current state of transition and because a single chapter isn't enough for a thorough proposition, this chapter focuses on a single unifying principle for a literary signature pedagogy without any assertions of comprehensiveness or conclusiveness. Many literary scholars, without using the specific language, have been calling for a literary signature pedagogy for years—most notably Scholes (1985), Graff (1987; 2006), Bass (1999), Blau (2003), Showalter (2003), and Salvatori and Donahue (2004)—in projects that, when brought together, begin to form ways of teaching literature that invoke the discipline's habits of mind, values, and moves in the classroom. My hope is to join and advance this disciplinary conversation, narrowing the focus to how we teach students to think like literary scholars.

A Literary Signature Pedagogy: Unpacking the Conflicts, Conversations, and Questions

One principle around which we can organize a literary signature pedagogy that would essentially unpack the discipline, its significant questions, and its major moves and values is the concept of "teaching the conflicts" (Graff, 1992). Although Graff coined the phrase (with Gibbons, 1985), has developed the concept in many publications,[8] and coedited critical editions of two major texts explicitly presented as *Case Studies in Critical Controversy*, literary studies has a long tradition of critical editions presenting differing (even opposing) perspectives about major literary texts, and the value of situating literary texts within larger literary, social, and cultural conversations and debates is not new. However, Graff's diligence and the critical attention to his work have placed the varying iterations of teaching the conflicts at the center of key conversations about teaching in literary studies, including a roundtable at the 2001 MLA Conference, a seven-essay "Teaching the Conflicts at Twenty Years" symposium in *Pedagogy* (2003), another five-essay *Pedagogy* symposium in 2007,[9] and countless conference panels and individual essays.

According to this principle, rather than confining to our professional presentations and publications the debated issues, controversies, and larger discussions about and within the discipline, these conversations should be guiding principles in our classes. Too often, we seal off from the classroom such larger questions about literature, its relationship to the world, and the discipline itself—in short, "the way intellectual work in the field is done" (Graff, 2006, p. 380). This exclusion has serious consequences for students' understanding of literary studies, of what it means to do literary studies, and of academic culture in general, not to mention their interest in pursuing a literature major or even further literary reading. Integrating this approach into our pedagogy opens up or unpacks the discipline by engaging students in the conversations, questions, and debates central to what we do professionally and, most importantly, in the processes used to carry on these conversations, rather than hiding them altogether or merely exposing students to the results of such debates.

Significantly, this approach is Graff's first proposal for overhauling how graduate students are socialized into the discipline, not only for their benefit as future literary scholars but also as future literature teachers. Because conventional ways of teaching literature make the discipline itself "elusive" or "mystifying," from introductory courses all the way up through graduate school (2006, p. 376), many graduate students don't even know "what it means to be part of 'the profession'" of literary studies. As a result they teach by relying on the default of professorial packing (which contributed to their own disorientation) and thus perpetuate the cycle of confusion and lack of disciplinary understanding (p. 375). Graff argues that graduate students in literature should be learning the conflicts and how to teach them.

Perhaps appropriately, the meaning of the approach has been a point of contention.[10] Because the phrase "teaching the conflicts" implies antagonism, polarity, and even dualistic thinking, it is easily misunderstood and misrepresented, despite attempts at clarifying the principle to include a sense of dialogue, conversation, and even negotiation (Benton, 2003; Graff, 2003; Tompkins, 2003). Another misconception is that this approach prescribes certain conflicts or debates. On the contrary, the specific themes or topics will vary at least according to context and don't by themselves provide the ultimate value of the approach (Graff, 2003). Instead, the value comes from the intellectual, emotional, and pedagogical moves used in teaching and learning this way. It's in line with at least two key elements of current learning theory: first, it confronts and contradicts specific misconceptions about the discipline itself, why and how we read literature, and what literature is ultimately about (Chick, Hassel, & Rybak, 2008). Also, by invoking large, complex questions which can't be answered by singular answers and simple pro-con debates, it nudges students out of dualistic thinking (Graff, 2003; Kloss, 1994; Shumway, 2003). Emotionally, when literature is placed in larger, more meaningful contexts, it's easier for students to recognize a sense of both personal relevance and the greater significance of literature than is possible with the more traditional practice of narrowly focusing on textual analysis, to the exclusion of any extra-textual considerations. Ultimately, the essence of this signature approach is twofold: organize teaching and learning around the conversations that engage literary scholars and readers (including students), and share, teach, and have students practice the disciplinary moves we make within these conversations.

By involving students in the conflicts and conversations that make our disciplinary processes meaningful, this literary signature pedagogy is guided not by the answers asserted in the singular perspective of professorial packing but by questions and by multiple perspectives. These key principles undergird everything from course design and text selection to assignments, in-class activities, and class dynamics. Students participate in conversations (oral and written) evaluating and negotiating different interpretations, theories, critical responses, and contexts for texts—appropriately adjusted to considerations of depth and course level. Certainly, no single course or teaching practice will create literary scholars or experts in a semester, but that's neither the claim nor the objective of a signature pedagogy. Instead, its goal in lower-level courses is to help students begin to recognize, value, practice, and internalize these essential moves of literary studies, and then continue this process in upper-level courses—or, to follow the disciplinary metaphor, as students participate in unpacking the discipline, they gain the skills to unpack it further themselves.

Such courses engage in inquiries about the literature, disciplinary processes, and the discipline itself. For instance, textual conversations might include showing students how to unpack the ambiguous and seemingly contradictory meanings within a single text, such as the ending of Kate Chopin's *The Awakening* or Theodore Roethke's "My Papa's Waltz" (Chick, Hassel, & Haynie, in press); placing texts that are in conflict side by side, such as the Booker T. Washington–W. E. B. DuBois debate; examining the social value and impact of texts, such as the discussions about *The Adventures of Huckle-*

berry Finn as a racist text; evaluating the insights offered through different theoretical perspectives (e.g., New Criticism, New Historicism, postcolonial theory, feminist theory); engaging in canon debates by considering what should be read (popular works such as *Harry Potter*? non-print genres such as film and song lyrics?) and why; or exploring the "newness" of such genres as the short story cycle or flash fiction. Inquiries about disciplinary processes might include examining the role of the author in interpreting a text. A common novice practice is the intentional fallacy, or the assumption that an author's intended meaning is the privileged and perhaps only meaning of a text (Chick, Hassel, & Rybak, 2008), but the disciplinary caution against relinquishing interpretive authority to the author is a product of the New Critics from the mid-20th century and isn't universally applied, as lyric poetry may be seen as the voice of the poet and not a separate persona (Blau, 2003). These complications make the reader's relationship to the author an ongoing site of negotiation. More broadly, an effective metacognitive and meta-disciplinary pursuit would be considering how literary reading processes overlap with and differ from what's commonly perceived as its opposite: "beach reading" or "reading for pleasure." Questions about the discipline itself might involve defining the discipline and its moves, discussing how it's related to other disciplines, how it's relevant to the world outside of academia, why it values reading, and what disciplinary practitioners can do about the nation's decline in reading and reading abilities (Graff, 2006).

This principle of teaching the conflicts, conversations, and questions speaks to how literary scholars view literature itself. First, it reflects the discipline's sense of the canon as a contested issue that invites critical evaluation and debate, a *conversation about* rather than a predetermined *list of* what literature we value and why. It also captures the discipline's approach to texts and what they mean: they are multiplicitous, layered, ambiguous, and influenced by contexts, rather than singular, flat, definitive, and decontextualized—as professorial packing erroneously suggests. In other words, rather than teaching that a text and its meanings are fixed or even dead, remains from a bygone era ready to be autopsied by contemporary readers, this element of a signature pedagogy teaches that texts are still alive, generative, and inviting of new questions, approaches, interpretations, and significance. After all, we talk about what happens in literary texts using what's called the literary present tense because we consider the text, its events, and its characters alive every time we look at the page. Each time we read *Hamlet*, he agonizes over what to do about his father's death; each time we read *Moby-Dick*, Ishmael joins Captain Ahab in search of the white whale; and each time we read *The Adventures of Huckleberry Finn*, Huck decides that helping Jim escape the slave-catchers is worth going to hell. We talk about the texts we love as offering something new with each reading. For us, literature and literary study can't be captured in a lecture or a pseudo-Socratic dialogue focused on one interpretation. It's the conversation—indeed many conversations—about the texts, what to make of them, and why we do it in the first place that makes literature and the discipline meaningful to us and to our students (Blau, 2003; Wallen, 2003).

By foregrounding significant conversations and debates, this pedagogical principle also heightens the awareness of perspective and differences in perspective. In doing so, it draws on the key literary element of the point of view or persona from which a narrative is told. For example, *The Adventures of Huckleberry Finn* would be a very different book if—instead of being limited to 13-year-old Huck's first-person perspective—it were told by the runaway slave Jim or by an omniscient narrator who gave equal insight into the minds of Huck, Jim, Tom Sawyer, and Pap. Similarly, the shifting perspectives of Toni Morrison's *Beloved* speak to the differing impacts of slavery on blacks and whites, on women and men, on adults and children, on Southerners and Northerners, on humans and animals. This literary signature pedagogy emerges when we ask students to examine how different characters in *Beloved* experience slavery and its aftermath, or the differences between characters in *Huck Finn* and *Beloved*, or how the two novels—one from 1885 and one from 1987—talk to and talk back to each other.

This signature pedagogy also reflects what literary scholars do. We invariably develop our responses to texts in dialogue and conflict with others: we exhaustively research what others have written about the texts, apply our perspectives influenced by larger theories, present our work at conferences, publish our written responses for our peers, and often share (or impose) our interpretations in our classes. Yet when students read only the literary texts, get only a single way (the professor's) of reading and responding to the texts, and miss the larger conversations within and about the texts, they are not participating in literary studies. On the other hand, this literary signature pedagogy has students reading literary criticism and perhaps even theory to engage in what scholars have said and continue to say, as well as how they say it. These disciplinary genres provide students with models of the moves they're expected to make, such as how to ask questions of texts, how to respond to these questions, how to use textual evidence, and how to place texts in dialogue with other texts and with broader contexts. Students learn something about the literary, historical, and cultural contexts in which the texts are produced and then read, as the literature itself is often in dialogue with these contexts. In such class discussions and in writing assignments, students are producing their own literary criticism, even if preliminary, rather than what some consider the more artificial assignments that require them to simply describe elements of setting, symbolism, theme, or character (Blau, 2003; Graff, 2006; Stephens, Corey, & Chapman, 2003).

As literary teacher-scholars answer the calls for SoTL that reflects the discipline and for SoTL-informed teaching that helps students do literary studies, the resulting conversations will continue to explore ways of teaching that embody what makes the discipline so meaningful to us: how literary texts, the meanings they suggest, the questions they raise, and the conflicts they provoke are connected to the larger concerns of the world we all live in. Applying the signature pedology discussed here, this conversation about a universal activity in literary studies—teaching—this needs to make its way into the literature classroom, as students participate in the further development of literary signature pedagogies. Such a pedagogical disciplinary conversation about "Why take literature—how do we teach our students?" will indeed be "really worthwhile."

References

Alonso, C. J. (2002). Editor's column: my professional advice (to graduate students). *PMLA, 117*(3), 401–406.

Ardizzone, T., Breithaupt, F., & Gutjahr, P. C. (2004). Decoding the humanities. In J. Middendorf & D. Pace (Eds.), *Decoding the disciplines: Helping students learn disciplinary ways of thinking. New directions for teaching and learning.* (pp. 45–56). San Francisco: Jossey-Bass.

Bass, R. (1999). The scholarship of teaching: What's the problem? *inventio, 1*(1). Retrieved February 11, 2007, from http://www.doit.gmu.edu/archives/feb98/randybass.htm

Benton, S. (2003). Conflict over conflicts. *Pedagogy, 3*(2), 245–249.

Blau, S. D. (2003). *The literature workshop: Teaching texts and their readers.* Portsmouth, NH: Heinemann.

Bransford, J. D., Brown, A. L., & Cocking, R. C. (Eds.). (2000). *How people learn: Brain, mind, experience, and school.* Expanded Edition. National Research Council Committee on Behavioral and Social Sciences and Education. Washington, DC: National Academy Press. Retrieved February 10, 2007, from http://www.nap.edu/books/0309070368/html/

Briggs, J. C. (2005, August 12). Introduction to critical methods. *Chronicle of Higher Education, 51*(49). Retrieved September 28, 2007, from EBSCOhost Academic Search Elite.

Calder, L. (2006). Uncoverage: Toward a signature pedagogy for the history survey. *Journal of American History.* Retrieved November 3, 2006, from http://www.indiana.edu/~jah/textbooks/2006/calder.shtml

Chatterjee, P. (2001). Encountering "third world women": Rac(e)ing the global in a U.S. classroom. *Pedagogy, 2*(1), 79–108.

Chick, N. L., Hassel, H., & Haynie, A. (in press). "Pressing an ear against the hive": Reading literature for complexity. *Pedagogy, 10*(2).

Chick, N. L., Hassel, H., & Rybak, C. (2008) "All they want to do": Novice practices and misconceptions in literary studies. *Manuscript under review.*

DeVoss, D. N., & Selfe, C. N. (2001). "This page is under construction": Reading women shaping on-line identities. *Pedagogy, 2*(1), 31–48.

Downs, D., & Wardle, E. (2007). Teaching about writing, righting misconceptions: (Re)envisioning "first-year composition" as "introduction to writing studies." *CCC, 58*(4), 552–584.

Garrard, G. (2007). Ecocriticism and education for sustainability. *Pedagogy, 7*(3), 359–383.

Graff, G. (1992). *Beyond the culture wars: How teaching the conflicts can revitalize American education.* New York: Norton.

Graff, G. (2003). Conflict clarifies: A response. *Pedagogy, 3*(2), 266–275.

Graff, G. (2006). Toward a new consensus: The Ph.D. in English. In C. M. Golde, G. E. Walker, & Associates (Eds.), *Envisioning the future of doctoral education: Preparing stewards of the discipline. Carnegie essays on the doctorate* (pp. 370–389). San Francisco: Jossey-Bass.

Graff, G., & Gibbons, R. (1985). The university and the prevention of culture. In G. Graff & R. Gibbons (Eds.), *Criticism and the university* (pp. 62–82). Evanston, IL: Northwestern University Press.

Gregory, M. (2005). Turning water into wine: Giving remote text full flavor for the audience of *Friends. College Teaching, 53*(3), 95–98.

Guillory, J. (2002). The very idea of pedagogy. *Profession*, pp. 164–171.

Jones, D. C. (2007). Thinking critically about digital literacy: A learning sequence of pens, pages, and pixels. *Pedagogy, 7*(2), 207–221.

Kahn, M. (2004). "Why are we reading a handbook on rape?": Young women transform a classic. *Pedagogy, 4*(3), 438–459.

Kloss, R. J. (1994). A nudge is best: Helping students through the Perry scheme of intellectual development. *College Teaching, 42*(4). Retrieved October 22, 2007, from EBSCOhost Professional Development Collection.

Linkon, S. (2005). The reader's apprentice: Making critical cultural reading visible. *Pedagogy, 5*(2), 247–273.

Mack, N. (2006). Ethical representation of working-class lives: Multiple genres, voices, and identities. *Pedagogy, 6*(1), 53–78.

McKeown, B. (2006, April). What is your fascination with these outcomes? *English Leadership Quarterly,* 3–6.

Miller, T. (2006). What should college English be . . . doing? *College English, 69*(2), 150–155.

Nash, J. (2007). The attitudes of English majors to literary study. *Changing English, 14*(1), 77–86.

National Endowment for the Arts (NEA). (2004). Reading at risk: A survey of literary reading in America. Washington, DC: Author. Retrieved October 15, 2007, from http://www.nea.gov/pub/ReadingAtRisk.pdf

National Endowment for the Arts (NEA). (2007). To read or not to read: A question of national consequence. Washington, DC: Author. Retrieved November 25, 2007, from http://www.nea.gov/research/ToRead.pdf

Pope, R. D. (2002). Why major in literature—what do we tell our students? *PMLA, 117*(3), 503–506.

Salvatori, M. R. (2002). The scholarship of teaching: Beyond the anecdotal. *Pedagogy, 2*(3), 297–310.

Salvatori, M. R., & Donahue, P. (2002). English studies and the scholarship of teaching. In M. T. Huber & S. P. Morreale (Eds.), *Disciplinary styles in the scholarship of teaching and learning: Exploring common ground* (pp. 69–86). Washington, DC: American Association for Higher Education and the Carnegie Foundation for the Advancement of Teaching.

Salvatori, M. R., & Donahue, P. (2004). *The elements (and pleasures) of difficulty.* New York: Pearson Longman.

Scholes, R. (1985). *Textual power: Literary theory and the teaching of English.* New Haven: Yale University Press.

Schwartz, R. B. (1999). Literature's year 2000 problem. *College Literature, 26*(3). Retrieved September 28, 2007, from EBSCOhost Academic Search Elite.

Shirane, H. (2002). Terrorism, culture, and literature. *PMLA, 117*(3), 513–514.

Showalter, E. (2003, January 17). What teaching literature should really mean. *Chronicle of Higher Education 49*(19). Retrieved May 2, 2007, from EBSCOhost Professional Development Collection.

Shumway, D. R. (2003). Graff and the left. *Pedagogy, 3*(2), 259–262.

Stephens, J., Corey, J., & Chapman, I. (2003). Between the lines: Reading and misreading student writers. *Journal of College Reading and Learning, 33*(2), 197–213.

Tompkins, J. (2003). Jerry's blind spot. *Pedagogy, 3*(2), 250–252.

Wallen, J. (2003). We really do not know how to disagree with each other. *Pedagogy, 3*(2), 253–256.

Weimer, M. (2006). *Enhancing scholarly work on teaching & learning: Professional literature that makes a difference.* San Francisco: Jossey-Bass.

Whitman, P. D., & Richlin, L. (2007). The status of the scholarship of teaching and learning in the disciplines. *International Journal for the Scholarship of Teaching and Learning, 1*(1). Retrieved February 15, 2007, from http://www.georgiasouthern.edu/ijsotl/v1n1/essays/witman/IJ_witman.pdf

Wilner, A. (2002). Confronting resistance: Sonny's blues—and mine. *Pedagogy, 2*(2), 173–196.

Notes

1. I'm grateful to my colleague Holly Hassel for her ongoing support and collaboration, as well as Aeron Haynie and Chuck Rybak, whose work on other collaborations has been invaluable. I also wish to thank Aeron Haynie and Regan Gurung, my fellow editors of this book, for their thoughtful feedback on this chapter.

2. The title of Schwartz's 1997 book *After the Death of Literature* speaks to what he sees as the consequences of these theorists.

3. In fact, Downs and Wardle (2007) articulate what may be a composition signature pedagogy, which they call "writing studies pedagogy" (p. 578), in their description of a course that "does not teach from principles that contravene writing studies research. Instead, it draws on research from the field and principles and ethics that shape the field to help students understand the nature of writing and to explore their own writing practices. Unlike pedagogies that are so detached from writing studies' specialized knowledge as to deny it, [this] pedagogy emerges from that knowledge and ethos" (p. 560).

4. Weimer (2006) validates the "wisdom of practice" found in personal narratives for their potential to motivate "the observation, adaptation, and application of those specifics in another context" (p. 90).

5. Given the focus of this book and the parameters of a single chapter, my summary of the disciplinary history and its traditional ways of teaching is limited to its practice in the United States.

6. Brookfield's *Becoming a Critically Reflective Teacher* (1995) is an extended

exercise in overcoming such self-deception, or nostalgia, or pedagogical narcissism by learning to empathize with students and see what happens in the classroom and how we teach through their eyes, rather than through our own reflections.

7. Bass (1999), Blau (2003), Ardizzone, Breithaupt, and Gutjahr (2004), Briggs (2005), Nash (2007), and Chick, Hassel, and Rybak (2008) articulate some of the major disciplinary misconceptions in literary studies. Chick, Hassel, and Rybak offer the most systematic and detailed study, resulting in a taxonomy of three types of misconceptions: those about the discipline itself, those about interpretive authority, and those about disciplinary processes.

8. The bibliography that accompanies the 2003 *Pedagogy* symposium on "Teaching the Conflicts at Twenty Years" is useful in tracing Graff's development of the concept (p. 274). It's also worth noting that, although Graff has extended his challenge more broadly across the disciplines, his concept originated in and has gained the most traction in his discipline.

9. This later symposium focuses on Graff's more recent and broader concept of students' "cluelessness" to the moves we make, as explained in *Clueless in Academe: How Schooling Obscures the Life of the Mind* (2003). The central moves Graff says we fail to teach students have to do with recognizing and engaging in debates, conflicts, dialogues, conversations. *They Say / I Say* (Graff & Birkenstein, 2006), his textbook companion to *Clueless in Academe*, teaches students how to make these moves. It's also worth noting that Calder, a leading SoTL scholar in history and author of "Uncoverage: Toward a Signature Pedagogy for the History Survey" (2006), called *Clueless in Academe* "the best SoTL book" he's read in years in his presentation at the 2006 CASTL Institute in Chicago.

10. For greater detail on the debates surrounding the "teach the conflicts" approach, see the 2003 *Pedagogy* symposium (pp. 245–275).

SECTION TWO

FINE ARTS

4

VISION AND RE-VISION IN CREATIVE WRITING PEDAGOGY

Rebecca Meacham

Moments before an Introduction to Creative Writing class, I realized a crisis was imminent. When my class convened, it would be the first time we'd engaged a signature element of creative writing pedagogy—the writing workshop. A student's short story would be discussed by the full class of 25 students and me while the student silently took notes until the discussion's conclusion, when she was permitted to speak. Although for weeks my class had been talking, exchanging drafts in groups, and free-writing—building our classroom community as well as each student's confidence to articulate and receive criticism—what happened during the workshop portion of the class, especially the first workshop session, was vital. For 75 minutes, I would solicit, direct, and refine often contradictory comments from a circle of students about the work of another student and attempt to add my opinions, all while diffusing the anxiety of a writer whose draft—her labor and passion—was on the pages before us. Handled poorly, this class session could create bitterness and fear: Our classroom community could fracture, anxiety could rule, and students might never again voice their true feelings in class or on the page.

Our first workshop discussion was a rape story. A pornographic, victim-blaming rape story. It was a rape story written from the victim's point of view, unfolding as the attack occurred. As her body is violated, the victim flashes back to buying new panties and kinky sexual encounters. As she's strangled with her own belt, the victim recognizes her attacker as a loser she's overlooked in her wilder days. Then she dies. The story was entitled "Attention."

As woman and professor of Women's Studies, I was deeply offended at the story's conflation of sexual pleasure with rape and strangulation. As a writer and professor of English, however, I was beset by different impulses. First, I noticed talent: If you removed the content, the story was gracefully written; the writer had considerable power but inadvertently (or so I hoped) had used that power for evil. Second, I saw errors of literary realism: The actions of the character's mind were out of sync with the actions inflicted on her body, including her own death. Internally, the cool detachment of writerly analysis sparred with the heat and nausea of my personal reaction. So how was I to react publicly, before my students, as their professor?

Stepping into the classroom, I could picture the writer being vilified by her peers, while at least one as-yet-unannounced rape victim fled the room in tears. Taking my seat, I imagined myself denouncing the story as pornographic and irresponsible, while the humiliated writer fled the room in tears. None of these scenarios prepared me for what actually happened: nothing. When it came time to discuss the piece, I was poised to soothe what I hoped would be some productive, useful outrage. Yet nobody voiced offense. Instead, my students applauded the writer's efforts and, applying many of my own lessons, added suggestions for revision. I stared at 25 placid, bright-eyed faces, and I felt newly offended as a woman, a writer, and a teacher. To my surprise, I found myself pushing hard for my students' resistance to a story I'd planned to defend. Afterward, in my written feedback, I was harsh and suggested the writer read the work of Alice Sebold, a rape survivor who has drawn on her trauma to craft a memoir and a best-selling novel.[1] Weeks later, after my student had read those books, we spoke about her newfound understanding of the story's problems. Years later, in my Advanced Workshop course, the student vowed to aim for the lyric empathy of her new favorite writer, Alice Sebold.

While this story has an unexpected ending, what's even more unusual is that I—a professor of creative writing who does not teach composition and who has literary publications as well as an M.F.A. and Ph.D.—am relating it on these pages, in a forum about pedagogies. Indeed, had I sought teaching advice from books and articles penned by other creative writers, I'd have found few answers, because little has been written about the practices and problems of creative writing pedagogy in U.S. higher education. In fact, as noted by the handful of scholars of teaching and learning in the field, writing about teaching is simply not what creative writing teachers do. Rather, creative writing professors write, and what we write is always "creative"—books, poems, novels, memoir, short stories, plays—unless we are solicited for a book review or wish to apply for a writerly grant to support more of our writerly activities. Teaching is how we support our writing. When and if we choose the classroom as a subject for writing, we do so with equal parts empathy and eye-rolling, crafting poems about students who torture confessions out of a poem instead of "waterskiing across" its surface,[2] honing images of the "dull roar of air forced to spend its life indoors" in a Florida classroom while in colder climates, plum trees explode with petals.[3]

Thus, what follows here could be called neither "writing" nor "creative," according to the assumptions made by and about my discipline, and I will explore why by reviewing selected articles and books from the last 20 years of the scholarship of teaching and learning (SoTL) in the field. As evidence of the nascent state of creative writing SoTL, my analysis will include questions long since settled by other disciplines, including whether the subject—creative writing—can be taught, and if so, by whom. I will then identify two major elements of creative writing's signature pedagogy: the lessons we teach about the writing process, including how to "read as a writer" and hone perception; and the most enduring method of critique, the writer's workshop. Finally, I will suggest some ways to broaden our perspectives as creative writing teachers, researchers, and scholars—to open up our discipline, reflect, and re-see, or *re-vision*, in all of its splendor and its squalor, the panoramic potential within the academy, our identities, and our students.

Unnatural Settings: The SoTL Grid and the Creative Writing Wilderness

With over 720 degree-conferring programs in the United States (Fenza, 2007), creative writing is clearly a discipline worth investigating. It is also a major growth area in English studies: in just eight years, the number of programs offering the B.A. or B.F.A. in creative writing skyrocketed from 10 programs in 1996 to 86 in 2004; the number of graduate programs, including the Ph.D., nearly doubled (Fenza, 2007).

Despite the burgeoning of creative writing programs, scholarship on its teaching practices—particularly scholarship supported by evidence, data, and assessment—is minimal (Light, 2002; Mayers, 1999; Ritter & Vanderslice, 2007). In fact, in an analysis of the past 15 years of SoTL in various disciplines (Witman & Richlin, 2007), creative writing doesn't even register. The omission of creative writing from this study—as well as the Fine Arts as an entire category of disciplines worth investigating—reveals two core problems of conducting SoTL in creative writing: the problem of procedure and the problem of publication. First, there is the perception of writers, teachers, and analysts alike that because creative writing, like the Fine Arts, is expressionistic, individualistic, personal, and instinctive (Light, 2002, p. 259), it cannot be assessed using the methodology of SoTL. Indeed, teachers in other, less "personal" disciplines struggle to apply a grid of baselines and hypotheses to their classroom practices (Richlin & Cox, 1990, p. 6, cited in Witman & Richlin, 2007).

Already an "unnatural setting" for creative writing instructors, the work of SoTL becomes even more challenging in its accepted procedures and common terminology. Indeed, as the authors assert, to qualify as SoTL work, a new teaching method must be applied and systematically documented. In the final step of SoTL before publication, the overall project is assessed based on "student achievement of learning objectives" in the course (Witman & Richlin, 2007, p. 3), a seemingly simple endeavor. Yet however elementary these terms and procedures seem for other disciplines, "student achievement" and "learning objectives" are particularly vexing for the teacher of creative writing, for when it comes to determining achievement for writers, especially student writers, age-old questions raise their grizzled heads: how can we quantify "success" in art? What about the efforts of novice practitioners? What measures can we use to assess "student achievement"—innovation? Consistency? Favorable student critiques? Our own favorable critiques? Publishing one's work would appear to be the gold standard of success for writers, but aside from the tastes and tides that drive the literary market, such validations occur outside of the classroom and often several years later—beyond the usual timeline of SoTL research.[4]

For creative writing, the problem of assessment is not only the "how," but also the "what" and "when." At the undergraduate level, instructors are aware that most students will not pursue creative writing as a vocation: in Gaffigan's 1995 survey, "71% of poetry instructors believed that ten percent or less of their students would pursue an M.F.A. . . . [and nearly the same number] doubted their students would continue to write poetry three years after the course" (1995, p. 3). So many undergraduate-level teachers might ask, just what are we trying to do? What *are* our "teaching objectives"? The answers are unknown, because, although creative writing has signature pedagogies to be detailed below, few teachers have defined in public forums their pedagogical goals. As Gaffigan concludes, though most agree that the goal of teaching graduate students is to train publishable, and published, writers (a goal very few M.F.A. or Ph.D. graduates accomplish), "the goals of teaching workshops to undergraduates are not as clearly established" (p. 10).

At the same time, both the Gaffigan survey and Bizarro's (2007) discussion of Robert Browning's career reveal that creative writing teachers have distinct objectives, or at least hopes, for students: to build their long-term development of writerly skills and perspectives. For example, many instructors realize that finding one's way into a character or resolving a story's conflicts may take years, as classroom lessons blend with personal maturity. Similarly, Uppal's (2007) teaching objective is to build in her students a lifelong understanding of audience awareness, modes of criticism, and critical reading skills. Yet again, however, such goals conflict with boundaries of the academic term and standard measures of assessment, as Uppal notes:

> I've always thought that creative writing students ought to be asked to evaluate their course experiences not at the end of the term, but after a few years of writing on their own. It is a teacher's goal to create an atmosphere conducive to learning and, in the process, teach students how to continue the learning process once out of the classroom. (2007, p. 53)

Another problem in assessing teaching objectives is that in creative writing, many students harbor no other aspiration than to sing songs of themselves, and they actively resist any lesson that challenges their pure self-expression.

To be sure, creative writing instructors do find ways to assess student achievement in the short term, to identify and address "problems" in teaching, and to reflect upon their practices. However, most pedagogical scholarship in the field overlooks these elements in various ways. For example, Light's survey of British students who had taken at least one creative writing course (2002) presents a good taxonomy of student perceptions—how students think creative writing is different from other kinds of writing; what students articulate, if anything, about writing for readers—but it includes no mention of their *preconceptions* before taking creative writing classes, or of the actual teaching practices that shaped their perceptions. On the other side of the coin, Gaffigan's survey (1995) of poetry workshop instructors investigates the influences affecting a range of their practices, but teaching problems, student feedback, and actual assignments are neither included nor assessed.

Beyond these studies, the major writings about the discipline might be described as "reflections from experienced teachers" (Witman & Richlin, 2007, 3) and fall into distinct genres: anthologies featuring famous writer-teachers discussing the myths and problems of writing programs (Moxley, 1989; Siegel, 1989); histories of the discipline (Myers, 1996); calls for change in teaching practices and attitudes, including collaborations with fields like composition (Bishop 1994; Mayers, 1999; Mayers, 2007); the uses of creative writing in other kinds of courses such as literature (Rakoff, 2001); teaching tips and collected wisdom; and anecdotes about writerly experiences, such as studying with famous authors. Selected works from some of these genres—and works closer to conventional SoTL—will be reviewed in more depth below.

At the same time, we must keep in mind the second problem of SoTL for creative writing teachers: the perception by *others*, including tenure and promotion committees, that the publication of SoTL is an unnatural—and unworthy—endeavor for creative writers. As Witman and Richlin acknowledge, "[T]he sad truth is that many departments, disciplines, and institutions do not count 'pedagogical scholarship' as part of a faculty member's scholarly production" (2007, p. 3). Thus, institutional pressure to publish novels and collections—not to mention the years such projects consume—helps explain why the signature pedagogy of creative writing has remained largely unexamined, unchallenged, and unrevised for over 70 years. Moreover, those who do publish SoTL are often already expected to analyze writing processes and assessments: Most scholars of teaching and learning in the field are trained and practice equally in composition studies, routinely publishing their work in such journals as *College English* and *College Composition and Communication.* On the other hand, few articles on teaching practices appear in the *Writer's Chronicle,* the sole journal marketed to creative writer-teachers in academia. Published by the Association for Writers and Writing Programs (AWP), the *Chronicle* features author interviews, articles on craft, reports on the job market, and forums on controversial topics. But despite the annual "Pedagogy Forum" at AWP Conferences, only around 7% of the *Chronicle's* content since 1989 has focused on teaching.[5] In addition, according to insiders, the "Pedagogy Forum" is a forum that "real writers" aren't supposed to attend, but rather use to justify departmental funding for the travel to the conference, because creative writers simply "don't give papers at conferences" (Bizarro, 1998, p. 286). Reinforcing the notion that for creative writers, even mentioning teaching practices is unnatural, AWP Executive Director D. W. Fenza makes no mention of the word "pedagogy" in his organizational overview (2008).

Conflicts at the Heart: Can Creative Writing Be Taught?

Given the unsettled nature of creative writing's pedagogical scholarship, it's no surprise that a recent anthology on creative writing pedagogy still asks, as its title, *Can it really be taught?* (Ritter & Vanderslice, 2007). This question is as old as the field, which emerged in the 1880s with a course in advanced composition at Harvard University (Myers, 1996). To some extent, asking if writing can, or must, be taught seems logical. After all, somehow Hemingway became Hemingway before the emergence of graduate writing programs in the 1930s. Even today, the romanticized image of the "self-made" writer persists: While graduate students hob-knob with luminaries around seminar tables, "real writers" sit in a "drafty attic garret, confront demons alone in the twilight, and write" (Wells, 2005, p. CM 12). The various contributors to the anthology cite dramatic pronouncements about the (un)teachability of creative writing, from Robert Harlow's statement that "one cannot teach originality; one can only preach awareness of the conditions which allow originality," (1966, cited in Uppal, 2007, p. 49) to Mary Oliver's assertion that "Everyone knows that poets are born and not made in school . . . something that is essential can't be taught" (1994, cited in Mayers, 1997, p. 3).

As a work of SoTL, the anthology offers some excellent insights into the practices and major questions of the field. Chief among these is the editors' review of previous pedagogical analysis, most of which "sidesteps scholarship" and consists mainly of "'stories'—literally *lore*—rather than contextualized discussions discussion of teaching as a profession or analyses that relate theories of writing to theories of teaching" (Ritter & Vanderslice, 2007, p. xiv). Significantly, Ritter and Vanderslice place their literature review in a context of "lore," defined by Stephen North as "the accumulated body of traditions, practices, and beliefs . . . that influence how writing is done, learned, and taught" (as cited in Ritter and Vanderslice, p. xiv). In contrast, in assembling their anthology, the editors asked "teachers to reconsider commonly held assumptions about how creative writers 'learn' to write . . . and to move beyond personal anecdote and myth" (p. xvi). However, only a handful of contributors (Uppal, Leahy, and Healy & Starkey) directly address and at least partially assess teaching methods and objectives. The remaining essays, though fascinating, discuss typologies of teaching (Cross) and personal experiences (Haake, Cain, and Bizarro & McClanahan) or call for programmatic changes and cross-disciplinary collaborations (Mayers)—the very genres disdained by the editors, including personal anecdote and myth.

An oft-referenced text in SoTL publications is D. G. Myers's (1996) spirited history of creative writing. Although not a work of SoTL, Myers's study is useful for understanding the origins and philosophies guiding the signature pedagogies of creative writing. In it, Myers chronicles the formation of creative writing as an academic field, as well as the emergence of the "writer-teacher" among English department faculty. In 1934, for example, Dorothea Brande asserted in *Becoming a Writer* that writing can be taught to anyone, even women, who had long been excluded from the male ranks of "genius." According to Myers, at roughly the same time as Brande was pioneering the signature pedagogy of "reading as a writer," professor Norman Foerster founded creative writing as a discipline at Iowa University—and what would eventually become the signature pedagogy of the writers' workshop—in an effort "to give all types of literary students a rigorous and appropriate discipline" (as cited in Myers, 1996, p. 126). Interestingly, in Foerster's conception, writing could indeed be taught, but it was actually the *geniuses* who were most in need of schooling, because contemporary writers were "lamentably uneducated" about literature and culture (1929, as cited in Myers, 1996, p. 134). Placing creative writing within a humanist context, as a means of examining literature from "the inside," Myers calls for a return to creative writing's disciplinary origins: a pedagogy that promotes connectedness among the fields of literary study, instead of the divides that characterize creative writing programs today.

Another landmark response to the "Can it be taught?" question comes from Wallace Stegner, a novelist and the founder of Stanford's Creative Writing program. Transcribed from a live discussion before Dartmouth audiences in 1980 and published in 1988, Stegner's *On the Teaching of Creative Writing* is not a work of SoTL, but rather an excellent explication of the typical writer-teacher's approach—something akin to creative writing's signature mindset. He begins by asking, "How can anyone 'teach' writing, when he himself, as an author, is never sure what he is doing?" (1988, p. 9). Comparing literature to a voyage, Stegner states,

> Nobody can teach the geography of the undiscovered. All he can do is encourage the will to explore, plus impress upon the unexperienced a few of the dos and don'ts of voyaging. A teacher who has been on those seas can teach certain things: equivalents of the use of compass and sextant; the language and its uses and certain tested literary tools and techniques and strategies and stances and ways of getting at the narrative . . . . (1988, p. 10)

Indeed, in my own classes, I've found that discussing the mis-steps of particular short stories—supplemented with my drafts, notes, and excised scenes—has demystified the process of writing for my students, and deglamorized the polish of published work. In doing this, I am careful to qualify that my work is not to be taken as a paradigm of the writing I expect; instead, I discuss my stories as if they are living things, still animate with possibility.

Dangerous Characters and Departmental Drama: The Writer as Teacher

Central to Stegner's characterization of creative writing teacher is the fact that he/she has been "on those seas"—significantly, Stegner imagines a writer who teaches. Moreover, in terms of pedagogical practices, this writer-teacher operates self-consciously as *another writer in the classroom*—one who never fully understands, nor masters, the creative process. Unlike professors in other disciplines who command facts and certainties, Stegner's writer-teacher professes from the personal experience of uncertainty and error, of sudden inspirations and bedeviling silences, and of passionate reactions to the work of other writers. Even if a writer-teacher can articulate "what worked" in a particular piece of writing, each poem or story is individual—as each student writer is individual—so the writer-teacher's formula for success may never again be repeated. Author William Hollinger elaborates on this in *Creative Writing in America: Theory and Pedagogy:* "My own writing process varies considerably from one project to another. I never write the same way twice; each new story and novel grows differently" (as cited in Moxley, 1989, p. 256). This is in stark contrast to the writing process usually taught in composition courses, which leads all students through the same orderly, if recursive, stages of brainstorming topics, proposing theses, outlining, researching, drafting, receiving feedback, and revising for every project—and assigns points for the work done in each stage.

But in creative writing courses, wherein the semester's end carries no guarantee of a finished final product, and assignments completed for identical exercises will look far more different than alike, a stance of professorial not-knowing is akin to the authorial not-knowing—Stegner's "geography of the undiscovered"—necessary to creativity. A commonplace in the anecdotes and aphorisms of hundreds of books on craft, this writerly not-knowing threads the very fabric of creative writing's signature pedagogy. As writer Robin Hemley observes, "Any new approach, any new way of seeing the world or one's work, is what we're after. That's the hallmark of creation, after all. If we only teach our certainties, then we might as well just record our lofty thoughts and prescriptions and hit 'play' at the beginning of the term" (2000, ¶ 38).

Hemley learned to teach his uncertainties from a famous writer-teacher, Barry Hannah, who in his workshops "always approached the process of writing as an ongoing experiment" (Hemley, 2000, ¶ 32). In the greater context of creative writing pedagogy, Hemley's admiration for his mentor leads to another set of questions: who should teach creative writing? Is the subject best taught by its best practitioners? The answer is complex. One the one hand, the exploits of Famous Author-Teachers are the "campfire stories" of our field. On the other hand, courses helmed by published authors can be "a wonderful thing: the opportunity for students to talk with writers actively engaged in finding solutions to the same kinds of problems in writing the students must solve for themselves" (Bizarro & McClanahan, 2007, p. 86)—be they problems of process or of publication, like finding an agent and promoting one's work.

Still, as Bizarro notes, aside from problems of personality, other issues complicate students' relationships with the Famous Author-Teacher. First, there is the imbalance of authority and power in the classroom, which can lead to a "master-apprentice" relationship—"the teacher having near dictatorial control over the students' texts" and, according to some reports, failing students who do not implement the teacher's suggestions (Bizarro & McClanahan, 2007, p. 86). As a result, a second problem can occur: "a generation of clones—students who sound amazingly like teachers. And because their teachers have some influence over what gets published and wins awards, this sameness is perpetuated in the magazines and journals that publish creative writing" (p. 86). Finally, and most importantly, scholar Kelly Ritter asserts that "the notion that a writer who succeeds as a writer by trade need [not] be trained in any formal, academic sense" is at least partly to blame for the dearth of teacher-training classes in most graduate writing programs (2001, p. 215). Ritter found that as of 1999, four of 25 Ph.D.–granting institutions required training in creative writing teaching; on the other hand, nearly all required coursework in the teaching of composition (p. 218). Consequently, creative writing Ph.D.s mainly learn to teach by osmosis—by watching their own workshop teachers in action—and conflation, relating the techniques of composition pedagogy to the creative writing classroom, despite vast differences in assessment, goals, and student populations.[6]

Point-of-View and Dialogue: The Signature Pedagogy of Creative Writing

Despite, or perhaps because of, the lack of teacher training, the practices of the discipline are remarkably uniform. Two basic principles underlie the activities that constitute creative writing's signature pedagogy. First, in order to discover images, characters, plots, and metaphors of their own, students must learn to see anew: to change their usual points-of-view on assigned literature as well as their lives, reading both text and experience "as writers." Second, once stories and poems have been drafted, students must learn to give and receive criticism in the full-class dialogue known as the writing workshop.

More than any other recommendation, writing teachers advise students to read extensively, believing "that students cannot create works of art, much less popular works of fiction or poetry, if they are not avid readers and aware of literary trends and genres" (Moxley, 1990, ¶ 8). Essential to this reading process is "reading as a writer." Introduced by Dorothea Brande in 1934 and refined by AWP founder R. V. Cassill in his handbook, *Writing Fiction* (1975), key to the concept is reading literary works not for their "aboutness," but for their "madeness." For many pedagogy scholars, "aboutness" describes the kind of reading done in literature classrooms, wherein a text is "understood as the result of unseen forces—in society, the times, the structure of the language—that produce it," or run through the "interpretive machine" of a critical approach (Myers, 1994, ¶¶ 13, 10). In contrast, Brande and Cassill advocate reading that examines the text's construction, asking what effect a story has achieved and what techniques the author used to do so—all in an effort to see how the student might (or might not) deploy similar tools in his or her own work. Illuminating the author's choices, texts are discussed as still brimming with alternatives: we might ask, "Could Toni Cade Bambara have written 'The Lesson' from Miss Moore's—or even a polished third-person narrator's—point of view?"[7] Or "Why did Li Young Lee describe his father's voice as a 'well of dark water, a prayer,' instead of as a birdsong, or thunder?"[8] In reading, "what a writer wants to note . . . is how the [work], its language, and all its parts have been joined together" (Cassill, cited in Dawson, p. 93). In my classes, I compare this process to looking under the hood of a car to see what makes it go (or stall out, or sputter along)—a technician's approach to examining a machine whose mission is to move.

Thus, "reading as a writer" situates published texts within the writing process, which prepares our students in several ways for creating their own works. First, it offers students models of what they might do on the page, granting a kind of "permission" to take risks as other authors have. Second, reading models makes students aware of the "aesthetic criteria separating 'good' from 'not so good' literature," and through discussion and reflection, they learn to use the critical vocabulary necessary to discuss each other's work (Clair, 1991, ¶ 4). Third, to disabuse students of the myth that "writing poems and stories means being suddenly inspired, and with little more than desire, creating a masterpiece in one draft" (¶ 3), reading as a writer allows us to discuss published work as a collection of choices, revisions, and reconsiderations. Finally, when students put down Robert Coover's "The Babysitter," puzzled by the multiple endings, or when they throw a poem across the room for being clichéd, they understand that the work *they* write can confuse or irritate a reader, too. Writing is no longer a private act but a performance before an audience. By reading as writers, students also begin to write as readers.

Some scholars have begun to challenge this pedagogy, asking what, exactly, students should *do* with all this reading. As Katherine Haake writes, "It's not enough to assert that writers are readers first, or even supply exhaustive models," because "all such work serves to reinforce the choices of the teacher and hence, the perpetuation of his or her aesthetic biases" (2007, p. 21). Haake asserts that presenting literature only as a standard of greatness is an "imitative pedagogy," and, believing they're reading what the professor admires, students will seek to reproduce it (p. 21). One of Haake's solutions to "look beyond the lure of the idealized text" and to make students aware of the "pressures—trends, market censorship, literary traditions, the classroom parameters of taste—that exert themselves on reading/writing, in general, and their own, on particular" (p. 21). In other words, teachers should actively discuss the factors shaping their own, and cultural, standards of "greatness," rather than passively perpetuating "greatness" as its own objective standard. In turn, Haake speculates, students may question their own aesthetics and rediscover the pleasures of the text, as well as what it might teach them.

In the classroom, writer Maxine Clair (1991) incorporates assignments based on oral literature. By reading oral literature as writers (or in this case, as oral performers), Clair's students became empowered to use the materials of their own memories and traditions as subject matter. As Clair reminds us, reading as a writer encompasses the reading of our own lives: in order to find material, students must sift through the ordinary activities of their days. Most creative writing teachers urge their students to take notes, be observant, and "read" the life around them by listening to conversations in grocery aisles or noting the way their landlord wears his toupee. In this way, "reading as a writer" also means collecting details, images, pieces of dialogue, memories, random thoughts, newspaper articles, gossip, and so on—usually in a writing journal.

Another element of creative writing's signature pedagogy, the writing journal is both a receptacle for gathered bits and a kind of text—one to be read as a writer, with an eye for possibility. Much as students discuss the choices published authors have made on the page, so too do they learn to select, reject, and combine the pieces they've gathered. Looking over her journal, a writer might wonder why her landlord even has a toupee—and in this manner, she begins to imagine a character's desires. When the student merges that landlord with a memory she jotted down—"the girl loved brushing her horse's mane"—a second character enters the picture, and an unlikely love story has begun.

From this example, we can discern what might be called the "signature sensibilities" of creative writing pedagogy: an attunement to possibility, the encouragement of serendipity, and the abandonment of outlines or any kind of map. A mapless journey can be terrifying and messy, we warn our students, but often, where they arrive is thrilling. By guiding them through the process of reading their own environments with selectivity, we teach our students to see "the angel in the marble" discussed by Michelangelo (Bizarro & McClanahan, 2007, p. 78)—and nudge it to take wing.

Once in flight, however, student writing usually goes through the writing workshop, a process that sometimes launches a work to the heavens, while others crash, wings clipped, to Earth. Largely unchanged in some scholars' estimation for the past 100 years, the workshop method is the most prevalent—and most maligned—element of creative writing's signature pedagogy. And although many calls for change in workshop practices have been issued in articles of the anecdotal and "teaching tips" genres, few if any have approached workshop as a teaching "problem" requiring hypothesis, solution, and assessment. In fact, even its "problem-ness" has yet to be adequately addressed via the methods of SoTL.

As described in the opening of this article, the basic operations of workshop involve the dissemination of a student's writing to the entire class, who then discuss the work. Many professors also require that students prepare written comments for the writer. In the classic workshop model, the writer remains silent until discussion is over so that he/she cannot explain nor defend the work. Indeed, the workshop is not about the writer at all, but rather, about the work. And yet, when a major national magazine editor has just eviscerated one's story, as happened to me in one workshop, it isn't the story that limps out at break and calls its mother in tears. It is the writer. This is perhaps the most difficult—and valuable—aspect of having one's writing workshopped: Nobody cares about the writer's feelings. Readers care about the story, what's under its hood, and what makes it go—and how it might go even farther.

To be sure, the workshop model succeeds on many levels, which is one reason it endures. First and foremost, the practice introduces a writer's work to readers—mouthy, learned, passionate readers—a whole bunch of them at one time. The sole focus of the class is the work a writer has crafted, and ideally, discussion incorporates not only reactions ("I hated the landlord") but also suggestions for reaching the writer's apparent goals ("If this is a love story, can the horse trainer seem more loveable?"). The writer's choices and their effects are considered, discussed, refined, and contested—as are the myriad suggestions offered by his or her readers. The sheer volume of commentary can be both confusing and inspiring: "workshop members . . . can learn much more than even the most diligent writer could ascertain in the same amount of time while working alone" (Oliver, 1994, ¶ 4). In addition, because so many experienced readers, including the professor, are analyzing one's work, performance anxiety can motivate writers to try harder. Beyond "forc[ing] students to escape their own perspectives and better understand the need for, and possibilities of, revision" (Moxley, 1990), workshop introduces students to the language of their craft, sharpens their editorial skills, and sets writing deadlines (Guevara, 1998)—an impressive list of benefits, to be sure. Likewise, Light (2002) found that through group peer critique, many students begin to integrate the reader into their writing.

However, workshop pedagogy is also suffering from exhaustion, and its ills are varied and numerous. The problems fall into three broad categories: the students, the teacher, and the content. Not surprisingly, when teachers discuss the pitfalls of workshop, they mainly focus on the students. According to Gaffigan (1995), chief among poetry instructors' complaints were student arrogance and intractability, which in workshop, manifested as resistance or condescension toward comments and peer work. Additionally, instructors noted that despite our entreaties to read, students often refused, preferring to read only their own work. Such self-centeredness can lead to a workshop "culture of narcissism" in which "students write like one another" (Solataroff; William H. Gass, cited in Moxley, ¶¶ 5 and 8). Moxley (1990) delineates other problems:

> [E]ven the boldest students are reluctant to mention aspects of craft they do not understand. Even one student—if he is forceful, articulate, and extremely negative—can shatter the ambiance of openness and trust that is essential to critical inquiry. And meeker, introverted students might be inclined to shy away from submitting experimental work [that] goes against the grain of what other students in the class are producing. (¶ 4).

Furthermore, because workshop "is built upon *personal*, rather than professional relationships [and] the writing is *raw* effort, and therefore, closely connected to the self" (Leahy, 2007, p. 58), students must talk and listen while suppressing anxiety, defensiveness, and vulnerability. In poetry, and underlying much fiction, students are often "exposing their most personal and private thoughts . . . to the room, and many lack the maturity and/or the objectivity to handle criticism of their 'writings' appropriately" (Uppal, 2007, p. 52, footnote). Although we might discuss the voice of "the poetic speaker," terminology cannot mask the fact that we're also discussing the life of a writer whose abortion, molestation, or other trauma is the topic of the day. In workshop, content—even in the works of others—hits home.

The anxieties of workshop, then, offering intriguing possibilities to future pedagogical scholarship, and it would be fascinating to examine these practices through a lens of "CAL," or Cognitive-Affective Learning. As described by Patti Owen-Smith, CAL scholars ask such questions as "How do we construct emotional practices that help learners (and ourselves) make the connection between the heart and mind?" (2004, p. 11). Moreover, the emotions of workshop seem to challenge prevailing assumptions. Presently, many scholars contend that high anxiety leads students to abandon their goals rather than fail—and that "requisite skills and self-confidence must be present in order for a student to persist toward a goal" (Wallace & Truelove, 2006, p. 22). However, an experience in one of my recent courses illustrates just the opposite. For an undergraduate Advanced Workshop, a painfully shy student submitted the first 40 pages—of 300 pages she'd already written—of a novel years in the making. The work didn't fare well. The workshop expressed concerns about clichés and preciousness, as the draft told the story of a dead teenaged girl guided through her memories by a mischievous fairy. Afterward, as I spoke with her about revision, tears rolled down her face. Neither of us acknowledged her weeping, and I felt as if I'd become a Bad Workshop Leader; that evening, I expected to receive notice that she had abandoned the course. But the next day, she reported she'd thrown out the old novel and had begun again, this time with a live character and no fairies. She'd already drafted 30 pages.

To my great surprise, the workshop had produced a usefully "*disorienting* moment" significant to enduring learning (Owen-Smith, 2004, p. 11, emphasis hers). Why does a painful workshop lead one student to amazing growth, while another sits quietly and mentally defends her writing, resisting all revision? How can instructors acknowledge feelings in the workshop without collapsing into group hugs and "reducing the materials of our courses to secondary status" (2004, p.11)? From these examples it's clear that as a site of future SoTL, workshop is rich with possibility.

Of course, feelings aren't the sole property of writers; readers are often offended by the work of their peers. Dangerous topics enter workshop conversations, and as instructors, we are endangered, too. Much as I fretted over how to workshop my student's rape story, David Schanker wondered, "Should students be free to bring to class stories that glorify violence, stories that may be regarded as sacrilegious or blasphemous, stories that are homophobic or misogynist or pornographic?" (2005, p.5) After a few students voiced offense, Schanker implemented warning labels—cover sheets students they could put their work if "they felt [it] contained material that other students may find objectionable." Then a student's cover sheet warned "this story contains homosexuality," but the story itself was not graphic; it "was simply a 'breakup story'" between two men (p. 2). In this case, from the professor's good intentions grew the student's perception that Schanker, or the class, was homophobic—and that Schanker permitted students to reject reading the work of others because of their own prejudices. Ultimately, Schanker proposes three solutions for troublesome workshop content—ranging from student self-censorship or professor censorship, to the warning label system, to a "no censorship, no cop-outs" (p. 6) policy where anything goes. Yet he rests uneasy with each. It remains a problem worth investigating: how should creative writing professors balance student feelings with academic freedom? Is it appropriate for instructors to suppress students' work, or is this a kind of bullying?

As Guevara (1998) notes, the worst workshops are teacher-dominated, and student participation is fastidiously controlled: they operate as a kind of "public judging of a text-in-progress, with the instructor acting as magistrate or foreman of the jury" (¶ 9)—or worse yet, as a prosecutor. Indeed, bad students can undermine the workshop community, but bad teachers do even greater damage. Bad workshop leaders embed their own judgments in questions to the class, issue pronouncements, and talk far more than their students, itemizing fault without offering suggestions. Consequently, quite often, the writer leaves feeling condemned.

The scholarship on workshops proposes many cures for these ills, including creating peer partnerships (Guevara, 1998) and assigning topics for students to write about. But largely overlooked are ways to build a pedagogy of reflection—how we might teach students to deal with criticism from various sources, peer and professor alike. Certainly, reflective practices have been defined, assessed, and studied in other disciplines (Russo & Ford, 2006), and the applications to creative writing could be particularly fruitful. Such a practice is not without risk:

> Reflection can be a painful process because it disrupts our taken-for-granted ways of thinking and acting . . . . [similar processes] can be

> impeded by defensive reasoning, which we experience when we try to avoid feeling embarrassed, incompetent, vulnerable, or when our egos are threatened. (p. 2)

And yet, creative writers manage such feelings all the time: finding inspiration despite writers' block, revising work that won't cooperate, sharing work with tough readers, receiving rejections from publishers. All of these rattle our taken-for-granted ways of thinking. Such pain is the writerly condition.

Perhaps one solution is to incorporate more student self-reflection, more regularly, into creative writing classes—and to forefront our own ways of interpreting, working with, and being productive with the various obstacles writers encounter. To this end, I assign my advanced undergraduates "self-diagnostics"—a kind of dissertation abstract, minus the dissertation—about their writing habits and recent work. In addition, I bring a stack of editors' rejections my fiction has received, mainly to illustrate to students perseverance ("This story was rejected 40 times before it won a major award!"). What would happen, though, if I discussed what I, as a writer, did with this stack of feedback? What rankled me, and what worked? Or, what if I furnished the workshop comments and drafts of a student writer's final portfolio and laid bare the way criticism helped shape revision? What if I showed my students how writers connect the dots?

Toward Resolution(s)

My review of the signature pedagogy and scholarship of creative writing reveals, overall, a need to connect the dots within and outside of the classroom. Currently, students are often left on their own to discern what good literature is; in workshop, they must sublimate personal connections and feelings in favor of detached critique and sort through a mass of self-contradictory feedback, wondering how to link any of it to revision. On a broader level, creative writing students are often isolated from the practices of other fields like literature, composition, theory, and pedagogy. Meanwhile, students who aspire to teach creative writing remain largely disconnected from field-specific pedagogy. As professionals, we writer-teachers uneasily inhabit the academy, ignoring conference sessions on pedagogy and anticking as "eccentricity delegates" (Saul Bellow, cited in Camoin,1984, ¶ 5)when we're not writing behind closed office doors. According to the lore we help create, all we wish to see is writing, our writing—the brightness of our own stars. But now it seems our reflections are blinding us, and we no longer see the sky.

As writer-teachers, let's change our perspective on what we do; let's get over ourselves. To start, let's erase the hyphen: we are writers *and* teachers, in equal parts, and we should examine both as processes. Let's encourage our students to see the world anew, too: to explore their own multiple identities; to take courses in literature, theory, social dance, ceramics, botany, astronomy; to find metaphors in mitosis or to re-envision the story of Orion's belt. In return, let's listen to the voices our students hear, the shows they watch and the fantasy novels they read—as long as we can stand it—and try to enlarge our powers of empathy, to understand what they *want* to write, and why. While we're at it, let's revise our reading lists and include models outside of literary realism. Let's stop banishing topics like ghosts, aliens, vampires, and fairytales. Instead, let's show them how to do it better. Finally, let's stop seeing students as our apprentices or viewing their works as reflections of our high standards. Let's treat them like writers and push them to articulate their processes, failures, and inspirations. Let's show them how to see their own work, however nascent, as a body of writing with patterns. Let's ask them to analyze their habits—then to write against them. As writers and teachers, we know there's too much safety in surrounding ourselves with likenesses, consensus, traditional practices, lore, and legend. Instead, let's be writerly and teacherly, and make our students and selves uncomfortable. In doing so, maybe we'll glimpse the winking of other lights around us and see the possibility in constellation—the new stories that can take shape among what gathers.

References

Bizarro, P. (1998). Review: Should I write this essay or finish a poem? Teaching writing creatively. *College Composition and Communication, 49*(2), 285–297.

Bizarro, P., & McClanahan, M. (2007). Putting wings on the invisible: Voice, authorship, and the authentic self. In K. Ritter and S. Vanderslice (Eds.), *Can it really be taught?* (pp. 77–90). Portsmouth, NH: Boynton/Cook.

Cain, M. A. (2007). Charming tyrants and faceless facilitators: The lore of teaching identities in creative writing. In K. Ritter and S. Vanderslice (Eds.), *Can it really be taught?* (pp. 28–37). Portsmouth, NH: Boynton/Cook.

Camoin, F. (1984). The writer and the English department. Retrieved January 1, 2008, from http://elink.awpwriter.org/m/awpChron/articles/fcamoin01.lasso

Clair, M. (1991). On literature in the teaching of creative writing. *AWP Chronicle.* Retrieved January 8, 2008, from http://elink.awpwriter.org/m/awpChron/articles/mclair01.lasso

Cross, M. (2007). Writing in public: Popular pedagogies of creative writing. In K. Ritter and S. Vanderslice (Eds.), *Can it really be taught?* (pp. 67–76). Portsmouth, NH: Boynton/Cook.

Dawson, P. (2004). *Creative writing and the new humanities.* New York and London: Routledge.

Fenza, D. (2007) About AWP: The growth of creative writing programs. Retrieved December 30, 2007, from http://www.awpwriter.org/aboutawp/index.htm

Fenza, D. (2008) A letter from AWP's Executive Director. In *AWP director's handbook* (pp. 1–2). Retrieved July 8, 2008, from http://www.awpwriter.org/pdf/DirectorsHandbook2008.pdf

Gaffigan, M. (1995). Reinventing the undergraduate poetry workshop: Reports from a nationwide survey of undergraduate poetry writing instructors. *AWP Chronicle.* Retrieved January 6, 2008, from http://elink.awpwriter.org/m/awpChron/articles/mgaffigan01.lasso

Guevara, M. K. (1998) Out of the ashtray: Revivifying creative writing classes. *AWP Chronicle.* Retrieved January 8, 2008, from http://elink.awpwriter.org/m/awpChron/articles/mguevara01.lasso

Haake, K. (2007). Against reading. In K. Ritter and S. Vanderslice (Eds.), *Can it really be taught?* (pp. 14–27). Portsmouth, NH: Boynton/Cook.

Healy, E. K., & Starkey, D. (2007). A better time teaching. In K. Ritter and S. Vanderslice (Eds.), *Can it really be taught?* (pp. 38–45). Portsmouth, NH: Boynton/Cook.

Hemley, R. (2000). Teaching our uncertainties. *AWP Chronicle.* Retrieved January 6, 2008, from http://elink.awpwriter.org/m/awpChron/articles/rhemley01.lasso

Light, G. (2002). From the personal to the public: Conceptions of creative writing in higher education. *Higher Education 43,* 257–276.

Leahy, A. (2007). Creativity, caring, and the easy 'A': Rethinking the role of self-esteem in creative writing pedagogy. In K. Ritter and S. Vanderslice (Eds.), *Can it really be taught?* (pp. 55–66). Portsmouth, NH: Boynton/Cook.

Mayers, T. (1999). (Re)writing craft. *College Composition and Communication 51*(1), 82–89.

Mayers, T. (2007). Figuring the future: Lore and/in creative writing. In K. Ritter and S. Vanderslice (Eds.), *Can it really be taught?* (pp. 1–13). Portsmouth, NH: Boynton/Cook.

Moxley, J. M. (1989). *Creative writing in America: Theory and pedagogy.* Urbana, IL: NCTE.

Moxley, J. M. (1990). Creative writing and composition: bridging the gap. *AWP Chronicle.* Retrieved January 1, 2008, from http://elink.awpwriter.org/m/awpChron/articles/jmmoxley01.lasso

Myers, D. G. (1994). The lesson of creative writing's history. *AWP Chronicle, 26*(1), 12–14. Retrieved July 8, 2008, from http://www-english.tamu.edu/pers/fac/myers/lesson_of_its_history.html

Myers, D. G. (1996). *The elephants teach: Creative writing since 1880.* Chicago: University of Chicago Press.

Oliver, M. (1994). Workshops and solitude. *AWP Chronicle.* Retrieved January 8, 2008, from http://elink.awpwriter.org/m/awpChron/articles/moliver01.lasso

Owen-Smith, P. (2004). What is cognitive-affective learning (CAL)? *Journal of Cognitive Affective Learning, 1*, 11.

Rakoff, J. S. (2001) "I walk the line: creative writing in the literature and composition classroom." *inventio, 3*(1). Retrieved March 1, 2008, from http://www.doit.gmu.edu/inventio/issues/Spring_2001/Rakoff_1.html

Richlin, L., & Cox, M. D. (1990). The scholarship of pedagogy: A message from the editors. *Journal on Excellence in College Teaching, 2*, 1–8.

Ritter, K. (2001). Professional writers/writing professionals: Revamping teacher training in creative writing Ph.D. programs. *College English, 69*(2), 205–227.

Russo, T. C., & Ford, D. (2006). Teachers' reflection on reflection practice. *Journal of Cognitive Affective Learning, 2*(2), 1–12.

Schanker, D. Academic freedom and the creative writing classroom. *AWP Chronicle.* Retrieved January 8, 2008, from http://elink.awpwriter.org/m/awpChron/articles/dschanker01.lasso

Stegner, W. (1988). *On the teaching of writing.* Hanover, NH: University of New England Press.

Uppal, P. (2007). Both sides of the desk: Experiencing creative writing lore as a student and as a professor. In K. Ritter and S. Vanderslice (Eds.), *Can it really be taught?* (pp. 46–54). Portsmouth, NH: Boynton/Cook.

Wallace, B. A. & Truelove, J. E. (2006). Monitoring student cognitive-affective processing through reflection to promote learning in high anxiety contexts. *Journal of Cognitive Affective Learning, 3*(1), 22–27.

Wells, J. (2005, August 21). Great expectations: Might one get published—or just enjoy a couple of years off from reality—in one of our many packed creative writing programs? *SF Gate,* p. CM-12.

Witman, P. D., & Richlin, L. (2007). The status of the scholarship of teaching and learning in the disciplines. *International Journal for the Scholarship of Teaching and Learning, 1*(1). Retrieved March 1, 2008, from http://www.georgiasouthern.edu/ijsotl/v1n1/essays/witman/IJ_witman.pdf

Notes

1. Sebold's memoir of her rape and recovery is *Lucky*; her novel is *The Lovely Bones* (both published in 2002, New York: Little, Brown).

2. Collins, B. (1988). Introduction to poetry. *The apple that astonished Paris.* Fayetteville, AR: University of Arkansas Press.

3. Gregor, D. (2006). The poetry of bad weather. *The Southwest Review, 91*(1), 90.

4. Regarding using publication as evidence of the success of writing courses, Bizarro and McClanahan (2007) articulate another factor that's been buzzed about for years: "85 percent of the 135 poets chosen to appear in *The Best American Poetry* for 1990 and 1991 were graduates, professors, or administrators of creative writing programs . . . [But] . . . the 85 percent statistic might not mean that writing programs are working, but that writing teachers who 'succeed' might select work for recognition when it sounds like their own" (p. 78).

5. These estimates (rounded up) have been culled from both a topic search and a year-by-year search of the online archives of *The Chronicle* from 1989 to 2007. Author interviews mentioning teaching, reports on teaching jobs, articles on programs generally, and comparative studies with other countries programs were excluded from this total.

6. One indication that times may be changing is the "Post-Graduate Certificate in the Teaching of Creative Writing," a track in the Low-Residency M.F.A. program at Antioch College—LA. For more on this program, see Healy & Starkey (2007).

7. Bambara, T. (1992). The lesson. *Gorilla, my love.* New York: Knopf Publishing Group.

8. Lee, L. Y. (1986). The gift. *Rose.* Rochester, NY: BOA Editions.

5

THEORY AND PRACTICE

Signature Pedagogies in Music Theory and Performance

Gary Don, Christa Garvey, and Mitra Sadeghpour

Pedagogy in music at the undergraduate level is designed to educate the "whole musician." A series of integrated courses helps undergraduate music students understand what it means to be a musician. Each course provides students with an increased understanding of analysis, performance, and music in a socio-historical context. These courses train students to know, think about, and value music like professional musicians. Professional musicians often have multiple roles: they perform, conduct research, teach applied lessons, direct ensembles, and teach core courses in the undergraduate curriculum. They must be well rounded yet highly specialized at the same time. In fact, the sub-disciplines of theory and performance are integrated until the end of the separate terminal degrees. Both are crucial to knowing, thinking, and doing music, but each of the sub-disciplines of theory and music performance has a unique history. Understanding the historical transformations of these sub-disciplines gives us insight into the signature pedagogies that have developed today.

A Brief History

Music as a discipline has a long and rich history. Greek sources such as the *Harmonic Elements* of Aristoxenus (ca. 375 BCE) regard music theory as an area of mathematics, seeking to reveal "universal patterns of order, leading to the highest levels of knowledge and understanding," as opposed to "the descriptive or analytical study of pieces of music" or the explanation of compositional or performance practice (Mathiesen, 2002, p. 112). The tradition of theory (*musica*) as the knowledge of abstract truths continued into the Middle Ages. "Yet *musica* could not remain unmoved by the vital, contemporaneous culture of liturgical chant [*cantus*], as that movement gained momentum in the 9th and 10th centuries," giving rise to "the intellectual and artistic synthesis that represents the beginnings of 'music theory'" (Bower, 2002, p. 136). This synthesis has resulted in a broad spectrum of activities united under the rubric of "music theory." For example, some theorists continued the work of the Greeks on tuning systems in the 17th and 18th centuries, and others focused on practical training for performers and composers.

The education of performing musicians has also evolved continually, reflecting changing needs of musicians, educational philosophies, and the role of music in society. Until the advent of the conservatory system, the largest percentage of musicians were trained by family members, who provided individual instruction. The earliest formal institution for music study was the Christian Church, which sought to improve singing in the church service. These medieval church singing schools (*scholae cantorum)* provided instruction in singing, musical instruments, composition, and harmony and sometimes taught writing, literature, and rhetoric as well (Dyer, 2001). These professional schools, directly associated with providing music for church ceremonies, were separate from the medieval universities, which incorporated only the study of music theory in their curricula.

An outgrowth of the church singing school is the conservatory, which differed from the *scholae cantorum* in several ways. Like the *scholae cantorum*, the earliest conservatories, which were founded in Venice and Naples, were orphanages (*conservatorio*). Perhaps one reason orphans were trained as musicians was that the profession was considered appropriate for members of the lower social classes. Additionally, the traveling life of a performing musician would not trouble someone without family ties (Abeles, Hoffer, & Klotman, 1994, p. 7). In 1667 the Neopolitan Conservatorio di S Maria di Loreto was the first to charge tuition and board to train talented nonorphaned students (Weber, 2001).

The modern conservatory, as we know it today, was a 19th-century European product that arose out of the political shifts among the church, monarchies, and newly powerful state institutions. The conservatory was different from the church-financed schools in several ways: It trained musicians for diverse careers that filled the needs of a changing private and public musical life, not just for church services, and the institutions were often state run or managed by wealthy individuals, not the church (Weber, 2001).

At many of these conservatories, the training was for musicians with professional prospects and wealthy dilettantes alike. The education in music, however, had only loose ties to an academic education, and some conservatories did little more than match teachers with students for lessons. It is important to note that formal conservatory training and informal training in the form of apprenticeships existed together throughout the 19th century to train aspiring musicians (Weber, 2001).

Twentieth-century reforms in education, especially in the United States, created huge changes to the educational system in music. The European conservatory model for training musicians became just one of several models. Many music schools became part of a larger university system, in which music was studied as part of the larger liberal arts education. With a uniting of the conservatory and university curricula, it became common to provide a coordinated study of performance, music theory, music history, and keyboard skills, as well as general education classes that rounded out a liberal arts education. Since World War II, a broader specialization in music has been offered, with advanced degrees in traditional art music, as well as newly developed curricula in jazz, church music, music education, music therapy, and arts management (Ritterman, 2001).

The current pedagogical practices in U.S. colleges and universities in the areas of performance, composition, education, theory, and history are the result of a long process in which practices evolved to fit changing roles of music in society. Consequently, the relationships among these subdisciplines have continually shifted over time. This chapter discusses traditional pedagogical practices in music theory and performance, recent revisions to these practices, and the emerging signature pedagogies that combine the strengths of traditional and contemporary approaches. This chapter also provides a survey of research that has examined assumptions, frequently implicit, about student learning outcomes of both traditional and contemporary pedagogical practices and discusses the ways in which pedagogical research can aid in the development of disciplinary signature pedagogies.

Traditional and Signature Pedagogies in Music Theory

Contemporary music theory instruction and research seeks to combine the quest for universal patterns of order from its Greek roots with the more recent descriptive or analytical study of pieces of music. Most undergraduate music programs in contemporary U.S. colleges and universities require the study of theory and musicianship skills (including keyboard study, singing melodies at sight, and notation of performed passages of music), along with the study of voice or an instrument, regardless of the students' areas of specialization. The two-year sequence of theory courses for undergraduate music majors is designed to cultivate practical skills and knowledge to benefit all music majors, regardless of their specialties or whether they plan to pursue graduate studies.

The focus of study is the "common practice" period; that is, the works of composers primarily from Western Europe, written in the 18th and 19th centuries. Lesson plans begin with rudiments of musical notation, proceed to exercises in figured bass (a shorthand notation for chords above a bass line, employed primarily in the 17th and 18th centuries) and the writing of four-voice chorales (referred to as part writing), then to the descriptive or analytical study of pieces of music for formal attributes and stylistic similarities. The practices of figured bass and part writing are mostly based on the music of J. S. Bach (1685–1750), in particular his works for harpsichord and four-voice chorus (soprano, alto, tenor, and bass).

At the graduate level, students specializing in performance and composition pursue a doctor of musical arts (DMA) or doctor of music (DM) degree, and students in music education, theory, and history programs customarily pursue a Ph.D. Graduate students in theory conduct research in a wide variety of approaches to understanding music, from the use of mathematical models to the analysis of musical compositions and the social and historical contexts underlying the composition, performance, and reception of music.

There are distinct differences as well as significant areas of intersection between the objectives of graduate and undergraduate theory study, which result in different "surface structures" and "deep structures" in the signature pedagogies (Shulman, 2005, p. 2). The "surface structures," or "concrete operational acts of teaching and learning" for undergraduates (figured bass and chorale exercises), are designed to inculcate an understanding of musical grammar from the inside out (the "deep structure") through small-scale composition exercises that apply principles derived from the direct study of the music itself. At the end of the two-year sequence, students analyze entire pieces of music and describe the compositional procedures evident within these pieces, applying lessons learned about musical grammar to larger-scale contexts.

Composition and theory majors, along with advanced performers, then take courses and seminars on specialized topics such as counterpoint (the study of the interactions of individual musical lines). Graduate composition and performance students prepare doctoral recitals, and graduate theory students pursue individual research projects culminating in a dissertation. Specific teaching techniques at the graduate level involve having students learn by doing. The assumption is that graduate students will become high-caliber composers, performers, and researchers in their own right through this process. There is also an assumption that graduate students will learn to teach through their experiences as teaching assistants.

Traditional pedagogical practice in music theory has the dimensions of a signature pedagogy. It has a surface structure and a deep structure, "a set of assumptions about how best to impart a certain body of knowledge" (Shulman, 2005, p. 2). It is "both pervasive and routine" (Shulman, 2005, p. 3) because theory pedagogy is remarkably similar in most U.S. colleges and universities.

However, the transfer of a predominantly European model for the practice and content of theory study to the U.S. classroom has rekindled centuries-old debates on the nature and role of theory instruction at the undergraduate and graduate levels. In fact, the debates have been intensified by factors not present to the same extent in earlier times, including the need to balance breadth and depth, process and content, the integration of the sub-disciplines of music and the maintenance of their unique identities, and the study of the Western European canon as opposed to indigenous American music and the music of other cultures. Although theory in the past was taught primarily as individual lessons for professional musicians and talented amateurs, theory teachers today often face large classes of students with a wide variety of aspirations.

The original European context differs from the realities of the U.S. academy to such a degree that the goals of the teacher frequently do not match the expectations of the students. The deep structure assumptions are that students will gain an understanding of the principles of musical grammar as a result of the traditional curriculum and teaching methods and that they will perceive the connections between the principles discussed in class and the principles underlying the music that they play. It is also assumed that students will discover rich and vital connections hitherto unknown to them and will be better musicians as a result.

Although this optimistic scenario plays out among the best students in the class, for many students it does not. Many enter music programs with more exposure to and interest in jazz and rock than the music of Bach, Haydn, Mozart, Beethoven, Brahms, and their contemporaries. Few students are composition majors or view themselves as composers, and many do not play keyboard instruments. As a result, some students regard theory as difficult and/or completely irrelevant to their other musical activities.

In recent decades, there have been numerous responses to lack of student engagement in the theory classroom. The Comprehensive Musicianship (CM) movement of the 1960s and 1970s sought to break down the compartmentalization of the sub-disciplines of music by combining aspects of music theory, musicianship, music history, composition, and performance in one class (Rogers, 1984, p. 19). CM also broadened the scope of the subject matter beyond the common practice repertoire to include jazz and the music of other cultures. CM sometimes involved sight singing, dictation, analysis, improvisation, and the performance of student compositions all in one class. On one hand, this interactive and inclusive atmosphere was invigorating, and connections among the sub-disciplines became abundantly clear to the students through frequent hands-on projects. On the other hand, CM placed intense demands on faculty to teach material that was not part of their specialties and on students to come to grips with a bewildering array of diverse activities and musical material. Topics not part of a faculty member's specialty were often covered in a superficial manner. Team teaching was a possible solution to this problem, but it required close cooperation that was sometimes sacrificed to busy teaching schedules.

Rogers points out that "many of [these] problems are applicable not just to CM but involve difficulties of music teaching in general . . . . Perhaps it would be best if CM were defined as a teaching method rather than as a way of naming courses or organizing curricula. Many of the goals and ideals of CM can be achieved, in other words, in courses that appear (on paper in a college catalog) to be narrow in scope" (1984, p. 23).

Current efforts are afoot to adopt the goals of CM in this way. The cohort model, in which the same students in the same semester take separate classes in theory, musicianship, and music literature with faculty who stress the interconnections, is gaining momentum. The National Association of Schools of Music, a major accreditation organization, calls for a "common body of knowledge and skills" that includes performance, musicianship skills and analysis, composition and improvisation, history and repertory, technology, and a synthesis of all of these activities for all students earning professional baccalaureate degrees in music (NASM, 2007, p. 84). Music faculty members are seeking more interactions with their colleagues from other subdisciplines. As a result, theory faculty deliver guest lectures for ensemble rehearsals, and performance faculty are often guest lecturers in the theory classroom.

This integrative model is reflected in recent music theory textbooks that have reduced or eliminated student work in figured bass and chorale writing and moved directly to the musical grammar displayed in the instrumental music of Bach and later common-practice composers, and in jazz and rock. Laitz writes that "music students often suffer through their tonal theory and ear-training courses" and "view part-writing and figured bass as arcane and antiquated activities" (Laitz, 2003, p. xvii). He bypasses work in part writing and figured bass, immersing students immediately in instrumental works such as Bach's Violin Partita in E Major (Laitz, 2003, p. 4), combining work in theory and musicianship by introducing "techniques for taking two-voice dictation," a topic not usually covered in a theory textbook (Laitz, 2003, p. 69). However, it is important to note that more traditional theory texts such as Kostka and Payne (2004) are still viable and widely used; these textbooks can be adapted to an integrative setting.

Although vigorous debate about the purpose of theory within the music curriculum is likely to continue for some time, a consensus appears to be emerging that theory as a purely abstract study separate from the other subdisciplines of music is becoming, or has become, untenable at the undergraduate level. And though the study and development of highly abstract models of music are an important part of graduate theory study, graduate students must also prepare for future involvement in undergraduate pedagogy because there are very few "pure" research faculty positions in music theory. Given that Laitz's objective of introducing students to the "processes [that] underlie all tonal music" (2003, p. xvii) is strikingly similar to the Greek objective of revealing "universal patterns of order, leading to the highest levels of knowledge and understanding" (Mathiesen, 2002, p. 112), it is clear that the current environment of debate and revision is part of a continuing process spanning centuries.

Many recent publications by music faculty embrace this integrative model. They focus on modes of instruction that foster creativity, including cooperative and collaborative methods, composition assignments, and the use of improvisation in the classroom. Barkley, Cross, and Major (2005) is an example. The authors distinguish between *cooperative* learning, where the teacher retains the traditional dual role of subject-matter expert and authority in the classroom, designs and assigns group learning tasks, manages time and resources, and monitors student learning, checking to see that they are on task and that the group process is working well, and *collaborative* learning that assumes knowledge is socially produced by consensus among knowledgeable peers (p. 5).

The study of music theory offers opportunities to foster both cooperative and collaborative learning styles. For example, if the topic is the principles of notation or some other well-established aspect of musical vocabulary, cooperative learning is appropriate because students can work in groups to reinforce an understanding of existing concepts. If the topic is improvisational or compositional creativity, then students can actively create their own means of assessment. Research indicates that although there is no standard basis for measuring creativity in music and there are subjective elements involved in each person's definition of creativity, there is a "relatively high level of agreement by independent observers as to what products or responses are more or less creative" (Priest, 2001, p. 246).

Young's work is an example of collaborative learning, emphasizing the importance of hands-on creative work and faculty collaboration in the music theory and aural skills classroom. He describes a class that integrates music theory, aural skills, composition, and performance in a manner similar to that of Comprehensive Musicianship (Young, 1998). His work on student improvisation in the theory classroom and the parallels between educational methods in improvisation and foreign language instruction (Young, 2007) offers a striking example of the revival of the ideals of the Comprehensive

Musicianship movement. Young's colleagues from music and foreign languages observed student improvisation exercises and wrote evaluations. Students also evaluated their peers. Of the students responding to the survey conducted after the exercises, 93% indicated perceived improvement in their improvisatory skills. Young reported that his colleagues' evaluations were helpful to him for planning future improvisatory activities.

Don (2006) focused on rubrics, guidelines, and models for composition assignments in the theory classroom, with the goal of providing students with a structure that encourages creativity and experimentation. He created rubrics similar to those used by Hickey (1999), explaining to students how the teacher evaluates the compositions. These rubrics emphasize a demonstrated comprehension of the compositional techniques employed in the creation of the composition and an integration of these techniques into a comprehensive and satisfying whole that exhibits contrast within unity. Priest (2001) notes that limitations "that are perceived as informational rather than constraining, actually increase intrinsic motivation, thereby increasing creativity levels" (p. 247) and that the use of models (i.e., compositions that the students and teacher consider successful) also enhance creativity. Student surveys conducted after completion and performance of the compositions indicated that a majority of students perceived that completing the project helped them to understand key course concepts.

There is potential for more scholarship of teaching and learning (SoTL) research on the integrative model of music instruction. For example, Don (2006) could be expanded to include a pretest before the composition assignment, a post-test to assess student retention of course concepts, and a breakdown by grade assigned for the project. It is likely that the interest in fostering creativity in the theory classroom will produce additional SoTL work in this area.

Signature Pedagogies in Performance

Private lessons are a central element of music performance education. The pursuit of any undergraduate music degree requires study of an instrument or voice. This is true of students working toward performance, music education, music theory, music history, and liberal arts music degrees. Depending on the instrument, aspects of applied study (private lessons) and the repertoire studied necessarily vary. There is, however, a basic pedagogy used in undergraduate applied music study that can be traced back to the music apprenticeship relationship and the conservatory system of study that followed. This basic pedagogy can be seen as a signature for the sub-discipline.

Students' private lessons continue over multiple semesters and include elements of applied performance. The major goals of this type of study are to gain technical facility (e.g., how to breathe correctly, how to play and sing with agility) and musical expression (e.g., phrasing, line, and emotion). Ideally, this study occurs simultaneously with the study of musical analysis and historical context. Once or perhaps twice a week, each student meets individually with the teacher, who is both a skilled performer and a teacher of the applied instrument. The lesson time is either half an hour or an hour, during which the student demonstrates the repertoire and/or exercises previously assigned. The master teacher critiques the performance, providing immediate feedback on the student's application of technique and musical expression. A variety of methods are used during this stage to provide guidance. These methods include modeling passages or phrases for the student on his or her own instrument, employing imagery, coaching or conducting as the student plays, or, in singing, explaining the physiology of the vocal mechanism as it functions to create sound. Woody (2006) provides an excellent exploration of several of these methods, such as imagery and modeling, and their effectiveness in facilitating improved musical expression.

Applied music study uses the standard repertoire of the individual instrument, complemented by exercises such as scales and arpeggios, to ensure that the student gains technical facility, musical expression, and knowledge of the repertoire and musical style. Study with the same applied teacher continues throughout the four years of the student's degree, during which time the amount and difficulty of literature studied increase. The opportunity to work closely with the teacher over an extended period of time and regularly receive this type of coaching and critique provides the student with a direct model of the habits of mind of a performer.

In addition to one-on-one work, all the students of one teacher meet regularly at a studio, either once a week or once a month, to perform in front of their peers in a "master-class" setting. They then receive public critique from the applied teacher. This setting gives the student an opportunity to perform in front of others and also to learn by watching the teacher work with other students on issues different from his or her own. Performing in ensembles such as choir, band, orchestra, and opera workshop is also an important application of what is learned in lessons and provides other opportunities to see the teacher work with other students. This, in turn, raises questions that can be addressed in lessons, thus creating a circular process of performance study.

A final common element of applied music study is the performance "jury" at the end of the semester. The student performs for multiple members of the music faculty from the particular applied area or division who evaluate his or her performance technically and musically. A jury provides the student with a variety of opinions on the performance, supplementing the perspective of the applied teacher on the student's improvement over time.

Is this one-on-one performance- and critique-based pedagogy effective in achieving the desired disciplinary learning in students? There are some aspects of the pedagogy of one-on-one performance and critique that powerfully facilitate deeper learning of what performers do, think, and value. This frequent and immediate assessment motivates the student to be prepared, evaluates current work, guides the student toward the next step, and helps form the student's own understanding of the expectations for technique and expression in performing.

Additionally, the student finds a learning community in the other students in the applied studio. A performer spends the majority of his or her time practicing alone, and the journey can be long and frustrating. The learning community of the studio provides motivation, competition, a support system, and a group of musicians who are all working toward the same technical and artistic goals. The importance of peers with a common goal cannot be overestimated.

The one-on-one, extended nature of applied lesson study allows for mentoring relationships between student and teacher that are more difficult to cultivate in larger classes. Because the applied teacher is a performer on the applied instrument, he or she can be an invaluable model for the student of what it looks like to be a successful performer.

Because of the extended amount of time an applied teacher and a student work together—often four years or longer—most students eventually do improve technically and musically. It can take up to several semesters for this improvement to be displayed consistently. Perhaps the biggest initial barrier is the attitude with which many students begin their music study: They assume that music is "fun." It is necessary to enjoy, love, and have fun doing what one chooses to study, but too often a new undergraduate's understanding of "fun" does not include any notion of the discipline and application it takes to be a successful musician. There is an expectation that all facets of music-making will be fun, when in reality they require many solitary hours in the practice room: Practice requirements range from one hour a day to six or seven hours a day, depending on the instrument and the student's career goals.

Success in applied music depends on students practicing regularly and effectively outside of lesson time, something that Kostka (2002) suggests does not occur as consistently as is necessary because many students report that they have never been taught how to practice. Sadeghpour (2007) does suggest that over time students do learn to model their practice on their applied lesson structure and create a practice regimen for themselves. Clearly, however, students would benefit if instruction covering *how* to practice and not just *what* to practice was incorporated more intentionally into early applied study and reiterated as study continues.

Although regular access to and feedback from a professional musician provides a direct model of the profession, another possible weakness in this pedagogy of one-on-one performance and critique is the long course of study under a single teacher, which may limit the student's access to different points of view or teaching methods. There is a degree of subjectivity in what constitutes excellence in performance and what methods inspire that excellence. Studying with one teacher for the entirety of the degree exposes the student to one interpretation of that ideal. This problem is lessened to some extent by juries if the student receives written comments, not just a grade, on his or her performance. Many teachers also help their students gather a variety of opinions by encouraging them to perform in competitions, summer training programs, and master classes with prominent artists in the field. However, it is a commonly held belief that remaining with one teacher throughout an undergraduate career provides technical stability in a young musician. The communal aspect of the studio can counterbalance the solitary aspects of practice and performance preparation and provide a model for future professional collaboration.

Given that the role of a signature pedagogy is to teach students to do, think, and value what practitioners of the field do, think, and value, does the previously described traditional pedagogy of applied music succeed? There is potential for SoTL research to investigate this and other questions. For example, pedagogical research could explore whether students would benefit from working with multiple teachers during a degree program, especially as it relates to gains in technique or musical expression. Existent pedagogy is almost completely performance oriented, yet many of the students in applied music will be teaching in addition to performing. Music education majors student teach, but, as Shulman (2005) points out, it is impossible to predict or dictate the student teaching experience, and students may never teach on their primary instrument as part of this experience.

Courses devoted to pedagogical approaches for a specific instrument are not required in all music degree programs, so students may not receive the experience such courses offer. Although it is true that some innovative teachers do incorporate a number of strategies such as allowing students to teach each other in the regular master-class meetings, working with students in groups rather than individual lessons, and otherwise including ways for students to experience teaching, student teaching is not a current facet of the pedagogy of performance.

The major reason for the paucity of SoTL articles written by applied music professors most likely lies in the training of musicians and the teacher's own professional performing obligations. Studio music professors often lead double lives as teachers and professional performers. When considering the hours teaching individual lessons and preparing students for their own performances, then hours of daily practice to maintain one's own level of performance, coupled with even more time practicing for, rehearsing, and performing solo recitals, chamber music concerts, and orchestral concerts, little time is left for other projects.

More important, most applied music teachers/performers with terminal degrees of DMA or DM are not trained in systematic inquiry in their disciplines. When writing on the subject of teaching, applied teachers are most likely to explain their methodologies and discuss what worked for them and their students, but most never empirically examine teaching effectiveness. For instance, Holden (2002) outlines a new model of studio teaching that is based on a mixture of group and private lessons and gives interesting details into the process and methods used but does not assess whether the students had a deeper learning experience. This certainly does not mean that important learning did not take place but only that systematic inquiry or evidence was not used to reach that conclusion.

Experts in the field of music education have conducted most of the research on teaching and learning in music. The field of music education is a very important but separate field from music performance and music theory and it has its own methodology. The largest percentage of music education articles and research investigates teaching and learning at the primary and secondary education levels, which is the focus of teacher training for the bulk of music education students. However, there are some studies that inquire into the teaching and learning of college-level music students and are tied to applied lesson contexts. For example, Kostka (2002) summarizes previous research into the practice of music and brings to light surprising differences between college music professors and students in their attitudes and expectations about practicing. A questionnaire assessed four areas: attitudes about specific music skills, expectations about the use of practice time, expectations for routines and strategies of practicing, and attitudes of practice in general.

Kostka found that teachers expected more practice time than what students reported actually doing, and although most teachers expected students to follow a specific routine for practice, more than half of the students did not do so. Most teachers reported discussing practice strategies with students, yet 41% of students stated that their teacher does not discuss such strategies in lessons. Also interesting is the feedback on feelings about practice, where teachers overwhelmingly reported practice to be fulfilling and challenging, and only half of the students reported it to be challenging and fulfilling. Students were also twice as likely to consider practicing tedious but necessary. Kostka sees this information as a beginning that will lead to further studies that investigate strategies for structuring practice, resulting in optimal improvement and increased enjoyment for students.

The Kostka study is an important one for studio music teachers: It shows a gap between what teachers think they are teaching about practice and what students are actually taking from lessons about practice. It also gives us a look at what students are actually doing and how we as teachers can train students to transform their practice sessions in order to think and work as professionals. This topic deserves special time in studio class or applied lessons and may be a component of a signature pedagogy.

The music educator Robert Woody investigated the teaching of musical expression and has produced several studies that summarize much of the past research on the topic and provide new insights into student learning that are potentially very helpful to applied music professors. For example, Woody (2003) explores how expressive performance is affected by goal imagery (or a mental drawing of phrase shapes) and motor production skills when students are asked to create imitations of an aural model.

In the study, 25 college music students listened to piano excerpts that were played in both expressionless and musically expressive ways. The students then imitated the expressive examples and drew the musically expressive features (such as dynamics and tempo) on a chart to represent the goal imagery. Woody (2003) observed that some students were able to create an accurate goal image of the model but were unable to imitate it in performance. This finding suggests that those student need to work on motor skill acquisition to align the actual performance with the mental image of the phrase. Students who created goal imagery drawings that more closely allied with their own performances but not the recorded models might have created inaccurate mental images of the models.

Woody's study (2003) has important implications for students and studio teachers. By exploring goal imagery in lessons, we can teach students to identify what is being modeled more accurately before they try to imitate it. The approach might further be used to help a student plan out goal imagery in pieces for which they do not have models. By investigating goal imagery and the motor skills needed to transform these ideas into expressive sounds, a teacher can quickly surmise why a given phrase is not expressive and determine whether lack of proper imagery or inadequate motor skills inhibits optimal performance.

In another article, Woody (2006) compares three methods (aural modeling, verbal instruction using concrete musical properties, and verbal imagery or metaphor) of eliciting expressivity in musical performances by college music students. The author found that students were able to benefit from all three approaches, but he observed strengths and weakness in all methods, depending on the type of music performed and the individual preferences of the musicians. Furthermore, Woody found that some students use a form of cognitive translation that allows them to transform information from imagery into concrete actions (changing dynamics, articulation, tempo) for expressive purposes.

The sample studies cited in this chapter and similar others reveal what already works in our field and what doesn't. More important, they put our scholarship of music teaching and learning on a firmer foundation based on observable data. We already teach musical expressivity and likely also use some forms of modeling, metaphor, and goal imagery. But investigating musical expression by means of how different cognitive skills are used gives us concrete ways of looking into how learning takes place and where learning and teaching deficiencies exist.

Examining how musical performances are obtained by different approaches such as aural modeling, verbal instruction using concrete musical properties, and verbal imagery or metaphor also gives us information as to which method of teaching expression might work best in a given situation. This information also helps studio teachers understand the variety of ways that the teaching of musical expression can be considered. In the case of Kostka (2002), teachers' expectations of student practice are revealed to be woefully inadequate, and we see that there must be more communication between teachers and students to optimize practice effectiveness. Research that helps teachers develop students' expressive musical thinking and shows how to structure effective practice strategies reaches the heart of the signature pedagogy of music performance, which investigates the process of becoming a professional performing musician.

Conclusion

Traditional pedagogies in music are coming under increased scrutiny, as they are in other fields. The fact that pedagogical practice is "prone to inertia" (Shulman, 2005, p. 5) is counterbalanced by many factors, including audits by accrediting agencies such as the National Association of Schools of Music, competition for the best students, and recognition by faculty that engaged students not only learn more deeply but are also more enjoyable to teach.

To address these challenges, scholarly inquiry into the traditional pedagogies of music is beginning to take place, although there is opportunity and need for much further study. Many traditional pedagogical practices in music are also signature pedagogies in the sense that they inculcate disciplinary habits of mind for theory and performance. It is encouraging, however, to see a common element emerging in the signature pedagogies of music that recognizes the necessary integration of the abilities to analyze and understand music and to perform at a high level of technical mastery and musical expression.

Traditionally, music theory and music performance have been thought of as two elements of music study that are important but separate and have different intended outcomes. Music educators now recognize that to turn out well-rounded musicians who know how to think and do as those in the profession think and do, our pedagogies must reflect the interconnection of the two areas of study. In the teaching of music theory, this means a focus on thought processes and analysis, as opposed to coverage of broad content areas, and increased use of improvisation and composition assignments in the theory classroom to foster student creativity. The use of part writing and figured bass assignments and the analysis of examples from the western European canon are likely to remain as signature pedagogies of music theory because of faculty expertise in these areas and the value of part writing and figured bass in imparting lessons on musical grammar and structure.

However, expansion of the canon to include indigenous American music and the music of other cultures is already under way and is likely to continue. In the teaching of music performance, one-on-one applied study that provides weekly assessment of student progress, continues over multiple semesters, and includes a communal studio aspect and an applied performance element is an effective signature pedagogy for helping students achieve technical facility and musical expression and for developing some of the habits of mind and practice of musicians. These two signature pedagogies in combination successfully create a complete musician.

References

Abeles, H. F., Hoffer, C. R., & Klotman, R. H. (1994). *Foundations of music education* (2nd ed.). New York: Shirmer Books.

Barkley, E., Cross, P. K., & Major, C. H. (2005). *Collaborative learning techniques: A handbook for college faculty*. San Francisco: Jossey-Bass.

Bower, C. M. (2002). The transmission of ancient music theory into the Middle Ages. In T. Christensen (Ed.), *The Cambridge history of Western music theory* (pp. 136–167). Cambridge, UK: Cambridge University Press.

Don, G. (2006). *The music composition assignment as an aid to the study of form*. Retrieved from http://cte.rockhurst.edu/rockhurstuniv.aspx?pgID=1772

Dyer, J. (2001). *Schola cantorum*. Grove Music Online ed. L. Macy. http://www.grovemusic.com

Hickey, M. (1999). Assessment rubrics for music composition. *Music Educators Journal 85*(4), 26–34.

Holden, R. B. (2002). A new model for training the collegiate voice student. *Journal of Singing—The Official Journal of the National Association of Teachers of Singing, 58*(4), 299–303.

Kostka, M. J. (2002). Practice expectations and attitudes: A survey of college-level music teachers and students. *Journal of Research in Music Education, 50*(2), 145–154.

Kostka, S., & Payne, D. (2004). *Tonal harmony, with an introduction to twentieth-century music* (5th ed.). New York: McGraw-Hill.

Laitz, S. G. (2003). *The complete musician: An integrated approach to tonal theory, analysis, and listening.* Oxford: Oxford University Press.

Mathiesen, T. J. (2002). Greek music theory. In T. Christensen (Ed.), *The Cambridge History of Western Music Theory* (pp. 109–135). Cambridge, UK: Cambridge University Press.

National Association of Schools of Music (NASM). (2007). *National Association of Schools of Music handbook.* Retrieved from http://nasm.arts-accredit.org/site/docs/Handbook/NASM_HANDBOOK_2007-2008.pdf

Priest, T. (2001). Using creativity assessment experience to nurture and predict compositional creativity. *Journal of Research in Music Education 49*(3), 245–257.

Ritterman, J. (2001). Conservatories since 1945. *Grove Music Online.* Retrieved from http://www.grovemusic.com

Rogers, M. (1984). *Teaching approaches in music theory: An overview of pedagogical philosophies.* Carbondale: Southern Illinois University Press.

Shulman, L. S. (2005). *Signature pedagogies in the professions.* Cambridge, MA: MIT Press.

Sadeghpour, M. (2007). *What IS happening in the practice room?* Unpublished manuscript.

Weber, W. 2001. Conservatories. *Grove Music Online* (ed. L. Macy). Retrieved from http://www.grovemusic.com

Woody, R. H. (2003). Explaining expressive performance: Component cognitive skills in an aural modeling task. *Journal of Research in Music Education, 51*(1), 51–63.

Woody, R. H. (2006). Musicians' cognitive processing of imagery-based instructions for expressive performance. *Journal of Research in Music Education, 54*(2), 125–137.

Young, C. R. (1998). An integrated path to musicianship. *Wisconsin School Musician.* Retrieved July 11, 2008, from http://www.uwsp.edu/music/cyoung/resources/an2.htm

Young, C. R. (2007). *Teaching music as a foreign language.* Unpublished manuscript.

6

CRITIQUE AS SIGNATURE PEDAGOGY IN THE ARTS

Helen Klebesadel and Lisa Kornetsky

Articulating a signature pedagogy for the creative arts requires reflecting on which values and ways of knowing and doing are shared by the arts disciplines. It requires considering how we as educators most effectively introduce those concepts to our students and how we articulate the core issues to our colleagues who have less understanding about the kind of experiential learning that is central to the arts.

Those who teach and study in these disciplines understand that the arts are not just forms of entertainment to fill leisure hours for consumers who can afford them. Beyond the qualities of creativity, self-expression, and communication, the arts provide a way to understand and interpret the non-text-based language of the visual culture that surrounds us daily.

At the center of an excellent education in the arts is the development of critical and linguistic skills that enable students to describe, analyze, and interpret visual culture. Students of performance, however, are more rooted in the analysis of text and must develop skills and techniques that allow them to interpret and embody the meaning of those texts, both personally and culturally.

The arts deal with durable human concerns through the study of which we learn *how* and *on what* our society places value. Through study in the arts, students learn to understand that values shape all human efforts and that exposure to ideas presented through the arts and visual culture can affect our personal value choices. The arts express the highest and lowest aspirations of the human spirit. Because artists play a significant role in society as purveyors of values, it is important that they learn how to become discerning creative thinkers and ethical practitioners in their chosen art. The interesting questions for us are how are these habits and values taught, and how do we evaluate the effectiveness of our teaching in the arts?

Students in these disciplines seldom consider the creative arts easy majors because of the required dedication to long hours of study, practice, and production to fulfill even the most basic of course requirements. To be well-educated artists, students must also understand past and present cultures and develop their own capacity for creative expression and effective communication. Their education is a balance of gaining technical knowledge and skills along with developing critical, conceptual, and creative abilities, as well as an understanding of historical, multicultural, and global perspectives on the arts and future directions in their fields.

Our focus in this chapter is the use of critique as a signature pedagogy in the arts, specifically in the creation of art by undergraduate practitioners. The authors, who come from a theater and a visual arts background, restrict their observations and research to these two areas of study but believe that the discussion will have currency in other art disciplines and beyond.

Common Traits of the Creative Arts

The disciplines that come under the heading of the creative arts are rich and varied. They cover studio arts, such as painting, printmaking, photography, sculpture, ceramics, and architecture; performing arts, such as theater, music, performance art and dance; and written forms, such as playwriting, music composition, and other forms of creative writing. By their very nature, the majority of creative arts disciplines are interdisciplinary. They usually combine multiple artistic mediums to tell a story, capture a moment in time, and therefore make visible some aspect of our world for comment or reflection. There is tremendous diversity among and within the various forms of creative arts.

The disciplines that constitute the creative arts do, however, share many features. The studio arts and the performing arts use different mediums but have the same learning goals of introducing students to the discipline's foundational theories, techniques, and practices of the art form in combination with nurturing creative talent and mastery of the craft. Undergraduate creative arts education prepares students for further training and work in the profession, but it is hoped that broader learning goals are attained. Unlike many other disciplines, training in these fields is often rooted in an experiential approach to learning how to become an active practitioner, rather than based on a scholarly model of inquiry. Students study the history of the art form and its theoretical underpinnings while reading, writing, and doing research within the discipline. But the majority of students hope to make their careers as practitioners of these art forms, so much of the focus is on how to *be* that practitioner, rather than on creating new knowledge within a traditional scholarly mode. This is really quite different from the student studying history or biology and, not surprisingly, the research in these fields is also different.

Critique as a mode of giving both structured and unstructured feedback is common to all creative work in the arts. The visual and theater arts both use a variety of pedagogical strategies for teaching theory, history, and technique, or craft. Studio art education tends to focus on three main pedagogical strategies, all of which are effective, especially when employed in tandem. The most common strategies are lecture and demonstration to introduce an assignment or problem, hands-on student art-making as a means of solving a presented problem, and critique as a means of understanding and evaluating the students' work in progress and completed work.

Performance-oriented theater training, on the other hand, has its own fundamental teaching strategies, including guiding students through acting exercises and improvisation, which are important tools for enhancing imagination and spontaneity because they teach fundamental skills of the craft. Students learn to analyze a script and develop a character in connection with scene or monologue work, which is then critiqued in the classroom. In tandem with both of these ways of teaching performance are acting methodologies rooted in both theory and practice and used to further the actor's ability to match style with performance and to improve a variety of acting skills, such as the use of body, voice, and imagination.

Whatever the methodology or branch of the creative arts, critique—either formal or informal—ultimately comes into play as the one pedagogical strategy that remains standard in most undergraduate classrooms, yet it is rarely written about or studied.

Goals of Critique

Critique is a formative mode of feedback. As in other types of performance feedback, such as athletic coaching or medical rounds, the goal of the assessment is to give specific feedback on a performance or creation to reinforce technical skills, change behavior, or modify thinking to improve performance overall. Although all of the creative arts have specific content knowledge, critique occurs when the artist combines that knowledge with individual creative expression to demonstrate how he or she applies the learned elements of the craft with the less tangible facets of the art form.

In many ways, critique is the signature pedagogy in art and performance because of what it teaches students about the process of creating art, appreciating the form, and understanding objective and subjective assessment of particular styles and works of art. Students in the arts generally do not learn to critique art in order to become critics but to better appreciate their art form as critical and creative expressions and to understand underlying assumptions of their field. Through the process of critique, art students consider what it means to define a work as "art," examine diverse systems of representation, investigate differing approaches to and perspectives on interpretation, and confront issues of values and judgment. Critique can be an effective way to teach students that the existence of competing value systems with differing criteria of artistic excellence does not mean that the success of a work of art or performance is simply a relativistic judgment.

An object of art or a performance can be approached as a text that can be described, analyzed, and evaluated. Critique often becomes an actual goal toward which student production is directed. However, it is more accurate to think of each critique as a step on the path toward the more ambitious project of the students' development of mature artistic practice. As instructors examine larger educational goals for students, the purpose of critique moves beyond simple analysis of individual artworks or performance to the creation of an evaluative process that develops artistic literacy and facility through the discipline's creative and critical thinking skills. By critiquing the work of peers and professionals in the field, students learn what is valued in the discipline, along with the process for creating successful work within whatever framework or methodology is used. They then can apply these analytical skills to their own creative work, that of their peers, the larger creative culture, and their professional fields. In other words, the critique process develops artist practitioners who can self-assess objectively and become artistically successful: As students progress through the curriculum creating new performances or works of art, they develop the ability to learn from the evaluation of others and their own critical sensibility, which leads to their growth as mature artistic practitioners.

SoTL in the Arts

Many important questions about this pedagogy need to be investigated to inform our practice as instructors who care deeply about our students' learning experiences. Because the overarching goal of most critiques is growth, how do we set the tone for active, engaged, productive, and constructive discussion? How do we maintain high standards and keep students engaged through the discomforts of careful scrutiny? How do we recognize unsuccessful work? Ultimately, how do we leave students with the tools to function successfully in their fields when they leave their formal education behind them?

Because critique is a standard pedagogy in all of the arts, we expected to find a fair amount written about it and at least some studies on the questions in the preceding paragraph. In our literature review, however, we found some information on performance assessment, largely in K–12 but little to none on the use of critique at the undergraduate level. Witman and Richlin's 2007 review of the status of SoTL in the disciplines did not include the creative arts, presumably because, as our own research revealed, there was not enough SoTL in the discipline to review (Richlin & Witman, 2007).

Our review revealed a great deal of literature on the value of creative expression and active learning in the arts, but research on the pedagogical techniques for helping students find freedom of expression while developing the ability to assess the work of peers and to self-assess is minimal. There is some information on performance assessment, primarily in K–12, but the visual and performing arts at the college level are seldom addressed in SoTL literature and research, even though enrollments have almost doubled since 1990 (Warburton, 2006).

In theater, SoTL work has focused on portfolio assessment, understanding oppression, and using drama as an effective learning strategy. Theater is catching up with other disciplines with its attention to models of assessment, which is heartening, but the focus on the K–12 classroom or the history/dramatic literature classroom is on models that do not necessarily fit into the undergraduate performance classroom.

In studio art, again, much of the research is focused on high school studio art education. For instance, recent research on rigorous studio art teaching in high schools found critique to be one of the three key ways that good visual art teaching happens (along with lecture/demonstration and experiential practice) (Hetland, Winner, Veenema, & Sheridan, 2007). The larger purpose of the study was to explore what students learn in the art studio and how it applies to contemporary art practice and learning beyond the classroom. The researchers found that art educators used the process of critique as an effective way to ask students to step back, analyze, judge, and sometimes reconceive their projects entirely.

Along with this paucity of SoTL in the arts, little research specifically addresses the use of critique at the undergraduate level. In fact, the word "critique" simply does not appear in the literature on American actor training. Although a few articles discuss models of critique and performance review, they are primarily focused on new models or simply how to conduct critique, and few address critique as pedagogy (Alexander, 1999; 2002). Interestingly, acting textbooks and interviews with master teachers often refer to critique but do not discuss what it is and why it should be used (Bartow, 2006; Brestoff, 1995; Hodge, 2000; Mekler, 1998). Critique is so fundamental that there appears to be no need to talk about it, much less study its effectiveness and what students learn about the creative arts through the process. One future direction for SoTL work, for example, would be to explore student reflection and articulation on how critique informs their process and finished product.

There are many reasons why faculty in the creative arts are not as engaged in this form of scholarly work as their peers in other disciplines. First, most fine arts faculty do not see themselves as scholars in any traditional sense, and perhaps they feel they lack the skills for this kind of inquiry. They, like their students, see themselves as practitioners and do not function within the language or domain of traditional academic scholarship. As in many other disciplines, most art and theater faculty have no training as educators other than the models used in their own education. The forms of assessment used in many disciplines do not apply to the kinds of classroom activities and pedagogical strategies used in the arts, so methods for studying learning that make sense to fine arts faculty need to be developed and explored. This is not to say that teachers in the arts do not explore pedagogy in their professional societies or with their colleagues, but the dearth of models for how to investigate these questions in ways that make sense for the discipline and a lack of awareness for where they may exist have limited participation of the fine arts in SoTL.

This limited participation is unfortunate. If we understood what is happening in critique, we would be able to design models that lead to deeper learning and more explicit outcomes for students. Clearly, because of critique's role in education in the arts, more SoTL work is needed to fully examine its effectiveness in helping students learn, including what and how they are learning. In this chapter, we consider what critique teaches students about the discipline and about what it means to be practitioners in the arts.

Critique in Undergraduate Theater Education

In the undergraduate theater classroom and studio, actors perform scenes, monologues, or other activities for an audience of classmates and the instructor, who then assess the performance. The performance could come from a written text, a piece developed by the ensemble, or an improvisation or theatrical exercise determined by the instructor. In all of these examples, there is a performance in real time that is fluid rather than static, that is often repeated but not replicable, and that is completely dependent on a set of circumstances not fixed in time and space. In other words, multiple inputs—intangible factors, only some of which are controlled by the performer—impact not only the performance itself but the observation of that performance.

Some of these elements include what the actor does, such as interpret the script, create a character, use his or her body and voice, and move in space using gesture and actions. The less obvious parts of the performance include the space it is in, the quality of that space (lighting, room temperature, setting), and the physical or vocal limitations of that particular actor on that particular day. There are also the subjective elements the actors and audience bring with them: mood, temperament, world view, likes and dislikes, and whatever is carried into the studio from the hour before. These things—and more—greatly influence the performance and how it is perceived by observers. In the traditional theater classroom, students are expected to learn, grow, and develop as actors and/or directors primarily through performance and the critique of that performance.

In the performance classroom, instruction and critique are in many ways the same. Actors learn to act by doing, but they also learn to act by evaluating the work of others and applying it to themselves. The way the instructor structures critique and combines it with the traditional elements of actor training is fundamental to how students engage with the material, reflect on their work, and find their unique creative voice.

Critique is a powerful learning tool: The immediacy of the performance is mirrored by that of the evaluation, and critique happens in real time with much of the same lack of control. Those who critique are reacting as well—taking what they know and understand, building on it, and responding to what they have seen and felt. There is no waiting for a studied and measured evaluation. The performance happens, and the response follows.

A typical acting critique (if such a thing exists) depends on the purpose of the exercise or piece of work and where the student is in his or her preparation. The critique covers some areas that are fairly easy to assess with objective criteria, such as physicality (use of the body, control, freedom, physical development of a character); vocal work (articulation, volume, range, vocal development of a character); and energy, preparation, and focus. For example, if the performance is lackluster or the actor is not understandable or does not walk, talk, or handle himself or herself the way the character would be expected to, the critique will address that.

Where critique becomes more difficult is in the areas of believability, honesty, and interpretation, which are harder to assess objectively. Even here, however, character interpretation must be rooted in an understanding of the play's circumstances, meaning, and historical framework. Interpretation must be reasoned and arrived at through a process of textual analysis and study. In these elements, critique in actor training is more complex than simple task-based feedback: It is also a way for the instructor and fellow students to add nuance, suggest new perspectives, or bring the performance to the next level of complexity.

Critique is also a way of teaching students fundamental disciplinary points of view. Although the success of a work is often measured in ticket sales, individual judgment by those within the discipline and the profession is subjective yet rooted in disciplinary values and perspectives. What sells and what is successful are not always the same.

Critique evolved as a practical way of training, without great thought to its value as a pedagogical tool, in part because undergraduate theater departments are a relatively new addition to higher education. Actor training started with theater companies handing down techniques from one actor to another and led to master teachers running their own schools or studios (Bartow, 2006; Hodge, 2000). Acting processes were developed to aid the actor in developing technique and accessing his or her own creative source and inspiration. Actor training is unique in its roots in specific methods and techniques developed by well-known 20th-century theater practitioners, usually actors themselves.

As American theater training evolved from the Stanislavski tradition in the 1920s and 1930s, the teaching of dramatic literature in English departments expanded to an occasional theater department. By the end of World War II and leading into the 1960s, theater programs sprang up to teach performance (acting, directing, voice, design, etc.) and more traditional academic courses in theater history and dramatic literature. Much of the teaching in these programs, however, started with those trained in the professional theater—actors and directors without an academic degree. As master of fine arts programs began to grow in the 1970s and 1980s, more teachers were trained as actors and directors, but only very recently has there been much emphasis on teaching along with preparation for the professional theater or other nonacademic performance venues. Actor training is unique compared to other facets of theater education. It is rooted in specific methods and techniques developed by well-known theater practitioners of the 20th century. Acting processes have emerged to aid the actor in developing his or her technique and accessing creative sources and inspiration.

In this context, critique naturally emerged as the logical way to give feedback to a live performance. Whether a student is a first-time actor taking a beginning course or an actor at the end of a professional training program, critique is at the heart of actor training. In other words, it makes little difference whether someone is preparing for the profession; the basic use of critique is the same—performance evaluation by the instructor and peers through feedback after a performance in the classroom. Performance learning thus occurs in two moments: students first experience their learning internally and then externalize the experience to perform it, analyze it, repeat it, and grow from it. Teachers and, most likely, students commonly accept that the best way to learn is by being critiqued and by critiquing the work of others, coming to a common understanding of criteria and judging technique, skills, interpretation, and intangibles against those criteria.

However, there are significant, unanswered questions about critique and how it plays out in the theater classroom. How does this learning happen?

How can acting teachers help students balance their internal assessment with the external evaluation by their colleagues and instructors? How do we create a nurturing classroom environment that allows for that to happen, and maintain the necessary rigor to prepare students for the next level of training or for the intensely critical professional world?

Because critique arose as the central pedagogy in undergraduate theater education without examination, it is fundamentally flawed in many ways. It is messy, often subjective, highly personal, and, as an outgrowth of the more traditional master–teacher model of actor training, a very hierarchical, teacher-centered way of assessing students' work. The shared beliefs and common criteria for evaluation are often determined by the instructor's preference for a particular method or approach and can leave out multiple perspectives on what is valued by the class as a whole or even the larger profession. As the field evolves, however, there is a growing desire to move from that model to a student-centered classroom where everyone is invested in constructive, formative feedback and students learn the tools for using this method to help themselves and their peers.

Creative interpretation is relative. There is no right answer when it comes to artistic expression. After the evaluation of basic skills and techniques, what is believable and true in a performance is subjective. To some degree, the evaluation is based on the personal preferences, beliefs, and social perspective of the individual responding. Although the process of making art can be assessed, the inspiration of the moment and the "magic" that we talk of in the theater are much harder to evaluate objectively. The power in making those judgments is tremendous and can easily be misused. In the theater, we talk about honesty and believability, yet believability is connected to cultural norms, time period, and even regional differences. Artistic truth, therefore, is as much socially as personally constructed. If perspective (even to seemingly objective criteria) and reflection are not part of the critique process, the assessment becomes personal—as much about the one doing the critique as about the performance and the analysis of the text.

Because of this subjectivity, the criteria used in critique are at the heart of an ongoing debate about performance assessment across creative arts disciplines (Colwell, 1998; Salazar, 1992). How does one assess an art-based curriculum perceived as grounded in the affective rather than the cognitive domain? Will rubrics or other objective assessment criteria create barriers to students' creativity? These questions about the validity of objective criteria have allowed for a model of critique based primarily on the instructor's personality and ways of knowing.

Performance is also deeply personal. It engages the whole student—the head, the heart, and the body. One's experience, emotions, and sense of self are intimately tied up in the work. As one author states in his discussion of training actors within a particular acting methodology,

> Our feelings signify what the world means to us, and the knowledge of how we feel about things . . . is what we will ultimately draw on in acting. Students must learn what these feelings are, how to gain access to them and what to do with them. During this process they must be dedicated to finding their own truth in order to inhabit and serve the lives of the characters they will encounter in their work as actors. (Bartow, 2006, p. 55)

When acting, a student brings himself or herself to the character, analyzing it from firsthand experience as much as from a subjective understanding of the text. From the actor's perspective, textual analysis is personal as well as intellectual. The actor interprets the text within multiple frameworks, such as broader cultural, social, and historical contexts; style and given circumstances; and relating that character and his or her words and experiences to the actor's own imagination and life experience. When an actor "fails" in a performance, then, it is not just an intellectual failure or a failure of skill but often feels to the actor like a failure of self. A student receiving a negative critique may not have the experience or flexibility to see it as one measure, albeit an important one, of the work. The response of the observers, particularly of the instructor as the one with the greatest power, can be devastating to the student who has not yet learned to temper negative criticism with a strong sense of self and self-worth.

For the traditional-aged undergraduate, the development of a sense of self is much of what the college experience is about, both personally and intellectually. The research on affective learning suggests that students' personal experiences of the classroom either lead to deeper understanding or to a lack of engagement (Kuh, Kinzie, Schuh, & Whitt, 2005; Owen-Smith, 2004). Clearly, engaging the students beyond their intellectual skills to inspire them and help them find their passion is a significant part of the training of creative artists.

Performance anxiety is tripled by the threat of being judged negatively, not being allowed to defend or explain one's choices, and, in many cases, being humiliated and broken down in front of one's peers. This dynamic establishes tension between the desire to do what is expected as a performer (being spontaneous, open to one's feelings, and willing to go beyond one's comfort zone) and the fear of being publicly berated by teachers with strong personalities and clear personal preferences for certain students and certain types of performances. The struggle between the desire to perform and the need to protect one's ego is often tremendous. In fact, it's what eventually led coauthor Lisa Kornetsky away from performance to teaching.

Embedded in critique's subjectivity and its intensely personal experience is another fundamental flaw in actor training as it has been practiced in this country for the last 60 years. Training focuses on the teacher rather than the student, on the personality rather than the task at hand, and on the intangible rather than on the melding of its multiple inputs:

> Actor training is highly teacher-dependent. Most teachers have the information about acting but not many are greatly gifted at communicating it. And ultimately, acting isn't about the information anyway. The teacher must communicate the madness of the art, the passion of the craft, the excitement of inspiration. (Brestoff, 1995)

Although there are certainly pockets of change and a renewed interest in pedagogy, the traditions of this kind of classroom are very strong. As the field evolves, there is a growing desire to move from that model to a student-centered classroom where everyone is invested in constructive, formative feedback and where students learn to use this method to help themselves and their peers. In a field where the relationship between reality and imagination is often conflated, it is essential that critique become a forum for reflecting what is observed, comparing work to clearly understood standards, and providing opportunities for reflection that is centered on the affective as well as the cognitive realms of knowing.

Critique in Undergraduate Studio Art Education

Critique is signature pedagogy for studio art because it teaches core disciplinary understandings of how the visual arts and artists function in society. Recent culture wars over what and who is to be valued, taught, preserved, and held up for emulation play out in the creative arts more visibly than in many disciplines, as evidenced by National Endowment for the Arts (NEA) and National Endowment for the Humanities (NEH) funding fights in recent decades. These struggles enter the art studio through the social, political, ethnic, sexual, cultural, and economic identities of faculty and students. And, though varying value systems may be introduced in critique, one of the most important aspects of the process of critique is that it teaches the importance to the arts of understanding how value systems are introduced, articulated, and used to judge art.

From one course to another, in critique, students observe how their faculty articulate the criteria that will be used to assess their academic performance and come to understand how the emphasis placed on valuing different aspects of art-making can change with the concerns of the instructor (and, by extension, the curator, exhibiting institution, collector, and professional artists themselves).

Early in a student's studio art education, mastering technique and visual language may outweigh the innovation and effective communication expected in more mature artworks. Throughout their education, visual arts students are trained to look beyond learned assumptions to perceive the world as accurately as possible. Excellent technical craft and effective artistic expression are important, as is the development of visual–spatial abilities. Persistent effort over time and learning to use reflection and self-criticism to advance artwork are necessary abilities. Experimentation and risk-taking with permission to learn from mistakes in the service of innovation are core expectations.

Art students are most often taught to make clear connections between schoolwork and the world outside the classroom and to see their projects as part of the larger art world, past and present. There can be an emphasis on clarifying decision making and understanding what motivates the choices made in the pursuit of effective artistic expression. Which of these expectations are of primary concern in the assessment of a particular assignment or class can shift throughout an art student's education, demonstrating that they must ultimately define for themselves what voice and concerns they will bring to their professional work as artists.

The contemporary visual arts studio functions as an experiential learning space. Students devote 12 to 18 hours a week to completing assignments defined by the faculty or developed by the student within limits defined by the faculty. Approximately six of those hours are part of the regular meeting of the studio class. Students come to the studio expecting to work on their projects, but they also seek advice from peers and teachers, offer advice to peers, and expect to take part in the critique process throughout the semester.

Studio critiques are an essential part of college undergraduate art courses at all levels and may take place in every studio period once a week or less periodically, depending on the magnitude of the assignments and the level of instruction. The art critique usually takes place in the context of the art studio, a dedicated space usually assigned to a faculty member or a small group of faculty in the same discipline (2D, 3D, photography, weaving, drawing, painting, sculpture, etc.). Because it is a dedicated space for specific courses, it's not uncommon for completed works of previous classes and artifacts related to the discipline to be on display. Classes are limited to approximately 20 students, and access to the studio is usually granted at any time during the class day to any student enrolled in a class using that studio. It's not uncommon to see students of several different classes (and academic levels) working side by side or students working alone in the studio when classes are not meeting. In the visual art studio, the goal is usually the creation of new and unique images or artifacts that satisfy to varying degrees an array of preset constraints and goals in visual study. In performance art, the body becomes the medium for the visual text. In all visual art studies, larger academic goals usually couple with an additional objective for students to discover their own creative and critical voices as artists.

Within visual arts studio culture, the process of the critique often results in the students and the teacher developing a collaborative or teamlike relationship that influences all the projects in the class. Once this collaborative culture is accepted and students become accustomed to ongoing critique as central to the educational process of the studio, the role of the instructor is much easier. The instructor must eventually "judge" the student, but that judgment is based on a semester-long working relationship. When the process is working well, criticism is viewed positively and constructively, and students welcome the instructor's and fellow students' comments and attention, and, although even constructive criticism is often met with a little resentment, visual art students learn to accept, expect, and even seek it out.

There are variations on how the critique is conducted at each level. Initially, instructors have most of the authority in the critique. They are likely to assist students in evaluation by demonstrating the most appropriate and effective method of analysis to achieve the goals of the particular assignment, process, or project. Effective instructors set the tone and create a learning environment conducive to discussion and student interaction. Over the semester and through progressive courses as students advance in their university work, there is a shift in authority from an instructor-centered to an instructor-facilitated critical analysis focused on student-centered peer critique. As students learn the process, they are encouraged to conduct critiques in small groups without direct teacher supervision. Instructors committed to student-centered and student-engaged pedagogies learn to restrain themselves, fostering creativity and critical student voices as emerging artists learn to articulate their goals and become more self-critical about their progress toward them.

In introductory and foundation courses, the instructor introduces students to the culture of critique. Through regular practice and discussion, students are exposed to various critique strategies and to the visual vocabulary most commonly used in critique. At the most basic level, learning to critique demystifies visual art simply by breaking down art-making into easily understandable parts that can be described, analyzed, and evaluated. Introductory courses most often focus on achieving facility with visual language and developing design skills; intermediate courses usually focus on acquiring media- and discipline-specific knowledge and applying it in the service of strong artworks; and upper-level courses rely increasingly on student-defined projects that apply visual language, critical voice, and media-specific knowledge to develop a cohesive body of individual artworks that relay the student artists' intended visual concerns.

At the intermediate and advanced level during the studio period (normally three hours, twice a week), students work on their assignments while the instructor circulates informally throughout the studio, reviewing and commenting on each project. The idea of seeking help from peers as well as teachers is a central part of this pedagogy. Art students become accustomed to sharing ideas, consistent and sometimes unrequested advice, and the regularly scheduled critiques of their work. For the visual art student, these aspects of the studio are at the very heart of the studio concept. Well-prepared visual art students will receive some form of critique consistently throughout their undergraduate and graduate careers.

As new teaching technologies emerge, Web-based environments are increasingly used to teach studio art. Some course delivery vehicles allow course designers to employ digitized art images in an artificial environment, and instructors who extend the classroom to the Web usually bring critique pedagogies with them. Intentional reflection on the purpose and methods of critique is a happy consequence of the necessity for preplanning when working in virtual reality. Critique It™, a virtual learning system under development at the University of Wisconsin–Madison, uses the multiuser, virtual reality program Second Life (http://engage.wisc.edu/sims_games/phaseII/critiqueit/index.html). Clearly, critique will remain a relevant pedagogy as undergraduate arts education expands to embrace new media.

Barrett's (1988) research comparing the underlying goals of college-level studio critique with the stated goals of art education criticism reveals that, although the university art professors he interviewed considered critique important, how often and when they employed critique varied. Most considered successful critique to occur when students participated actively and frequently, although some teachers admitted that they talked more than their students. Faculty and students reported that ineffective critiques occur when faculty dominate the discussion or when students are hurt from their experience of having their work critiqued, especially when they find it difficult to separate critique of their art from a critique of themselves. Faculty also reported dismay with nonresponsive or apathetic students resistant to guidance and with student frustration or embarrassment during critique (Barrett, 2000).

For most instructors, the major goal of studio critique was the evaluation or "judgment" of student artwork, with many of the instructors emphasizing negative rather than positive aspects of their students' artwork. Barrett (1988) found several important differences between the goals for conducting critique identified by studio professors and the goals commonly found in art education literature articulating the strengths of criticism as a pedagogical method. Although art education literature considers criticism a subject matter in itself with a body of knowledge, logic, recommended procedures, and a variety of goals, the studio professors used critique primarily to assess their students' success at fulfilling their assignments and to improve their students' art-making through evaluation. Many art instructors specifically defined criticism as judgment, while art education literature articulated evaluation as just one aspect of criticism with greater emphasis on developing interpretation by building arguments based on evidence in and around the artwork (Barrett, 1988). Through strategies that emphasize descriptive analysis, interpretive argumentation, and evaluation as a critical process that makes underlying value systems visible, critique can introduce an approach to analyzing art that can be useful well beyond the studio classroom.

As an instructor of visual art practice coauthor Helen Klebesadel uses critique to encourage student artists to better understand that the norms they use to judge art and the unacknowledged conventions they may be using in their art-making are constructed, even though they've learned to accept them as norms. In recognizing the pressures to conform to norms, student artists are better able to resist and work toward more original artworks. Understanding and rejecting the pressure to conform to cultural norms can encourage students to immerse themselves in the research and analysis of unfamiliar artwork to gain a deeper understanding of art generated from impulses outside their own experience. These approaches encourage agency and create a valuable engagement with difference. Bringing student-directed, self-defined learning within the context of broad-based education to the foreground is the foundation for a studio critique process that encourages openness to the unknown. This approach models an educational process that makes room for many voices to enter our cultural dialogues.

Artists learn by being critiqued, but they also learn by critiquing the artworks of their peers. As in theater, studio art instruction and critique are essentially the same thing. Student artists learn through the act of making art and struggle to create a cohesive set of artwork or portfolio, but they also learn through having their work evaluated and evaluating the work of others. Participants come to a common understanding of the criteria for the judgment of the art and then assess their own and other artworks by those criteria, or they determine whether the medium, intention, audience, and form of the artwork under consideration requires another set of criteria to judge it appropriately. For example, although a painting may require attention to mark-making as an expressive element, a traditional quilt may require more attention to careful stitching. The significance of representational imagery could be analyzed in both but toward different ends. The use of color and the effectiveness of compositional concerns may overlap, but symmetrical compositional elements would be a more acceptable convention for the quilt than the painting. The effectiveness of the piece in communicating with intended audiences could be a topic for both. Students often state that during group critique they learn as much through the evaluation of other students' work as their own.

Ultimately, critique can encourage the intellectual and emotional engagement of student artists in critical thinking processes by encouraging them to recognize what they bring from their own lives as worthy subject matter for art. It can also engage students in their creative practice in a way that appreciates art-making as a critical work as well as a creative, cultural one.

Conclusion

Despite differences between the undergraduate studio art and performance classroom, the use of critique and the dynamics connected to them are similar. It's a powerful tool for student growth and development that should be deeply situated in course objectives around the visual, performative, analytical, and intellectual goals of the course and each lesson. Through effective critique, students can and do learn theory, create arguments, and situate the performance or artwork into social, ethical, or political perspectives. Criteria for evaluation are transparent and understood by all, so the assessment is fair, and students have a way of measuring their progress and learning to use their creative voices positively to judge the work of peers. When instructors consider students as having the capacity to make sophisticated art statements, art will be produced that is varied and reflective of individual voices and experience. When instructors push students farther in the direction they're already going and facilitate their intellectual and technical growth, great things can happen. Students bring complicated and interesting understandings of the world with them to the art and acting studios, and—if allowed and encouraged through positive critique—they will make amazing creations from it.

Creating a community of learners in the performance or visual art classroom where ideas can be freely exchanged, perspectives openly shared, and performance used to understand and impact the world we live in is central to an open learning space for all, including the instructor. Where and how critique fits into that space in a holistic way is an area for research into this signature pedagogy, particularly how it is evolving and how it can be better understood and used most productively.

What we hope for is a richer discussion with our colleagues about the tools and methodologies of critique to ensure that they are used to bring out the best in our students and to nurture them as productive and valued creative artists. A student-active, student-centered classroom where the more limiting conventions in studio and performance practice are challenged and transparent evaluative processes are produced is something we strive for. One way to do this is to encourage more scholarly investigations into creative expression and student learning in the creative arts classroom. This objective can be accomplished through solidly designed SoTL research aimed at helping us identify and share the most effective strategies toward the larger goal of student success.

References

Alexander, B. K. (1999). Moving toward a critical poetic response. *Theatre Topics, 9*(2), 107–125.

Alexander, B. K. (2002). Intimate engagement: Student performances as scholarly endeavor. *Theatre Topics, 12*(1), 85–98.

Barrett, T. (1988). A comparison of the goals of studio professors conducting critiques and art education goals for teaching criticism. *Studies in Art Education, 30*(1), 22–27.

Barrett, T. (2000). Studio critiques of student art: As they are, as they could be with mentoring. *Theory and Practice, 31,* 29–35.

Bartow, A. (2006). *Training of the American actor.* New York: Theatre Communications Group.

Brestoff, R. (1995). *The great acting teachers and their methods.* Lyme, NH: Smith and Kraus.

Colwell, R. (1998). Preparing student teachers in assessment. *Arts Education Policy Review, 99*(4), 29–34.

Hetland, L., Winner, E., Veenema, S., & Sheridan, K. M. (2007). *Studio thinking: The real benefits of visual arts education.* New York: Teachers College Press.

Hodge, A. (Ed.). (2000). *Twentieth century actor training.* New York: Routledge.

Kuh, G., Kinzie, J., Schuh, J. H., & Whitt, E. J. (2005). *Student success in college.* Indianapolis: Jossey-Bass.

Mekler, E. (1988). *The new generation of acting teachers.* New York: Penguin Books.

Owen-Smith, P. (2004). What is cognitive–affective learning (CAL)? *Journal of Cognitive Affective Learning, 1*(1).

Richlin, L., & Witman, P. D. (2007). The status of the scholarship of teaching and learning in the disciplines. *International Journal for the Scholarship of Teaching and Learning, 1*(1), 1–17.

Salazar, L. G. (1992). Assessment in theatre education. *Design for Arts in Education, 93*(5), 41–46.

Warburton, E. C. (2006). Access to arts beyond high school: Issues of demand and availability in American higher education. *Arts Education Policy Review, 107*(6), 11–16.

SECTION THREE

SOCIAL SCIENCES

7

MOVING TOWARD A SIGNATURE PEDAGOGY IN GEOGRAPHY

A Close Reading of the Landscape

Cary Komoto

The average person is likely to define geography as a collection of trivial facts about a place, such as depicted on the TV game show *Jeopardy*. Defined in this way, U.S. citizens' knowledge of geography is poor. Roach (2006) reported that "young adults in the United States fail to understand the world and their place in it, according to a survey-based report on geographic literacy" (p. 1). More than 10 years ago, Gilbert Grosvenor (1995), chairman of the board of trustees of the National Geographic Society, wrote about an ongoing effort by the society to support geographic education to eliminate geographic illiteracy in the United States (p. 410). Despite this effort, most U.S. college geography teachers would probably agree that most U.S. citizens still do not know much about geography; furthermore, the teachers would probably disagree with the assumption that geography is merely a collection of trivial facts. Geographic facts are to geography like words are to literature: Both facts and words are important, but even more important are how those facts and words can be put together and interpreted.

In part, the state of geographic knowledge in the United States is a result of what happens in the college classroom. What is happening in the college classroom that contributes to this misunderstanding about geography? This chapter will attempt to answer this question by explaining the traditional pedagogies used to teach geography content and skills and suggesting how these pedagogies should be revised. In keeping with the theme of this volume, the chapter also identifies a signature pedagogy for geography that would help students develop the geographic skills used by experts in the discipline.

Thinking like a Geographer

Geography comprises a wide range of topics from human or cultural geography (which focuses on features and topics of human activity on Earth) to physical geography (which focuses on features and topics of the natural world). In between these two is human–environmental geography, which focuses on the interaction of human activity with the natural world. These three broad classes do not have well-defined boundaries, and some topics studied by geographers may not neatly fit into any one category.

Geography as a discipline is also defined by a set of geographic skills that help in answering geography questions. Among the most fundamental of these are map skills that allow a geographer to use maps as a tool. Maps can be used to raise questions as well as to answer questions. Also fundamental to geography is the ability to think spatially; that is, to understand concepts such as location, place, relationships between and among locations, and diffusion over space. This ability is known as spatial cognition. In addition, depending on the particular subfield within geography, other skills such as quantitative and qualitative analysis may be important.

The academic discipline of geography is a way of thinking about the spatial aspects of both the human and natural worlds. Thinking like a geographer usually starts with a question about space. For example, in the human realm, one question might be where is Christianity practiced? Or, in the natural realm, where is big bluestem prairie grass found? Geographers use a wide variety of approaches and types of evidence to try to answer these questions. Acceptable answers to these questions often stimulate further questions that require further research. For example, the answer to the question of where Christianity is practiced might stimulate further questions about why it is practiced in certain locations but not in others. Similarly, investigating the locations of prairie grass might stimulate questions about what factors control its distribution.

The geographer is a content and skills expert. Given an aerial photograph of a city, an urban geographer will typically be able interpret the city landscape in a much more sophisticated way than the average person.

Both may notice the same visual elements in the photo that represent real-world things—roads, houses, office buildings, parking lots, rail lines, green spaces, warehouses, stores, gas stations, golf courses, cemeteries, churches, factories, clinics, government offices, libraries, and all of the other cultural artifacts that make up a city—but the urban geographer will also note structures in the landscape that the average person may not. The geographer may recognize residential neighborhoods and distinguish them based on where they are located within the city. The geographer will understand why residential neighborhoods are located and distributed in particular ways, what land uses are missing or occupy more land than expected, and whether the city is located in a developed country. The photo will also provoke questions about what is happening in the city. Why is office building development happening in a particular part of the city? Why are all water bodies buffered by green space? In short, the urban geographer has the ability to use geographic skills, concepts, theories, and models to understand and interpret the city landscape. In addition, the geographer has the ability to formulate sophisticated questions about the city and understand how to design research that can answer these questions.

The goal of geography education in most colleges and universities in the United States today is to teach students to think like geographers do. Students should progress along the continuum from novice to expert geographer both in understanding content and in acquiring skills. A signature geography pedagogy must move students along this continuum. The learning goals of most geography courses must focus on geography content but also implicitly focus on fostering the development of geographic skills and spatial cognition abilities to help students become geography experts.

The difference between a geography expert and a novice can be understood by considering a modified framework from Bransford and Donovan (2005). In this adapted framework, the geography expert is characterized by the following:

- An understanding of geography's concepts, theories, and models;
- An understanding of how geography knowledge is generated and justified;
- The ability to use an understanding of geography's concepts, theories, and models, combined with geography knowledge creation to ask and answer new geography questions; and

- The ability to use mental processes that monitor and control the cognitive activity focused on geography content and skills—processes known as metacognition.

SoTL in Geography

A review of the geography education literature will help explain how geography is taught and also help assess characteristics of geography's traditional pedagogies to facilitate the identification of a signature pedagogy.

In general, SoTL is not a widely recognized type of scholarship within geography. Although Boyer (1990) essentially coined the term SoTL more than 15 years ago, there is still little recognition in geography for this type of scholarship, despite the fact that many geographers have engaged in SoTL for a long time. It is difficult to classify SoTL work in geography over the last 15 years into discrete categories. One characteristic of SoTL in geography literature is that it hasn't been synthesized: Many articles are indirectly linked to each other, but there has been little done to put the SoTL work together into a more coherent whole. SoTL in geography also tends to emphasize teaching and learning of geographic *skills* rather than what specific content should be taught.

Currently, only a few journals regularly publish SoTL work in or related to geography. These include the *Journal of Geography* and the *Journal of Geography in Higher Education.* The articles in these two journals typically deal with geography education, but most articles do not have all of the elements of true SoTL work. Most articles describe how an individual instructor is engaged in scholarly teaching but not in SoTL. The articles usually report whether a particular method or assignment improved student learning, although evidence of this improved learning is not always well documented, often because the instructor tried something new without comparing it to any other methods and did not use a robust research design. Two other journals also publish SoTL in geography: the *Journal of Geoscience Education* and *Research in Geographic Education.*

The two major traditional research journals in geography, the *Annals of the Association of American Geographers* and *The Professional Geographer,* also have published a few SoTL articles. Healey (2003) argued that faculty in higher education need more professional development in SoTL. In an attempt to bridge the gap between traditional research and geographic education issues, Warf (1999) argued for more collaboration between the areas, essentially recognizing the need for SoTL in geography without calling it such. As those interested in SoTL in geography in the late 1990s began to develop a research agenda, Shelley (1999) argued the need to pay attention to the state of national education and its increased attention to learning, not just teaching, thus putting the "L" in SoTL.

Another source for understanding how geography content and skills have been taught and what students are learning is a widely used text for teaching college geography, *Teaching Geography in Higher Education: A Manual of Good Practice* (Gold, Jenkins, Lee, Monk, Riley, Shepherd, & Unwin, 1991). This text is a summary and synthesis of general educational practice and specific geography pedagogy. Illustrative of the state of SoTL in geography at the time the book was published, the majority of the book (approximately 60% as based on the cited references) is derived from the general education literature or pedagogical literature from other disciplines as opposed to specific geography education literature. The purpose of the book is to provide college geography teachers with an understanding of traditional pedagogies and how to use them effectively—hence the subtitle *A Manual of Good Practice.*

Generic Pedagogies Used in Geography

A broad range of generic pedagogies has been fine tuned by geographers to help train students to think like geographers. This section addresses five in particular: Internet use, writing exercises, role-playing, active learning and discussion techniques, and case studies.

Using the Internet to improve student learning has also received attention in geography SoTL literature. Studies on use of the Internet have generally found the Web to be an effective tool for enhancing student learning in both geographic content and skills. Most of the studies have found that the Web, when combined with another technique such as collaborative learning or inquiry-based learning, allows for greater achievement as assessed in different ways (Hill & Solem, 1999; Hurley, Proctor, & Ford, 1999; Mitchell & Reed, 2001; Solem, 2000; Steinberg, Walter, & Sherman-Morris, 2002; Sui & Bednarz, 1999; Taylor, 2000; Warf, Vincent, & Purcell, 1999). Furthermore, a study by Smith, Edwards, and Raschke (2006) not only supports the general findings of the previous studies, but it also reinforces the importance of articulating learning objectives to students.

Research into writing as a means of creating new knowledge and as a means to help students understand concepts has contributed to SoTL in geography literature. Representative of this research is Hooey and Bailey's (2005) study of the use of journal writing as a learning exercise for students in world regional geography. Their conclusion was that journal writing helped students' "progression in the development of critical and geographic thinking skills" (p. 261). Heyman (2004) argued that having students participate in knowledge production through writing assignments enhanced their understanding of social justice in geography. Fouberg (2000) and Proctor, Sutton, and Michaels (1995) also found that various writing exercises were effective in introductory geography courses. Thus, using the Internet and writing can help students learn how to think like a geographer and are potential elements of a signature pedagogy.

Student engagement has been shown to increase when specific techniques are used, such as simulations in which students assume the role of particular persons within a hypothetical scenario. Several studies have demonstrated through various types of evidence that role-playing exercises are useful for student understanding of some types of cultural geography topics. Oberle (2004) used student evaluations to find that a role-playing scenario about public land management was effective for student learning. Kurtz (2004) determined that student engagement increased with a role-play about the global economy. Other studies involving cultural geography topics with different scenarios also argue that role-playing is an effective technique for students (Masilela, 1994; Van DeVort, 1997).

A number of studies in the SoTL in geography literature have tried to determine effective ways of engaging students in geography content and skills so that they are more motivated to learn. These studies span a range of content and skills. Studies by Aspaas (2003), Klein (2003), and Mowell (2003) suggested that various forms of active learning are effective in improving knowledge and skills in world geography courses, which are often part of a core in the geography major. These active learning strategies include using case studies (Aspaas, 2003) and food (Mowell, 2003) to engage student interest.

Other studies reported on a variety of means to engage students in learning both content and skills (Alderman & Popke, 2002; Brady, 1999; Rodrigue, 1996). Buckley, Bain, Luginbuhl, and Dyer (2004) found evidence based on student evaluations and exit interviews that active learning exercises such as journals and group-based assignments in large lecture courses were effective in improving student understanding. Similarly, Oldakowski (2001), and Sommers (1997) found improved student engagement and learning through the use of active learning techniques in introductory geography courses and in freshmen-year experience courses. Additionally, there are examples of different techniques such as problem-based learning exercises, journal writing, and using popular culture that utilize the idea of engagement to improve student learning.

One potential advantage of classroom discussion as a teaching method is the possibility of students hearing multiple perspectives which, if done right, can improve student engagement. Oberhauser (2002) reported on a growing body of literature in critical geography, which includes feminist perspectives that emphasize the multiple perspectives of those being studied as well as the perspectives of students in the classroom. Browne (2005) argued for drawing on personal experience in class discussion, but she also suggests that the complexity of personal experience requires special care for this discussion to be effective (pp. 339–354).

Case studies, another generic pedagogy, can also be very useful in teaching geography as seen in an example from an economic geography class. In this class, a video case study on Nike shoe manufacturing in Guangdong, China, is shown to students. The case study can help students build their visual vocabulary, a process that is ongoing throughout the course. For example, a factory may mean different things in different places in the world. In the Guangdong case study, this includes the geographic concept of globalization of the labor force. The case can also prompt questions, such as what are the implications of the transfer of manufacturing jobs to China? The case study can also be better understood by examining a map that shows that Guangdong Province is close to Hong Kong, which has the transportation facilities and business know-how to effectively compete in a global economy. Map interpretation skills help the expert geographer make the connections. The high population growth and large population results in China having an abundance of low-cost labor. An understanding of political and economic geography also helps in understanding the case because China's government is committed to encouraging capitalist enterprise. So, although the novice might view the case simply as a factory in China making shoes, the geography expert uses geography content knowledge and geographic skills to understand that the case illustrates many geographic concepts all coming together in one place. The close reading of the Guangdong landscape reveals much more meaning to the expert.

To reiterate, the geography education literature focuses on specific ways to effectively teach particular geographic content and skills. As suggested by the literature, student engagement through techniques such as role-playing simulations, class discussions, and other active learning techniques, along with other approaches such as case studies, can be effective in helping students to think like a geographer and therefore should be considered as part of a signature pedagogy.

Developing a Signature Pedagogy in Geography

Many traditional methods of teaching geography do not always teach students to think like experts in geography. Consequently, after completing a geography course, students have not made progress in moving along the continuum from geography novice to expert. The geography education literature and the SoTL in geography literature have not addressed this issue specifically and have focused more on examining various elements of teaching and learning in geography.

Spatial Information Skill

Spatial information is a fundamental aspect of geography, and developing it in students forms a key element of geography's signature pedagogy. Surprisingly, there is little focus on spatial cognition in existing pedagogical research. Most of the explicit concern with spatial cognition tends to occur with two broad groups of research topics: geographic information systems (GIS) and interpreting and creating maps. Despite the lack of direct focus on spatial cognition, pedagogical research related to spatial cognition is important for identifying a signature geography pedagogy.

GIS usually refers to computer software that enables a user to store, retrieve, and process information that has some location component, such as a street address. Although not exhaustive of the literature, four studies are representative of the SoTL work done in this area. Each has to do with GIS and students' acquisition of spatial cognition skills through different learning activities. West (2003) focused on how GIS can impact thinking skills and motivation. Lloyd (2001) argued for the effectiveness of GIS as tool for students to engage in active learning. Bunch (2000) found differences between adults and children in terms of their abilities to develop cognitive skills. Koch and Denike (2007) pointed out the potential pitfalls of using GIS to teach spatial cognition as demonstrated by the failure of one of their students to understand some important concepts, despite developing a seemingly sophisticated solution to a problem. Although there are some potential problems for student learning with such methods, these studies generally argued for the effectiveness of GIS in teaching spatial cognition and suggested that teaching how to use GIS is part of a signature pedagogy.

One explicit way to develop spatial cognition skills is the geography lab, but some potential problems need to be addressed. Knight (2004) reported that in a study of key skill development in students, the students preferred individual learning, contrary to the finding that group work was shown to increase skill development. In another study, Folkard (2004) found that mathematical skills related to spatial cognition were not effectively learned in labs focused on the development of quantitative geography skills. Finally, Bransford and Donovan (2005), in a synthesis of educational research, argued that many labs reinforce incorrect ideas held by students rather than help them correctly understand concepts when students do not account for data that do not support their preconceptions (p. 400). This last general statement is important for a signature geography pedagogy because if geography labs are not well designed, they will not help students learn how to think like a geographer.

Fieldwork

Fieldwork is a clear example of an explicit signature pedagogy for geography. Fieldwork entails students spending time out of the classroom at a particular location engaged in some type of learning activity. At the lowest cognitive level, this might be a simple guided field trip in which the learning objective is primarily one of student observation to build a visual vocabulary (e.g., what does term "residential neighborhood" mean?). At the other end of the cognitive continuum is collecting of data by students for research about a particular geographic question (e.g., recording observations of how gender affects people's movements). Given the discipline's concern with space and place, fieldwork is arguably one of the most important pedagogies for geography. For example, Mires (2004) argued that fieldwork can build geographic skills important for "attaining the geographer's eye for landscape" (p. 13), and Gold et al. (1991) provided a comprehensive list of different types of geographical learning objectives addressed through fieldwork, which can range from developing observation skills to facilitating experiential learning to experiencing research.

The SoTL in geography literature includes a significant number of studies that reported on the effectiveness of fieldwork for student learning. Given that most geography is rooted in the real world and that much geographic research is based on work from the field in locations of interest to the study, it seems intuitive that fieldwork should be effective for student learning and skill building. The geography SoTL has examined issues of location, length of field studies, content, logistics, and planning of fieldwork to support this intuition. For instance, though fieldwork can vary in length from a couple of hours in a single lab class to semester-long studies, Stanitski and Fuellhart (2003) argued for the effectiveness of short-term, study-abroad classes (pp. 202–215). Fuller, Edmondson, France, Higgitt, and Ratinen (2006) also supported the idea of the effectiveness of international fieldwork for student learning (pp. 89–101). Others argued that other fieldwork experiences, such as those possible on campus, are also valuable for student learning (Hudak, 2003; Jennings & Huber, 2003).

Fieldwork has been shown to be a useful and effective way to learn a wide variety of content and skills that range as widely as the discipline. For example, a study on applied tourism geography included elements of cooperative learning within student teams (De Bres & Coomansingh, 2006). Other articles about fieldwork concerned with cultural topics such as American Indian geography and history (Hurt & Wallace, 2005), general human geography (Panelli & Welch, 2005), and teaching field methods to cultural resource management technicians (Mires, 2004) showed that fieldwork resulted in improved understanding of geography content. Based on their investigations of teachers' perceptions, Scott, Fuller, and Gaskin (2006) reported that fieldwork was effective in putting theory into context and in teaching skills to students. Additionally, fieldwork is certainly not limited to cultural geography topics. Ellis and Rindfleisch (2006) reported that a combined field and lab activity for students studying geomorphology allowed to students to increase their concept understanding and enjoy the learning experience.

The common thread for all of these studies is that fieldwork is effective in promoting student learning of content and skills in geography. This notion was extended by Hasse and Colvard (2006) and by McMorrow (2005), all of whom argued that fieldwork can also be enhanced by online materials.

Despite these studies affirming the value of fieldwork, Nairn (2005) argued that students' experiences with the complexities of "the real world" may make it difficult for them to grasp underlying geographic concepts or theories that were the objective of the field experience. Students conducting fieldwork may not yet have the ability to separate the key features of a real-world situation in order to achieve the learning objective. Finally, fieldwork may also reinforce wrong ideas rather than create correct understandings because students may pay attention only to evidence or features that they are familiar with and that support their preconceptions (Bransford & Donovan, 2005). These findings suggest there are features of fieldwork that are an integral part of a signature pedagogy, but care must be taken in designing the fieldwork so that it will meet particular learning objectives.

Visualization

Thinking like a geographer can involve a great deal of visualization. The SoTL in geography literature includes studies about the use of various visualization technologies, techniques, and exercises to help students learn geography and to improve their visualization skills. Many of the studies have focused on physical geography topics, but some of the findings are applicable to cultural geography as well. Both Anthamatten and Ziegler (2006) and Slocum, Dunbar, and Egbert (2007) provided evidence that the three-dimensional visualization technology known as GeoWall enhances student learning of physical geography concepts and processes and landscape features. Student evaluations and comments from focus group experiments provided evidence of the effectiveness of this technology in aiding student understanding. Although this technology was evaluated in terms of its application to understanding physical geography, it seems logical that it would help students understand cultural geography as well.

Some studies have argued that various visual technologies combined with particular techniques can enhance student understanding of physical geography (Brown & Olson, 2001; Butler, 1994). Other studies suggested ways to use visualization to aid and assess student understanding of geography content and skills. Castner (2003) focused on the use of photos, and

Walk (1994) focused on videos as a means for building content and skills. Fredrich and Fuller (1998) found that photographic slide tests are an effective assessment of student knowledge and skill. Combined, these studies suggest that visualization skills are an integral part of a signature pedagogy.

Map Use

Another element of geography's signature pedagogy relates to using maps. In terms of improving student map interpretation and map-making skills, the SoTL in geography is relatively rich in studies. Several studies have tested various approaches to developing map interpretation skills. Map-making can improve students' knowledge of geography, along with improving their map-making skills (Acheson, 2001; Cravey, Arcury, & Quandt, 2000; Lee & Bednarz, 2005). One significant finding is that making the intent of the skill-building assignment clear to the students can improve the effectiveness of the assignment (Battersby, Golledge, & Marsh, 2006). Another study found no difference in student achievement between the use of paper maps and electronic or computer maps (Pedersen, Farrell, & McPhee, 2005). Other studies focused on improving the effectiveness of map assignments for building student map interpretation skills (Chiodo, 1997; Linn, 1997; Thomas, 1994).

Skills and Concepts

Gersmehl (2005) identified one problem with geography education that may inhibit students from becoming experts. In *Teaching Geography*, Gersmehl identified a problem in the traditional ways of teaching geography, which tend to separate skill building, such as map interpretation skills, from more abstract ideas, such as a geographic region. The problem is based on the idea that "the human brain is structured to acquire knowledge . . . through several (cognitive) pathways simultaneously" (p. 28). Thus, good geography teaching means structuring a course and individual teaching units (class periods or particular topics) within the course so that they address different cognitive pathways more or less at the same time like a "multi-strand rope" (pp. 27–49). The most effective geography teaching occurs, for example, when students learn map skills while learning about geographic regions and also learning about a specific region, such as the U.S. Midwest. This also how a geographer thinks; therefore, Gersmehl's ideas are useful in a signature geography pedagogy. Along with the signature skills identified in this section, the activity of fieldwork can act as a way of combining these skills into an integrated, but not complete signature pedagogy. A well-designed fieldwork project will engage students to think like a geographer and use spatial information skills that can be learned through GIS labs and other lab exercises. GIS can also be an integral part of the fieldwork both as part of the preparatory work for the actual fieldwork project and as a means to analyze the results of the fieldwork. Visualization skills and map use can also be integral to the fieldwork project. Designed correctly, a fieldwork project can address Gersmehl's ideas of teaching several things, such as skills and content, at the same time. It makes sense that fieldwork combined with spatial skills is part of a signature pedagogy because fieldwork is essentially how most geographers do a close reading of the landscape.

Concluding Thoughts

Identifying elements of a comprehensive signature pedagogy in geography based on current practices and suggesting what it *should do* is easy, but outlining a concrete guide for actual classroom practice, is more difficult. At a general level a signature pedagogy should take into account student preconceptions, enable students to understand how geography works, and help students master the ability to use mental processes that monitor and control cognitive activity focused on geography content and skills (Donovan & Bransford, 2005). A signature pedagogy should enable students to move along the continuum from being disciplinary novices to disciplinary experts. A signature pedagogy should also engage students on several cognitive pathways, such as understanding abstract geographic concepts, learning geographic skills, and learning how to think like a geographer at the same time (Gersmehl, 2005).

The geographic education and SoTL literature suggests that the different elements of a signature pedagogy for geography described in this chapter—fostering spatial cognition with GIS, map reading, fieldwork, and visualization instruction—together with variations on traditional pedagogies such as role-playing and case studies, should together enable a student to begin to think like a geographer and engage in close readings of the landscape. Both the novice and expert are able to identify some of the basic features of the landscape, much like words in a text. These features are things that make up that landscape, whether they are human created, such as a fence, or natural, such as a tree. The rules of geographic concepts and theories (such as the link between plant distribution and climate) are much like grammar rules that indicate appropriate arrangements of words for sentences and entire texts.

A landscape may also be impacted by factors outside of what is visible. For example, federal laws regulate what activities can occur in certain areas, which is analogous to the different contexts within which a text might written. The novice in geography is not equipped to go much beyond some simple observations and ideas about what features are and why they might be there, much like a novice in literature is able to glean some meaning from a text. Yet both are, in effect, skimming. On the other hand, the expert in geography is able to make more complex observations and apply concepts and theories that help explain the landscape. The landscape may stimulate additional questions that compel the expert to do more study. The expert will also recognize the limitations of his or her own knowledge. The geography expert is able to do a sophisticated interpretation of the landscape.

Teaching students to closely read the landscape can ultimately help them move beyond their status as novices and to understand how geography as a discipline works. The spatial perspective that geographers use is a unique and fascinating way to interpret and understand the world. There is no greater reward for a geography teacher than seeing students understand and appreciate geography as they move towards thinking like geographers and being able to do their own close readings of the landscape.

References

Acheson, G. (2001). Teaching the tool of the trade: Understanding teachers' beliefs, knowledge, and practices about map skills. *Research in Geographic Education, 3,* 71–75.

Alderman, D. H., & Popke, E. J. (2002). Humor and film in the geography classroom: Learning from Michael Moore's *TV Nation. Journal of Geography, 101,* 228–239.

Anthamatten, P., & Ziegler, S. S. (2006). Teaching geography with 3-D visualization technology. *Journal of Geography, 105,* 231–237.

Aspaas, H. R. (2003). Integrating women and environmental issues into world regional geography. *Journal of Geography, 102,* 158–166.

Battersby, S. E., Golledge, R., & Marsh, M. J. (2006). Incidental learning of geospatial concepts across grade levels: Map overlay. *Journal of Geography, 105,* 139–146.

Boyer, E. L. (1990). *Scholarship reconsidered: Priorities of the professoriate.* New York: The Carnegie Foundation for the Advancement of Teaching.

Brady, S. (1999). Using a travelogue to learn a region. *Journal of Geography 98*, 79–85.

Bransford, J. D., & Donovan, M. S. (2005). Scientific inquiry and how people learn. In M. S. Donovan, & Bransford, J. D. (Eds.), *How students learn* (pp. 397–419). Washington, DC: The National Academies Press.

Brown, D. G., & Olson, J. M. (2001). Integrated teaching of geographic information science and physical geography through digital terrain analysis. *Journal of Geography, 100*, 4–13.

Browne, K. (2005). Placing the personal in pedagogy: Engaged pedagogy in 'feminist' geographical teaching. *Journal of Geography in Higher Education, 29*, 339–354.

Buckley, G. L., Bain, N. R., Luginbuhl, A. M., & Dyer, M. L. (2004). Adding an 'active learning' component to a large lecture course. *Journal of Geography, 103*, 231–237.

Bunch, R. L. (2000). GIS and the acquisition of spatial information: Difference among adults and young adolescents. *Research in Geographic Education, 2*, 67–97.

Butler, D. R. (1994). Repeat photography as a tool for emphasizing movement in physical geography. *Journal of Geography, 93*, 141–151.

Castner, H. W. (2003). Photographic mosaics and geographic generalizations: A perceptual approach to geographic education. *Journal of Geography, 102*, 121–127.

Chiodo, J. J. (1997). Improving the cognitive development of students' mental maps of the world. *Journal of Geography, 96*, 153–163.

Cravey, A., Arcury, T. A., & Quandt, S. A. (2000). Mapping as a means of farmworker education and empowerment. *Journal of Geography, 99*, 229–237.

De Bres, K., & Coomansingh, J. (2006). A student run field exercise in applied tourism geography. *Journal of Geography, 105*, 67–72.

Donovan, M. S., & Bransford, J. D. (2005). Introduction. In M. S. Donovan & J. D. Bransford (Eds.), *How students learn* (pp. 1–28). Washington, DC: The National Academies Press.

Ellis, J. T., & Rindfleisch, P. R. (2006). A coastal environment field and laboratory activity for an undergraduate geomorphology course. *Journal of Geography, 105*, 216–224.

Folkard, A. M. (2004). Mathophobic students' perspectives on quantitative material in the undergraduate geography curriculum. *Journal of Geography in Higher Education, 28*, 209–228.

Fouberg, E. H. (2000). Concept learning through writing for learning: Using journals in an introductory geography class. *Journal of Geography, 99*, 196–206.

Fredrich, B., & Fuller, K. (1998). What we see and what they see: Slide tests in geography. *Journal of Geography, 97*, 63–71.

Fuller, I., Edmondson, S., France, D., Higgitt, D., & Ratinen, I. (2006). International perspectives on the effectiveness of geography fieldwork for learning. *Journal of Geography in Higher Education, 30*, 89–101.

Gersmehl, P. (2005). *Teaching geography*. New York: The Guilford Press.

Gold, J. R., Jenkins, A., Lee, R., Monk, J., Riley, J., Shepherd, I., & Unwin, D. (1991). *Teaching geography in higher education: A manual of good practice*. Oxford, UK: Blackwell.

Grosvenor, G. (1995). In sight of the tunnel: The renaissance of geography education. *Annals of the Association of American Geographers, 85*, 409–420.

Hasse, J., & Colvard, C. (2006). Inverse distance learning: Digitally enhancing a geography field-course. *Journal of Geography, 105*, 167–174.

Healey, M. (2003). Promoting lifelong professional development in geography education: International perspectives on developing the scholarship of teaching in higher education in the twenty-first century. *The Professional Geographer, 55*, 1–17.

Heyman, R. (2004). Inventing geography: Writing as a social justice pedagogy. *Journal of Geography, 103*, 139–152.

Hill, D. A., & Solem, M. N. (1999). Geography on the Web: Changing the learning paradigm. *Journal of Geography, 98*, 100–107.

Hooey, C. A., & Bailey, T. J. (2005). Journal writing and the development of spatial thinking skills. *Journal of Geography, 104*, 257–261.

Hudak, P. F. (2003). Campus field exercises for introductory geoscience courses. *Journal of Geography, 102*, 220–225.

Hurley, J. M., Proctor, J. D., & Ford, R. E. (1999). Collaborative inquiry at a distance: Using the internet in geography education. *Journal of Geography, 98*, 128–140.

Hurt, D. A., & Wallace, M. L. (2005). Teaching American Indian geography and history with new perspective: The Lodge Pole River Project example. *Journal of Geography, 104*, 187–193.

Jennings, S. A., & Huber, T. P. (2003). Campus-based geographic learning: A field oriented teaching scenario. *Journal of Geography, 102*, 185–192.

Klein, P. (2003). Active learning strategies and assessment in world geography classes. *Journal of Geography, 102*, 146–157.

Knight, J. (2004). Comparison of student perception and performance in individual and group assessments in practical classes. *Journal of Geography in Higher Education, 28*, 63–81.

Koch, T. & Denike, K. (2007). Aaron's solution, instructor's problem: Teaching surface analysis using GIS. *Journal of Geography, 106*, 69–77.

Kurtz, H. E. (2004). Reflecting on role play in geographic education: The case of the banana war. *Journal of Geography, 103*, 16–27.

Lee, J., & Bednarz, R.S. (2005) Video analysis of map-drawing strategies. *Journal of Geography, 104*, 211–221.

Linn, S. E. (1997). The effectiveness of interactive maps in the classroom: A selected example in studying Africa. *Journal of Geography, 96*, 164–170.

Lloyd, W. J. (2001). Integrating GIS into the undergraduate learning environment. *Journal of Geography, 100*, 158–163.

Masilela, C. O. (1994). Teaching American students about urbanization in developing countries: The use of role-playing. *Journal of Geography, 93*, 114–124.

McMorrow, J. (2005). Using a web-based resource to prepare students for fieldwork: Evaluating the Dark Peak virtual tour. *Journal of Geography in Higher Education, 29*, 223–240.

Mires, P. B. (2004). Teaching geographic field methods to cultural resource management technicians. *Journal of Geography, 103*, 8–15.

Mitchell, B., & Reed, M. (2001). Using information technologies for interactive learning. *Journal of Geography, 100*, 145–153.

Mowell, B. D. (2003). Edible geography: International foods in the world geography classroom. *Journal of Geography, 102*, 140–145.

Nairn, K. (2005). The problems of utilizing "direct experience" in geography education. *Journal of Geography in Higher Education, 29*, 293–309.

Oberhauser, A. M. (2002). Examining gender and community through critical pedagogy. *Journal of Geography in Higher Education, 26*, 19–31.

Oberle, A. P. (2004). Understanding public land management through role-playing. *Journal of Geography, 103*, 199–210.

Oldakowski, R. K. (2001). Activities to develop a spatial perspective among students in introductory geography courses. *Journal of Geography, 100*, 243–250.

Panelli, R., & Welch, R. V. (2005). Teaching research through field studies: A cumulative opportunity for teaching methodology to human geography undergraduates. *Journal of Geography in Higher Education, 29*, 255–277.

Pedersen, P., Farrell, P., & McPhee, E. (2005). Paper vs. pixel: Effectiveness of paper vs. electronic maps to teach map reading skill in an introductory physical geography course. *Journal of Geography, 104*, 195–202.

Proctor, J. D., Sutton, P. C., & Michaels, G. H. (1995). Multimedia guided writing modules for introductory human geography. *Journal of Geography, 94*, 571–577.

Roach, J. (2006, May 2). Young Americans geographically illiterate, survey suggests. *National Geographic News*. Retrieved January 5, 2008, from http://news.nationalgeographic.com/news/2006/05/0502_060502_geography.html

Rodrigue, C. M. (1996). Imaginary migration exercise in multicultural geography. *Journal of Geography, 95*, 81–85.

Scott, I., Fuller, I., & Gaskin, S. (2006). Life without fieldwork: Some lecturers' perceptions of geography and environmental science fieldwork. *Journal of Geography in Higher Education, 30*, 161–171.

Shelley, F. M. (1999). Geographic education research and the changing institutional structure of American education. *The Professional Geographer, 51*, 592–597.

Slocum, T. A., Dunbar, M. D., & Egbert, S. L. (2007). Evaluating the potential of the GeoWall for geographic education. *Journal of Geography, 106*, 91–102.

Smith, J. M., Edwards, P. M., & Raschke, J. (2006). Using technology and inquiry to improve student understanding of watershed concepts. *Journal of Geography, 105*, 249–258.

Solem, M. (2000). Differential adoption of internet-based teaching practices in college geography. *Journal of Geography, 99*, 219–227.

Sommers, B. J. (1997). The freshman year experience and geography: Linking student retention and the introductory geography curriculum. *Journal of Geography, 96*, 243–249.

Stanitski, D., & Fuellhart, K. (2003). Tools for developing short-term study abroad classes for geography studies. *Journal of Geography, 102*, 202–215.

Steinberg, P. E., Walter, A., & Sherman-Morris, K. (2002). Using the internet to integrate thematic and regional approaches in geographic education. *The Professional Geographer, 54*, 332–348.

Sui, D. Z., & Bednarz, R. S. (1999). The message is the medium: Geographic education in the age of the internet. *Journal of Geography, 98*, 93–99.

Taylor, J. S. (2000). Using the world wide web in undergraduate geographic education: Potentials and pitfalls. *Journal of Geography, 99*, 11–22.

Thomas, R. (1994). Data maps and correlation: Tools for inquiry. *Journal of Geography, 93*, 279–284.

Van DeVort, J. (1997). Our town's planning commission meeting. *Journal of Geography, 96*, 183–190.

Walk, F. H. (1994). The tale of the tape: Making video viewing more thoughtful. *Journal of Geography, 93*, 197–203.

Warf, B. (1999). Constructing a dialogue: Geographic education and geographic research. *The Professional Geographer, 51*, 586–591.

Warf, B., Vincent, P., & Purcell, D. (1999). International collaborative learning on the world wide web. *Journal of Geography, 98*, 141–148.

West, B. A. (2003). Student attitudes and the impact of GIS on thinking skills and motivation. *Journal of Geography, 102*, 267–274.

8

TEACHING AND LEARNING IN THE "INTERDISCIPLINARY DISCIPLINE" OF HUMAN DEVELOPMENT

Denise S. Bartell and Kristin M. Vespia

The purpose of this chapter is to explicate signature pedagogies for the field of human development. What makes this chapter unique is that human development is perhaps less well-defined than other social sciences because of its interdisciplinary nature. Furthermore, its pedagogical literature, which appears to be relatively limited in scope and in early stages of development, is not tied to a unified, disciplinary perspective. These factors make describing signature pedagogies in human development both more challenging and more exciting. They also require that we take time to describe the field and critically evaluate its relevant literature to ensure that the signature pedagogies outlined in the chapter are solidly grounded in theory and research, as well as within the context of this "interdisciplinary discipline."

What is Human Development?

Human development is a broad-based interdisciplinary field that incorporates information from psychology, biology, sociology, anthropology, and history, among others, in the study of growth and change across the human lifespan. Disciplinary fields typically have meaningful commonalities, such as a focus on a shared group of problems or issues, questions to be investigated, philosophical assumptions, perspectives about the world, and modes of inquiry (Newell & Green, 1988). Interdisciplinary study may, on the other hand, ask students to entertain competing foci, research methods, and worldviews. Interdisciplinarity can be seen as merely the use of more than one discipline in the examination of a problem, often referred to as multidisciplinarity (Nissani, 1997; Squires, 1992) or as the true integration of these elements into a new and more complete perspective (Klein, 1990; Klein & Newell, 1998; Lattuca, 2001).

As an interdisciplinary area of study, human development explores the interactive influences of multiple forces on the processes and mechanisms of physical, cognitive, emotional, and social development (Cornell University College of Human Ecology, 2007; CSULB Department of Human Development, 2007). However, within the field of human development, a diversity of approaches likely exists regarding the degree to which programs emphasize interdisciplinarity, as well as the extent to which they focus on interdisciplinarity as incorporating versus truly integrating multiple disciplinary perspectives on development.

Graduate programs in human development are relatively common; however, at the undergraduate level, which will be the focus of our discussions of signature pedagogy, human development is less likely to exist as a stand-alone major. Instead, undergraduate programs are more likely to co-occur with family studies (e.g., human development and family studies, child and family studies), human services (e.g., human and community development), or education (e.g., education and child development) (Hans, 2002). Many of these programs, even those whose title is solely "human development," include a strong emphasis on family issues and relationships in their objectives and curricula (e.g., Cornell University College of Human Ecology, 2007). Undergraduate programs in human development can help prepare students for work in social service agencies (e.g., family services, aging services) and education (e.g., early childhood education), along with graduate study in research and clinically focused programs.

The Pedagogical Literature in Human Development

Because it is an interdisciplinary "discipline," the study of human development may involve courses in many different fields, and its professors may include psychologists, sociologists, anthropologists, and biologists, as well as other professionals, all of whom bring their specific disciplinary perspectives to the traditional and signature pedagogies of the field. In addition, some faculty members in these programs have graduate degrees from interdisciplinary programs. Therefore, instructors in these departments likely ask different questions, rely on different methods of inquiry, vary in what they consider "evidence," and hold diverse ideas about effective teaching methods based on their own instruction. There is no unifying professional organization in human development, such as the American Psychological Association's Society for the Teaching of Psychology, which might facilitate the development and communication of established teaching methods. In essence, there is no dominant pedagogical model in this field, and the scholarship of teaching and learning (SoTL) literature related to human development reflects the fact that faculty come from different disciplines with sometimes quite distinct pedagogical models and practices.

One approach to facing this challenge in a review of pedagogical work in the field would be to summarize the pedagogies of different disciplines typically drawn upon in the study of human development, such as psychology and anthropology. This approach would be unwieldy, however, and would lack the integration of knowledge across different disciplines that is central to the field. Therefore, in this chapter we focus on pedagogical literature that deals specifically with courses defined as human development and/or family studies in an attempt to identify their traditional and signature pedagogies. In fact, most of the SoTL literature we review will relate to our subsequent description of signature pedagogies for the field.

In conducting this literature review, we found less work dealing solely with human development than with the often-related area of family studies. With the exception of gerontology, which has at least two pedagogical periodicals (*Educational Gerontology; Gerontology and Geriatrics Education*), we found no pedagogical periodicals for human development specifically. On the other hand, in the area of family studies there are at least two such journals (*Marriage and Family Review*; *Journal of Teaching in Marriage and Family*), as well as an applied publication in family studies that regularly includes pedagogical articles and special sections on pedagogy (*Family Relations*).

There are two ways to characterize the body of pedagogical literature generated by our review. The first is based on the type of work published. For example, although the literature includes discussions of broad, theoretical pedagogical issues (e.g., the use of feminist ideology in pedagogy; Allen, 1988) and descriptions of course design (e.g., developing an Internet course on child development; Graham, 2001), the most common type of article involves examples and/or assessment of specific teaching materials or techniques, such as readings, activities, and assignments (e.g., Glenn, 1997; Harper & Rogers, 1999). The second, and perhaps more interesting analysis of this pedagogical work, and the most useful given the objectives of this book, involves an exploration of the ways in which it informs and reflects more global themes that help to define human development as a field, as well as its pedagogical practices.

Guiding Themes of Human Development

A closer examination of the existing literature, along with the course offerings and objectives of several undergraduate programs, reveals at least five common guiding themes that describe human development: (1) a lifespan perspective, (2) interdisciplinarity, (3) critical thinking and reflexivity, (4) diverse contexts, and (5) application. These themes do not merely represent aspects of curriculum in human development; they are derived from its core values and reflect the specific types of thinking and problem solving (Middendorf & Pace, 2004) required of its students and professionals. As such, when used in pedagogy, these themes are critical to helping us educate our students in the ways of thinking and reasoning that are central to expertise in human development. In this section, we will describe the SoTL literature relevant to each theme. It is important to note that these themes are not mutually exclusive. Instead, they relate to each other in complex and multifaceted ways. Therefore, we will mention the ways in which they connect to and draw from each other, and we will ultimately explicate signature pedagogies for human development that integrate material from across the five themes.

Lifespan Development

The field of human development takes a lifespan perspective, emphasizing human growth and change as a lifelong process. An examination of the SoTL literature reflects this lifespan perspective with work that discusses aspects of teaching courses such as developmental theories (e.g., Sherman, 1990), child development (e.g., Graham, 2001), or adulthood and aging (e.g., Fingerman & Bertrand, 1999).

Most of these articles, however, do not explicitly address the importance of taking a lifespan perspective in teaching about human development; they merely provide descriptions of pedagogical techniques that can be used in such classes. And, with few exceptions, this work does not empirically assess the effectiveness of the teaching techniques and strategies presented. In fact, this is an overall trend in human development SoTL literature, which is, perhaps, not surprising given previously mentioned constraints on building a teaching and learning literature in an interdisciplinary field.

This dearth of empirical information on learning outcomes creates problems. One might argue that the lifespan perspective is simply inherent in this field and does not require formal assessment. However, if students are truly to think like "developmentalists," they must know that, for example, adolescence cannot be truly understood without appreciating what happens both before and after it. Given how central this learning outcome is to the field, more pedagogical work designed to evaluate whether it is being met would be a real contribution to the literature and to the articulation of signature pedagogy in human development.

Interdisciplinarity

The next guiding theme in human development is its interdisciplinary approach to the understanding of human growth and change. Underlying research and theory in the field is the belief that a true understanding of development requires the comprehension, use, and, most importantly, the integration of information from a variety of disciplinary fields (Cornell University College of Human Ecology, 2007). Interestingly, however, in our review of the SoTL literature pertinent to human development, interdisciplinarity was not typically discussed as a primary determinant of curricular design or of teaching techniques. A few sources discussed the interdisciplinary nature and objectives of their courses (e.g., Allen, Floyd-Thomas, & Gillman, 2001). Two articles dealt with the design and implementation of a truly interdisciplinary course, where faculty across disciplines worked together to integrate their areas of expertise into the collaborative teaching of a course (Allen et al., 2001; Schuster, Francis-Connolly, Alford-Trewn, & Brooks, 2003). In one case, the authors discussed the importance of providing students with this type of course experience because many of them will be required to work in interdisciplinary teams in their chosen professions (Schuster et al., 2003). Other sources identified their fields as interdisciplinary (e.g., Price & Brosi, 1992) or described the limitations of using purely disciplinary perspectives in human development courses (Guay-McIntyre, Grout, Jennings, & Poppei, 1996).

This overview is consistent with what authors have had to say about pedagogical research related to interdisciplinarity in general. Vess and Linkon (2002) argued that although a great deal has been done in terms of describing the goals and methods of interdisciplinary education, we need more research on the measurable effects of such coursework on student learning. The authors also asserted that effective assessment of the impact of interdisciplinary programs needs to involve multiple methods and measurement tools (Vess & Linkon, 2002).

Given that techniques designed to enhance interdisciplinary thinking will have to be part of any signature pedagogy in human development, future SoTL scholarship must examine interdisciplinarity as an explicit component of classes in the field. It should also include empirical examinations of the utility of an interdisciplinary perspective in helping students to (a) learn about the field, (b) develop skills for applying multiple perspectives to complex problems, and (c) appreciate the value of an interdisciplinary education.

Critical Thinking and Reflexivity

One of the most striking themes to emerge from our review of the literature involves the reflexive and constructivist goals of both human development and family studies. At the heart of these objectives are many of the central components of a feminist perspective on teaching, which include recognition of and respect for diversity, an attempt to create an inclusive and equal classroom atmosphere, and the intent to facilitate cooperative and active learning experiences for students (Allen, 1988). Reflexivity is defined as a critical reflection on one's beliefs, values, and behaviors given the context of the social system (Allen et al., 2001; Lewis, 1995). The goal of this reflexive perspective in human development education is to sensitize students to the viewpoints of others by increasing their self-awareness, so they can then decenter from their own experiences and become more effective in their work with others (Allen & Farnsworth, 1993). Thomson (1995) discussed this type of development as requiring a pedagogy of "care," where promoting students' attentiveness, empathy, and responsiveness to others can help them to focus on the life circumstances of others and become more effective human service professionals.

The pedagogical literature related to this theme focuses in large part on methods of encouraging critical thinking and reflexivity, and it is largely descriptive. Authors assert that this type of student development in classes requires a unique approach to teaching and learning that provides a supportive environment for discussing experiences and viewpoints (Sollie & Kaetz, 1992). A number of methods for producing these learning environments are proposed in this body of work, such as instructors indicating care for and involvement with students, sharing authority with students, being willing to voice their own opinions on issues while still being open-minded, and providing examples of multiple perspectives on issues in class through the use of texts and guest speakers (Allen & Farnsworth, 1993). The literature also examines student assignments and activities that might promote both critical thinking and reflection; examples include self-reflective journal writing (Allen & Farnsworth, 1993), engaging in activities whose intent is to directly address biases (e.g., addressing ageist beliefs; Young & Robson-Funk, 2004), exposing students to circumstances or situations common for certain groups (e.g., aging; Fingerman & Bertrand, 1999), and introducing conflict among the multiple perspectives in a class (e.g., having students generate comparative essay questions and model answers; Sherman, 1990).

This element of human development SoTL also links reflexive approaches to education and social action objectives, where the intent of certain educational experiences is to promote a sense of social justice, empowerment, and desire to help others (Allen & Crosbie-Burnett, 1992; Winsfield, 2003). These social action or social justice objectives relate to reflexivity in that understanding of self and awareness of others are necessary for effective and informed social action (Lewis, 1995). Thus, there are a number of articles that describe how teaching and learning in human development can encourage social action. Examples of such strategies include requiring students to become more knowledgeable about our social systems through writing policy briefs (Britner & Alpert, 2005) or simply providing students with accurate information about relevant societal concerns (Glenn, 1997). Authors also discuss encouraging social action by activities that explicitly attempt to develop students' sense of empathy (e.g., Johnson & Sullivan, 1995), such as assigning memoirs or ethnographies as readings (Thomson, 1995), bringing in guest speakers to discuss their experiences with the class (Allen, 1995), or requiring service learning (Thomson, 1995).

Although some of the teaching strategies discussed, such as bringing guest speakers to class, are likely traditional techniques used across fields, the extent to which reflexive techniques as a whole are described in the literature suggests that they are part of signature pedagogy in human development. However, this work tends to rely on a theoretical rationale for the value of these skills as a priori evidence for the utility of the reflexive activities and assignments. To provide comprehensive support for the value of this theme in human development education, we suggest additional SoTL work examining the extent to which course experiences truly foster reflexivity in students' thinking, particularly their thinking about developmental issues and concerns.

Diverse Contexts of Development

A fourth theme in the study of human development is emphasis on the diverse contexts within which development occurs. From this perspective, development is influenced not only by biological and psychological forces but also by a diverse array of environmental contexts, from family, community, and school or work environments to broader sociocultural contexts such as gender, race/ethnicity, and historical period (Cornell University College of Human Ecology, 2007; Washington State University–Vancouver Department of Human Development, n.d.).

The importance of this theme is clear in the pedagogical literature. For example, authors emphasize that infusing multiculturalism in human development course offerings is critically important to prepare students to work with diverse groups in human service careers (e.g., Smith & Ingoldsby, 1992) and to inform and promote advocacy and public policy work (e.g., Dixon, 2001). Diverse contexts are also defined broadly in this literature and include gender (e.g., Walker, 1996), sexual orientation (e.g., Allen, 1995), social class, and disability status, as well as elements of family structure (e.g., Coleman, Ganong, & Goodwin, 1994). By far the most common type of diversity addressed, however, is race/ethnicity (e.g., Dixon, 2001; Robila & Taylor, 2005; Shaw-Taylor & Benokraitis, 1995; Thomson, 1995).

Some of the existing empirical pedagogical literature that deals with the theme of diverse contexts investigates the prevalence of courses on international families in human development programs (Robila & Taylor, 2005) or the ways in which classes may address family diversity (Umana-Taylor & Wiley, 2004). Other work has examined the ways in which diverse contexts are included in textbooks in the field (Coleman et al., 1994; Shaw-Taylor &

Benokraitis, 1995) or has asked faculty members about the types of reading materials they need to effectively teach about family diversity (Smith & Ingoldsby, 1992). All of this work has been empirical but purely descriptive, providing information on what is taught as "diverse context" material but generating no real information on whether that content effectively prepares students to work with diverse populations.

There is also a small body of literature on pedagogical strategies to infuse diverse contexts into human development courses—strategies that we will argue inform signature pedagogy in the field. For example, Sollie and Kaetz (1992) discuss the need for faculty to foster a supportive classroom atmosphere so that students feel comfortable participating and are exposed to a diversity of experiences and viewpoints. Other techniques identified in the literature include using children's literature to promote students' understanding of cultural and ethnic influences on child development (Mulligan & Book, 1992); utilizing a "family strengths" perspective in course content as opposed to a more negative, comparative approach (Medora, 2005); and confronting heterosexism through classroom discussion and written self-reflection (Allen, 1995).

Application

A final theme that emerges from an examination of human development curricula and pedagogy involves an emphasis on application. Some articles explicitly discuss the human service goals of programs and courses (e.g., Johnson & Sullivan, 1995; Sollie & Kaetz, 1992). A few of the sources describe the importance of providing students with information about the actual human and/or family service fields they may enter (Schuster et al., 2003), and others focus more on teaching students a variety of skills that will be necessary in applied work, such as grant writing for program funding (Harper, 1980) and working with multidisciplinary teams (Schuster et al., 2003). These instructional strategies, along with others described in this chapter, will clearly emerge as important components of signature pedagogy in human development.

An emphasis on active learning, including service learning, is also an important component of this literature, in part because it is seen as crucial to preparing students for careers in human services (Smart & Berke, 2004). Particularly in the field of family studies, there has been an increase in explicit discussions of the need for more active learning experiences over the last 20 years (Allen & Crosbie-Burnett, 1992; Sollie & Kaetz, 1992), but this shift is also evident in the topics covered in the human development pedagogical literature (e.g., Fingerman & Bertrand, 1999; Harper & Rogers, 1999). Much of the literature on active learning involves discussion of application activities or experiences in the classroom. Some of this work describes techniques to help students to apply course material to their personal lives, such as generating lifelines in a lifespan development course (Yanowitz, 2001), writing a paper on their personal experiences with puberty in a course on adolescence (Johnson & Sullivan, 1995), or reading textbook material that is either made personally relevant to students themselves (Larson & Hickman, 2004) or can be used to assist them in making good decisions in their personal lives (Glenn, 1997).

On the other hand, some of the pedagogical literature in human development emphasizes application to nonpersonal, real-world experiences. For example, one article describes using films that relate to course content (Harper & Rogers, 1999), and another discusses using children's literature to facilitate an understanding of child development (Mulligan & Book, 1992). Others discuss using semester-long "family simulations" in an introductory family studies course to help students understand the variety of issues families face (Koropeckyj-Cox, Cain, & Coran, 2005).

Finally, given the applied emphasis of many human development programs, it is not surprising that many of the activities described in the literature relate directly to potential professional experiences. For example, one class on adulthood and aging asked students to design a retirement community (McGuire & Zwahr, 1999), and another required students in a family policy class to write policy briefs for judges and legislators (Britner & Alpert, 2005). In addition, a variety of sources described the use of simulations and role-playing activities to provide students with experience using skills required in their chosen professions (Browning, Collins, & Nelson, 2005; Crosbie-Burnett & Elsen, 1992).

One particular type of applied learning experience, service learning, has become an increasingly popular topic in the pedagogical literature and has clearly become an element of signature pedagogy in human development. These applied experiences in community settings, which often take the form of internships, are valuable learning strategies that can promote reflexivity, empathy (e.g., Allen & Farnsworth, 1993; Thomson, 1995), and comprehension of course material (Toews & Cerny, 2005), as well as knowledge about human service fields and professional skill development (e.g., Bliezner & Artale, 2001; Smart & Berke, 2004). The literature on service learning includes articles on its use in a course on parenting education (Richardson, Kraynak, Blankemeyer, & Walker, 2004) and in courses on adulthood and aging (e.g., Shapiro, 2002; Von Dras & Miller, 2002). Some of this literature focuses on the structure of the internship experience, providing information on the value of course portfolios as an indicator of the developmental process in internships (Bass, Barnes, Kostelecky, & Fleming, 2004) or on how to use Bloom's taxonomy of educational objectives in the design of the course (Von Dras & Miller, 2002).

What assessment exists in this work points to these applied learning experiences promoting the learning of course content and professional skills important to success in relevant professions (e.g., empathy; Browning et al., 2005; Walker, 1996). However, these data are largely qualitative (e.g., Walker, 1996) or descriptive (e.g., Harper, 1980), and they were not gathered using the rigorous methods of examination suggested for SoTL research.

A more challenging issue, but one that is critical to understanding the effectiveness of the courses and teaching techniques used as applied and active learning tools, is that of assessing the extent to which these experiences actually do promote success in the careers typical of human development majors. This could be examined not only through evaluation of the development of career-related skills but also of students' success in actual professional roles.

Key Principles of Signature Pedagogy in Human Development

Some authors have asserted that interdisciplinary education in general does not have its own distinct pedagogy (Klein & Newell, 1998). Examining the diversity of programs that identify as "human development" or "human development and family studies" might also suggest that identifying signature pedagogies for this specific interdisciplinary field would be impossible. However, we have already described in the context of the preceding literature review some of the signature pedagogies designed to help students think like developmentalists. We now turn to a more comprehensive articulation of signature approaches to teaching and learning, one which draws not only on the SoTL literature but also on previous discussions of the definition of human development and its unifying themes as a field of study.

Developmental Perspectives on Teaching and Learning

No matter the disciplinary training of the faculty member or the diversity of course offerings, the central core that unifies human development departments is a developmental perspective on everything from physiological processes to family relationships. As such, one of the key principles of signature pedagogy might involve implementing a developmental perspective on teaching and learning. For example, Lev Vygotsky used the term "zone of proximal development" when describing the cognitive development of children and the gap between their independent abilities and what they could accomplish with assistance, but these ideas have since been discussed in the context of college teaching (Doolittle, 1995). For Vygotsky, moving an individual's zone of proximal development could be facilitated by providing assistance with "scaffolding," promoting interactions among peers, and encouraging rehearsal of the component skills of more complex learning goals (Doolittle, 1995).

Teaching and learning in human development courses and programs should benefit from application of these principles. If, for example, an instructor wanted students to be able to fully conceptualize case studies using diverse theoretical models by the end of the semester, he or she might model that activity for the class during lectures, provide opportunities for small group work on related tasks in class, and even require shorter papers using brief cases and only one theoretical perspective in preparation for a final term paper involving a complex case study and several competing approaches.

Vygotskian principles are only one example of how a developmental perspective might be incorporated in teaching and learning. Theory and research on cognitive and socio-emotional development in adolescence and young adulthood (e.g., Perry's theory of college student development; Marcia's theory of identity status; Berk, 2008) can be used to design class assignments and activities that will effectively promote course objectives based on the developmental status of the students in the class. From this perspective, courses with predominantly freshman audiences should be taught in distinctly different ways from those with primarily upper-level students. Consistent with recommendations regarding college teaching and learning (e.g., Chickering &

Gamson, 1987), instructors might also acknowledge and accommodate different learning styles and use concepts from cognitive development, such as social learning and active learning, when developing curricula and course content.

A developmental approach to education is a signature pedagogy in human development because it models the field's lifespan perspective, relies upon views of education that are at least multidisciplinary, if not truly interdisciplinary, and provides approaches to teaching and learning (e.g., scaffolding, peer interaction) that will likely encourage critical thinking and application skills. Furthermore, these teaching and learning methods are very consistent with calls to help students gradually learn the manners of thinking associated with specific fields (Middendorf & Pace, 2004).

Intentionality with Curricular Design and Sequencing

Helping human development students think like and take the perspective of an expert in the field also relies heavily on intentional curricular design. Although this would seem to be an obvious element of pedagogy in general, we argue that it is a necessary signature pedagogy in human development because of the field's interdisciplinary nature and broad lifespan perspective. If the curricula of these programs are to promote integration of disciplinary perspectives and an understanding of development from infancy through death, careful attention will need to be paid to individual courses and to the structuring of their sequence. For example, Klein and Newell (1998) asserted that faculty members often include more content than necessary in interdisciplinary courses, noting that more narrowly defined classes offer greater opportunity for examining focused topics through a variety of lenses in a meaningful way. When faced with an introductory course designed to cover the entire lifespan, instructors will have to carefully weigh the needs for depth and breadth of content, for requiring critical analysis of students, and for providing integrative opportunities to foster interdisciplinary understanding and skill development (Klein & Newell, 1998).

On a related note, faculty members in human development programs will also have to consider how the classes are sequenced within the major to maximize the student experience. For example, where and when will students gain a firm grasp of the different disciplines important to human development? When will they first begin to integrate those perspectives, and how will those skills be acquired? If students take solely disciplinary courses at the lower level and then confront, as juniors and seniors, interdisciplinary classes that require integration of viewpoints, they will likely have much more difficulty doing so than if integration had been required of them from the beginning (Newell & Green, 1998). That said, students still need to have a very solid grounding in the relevant disciplines, including their research methods and theoretical perspectives, if they are to learn to use and integrate these perspectives effectively (Newell & Green, 1998).

Not having sufficient disciplinary background and lacking practice with integration early in one's education could lead to a specific type of obstacle to learning that Middendorf and Pace (2004) describe as creating difficulties for students trying to determine how to learn within the context of a specific field. Experts in the field of human development may naturally understand differences in the research methods of psychologists and anthropologists and easily synthesize findings on similar topics from these diverse fields, but students will need to have these complex tasks broken down into manageable pieces and demonstrated for them in order to effectively learn how to think as developmentalists. Thus, courses that provide the necessary foundational content (i.e., disciplinary information) and skill development (e.g., integration) should occur early in curricula, for example, before courses on specific phases of the lifespan or aspects of development. Alternatively, the foundational content and skill development could be integrated within courses, such as classes on infancy or adolescence, that are sequenced in a deliberate and developmentally appropriate way.

Team Teaching and Faculty Development

Team teaching is another potential signature pedagogy in human development. This educational practice can be very effective in integrating multiple disciplinary perspectives within the classroom. What better way to help students see what it means to think like developmentalists and integrate information from different disciplines than to model those processes for them in front of the classroom? Having a sociologist and biologist discuss their views on the topic of social development in adolescence, for example, would provide living examples of how those perspectives are different and how they might be integrated to create a more comprehensive view of the topic. Faculty members can also model the intellectual benefits of interdisciplinarity by being willing to discuss openly and in front of the class philosophical disagreements on issues with colleagues from other disciplines (Lattuca, 2001).

If team teaching is to be a significant component of human development signature pedagogy, however, considerable attention needs to be paid to faculty development. Using the definitions outlined earlier in this chapter, simply having faculty from different disciplines come together to lecture about a topic from their particular perspectives, with no attempt at integration, would be a multidisciplinary but not truly interdisciplinary experience for students. If faculty members, particularly those with only disciplinary training, are to feel comfortable teaching interdisciplinary courses and to have the expertise in component disciplines to integrate them effectively, they will likely need substantial support to do so, including team curriculum development and the opportunity to observe or team teach with an instructor who has taught interdisciplinary courses (Newell & Green, 1998). Substantial reading across disciplines, either individually or with colleagues, attendance at workshops, and ongoing conversations with colleagues from different fields may also be helpful (Klein & Newell, 1998; Lattuca, 2001).

Active Learning and Real-World Problem Solving

Another key component of signature pedagogy in human development is an emphasis on active learning and real-world problem solving. These experiences might involve brief class-time opportunities to apply course concepts to real-world examples, extended role-playing or simulation exercises, or service learning and practicum course experiences.

Many of the pedagogical articles we reviewed earlier discussed teaching techniques that incorporated some type of application. This emphasis on application is consistent with the goals of interdisciplinary pedagogy in general, which evolved in part as a way to address complex, social problems that do not fall easily within disciplinary boundaries (Lattuca, 2001). Interdisciplinarians also advocate teaching and learning strategies that include collaboration among students and active learning approaches such as role-playing (Klein & Newell, 1998).

In addition, the reflexive, constructivist paradigm discussed previously emphasizes these same types of learning experiences as critical to students' development of empathy, responsiveness, and a desire to engage in social action—all important objectives for careers in the human service professions (Allen & Farnsworth, 1993; Johnson & Sullivan, 1995; Thomson, 1995).

Finally, active learning is an important component of understanding diversity and the multiple contexts of development. Some examples of such relevant learning experiences with real-world applications include service learning with a local ESL program; writing a grant for a program to reduce prejudice against gay, lesbian, bisexual, and transgendered youth in local high schools; or developing a panel presentation on the experience of living in the community as a first-generation immigrant. Given its relevance to so many of the themes that define human development as a field, active learning is clearly one of its signature pedagogies.

An Emphasis on Context

An emphasis on context, broadly defined, is also important to human development signature pedagogy. Material on biological, psychological, and sociocultural aspects of development should be a significant part of courses in the curriculum. The interdisciplinary nature of the field requires that the unit of analysis in these courses is not only the individual but also the context in which that individual develops and the forces that work both to promote and restrict development. For example, a lifespan development course should not merely address biological and psychological aspects of development but should examine the ways in which government-sponsored pre-school education or national health care programs for children might influence developmental processes.

Of course, an emphasis on context also means that programs need to pay particular attention to addressing sociocultural diversity in their coursework, which the SoTL literature indicates is a clear priority in human development programs. Two common methods for incorporating cultural perspectives in the curriculum are by infusing such content throughout the coursework and/or by creating specific diversity classes (e.g., Umana-Taylor & Wiley, 2004). Both of these approaches have merit, but we would argue that a combination of both strategies will best promote student learning.

For example, one or two courses on diversity in child development or in family relationships with no supporting experiences in other coursework is unlikely to promote the type of integrative interdisciplinary understanding of diverse contexts that is key to the field. On the other hand, relatively brief coverage of diversity issues in courses whose topic areas are not diversity specific is unlikely to promote the depth of knowledge about diversity that is necessary for students to effectively apply this information. Helping students become more sensitive to the perspectives of diverse others will involve several strategies, but one that appears within the human development literature is that of developing self-reflexivity, or a critical understanding of one's own beliefs, values, and behaviors (Allen et al., 2001). From this perspective, human development coursework, to effectively teach about diversity, must provide students with opportunities to engage in a self-reflective process through activities such as regular journal writing, where they are asked to comment on their reactions to course material and on how their beliefs and behaviors are being influenced by the course experience (Allen & Farnsworth, 1993).

Attention to the Learning Environment

A final element of signature pedagogy we propose for the field involves careful attention to the learning environment. Learning to think like a human developmentalist is not easy, and it requires critical thinking, synthesis of diverse perspectives, attention to real-world problem solving, and active engagement with issues of context and diversity. One theme that recurs in the literature about these topics is the need to focus on support of the student throughout the learning process. For example, interdisciplinary educators argue that instructors need to be prepared to assist students who feel overwhelmed or intimidated by this type of learning by providing additional time and support, by acknowledging the challenges inherent in interdisciplinary courses, and even by sharing their own struggles as seasoned professionals with reading or using information from disciplines other than their own (Lattuca, 2001).

In a similar way, the literature on constructivist and reflexive approaches to human development education stresses the importance of creating a classroom environment that includes clear evidence of the teacher's care for and involvement in the educational experiences of the students (Allen, 1988), an atmosphere of equality where the teacher shares authority over learning with the students (Allen & Farnsworth, 1993), and the encouragement of students' exchange of ideas and experiences (Sollie & Kaetz, 1992). This type of environment can be promoted by strategies such as teachers disclosing carefully selected relevant personal experiences with the class or by providing small discussion sections in classes when discussing sensitive topics in a large group may be too intimidating for some students.

Concluding Thoughts

Human development as a field clearly presents unique obstacles for building a body of SoTL literature and creating and implementing signature pedagogies. Faculty members in these interdisciplinary programs bring to the classroom diverse perspectives on the world and diverse teaching approaches from their own, often disciplinary, training. Students, on the other hand, are asked, at the very least, to appreciate the mental operations required of experts in multiple disciplines. Ideally, they are then asked to integrate those perspectives into a unique framework for viewing the world, what might be called the perspective of a developmentalist.

Although these are challenging circumstances, we believe we have identified signature methods of teaching and learning that not only bind this field together but also provide a road map for future pedagogical work and suggest some of the learning outcomes SoTL research might assess. Ultimately, we hope the reward for facing these challenges will be students who bring a self-reflexive and multi-faceted approach both to understanding and solving the complex, real-world problems of a diverse society.

References

Allen, K. R. (1995). Opening the classroom closet: Sexual orientation and self-disclosure. *Family Relations, 44,* 136–141.

Allen, K. R. (1988). Integrating a feminist perspective into family studies courses. *Family Relations, 37,* 29–35.

Allen, K. R., & Crosbie-Burnett, M. (1992). Innovative ways and controversial issues in teaching about families: A special collection on family pedagogy. *Family Relations, 41,* 9–11.

Allen, K. R., & Farnsworth, E. B. (1993). Reflexivity in teaching about families. *Family Relations, 42,* 351–356.

Allen, K. R., Floyd-Thomas, S. M., & Gillman, L. (2001). Teaching to transform: From volatility to solidarity in an interdisciplinary family studies classroom. *Family Relations, 50*, 317–325.

Bass, B. L., Barnes, H. L., Kostelecky, K. L. & Fleming, W. M. (2004). Service learning and portfolios: Enhancing the scholarship of integration and application. *Journal of Teaching in Marriage and Family, 4*(1), 79–100.

Berk. L .E. (2008). *Exploring lifespan development.* Boston, MA: Pearson Education.

Bliezner, R., & Artale, L. M. (2001). Benefits of intergenerational service-learning to human service majors. *Educational Gerontology, 27*, 71–87.

Britner, P. A., & Alpert, L. T. (2005). Writing *amicus curiae* and policy briefs: A pedagogical approach to teaching family law and policy. In D. Berke & S. K. Wisendale (Eds.), *The craft of teaching about families: Strategies and tools* (pp. 7–23). Binghamton, NY: Haworth Press.

Browning, S., Collins, J. S., & Nelson, B. (2005). Creating families: A teaching technique for clinical training through role-playing. In D. Berke & S. K. Wisendale (Eds.), *The craft of teaching about families: Strategies and tools* (pp. 185–203). Binghamton, NY: Haworth Press.

Chickering, A. W., & Gamson, Z. F. (1987). Seven principles for good practice in undergraduate education. *AAHE Bulletin*, 3–7. Reprinted with permission in the *Wingspread Journal.* Retrieved August 12, 2007, from http://www.johnsonfdn.org/Publications/ConferenceReports/SevenPrinciples/SevenPrinciples_pdf.pdf

Coleman, M., Ganong, L. H., & Goodwin, C. (1994). The presentation of stepfamilies in marriage and family textbooks. *Family Relations, 43*, 289–297.

Cornell University College of Human Ecology. (2007). *Academics: Undergraduate.* Retrieved January 7, 2008, from http://www.human.cornell.edu/che/HD/Academics/Undergraduate

Crosbie-Burnett, M., & Elsen, M. (1992). Simulated divorced and remarried families: An experiential teaching technique. *Family Relations, 41*, 54–58.

CSULB (California State University–Long Beach) Department of Human Development. (2007). *Background and philosophy.* Retrieved January 7, 2008, from http://www.csulb.edu/colleges/cla/departments/hdev/about

Dixon, G. (2001). The development of course content: Teaching child development from a multicultural perspective. In *National Association of African American Studies and National Association of Hispanic and Latino Studies: 2000 literature monograph series* (pp. 55–71). Houston, TX. (ERIC Document Reproduction Service No. ED 456 182)

Doolittle, P. E. (1995, June). *Understanding cooperative learning through Vygotsky's zone of proximal development.* Paper presented at the Lilly National Conference on Excellence in College Teaching, Columbia, SC. (ERIC Document Reproduction Service No. ED 384 575)

Fingerman, K. L., & Bertrand, R. (1999). Approaches to teaching adult development within a lifespan development course. *Teaching of Psychology, 26*, 55–57.

Glenn, N. D. (1997). A critique of twenty family and marriage and the family textbooks. *Family Relations, 46*, 197–208.

Graham, T. A. (2001). Teaching child development via the internet: Opportunities and pitfalls. *Teaching of Psychology, 28*, 67–71.

Guay-McIntyre, J., Grout, L. A., Jennings, S. H., & Poppei, J. E. (1996, March). *Human development or developmental psychology: That is the question.* Paper presented at the 10th Annual Conference on Undergraduate Teaching of Psychology, Ellenville, NY. (ERIC Document Reproduction Service No. ED 405 029)

Hans, J. D. (Ed.). (2002). *Graduate and undergraduate student in marriage and family.* Columbia, MO: Family Scholar Publications.

Harper, G. F. (1980). A simulation technique to teach a graduate course in early childhood development. *Teaching of Psychology, 7*, 218–221.

Harper, R. E., & Rogers, L. E. (1999). Using feature films to teach human development concepts. *Journal of Humanistic Counseling, Education and Development, 38*, 89–97.

Johnson, E. J., & Sullivan S. M. (1995, March). *Thinking critically and teaching empathically: Techniques for teaching adolescent development.* Paper presented at the 9th Annual Conference on Undergraduate Teaching of Psychology, Ellenville, NY.

Klein, J. T. (1990). *Interdisciplinarity: History, theory, and practice.* Detroit, MI: Wayne State University Press.

Klein, J. T., & Newell, W. H. (1998). Advancing interdisciplinary studies. In W. H. Newell (Ed.), *Interdisciplinarity: Essays from the literature* (pp. 3–22). New York: College Entrance Exam Board. (Reprinted from *Handbook of the undergraduate curriculum*, Chapter 19, by J. Gaff & J. Ratcliff, Eds., 1996, San Francisco: Jossey-Bass)

Koropeckyj-Cox, T., Cain, C., & Coran, J. (2005). Small-group learning and hypothetical families in a large introductory course. In D. Berke & S. K. Wisendale (Eds.), *The craft of teaching about families: Strategies and tools* (pp. 205–223). Binghamton, NY: Haworth Press.

Larson, J. H., & Hickman, R. (2004). Are college marriage textbooks teaching students the premarital predictors of marital quality? *Family Relations, 53*, 385–392.

Lattuca, L. R. (2001). *Creating interdisciplinarity: Interdisciplinary research and teaching among college and university faculty.* Nashville: Vanderbilt University Press.

Lewis, E. A. (1995). Toward a tapestry of impassioned voices: Incorporating praxis into teaching about families. *Family Relations, 44*, 149–152.

McGuire, L. C., & Zwahr, M. D. (1999). Tying it together: Two comprehensive projects for adult development and aging courses. *Teaching of Psychology, 26*, 53–55.

Medora, N. P. (2005). International families in cross-cultural perspective: A family strengths approach. In D. Berke & S. K. Wisendale (Eds.), *The craft of teaching about families: Strategies and tools* (pp. 147–164). Binghamton, NY: Haworth Press.

Middendorf, J., & Pace, D. (2004). Decoding the disciplines: A model for helping students learn disciplinary ways of thinking. In D. Pace & J. Middendorf (Eds.), *Decoding the disciplines: Helping student learn disciplinary ways of thinking* (pp. 1–12). San Francisco: Jossey-Bass.

Mulligan, J. C., & Book. L. A. (1992, March). *Who is the child? Children's literature in a human development class.* Paper presented at the 6th Annual Undergraduate Teaching of Psychology Conference. Ellenville, NY.

Newell, W. H., & Green, W. J. (1998). Defining and teaching interdisciplinary studies. In W. H. Newell (Ed.), *Interdisciplinarity: Essays from the literature* (pp. 23–34). New York: College Entrance Exam Board. (Reprinted from *Improving College and University Teaching, 30*(1), 23–30, Winter 1982)

Nissani, M. (1997). Ten cheers for interdisciplinarity: The case for interdisciplinary knowledge and research. *Social Science Journal, 34*, 201–216.

Price, C. A., & Brosi, W. A. (2006). Resources for advancing family gerontology education and practice. *Family Relations, 55,* 649–662.

Richardson, R. A., Kraynak, A., Blankemeyer, M., & Walker, K. A. (2005). Service-learning in parenting education: Insights from students and parent participants. In D. Berke & S. K. Wisendale (Eds.), *The craft of teaching about families: Strategies and tools* (pp. 115–131). Binghamton, NY: Haworth Press.

Robila, M., & Taylor, A. C. (2005). Teaching about international families across the United States. In D. Berke & S. K. Wisendale (Eds.), *The craft of teaching about families: Strategies and tools* (pp. 133–145). Binghamton, NY: Haworth Press.

Schuster, E. O., Francis-Connolly, E., Alford-Trewn, P., & Brooks, J. (2003). Conceptualization and development of a course on aging to infancy: A life course retrospective. *Educational Gerontology, 29,* 841–850.

Shapiro, A. (2002). A service-learning approach to teaching gerontology: A case of a first-year undergraduate seminar. *Gerontology and Geriatrics Education, 23,* 25–36.

Shaw-Taylor, Y., & Benokraitis, N. V. (1995). The presentation of minorities in marriage and family textbooks. *Teaching Sociology, 23,* 122–135.

Sherman, L. W. (1990, July). *A cooperative pedagogical strategy for teaching developmental theories through writing: Dyadic confrontations.* Paper presented at the International Convention on Cooperative Learning, Baltimore, MD. (ERIC Document Reproduction Service No. ED 321 721)

Smart, L. S., & Berke, D. L. (2004). Developing professional standards in family science internships. *Journal of Teaching in Marriage and Family, 4*, 101–126.

Smith, S., & Ingoldsby, B. (1992). Multicultural family studies: Educating students for diversity. *Family Relations, 41*, 25–30.

Sollie, D. L., & Kaetz, J. F. (1992). Teaching university-level family studies courses: Techniques and outcomes. *Family Relations, 41*, 18–24.

Squires, G. (1992). Interdisciplinarity in higher education in the United Kingdom. *European Journal of Education, 27*, 201–210.

Thomson, L. (1995). Teaching about ethnic minority families using a pedagogy of care. *Family Relations, 44*, 129–135.

Toews, M. L., & Cerny, J. M. (2005). The impact of service learning on student development: Students' reflections in a family diversity course. In D. Berke & S. K. Wisendale (Eds.), *The craft of teaching about families: Strategies and tools* (pp. 263–280). Binghamton, NY: Haworth Press.

Umana-Taylor, A. J., & Wiley, A. R. (2004). Family diversity in the classroom: A review of existing strategies. *Journal of Teaching in Marriage and Family, 4*, 127–146.

Vess, D., & Linkon, S. (2002). Navigating the interdisciplinary archipelago: The scholarship of interdisciplinary teaching and learning. In M. T. Huber & S. P. Morreale (Eds.), *Disciplinary styles of research in the scholarship of teaching and learning* (pp. 87–106). Sterling, VA: Stylus.

Von Dras, D. D., & Miller, K. M. (2002). Learning outside the classroom: The undergraduate gerontology internship. *Educational Gerontology, 28*, 881–894.

Walker, A. J. (1996). Cooperative learning in the college classroom. *Family Relations, 45*, 327–335.

Washington State University–Vancouver Department of Human Development. (n.d.). *What is human development and other frequently asked questions?* Retrieved January 7, 2008, from http://www.vancouver.wsu.edu/hd/hdintro.htm

Winsfield, B. M. (2003). Turning the kaleidoscope: Telling stories in rhetorical spaces. *Journal of Sociology and Social Welfare, 30*, 23–40.

Yanowitz, K. L. (2001). Looking to the future: Students' evaluations of generating lifelines. *Teaching of Psychology, 28*, 209–210.

Young, M. H., & Robson-Funk, B. (2004). Perceptions of Generation X toward older persons: The role of education in ameliorating ageist attitudes. *Journal of Teaching in Marriage and Family, 4*, 147–174.

9

DEVELOPING HABITS OF THE MIND, HAND, AND HEART IN PSYCHOLOGY UNDERGRADUATES

Blaine F. Peden and Carmen R. Wilson VanVoorhis

We endeavor to explain how teachers of psychology imbue the discipline's fundamental habits of the mind, hand, and heart (after Shulman, 2005a) in undergraduates. In particular, we portray the signature pedagogy for undergraduate education in psychology and determine whether it resembles those of professions such as law and medicine (Shulman, 2005a), liberal arts disciplines such as history (Calder, 2006) and political science (Murphy & Reidy, 2006), or stands apart (Goodyear, 2007).

Psychology is an academic and applied discipline involving the scientific study of mental processes and behavior. Although there is some tension between scientific psychology (with its program of empirical research) and applied psychology (dealing with a number of areas), all psychologists share a common core (Stanovich, 2007). Nonetheless, portraying the signature pedagogy for undergraduate psychology majors is a challenging task. The major complication concerns what and how psychologists teach undergraduates about psychology. Despite a longstanding concern for pedagogical issues, psychologists have been slow to develop standards for collegiate pedagogy. To their credit, psychologists recently endorsed guidelines for learning outcomes of undergraduate education (APA, 2007); however, the guidelines

We thank Scott Bates, Linda Carpenter, David Carroll, and Joseph Hatcher for helpful comments on drafts of this manuscript.

are not mandatory, as they are in disciplines with national accreditation, such as social work. Furthermore, psychologists agree little about how to teach undergraduates, and efforts to identify best practices have just begun. With respect to best practices, annual conferences have produced a series of volumes (e.g., Dunn & Chew, 2006; Dunn, Halonen, & Smith, 2008; Dunn, Smith, & Beins, 2007), and the 2008 National Conference on Undergraduate Education in Psychology will publish best practices regarding such things as modes of teaching and the use of new technologies to promote student learning (see Halpern, 2008; Halpern et al., 2007).

In this chapter, we explore an emerging consensus about what and how to teach undergraduates, indicate what acting and thinking like a psychologist looks like, and characterize the signature pedagogy for undergraduate education in psychology. We conclude by considering whether the signature pedagogy for psychology is unique.

Do Psychologists Agree about What and How to Teach Undergraduates?

We answer this question by exploring the history of undergraduate education in psychology. Plans for the 1992 centennial of the American Psychological Association prompted scholarship on the history of teaching psychology in the United States (Beins, 1992; Brewer, 1997; Brewer et al., 1993; Daniel, 1992; McGovern, 1992; McGovern, 1993; McGovern, Furumoto, Halpern, Kimble, & McKeachie, 1991; Puente, Mathews, & Brewer, 1992; Street, 1994) that guides our review.

Psychologists know well that our discipline has a long past and a short history. Psychologists trace the origins of our discipline to various Greek philosophers and say our history began in 1879 when Wilhelm Wundt founded a laboratory in Leipzig, Germany. The first psychologists typically traveled to Leipzig for graduate or postdoctoral training in the new experimental and physiological psychology, or received their doctoral degrees from psychologists who pioneered the new psychology into American universities and colleges. For example, G. Stanley Hall completed a doctoral degree with William James in 1878 at Harvard University and then studied with Wundt. Hall subsequently established the first doctoral program in psychology in the United States at Johns Hopkins University and mentored Joseph Jastrow, who completed America's first doctorate in psychology, in 1886.

In 1892, psychologists formed the American Psychological Association (APA). Almost immediately, psychologists addressed questions about curriculum and pedagogy for undergraduate education in psychology. Wolfe (1895) argued that the new experimental and physiological psychology had not replaced the old philosophical psychology as a required course of study, despite the steady emergence of psychology laboratories in universities and colleges throughout the United States. Wolfe asserted that the new psychology should be "recommended to juniors and should occupy about one-fourth of their time for a year. At least two hours per week should be spent in the laboratory. The class work should not be formal and impersonal lectures, nor should it be time-killing oral quizzes. Informal conferences, mutual quizzes and explanations should be accompanied by frequent *written* reviews. If possible the *instructor* should be suppressed and the director and inspirer brought into his place" (p. 387). In contrast, French (1898, p. 512) claimed that "from the point of view of both the general and the special student [psychology major] there is no call for experimental psychology in the college, but that its proper place is in the graduate school."

According to Street (1994), the eighth annual meeting of the APA in 1899 featured the first session about teaching psychology: "How should psychology be taught?" George S. Fullerton, Joseph Jastrow, H. Austin Aikins, and Charles H. Judd unanimously agreed that psychology must be taught as a science. Benjamin (2000) noted that "by the first decade of the 20th century, a year-long laboratory course in experimental psychology had become a standard part of the curriculum for undergraduates studying psychology" (p. 321), and prominent psychologists had begun to publish textbooks for laboratory training of undergraduates.

Beins's (1992) statement that "the approach to research, the role of psychology in the undergraduate curriculum, and the content of its courses were still fairly amorphous" (p. 540) aptly portrays teaching and learning from the turn of the century through the 1940s. The growth of psychology departments following World War II and through the 1960s prompted interest in "the rationales, objectives, and implementation of undergraduate psychology programs" (Brewer, 1997, p. 434), explored in a series of conferences. Cornell University sponsored the first conference in 1951, whereas the most recent National Conference on Undergraduate Education in Psychology convened in 2008 at the University of Puget Sound. Between 1951 and 2008, psychologists issued a series of reports regarding the state of undergraduate education, confirming the interplay between psychology and liberal arts education and providing recommendations for curriculum and pedagogy: (a) 1952—improving undergraduate instruction in psychology, (b) 1961—undergraduate curricula in psychology, (c) 1973—undergraduate education in psychology, (d) 1985—the undergraduate psychology curriculum, (e) 1991—liberal education, study in depth, and the arts and sciences major—psychology, (f) 1993—handbook for enhancing undergraduate education in psychology, and (g) 2007—APA guidelines for the undergraduate psychology major. The 2007 report conveyed the longstanding interests about pedagogy by psychologists and also satisfied pressures for accountability in higher education.

The APA (2007) *Guidelines* for the undergraduate psychology major represent a consensus about what to teach undergraduates about psychology and provides hints regarding a disciplinary signature pedagogy. The *Guidelines* define the psychology major as a science and establish five goals for teaching and learning psychological content (i.e., "mind"), values (i.e., "heart"), and skills (i.e., "hand"), and another five goals regarding how undergraduate training in psychology contributes to liberal arts education. Goals 1 through 5, regarding "Knowledge, Skills, and Values Consistent with the Science and Application of Psychology," represent activities in psychology education through coursework and advising. These goals represent common thinking about the "habits of mind, hand, and heart" in the field of psychology to date. In contrast, Goals 6 through 10, regarding "Knowledge, Skills, and Values Consistent with Liberal Arts Education that are Further Developed in Psychology," represent activities typical of general education programs.

The *Guidelines* also convey some degree of agreement on how to teach undergraduates about psychology. A curriculum based on the *Guidelines* should make "use of a variety of pedagogical models, including service-learning, research and laboratory experiences, online applications, and traditional classroom approaches" (APA, 2007, p. 3).

What Does Acting and Thinking like a Psychologist Look Like?

It is clear that psychologists agree much more about what to teach in psychology than they do about how to teach psychology to undergraduates. Given our interest in portraying the signature pedagogy for undergraduate education in psychology, we explore our second question by reviewing recent pedagogical research in the premier disciplinary journal for teaching and learning, *Teaching of Psychology* (*ToP*). In the second issue, Jones, Saff, and Daniel (1974) published *ToP*'s first installment in a series of annotated bibliographies that cumulatively number entries. For 2006, there were 163 entries, and the cumulative total was 5,936 (Johnson & Schroder, 2007). In light of the large literature about teaching in psychology, we have restricted the scope of our content analysis. First, we limited our review to articles in *ToP* that address student learning outcomes for Goals 1 through 5 regarding "Knowledge, Skills, and Values Consistent with the Science and Application of Psychology" (APA, 2007). Second, we limited our review to 2003 through 2007, the five years following the APA Board of Educational Affairs (BEA) 2002 report by its Task Force on Psychology Major Competencies. Third, we excluded articles about graduate education, advising (e.g., introduction to major or career courses), computerized courses (e.g., converting to an online format), and techniques unrelated to specific pedagogies (e.g., characteristics of programs or successful teachers, reviews of textbooks). Our purpose is to discover what these articles reveal about whether psychologists weigh the goals equally and how psychologists teach undergraduates to think and act like psychologists.

From 2003 through 2007, *ToP* published 343 articles (excluding interviews and Society for the Teaching of Psychology news and awards); however, only 199 articles discussed pedagogical techniques or activities. A subset of 138 articles addressed Goals 1 through 5, regarding "Knowledge, Skills, and Values Consistent with the Science and Application of Psychology." The remaining 61 articles included pedagogical techniques or activities unrelated to any of Goals 1 through 5, even though many could be categorized in terms of Goals 6 through 10, for "Knowledge, Skills, and Values Consistent with Liberal Arts Education that are Further Developed in Psychology." Table 9.1 presents a cross-tabulation of the articles by Goals 1 through 5 (columns) and pedagogy (rows), rank-ordered in terms of frequency from left-to-right and top-to-bottom. If the technique or activity related to more than one goal, we categorized the article according to the author's statement of primary purpose. For example, we categorized an article about a research project to teach a content-specific concept as Goal 1, Knowledge Base in Psychology, even though a secondary outcome included Goal 2, Research Methods in Psychology. In our review, we selected articles that illustrated the goal and also could be used by teachers in other disciplines.

TABLE 9.1
Number of Articles Cross-tabulated by APA Student Learning Goal and Pedagogy

	APA Student Learning Goal						
Pedagogy	**Goal 1**	**Goal 2**	**Goal 4**	**Goal 3**	**Goal 5**	**Number**	**Percentage**
Activity/ Demonstration	22	12	12	7	3	**56**	**41%**
Writing/Problem Solving	10	2	3	3	2	**20**	**15%**
Course	4	2	3	2	4	**15**	**11%**
Methods/Content	2	5			1	**8**	**6%**
Example/Media	4	1	1	2		**8**	**6%**
Computer activity	5	2				**7**	**5%**
Service learning	1	1	4	1		**7**	**5%**
Presentation	1		2	2	1	**6**	**4%**
Miscellaneous	2	6		2	1	**11**	**7%**
Number	**51**	**31**	**25**	**19**	**12**	**138**	
Percentage	**37%**	**22%**	**18%**	**14%**	**9%**		**100%**

Goal 1: Knowledge Base of Psychology

Students will demonstrate familiarity with the major concepts, theoretical perspectives, empirical findings, and historical trends in psychology.

Of the 138 articles, 51 (37%) addressed basic content in psychology. Teachers of psychology clearly favor activities and demonstrations (22 articles) and writing and problem solving (10 articles) for teaching and learning the knowledge base of psychology.

Activity or Demonstration

Middlecamp (2003) described a "20 Questions" test-review method for abnormal psychology students. Individuals randomly drew a name of a psychological disorder and then determined other students' disorders by asking a series of yes/no questions. Because students must generate informative questions and answer questions correctly, the exercise allowed them to review course material and identify gaps in their knowledge. Almost all students rated the activity as helpful in consolidating their knowledge of various disorders. In addition, students' exam performance correlated with the number of disorders correctly identified.

Zehr (2004) required history of psychology students to role-play as faculty members who debated whether to hire William James, a founder of American Psychology. The professor randomly assigned students to advocate either for or against hiring James. Groups of students summarized their reasons, a spokesperson presented the reasons to the entire class, and then individuals cast votes. Students enjoyed the activity and reported that it helped them better understand James and his contributions.

Writing and Problem Solving

Typical writing assignments required students to apply concepts to real-world examples. For example, Miserandino (2007) asked students to analyze Johnny Carson's personality from obituaries and other information. Johnson (2004) asked abnormal psychology students to diagnose a famous person or fictional figure from interviews or other information. Mazur (2005) required adolescent psychology students to examine teen Weblogs (blogs) and write papers that demonstrated an understanding of social psychological concepts in the real world. Students analyzed the blogs in terms of several factors provided by the instructor. Students reported that the activity increased their knowledge about the concerns and computer use of adolescents.

Other writing activities helped students learn to organize information. Mayo (2004) required developmental students to complete a repertory grid in which they rated 10 major theorists on 10 bipolar continua. Students who completed the grid performed better on a cumulative final than students who did not, and reported the assignment helped them organize course content.

Computer Activities and Media Examples

About 20% of the 51 articles concerned either computer activities (5 articles) or media (4 articles). The virtual world often allows more controlled demonstrations than can be completed in vivo. Computers also can track response time or other data, and display the data to students.

Kahan and Mathis (2007) evaluated a computer simulation for how people search their memories. The computer presented the search problem in ways that conform to several competing theories. After completing the virtual task (i.e., searching under a number of cups for a ball), students viewed graphs of their reaction time and graphs of reaction times predicted by a particular theory. Students who completed the simulation performed better on questions related to memory models than two groups of control students who did not complete the simulation.

Various media provide a rich source of psychological constructs in action. Teachers of psychology have illustrated various psychological concepts with music (Daehler & Miller, 2004; Leck, 2006), film (Christopher, Walter, Marek, & Koening, 2004), and television shows (Eaton & Uskul, 2004). Generally, students find the activities enjoyable and useful, and students who participate tend to score higher on related exam questions (Eaton & Uskul, 2004; Leck, 2006).

Goal 2: Research Methods in Psychology

Students will understand and apply basic research methods in psychology, including research design, data analysis, and interpretation.

Of the 138 articles, 31 (22%) concerned research methods. Teachers of psychology employ activities and demonstrations (12 articles), comparisons of multiple techniques or type of content (5 Methods/Content articles), and research projects (4 of 6 miscellaneous articles) for teaching and learning research methods in psychology.

Activity or Demonstration

Psychology is unique in our use of human participants in research. In fact, participants in many psychological studies are introductory psychology students. Several studies investigated the educational benefits students realize from participating in research (Balch, 2006; Bowman & Waite, 2003; Rosell, Beck, Luther, Goedert, Shore, & Anderson, 2005). Other articles investigated techniques to teach research methods concepts, such as data collection (Madson, 2005) or random assignment (Enders, Stuetzle, & Laurenceau, 2006).

Finally, articles frequently described demonstrations of statistical concepts (Kelley, 2004; Kolar & McBride, 2003; Segrist & Pawlow, 2007). Bartsch (2006) describes several demonstrations used on the first day of a statistics class to decrease anxiety about statistics, by illuminating students' intuitions about numbers and statistics. In one activity, five to 10 students drew numbers out of a hat, and the instructor wrote the numbers on the board. Students then estimated the middle of the numbers and the average distance of each of the numbers from the middle, thereby estimating (whether they knew it or not) the mean and standard deviation. Student attitudes about statistics generally improved after the exercise. Moreover, students with the most fear of statistics showed the greatest improvement.

Methods and Content

Another group of articles described investigations of various methods or content, typically comparing groups exposed to different materials, instruction, or content (Lakin, Giesler, Morris, & Vosmik, 2007; Landau, & Bavaria, 2003; Lawson, Schwiers, Doellman, Grady, & Kelnhofer, 2003; Ruscio, 2003). By way of example, Benedict and Anderton (2004) evaluated a Just-In-Time teaching approach to statistics. Students completed pre-class problems online. The instructor evaluated the answers and presented a subset in class for discussion. Students identified any misconceptions and added information to improve the answers. Students in the Just-In-Time course performed better on a comprehensive final than students in a traditional course.

Miscellaneous

One of the best techniques to teach and learn about research methods is to require students to complete a research project. Several articles proposed and investigated the effectiveness of student research projects in achieving this goal (Dermer, 2004; Marek, Christopher, & Walker, 2004; The School Spirit Study Group, 2004). For example, LoSchiavo and Roberts (2005) described a semester-long research project in which students evaluated a software program for detecting deception (i.e., "lie detector" test). Students found the topic interesting and appreciated evaluating an actual product.

Goal 3: Critical Thinking Skills in Psychology

Students will respect and use critical and creative thinking, skeptical inquiry, and, when possible, the scientific approach to solve problems related to behavior and mental processes.

Of the 138 articles, 19 (14%) promoted critical thinking. Teachers of psychology endorse activities and demonstrations (7 articles) and writing and problem solving (3 articles) for teaching and learning about critical thinking.

Activities or Demonstrations

A popular method involved small groups of students discussing and evaluating media presentations of psychological material (Madsen, Van Abbema, Allen, & Schmidt, 2006). Given access to the Internet, students (like all Internet users) are inundated with information. As is true for most disciplines, newspapers, magazines, and Internet sites frequently report information from psychological studies. The presentations, however, do not include either the detail or subtleties of a journal article. To help students think critically about media presentations, Hall and Seery (2006) describe an activity in which students read both a media account and the original journal article and then completed a pre-class worksheet. During class, groups of students compared answers on their worksheets. The groups completed an in-class worksheet in which they identified discrepancies between the media account and the journal article and then explained reasons for the discrepancies. Students who completed the project were better able to evaluate a media headline than students who did not complete the project.

Other articles examined activities designed to help students critically evaluate more specific concepts (Akers & Hodge, 2006; Finken, 2003; Lawson, 2003). Merwin (2003) designed a game, modeled after the popular game Taboo, to encourage students to think critically about course material. Students generated a list of forbidden words for a particular concept, and then other students described the concept without using the forbidden words. Students reported that generating the forbidden words helped them learn class material and that the game was a good test review.

Writing and Problem Solving

Writing is a popular method to encourage critical and creative thinking in many disciplines, including psychology. Often, writing exercises engage critical thinking through evaluating peer work (Sung, Lin, Lee, & Chang, 2003) or creating concept maps (Anthis, 2005). Goal 3, "Critical Thinking Skills in Psychology," also includes creative thinking. Connor-Greene, Young, Paul, and Murdoch (2005) described an activity in which students in an abnormal psychology class earned extra credit for writing poems describing a concept related to the class. Although the students received no formal instruction about how to write poetry and the exercise was voluntary, 79% of students did write poems. Though they were apprehensive initially, students were very positive about the experience by the end of the semester.

Goal 4: Application of Psychology

Students will understand and apply psychological principles to personal, social, and organizational issues.

Of the 138 articles, 25 (18%) focused on the application of psychology. Teachers of psychology make greatest use of activities and demonstrations (12 articles) and service learning (4 articles) for teaching and learning application of psychology.

Activities or Demonstrations

Therapy is one of psychology's major applications, and many articles involved clinical and counseling skills. Some articles described learning to conduct structured interviews (Balsis, Eaton, Zona, & Oltmanns, 2006; Bartels, Nordstrom, & Koski, 2006) or simulate clinical training (Akillas, 2003). One common misconception is that any psychology student can give advice, diagnose, treat, assess, or the like. Although students of psychology are not qualified to conduct therapy, they should know how to best share their knowledge. Pury (2003) required small groups of abnormal psychology students to generate and write answers to questions that might be asked by friends or family. The instructor provided feedback to correct any misconceptions or inappropriate responses. Students reported that completing the activity increased their confidence in knowing the appropriate types of responses to a layperson, and improved their ability to apply research to real-world issues.

Other activities described applications of psychology to students' lives, such as creating a family health history to help them maintain their physical health (Sumner, 2003). Levine, Fast, and Zimbardo (2004) assigned students to engage someone trying to persuade them to do something (e.g., salesperson), and write a paper describing the tactics of the persuader. Students reported the assignment better prepared them to avoid undue influence in future situations.

Service Learning

The most direct way for students to apply psychology is to work in the community. Many classes involve some kind of service-learning project, and several articles described service-learning experiences (Harpine, 2007; Knutson Miller & Yen, 2005; Wells, 2003). Although working with people is popular, Kogan and Kellaway (2004) presented a service-learning activity in an applied animal behavior course. Students applied animal learning theory to train animals at the Humane Society. The students rated the course positively, and the staff at the Humane Society enjoyed the student presence and reported the experience was good for the animals and the Humane Society.

Writing and Problem Solving

Writing assignments lend themselves to application problems. Journaling was the most popular form of writing among articles on the application of psychology (Bolin, Khramtsova, & Saarnio, 2005; Graham, 2006; Kowalski & Lakey, 2004). Instructors require students to write a journal in a variety of classes (e.g., gender of psychology, social psychology, abnormal psychology), anywhere from several times per week to twice a month. Although the specific instructions vary, students frequently apply course material to what they observe in the real world. Students report that journals are helpful personally and academically, and useful in applying the material and encouraging reflective thinking.

Goal 5: Values in Psychology

Students will be able to weigh evidence, tolerate ambiguity, act ethically, and reflect other values that are the underpinnings of psychology as a discipline.

Only 12 of the 138 articles (9%) concerned values in psychology. Unlike Goals 1 through 4, the majority of articles described a unique course to raise students' awareness of diversity (Case, 2007; Kernahan & Davis, 2007; Michaelson, 2006; Probst, 2003).

Activities or Demonstrations

Articles describing activities and demonstration also focused on increasing students' awareness of diversity, or their understanding of the experiences of members of minority groups (Moradi, 2004; Moradi & Townsend, 2006;

Warren, 2006). For example, Battle (2004) described an experiential learning activity in which students wore Gay, Lesbian, Bisexual, or Transgender (GLBT) lapel pins for three days and recorded their thoughts, feelings, and observations while wearing the pin. Students reported better understanding of GLBT issues such as the coming out process, social rejection, and heterosexist attitudes.

What Is the Signature Pedagogy for Undergraduate Education in Psychology?

Our review reveals that the APA (2007) *Guidelines* constitute a workable heuristic for evaluating pedagogy and practices in psychology. Our classification of articles in terms of APA Goals 1 through 5 and pedagogical techniques provide some evidence about undergraduate education in psychology; however, we must evaluate our findings before we interpret them. First, our review focused exclusively on articles in *ToP* and neglected both interdisciplinary journals for the scholarship of teaching and learning, and international journals within the discipline, such as *Psychology Learning and Teaching*. Second, our review covered only five years; however, this period is appropriate, given that the BEA approved and published the *Guidelines* in March 2002. Third, topics rise and fall in popularity over time (Daniel, 1992); however, fads in teaching constitute molehills rather than mountains. Despite the limitations of focus, era, and fads in publishing, we are confident that the overall patterns of results would remain relatively constant across samples of articles from other journals and other eras.

One question is whether psychologists weigh the five disciplinary goals (Goals 1–5) and the five general education goals (Goals 6–10) equally. Table 9.1 reveals that almost one-third of the 199 articles addressed goals other than the five related to "Knowledge, Skills, and Values Consistent with the Science and Application of Psychology." Overall, psychologists devoted greater effort on Goals 1 through 5 (138 articles) than Goals 6 through 10 (61 articles) regarding "Knowledge, Skills, and Values Consistent with Liberal Arts Education that are Further Developed in Psychology." Hence, teachers of psychology primarily engage in instruction about psychology, and liberal arts education is a secondary consideration.

A second question concerns the relative emphases psychologists place on the various components of thinking and acting like psychologists. In other words, how much time do psychologists spend teaching the discipline's fundamental habits of the mind, hand, and heart (Shulman, 2005a)? Conveniently, Goals 1 through 5 map onto the fundamental habits. For example, Goal 1 corresponds to habits of the mind because the emphasis is on the knowledge base of psychology. Goals 2 through 4 correspond to habits of the hand with their respective emphases on research methods, critical thinking, and application. It occurs to us that that research methods and applications also represent that traditional distinction between basic and applied research in psychology. Finally, Goal 5 corresponds to habits of the heart because the focus is on values.

Table 9.1 shows that teachers of psychology strive most to promote habits of the mind and least to imbue habits of the heart. Over a third of all the articles endeavor to build the knowledge base of undergraduates (Goal 1). In contrast, relatively few articles (9%) concern values (Goal 5), even though psychologists profess to instill habits of the heart in their students. Moreover, the emphasis on diversity indicates that psychologists encourage respect for persons, a fundamental ethical principle of the discipline. At the same time, teachers of psychology fall short with respect to teaching and learning about tolerating ambiguity. With regard to imbuing habits of the hand, psychologists work equally hard on research methods and applications of psychology and less on critical thinking. Even more importantly, over half of the articles address habits of the hand (Goals 2–4) collectively. Clearly, these results confirm the common core that psychologists endorse only scientifically derived and tested applications of empirical findings or principles (Stanovich, 2007).

A third question concerns what our analysis reveals about how psychologists teach undergraduates to think and act like psychologists. Conveniently, Table 9.1 rank orders the pedagogical classifications from most common to least common and identifies two clusters.

"High Frequency" pedagogies include those with 11% to 41% of the 138 articles. The most frequent pedagogies are *Activities and Demonstrations* and *Writing and Problem Solving*, together accounting for 56% of articles addressing Goals 1 through 5. *Activities or Demonstrations* articles report a variety of activities both in and out of class. We included articles in the *Writing and Problem Solving* category if the primary activity required students to write papers. Most articles in this category describe an episodic event, an activity requiring part of a class period or a single writing assignment, although some were ongoing. In sum, these articles suggest that much of the teaching in psychology involves lectures, punctuated with asking students to do something with the information. The final category of articles included in the High Frequency pedagogies described novel and unique courses, generally including a description of curricula, assignments, and evaluations of the course.

"Low Frequency" pedagogies include those described by 4% to 6% of articles and together equaled some 26% of articles addressing Goals 1 through 5. Articles included in the *Method and Content* category compared two or more pedagogical techniques or different types of content. *Computer activities and Media examples* describe activities in which students watch a video clip, listen to music, or examine a news story. *Computer activities* included computer demonstrations or tutorials. *Service Learning* articles describe activities in which students work in the community and apply what they have learned in class to their experiences. We included articles in the *Presentations* category when the primary task was for students to create any type of presentation, such as oral, poster, or web-based presentations. Yet again, although the tasks are different, the basic structure of the psychology classes described in these articles is student activity interspersed within lecture.

Finally, "Miscellaneous" pedagogies include those described by fewer than 3% of articles and represented only 7% of the 138 articles. Almost half of the miscellaneous articles described research projects; however, the category also included thought (theory) papers proposing reasons for teaching various constructs or using various methods, or study aids.

Psychologists rely on empirical evidence to support their theories about behavior. Research on the scholarship of teaching and learning in psychology is no different. Almost all the articles evaluated the relationship between the activity, task, etc., and student learning, enjoyment, and/or interest in the material. Furthermore, the research often compared groups of students who either did or did not engage in the task or activity. In the majority of cases, students engaging in the activity or task achieved higher test scores, and/or reported greater enjoyment with or interest in the material. It seems that this style of lecture interspersed with activities is useful, in addition to commonplace.

Conclusions

Although the *Guidelines* (APA, 2007) indicate something about what we believe acting and thinking like a psychologists looks like, the goals alone do not indicate *how* teachers of psychology help students acquire and develop those skills. In some clear sense, this is the fundamental issue regarding what defines a signature pedagogy in psychology.

Shulman (2005b) contends that large lecture is the default pedagogy of liberal arts disciplines such as psychology. Our results are consistent with this idea; however, the role of large lecture has been and remains controversial. As early as 1895, Wolfe argued that lecture alone is insufficient, and the new experimental psychology "cannot be communicated to a large proportion of students by the most brilliant lecturer with a text-book assistant" (p. 385). As a counterpoint, Nevid (2006) discussed ways to apply psychological knowledge about learning in pursuit of the perfect lecture. Perhaps recommendations for best practices will emerge from the members of the work group at the 2008 National Conference on Undergraduate Education in Psychology, who will consider the advantages and disadvantages of various modes of teaching students content and context given that (a) the lecture method has long been the mainstay of instruction in all levels of education, and (b) teachers have developed a wide range of other teaching methods that may be as effective, or more effective than the traditional lecture (Halpern, 2007).

Although our review highlights both the goals and the episodic activities psychologists use in their teaching, what remains uncertain is the larger context. That is, how exactly do the goals and activities relate to the overall student learning outcomes? Periodically, *Teaching of Psychology* publishes special topics issues. Perhaps one future issue should address learning goals and activities within the larger context of courses and the undergraduate curriculum.

In the end, psychology faculties generally appear to use a common pedagogy: they lecture, and they ask students to do something with the information. It seems that our portrayal of the signature pedagogy in psychology conforms to Shulman's (2005a) liberal arts default pedagogy (with a bit of science tossed in). But is this "psychological tossed salad" a signature pedagogy?

It is clear that there is no single signature pedagogy for teaching undergraduates about psychology at this time. Nonetheless, we can ponder whether teachers of psychology will converge on a single signature pedagogy in the future or whether they will devise a cluster of psychological signature pedagogies. Quite simply, it is too much to expect that teachers of psychology adopt all five course goals (APA, 2007) and weight them equally in a single course. In addition to a primary course goal concerning foundational knowledge, an instructor can include and implement one or two of Goals 2 through 5.

Consider the case of instructors who want their students to think critically about foundational knowledge in a specific psychology course. In a volume on best practices for critical thinking, Carroll, Keniston, and Peden (2008) depicted two strategies. An infusion approach is one in which an instructor engages students in critical thinking activities intermittently during a period and across the course. All of the activities are discrete and represent ways to infuse critical thinking across assignments. This approach mimics the lecture-activities-lecture signature pedagogy typical of the articles in our review. An alternative approach is to weave critical thinking objectives into the fabric of the course. The key feature of this tapestry approach is that content and critical thinking are part of the same package. That is, critical thinking is not simply an incidental feature of learning. To the extent that psychologists could agree about what and how students should learn in a specific course, content area signature pedagogies could emerge.

Finally, we consider whether our depiction of a signature pedagogy is unique in some way when compared with other liberal arts disciplines. We are unable to answer this question in a single chapter; however, this is a rich area for further research. On one hand, answers may emerge by reading the other chapters about liberal arts disciplines throughout this volume. On the other hand, future research may require systematic observation of teaching and learning in vivo across the liberal arts curriculum. Perhaps a new subdiscipline within the scholarship of teaching and learning that examines signature pedagogies, within and across disciplines, is on the horizon.

References

Akers, K. G., & Hodge, F. K. (2006). The virtual cola challenge. *Teaching of Psychology, 33,* 125–127.

Akillas, E. (2003). Simulated clinical training in an advanced undergraduate seminar. *Teaching of Psychology, 30,* 147–148.

American Psychological Association (APA). (2007). *APA guidelines for the undergraduate psychology major.* Washington, DC: Author. Retrieved from www.apa.org/ed/resources.html

Anthis, K. (2005). From Freud to Erikson to Marcia: Concept maps in personality psychology courses. *Teaching of Psychology, 32,* 263–265.

Balch, W. R. (2006). Encouraging distributed study: A classroom experiment on the spacing effect. *Teaching of Psychology, 33,* 202–204.

Balsis, S., Eaton, N. R., Martin Zona, D., & Oltmanns, T. F. (2006). Teaching advanced psychopathology: A method that promotes basic undergraduate clinical and research experience. *Teaching of Psychology, 33,* 242–246.

Bartels, L. K., Nordstrom, C. R., & Koski, J. A. (2006). A structured interview demonstration. *Teaching of Psychology, 33,* 55–57.

Bartsch, R. A. (2006). Improving attitudes toward statistics in the first class. *Teaching of Psychology, 33,* 197–198.

Battle, C. L. (2004). Promoting increased understanding of sexual diversity through experiential learning. *Teaching of Psychology, 31,* 118–119.

Beins, B. C. (1992). Constancy and change: Teaching as depicted in psychology journals. In A. E. Puente, J. R. Matthews, & C. L. Brewer (Eds.), *Teaching psychology in America: A history* (pp. 525–551). Washington, DC: American Psychological Association.

Benedict, J. O., & Anderton, J. B. (2004). Applying the Just-In-Time teaching approach to teaching statistics. *Teaching of Psychology, 31,* 197–199.

Benjamin, L. T., Jr. (2000). The psychology laboratory at the turn of the 20th century. *American Psychologist, 55,* 434–441.

Bolin, A. U., Khramtsova, I., & Saarnio, D. (2005). Using student journals to stimulate authentic learning: Balancing Bloom's cognitive and affective domains. *Teaching of Psychology, 32,* 154–159.

Bowman, L. L., & Waite, B. M (2003). Volunteering in research: Student satisfaction and educational benefits. *Teaching of Psychology, 30,* 102–106.

Brewer, C. L. (1997). Undergraduate education in psychology: Will the mermaids sing? *American Psychologist, 52,* 434–441.

Brewer, C. L., Hopkins, J. R., Kimble, G. A., Matlin, M. W., McCann, L. I., McNeil, O. V., Nodine, B. F., Quinn, V. N., & Saundra. (1993). Curriculum. In T. V. McGovern (Ed.), *Handbook for enhancing undergraduate education in psychology* (pp. 161–182). Washington, DC: American Psychological Association.

Calder, L. (2006). Uncoverage: Toward signature pedagogy for the history survey. *The Journal of American History, 92,* 1358–1370. http://www.indiana.edu/~jah/textbooks/2006/calder/

Carroll, D. W., Keniston, A. H., & Peden, B. F. (2008). Integrating critical thinking with course content. In D. Dunn, J. Halonen, & R. Smith (Eds.), *Teaching critical thinking in psychology: A handbook of best practices.* London: Wiley-Blackwell.

Case, K. (2007). Raising white privilege awareness and reducing racial prejudice: Assessing diversity course effectiveness. *Teaching of Psychology, 34,* 231–235.

Christopher, A. N., Walter, J. L., Marek, P., & Koening, C. S. (2004). Using a "New Classic" film to teach about stereotyping and prejudice. *Teaching of Psychology, 31,* 199-202.

Connor-Greene, P. A., Young, A., Paul, C., & Murdoch, J. W. (2005). Poetry: It's not just for English class anymore. *Teaching of Psychology, 32,* 215–221.

Daehler, M. W., & Miller, K. W. (2004). Themes and principles of child development illustrated in music. *Teaching of Psychology, 31,* 195–197.

Daniel, R. S. (1992). Teaching of *Psychology,* the journal. In A. E. Puente, J. R. Matthews, & C. L. Brewer (Eds.), *Teaching psychology in America: A history* (pp. 433–452). Washington, DC: American Psychological Association.

Dermer, M. L. (2004). Using CHINS, a QuickBASIC 4.5 program, to teach single-subject experimentation with humans. *Teaching of Psychology, 31,* 285–288.

Dunn, D. S., & Chew, S. L. (Eds.). (2006). *Best practices for teaching introduction to psychology.* Mahwah, NJ: Erlbaum.

Dunn, D. S., Halonen, J., & Smith, R. (Eds.). (2008). *Teaching critical thinking in psychology: A handbook of best practices.* London: Wiley-Blackwell.

Dunn, D. S., Smith, R. A., & Beins, B. C. (Eds.). (2007). *Best practices for teaching statistics and research methods in the behavioral sciences.* Mahwah, NJ: Erlbaum.

Eaton, J., & Uskul, A. K. (2004). Using *The Simpsons* to teach social psychology. *Teaching of Psychology, 31,* 277–278.

Enders, C. K., Stuetzle, R., & Laurenceau, J.-P. (2006). Teaching random assignment: A classroom demonstration using a deck of playing cards. *Teaching of Psychology, 33,* 239–242.

Finken, L. L. (2003). The complexity of student responses to in-class debates in a human sexuality course. *Teaching of Psychology, 30,* 263–265.

French, F. C. (1898). The place of experimental psychology in the undergraduate course. *Psychological Review, 5,* 510–512.

Goodyear, R. K. (2007). Toward effective signature pedagogy for psychology: Comments supporting the case for competent supervisors. *Professional Psychology, 38,* 273–274.

Graham, S. M. (2006). Understanding the applicability of social psychology: The benefits of a semiweekly journal assignment. *Teaching of Psychology, 33,* 54–55.

Hall, S. S., & Seery, B. L. (2006). Behind the facts: Helping students evaluate media reports of psychological research. *Teaching of Psychology, 33,* 49–51.

Halpern, D. F. (2007). Redesigning undergraduate education in psychology: Imagine the possibilities. *Psychology Teacher Network, 17(3),* 1–3. Retrieved January 3, 2008, from http://www.apa.org/ed/pcue/ptn_halpern.pdf

Halpern, D. F. (2008). *The National Conference on Undergraduate Education in Psychology: A blueprint for the future of our discipline.* Retrieved March 28, 2008 from http://www.apa.org/ed/pcue/blueprint.html?tag=bubbl_3

Harpine, E. C. (2007). Applying motivation theory to real-world problems. *Teaching of Psychology, 34,* 111–113.

Johnson, D. E., & Schroder, S. I. (2007). Annotated bibliography on the teaching of psychology: 2006. *Teaching of Psychology, 34,* 268–279.

Johnson, W. B. (2004). Diagnosing the stars: A technique for teaching diagnosis in abnormal psychology. *Teaching of Psychology, 31,* 275–276.

Jones, C. S., Saff, J. L., & Daniel, R. S. (1974). Annotated bibliography on the teaching of psychology: 1973. *Teaching of Psychology, 1,* 75–79.

Kahan, T. A., & Mathis, K. M. (2007). Searching under cups for clues about memory: An online demonstration. *Teaching of Psychology, 34,* 124–128.

Kelley, M. R. (2004). Demonstrating the Monty Hall dilemma. *Teaching of Psychology, 31,* 193–195.

Kernahan, C., & Davis, T. (2007). Changing perspective: How learning about racism influences student awareness and emotion. *Teaching of Psychology, 34,* 49–52.

Knutson Miller, K., & Yen, S.-C. (2005). Teaching application and personal relevance through writing in courses on gender. *Teaching of Psychology, 32,* 56–58.

Kogan, L. R., & Kellaway, J. A. (2004). Applied animal behavior course: A service-learning collaboration with the Humane Society. *Teaching of Psychology, 31,* 202–204.

Kolar, D. W., & McBride, C. A. (2003). Creating problems to solve problems: An interactive teaching technique for statistics courses. *Teaching of Psychology, 30,* 67–68.

Kowalski, R. M., & Lakey, C. E. (2004). Teaching application and personal relevance through writing in courses on gender. *Teaching of Psychology, 31,* 279–281.

Lakin, J. L., Giesler, R. B., Morris, K. A., & Vosmik, J. R. (2007). HOMER as an acronym for the scientific method. *Teaching of Psychology, 34,* 94–96.

Landau, J. D., & Bavaria, A. J. (2003). Does deliberate source monitoring reduce students' misconceptions about psychology? *Teaching of Psychology, 30,* 311–314.

Lawson, T. J. (2003). A psychic-reading demonstration designed to encourage critical thinking. *Teaching of Psychology, 30,* 251–253.

Lawson, T. J., Schwiers, M., Doellman, M., Grady, G., & Kelnhofer, R. (2003). Enhancing students' ability to use statistical reasoning with everyday problems. *Teaching of Psychology, 30,* 107–110.

Leck, K. (2006). Teaching personality theories using popular music. *Teaching of Psychology, 33,* 34–36.

Levine, R. V., Fast, N., & Zimbardo, P. (2004). The power of persuasion: A field experience. *Teaching of Psychology, 31,* 136–138.

LoSchiavo, F. M., & Roberts, K. L. (2005). Testing pseudoscientific claims in research methods course. *Teaching of Psychology, 32,* 177–180.

Madsen, S. D., Van Abbema, D. L, Allen, C. C., & Schmidt, R. E. (2006). Questioning claims of baby genius: Students evaluate advertisements of infant stimulation products. *Teaching of Psychology, 33,* 134–135.

Madson, L. (2005). Demonstrating the importance of question wording on surveys. *Teaching of Psychology, 32,* 40–43.

Marek, P., Christopher, A. N., & Walker, B. J. (2004). Learning by doing: Research methods with a theme. *Teaching of Psychology, 31,* 128–131.

Mayo, J. A. (2004). Repertory grid as a means to compare and contrast developmental theorists. *Teaching of Psychology, 31,* 178–180.

Mazur, E. (2005). Online and writing: Teen blogs as mines of adolescent data. *Teaching of Psychology, 32,* 180–182.

Merwin, M. M. (2003). Forbidden words: A strategy for studying psychology. *Teaching of Psychology, 30,* 242–244.

McGovern, T. V. (1992). Evolution of undergraduate curricula in psychology: 1892–1992. In A. E. Puente, J. R. Matthews, & C. L. Brewer (Eds.), *Teaching psychology in America: A history* (pp. 13–38). Washington, DC: American Psychological Association.

McGovern, T. V. (Ed.). (1993). *Handbook for enhancing undergraduate education in psychology.* Washington, DC: American Psychological Association.

McGovern, T. V., Furumoto, L., Halpern, D. F., Kimble, G. A., & McKeachie, W. J. (1991). Liberal education, study in depth, and the arts and sciences major—psychology. *American Psychologist, 46,* 598–605.

Michaelson, C. (2006). Integrating Eastern and Western approaches to psychology: An undergraduate senior seminar. *Teaching of Psychology, 33,* 142–144.

Middlecamp, M. (2003). Uncover the disorder: A review activity for abnormal psychology courses. *Teaching of Psychology, 30,* 62–63.

Miserandino, M. (2007). Heeeere's Johnny: A case study in the Five Factor Model of personality. *Teaching of Psychology, 34,* 37–40.

Moradi, B. (2004). Teaching about diversities: The shadow/role-play exercise. *Teaching of Psychology, 31,* 188–191.

Moradi, B., & Townsend, D. T. (2006). Raising students' awareness of women in psychology. *Teaching of Psychology, 33,* 113–115.

Murphy, M. C., & Reidy, T. (2006, Winter). Exploring political science's signature pedagogy. *Academic Exchange Quarterly, 10*(4), 130–134.

Nevid, J. S. (2006, February). In pursuit of the "perfect lecture." *APS Observer, 19*(2). Retrieved from http://www.psychologicalscience.org/observer/get Article.cfm?id=1933

Probst, T. M. (2003). Changing attitudes over time: Assessing the effectiveness of a workplace diversity course. *Teaching of Psychology, 30,* 236–239.

Puente, A. E., Matthews, J. R., & Brewer, C. L. (Eds.). (1992). *Teaching psychology in America: A history.* Washington, DC: American Psychological Association.

Pury, C. L. S. (2003). What are students telling their friends? Teaching responses to lay psychopathology questions. *Teaching of Psychology, 30,* 145–146.

Rosell, M. C., Beck, D. M., Luther, K. E., Goedert, K. M., Shore, W. J., & Anderson, D. D. (2005). The pedagogical value of experimental participation paired with course content. *Teaching of Psychology, 32,* 95–99.

Ruscio, J. (2003). Comparing Bayes's theorem to frequency-based approaches to teaching Bayesian reasoning. *Teaching of Psychology, 30,* 325–328.

Segrist, D. J., & Pawlow, L. A. (2007). The mixer: Introducing the concept of factor analysis. *Teaching of Psychology, 34,* 121–123.

Shulman, L. (2005a, Summer). Signature pedagogies in the professions. *Daedalus, 134,* 52–59.

Shulman, L. S. (2005b, Spring). Pedagogies of uncertainty. *Liberal Education,* 18–25. Retrieved November 12, 2007, from http://www.aacu.org/liberaleducation/le-sp05/le-sp05feature2.cfm

Stanovich, K. E. (2007). *How to think straight about psychology* (8th ed.). Boston: Allyn & Bacon.

Street, W. R. (1994). *A chronology of noteworthy events in American psychology.* Washington, DC: American Psychological Association.

Sumner, K. E. (2003). Constructing a family health history to facilitate learning in a health psychology seminar. *Teaching of Psychology, 30,* 230–232.

Sung, Y.-T., Lin, C.-S., Lee, C.-L., & Chang, K.-E. (2003). Evaluating proposals for experiments: An application of web-based self-assessment and peer-assessment. *Teaching of Psychology, 30,* 331–334.

The School Spirit Study Group (2004). Measuring school spirit: A national teaching exercise. *Teaching of Psychology, 31,* 18–21.

Warren, C. S. (2006). Incorporating multiculturalism into undergraduate psychology courses: Three simple active learning activities. *Teaching of Psychology, 33,* 105–109.

Wells, C. V. (2003). Service learning and problem-based learning in a conflict resolution class. *Teaching of Psychology, 30,* 260–262.

Wolfe, H. K. (1895). The new psychology in undergraduate work. *Psychological Review, 2,* 382–387.

Zehr, D. (2004). Two active learning exercises for a history of psychology class. *Teaching of Psychology, 31,* 54–56.

10

SIGNATURE PEDAGOGY AND THE SOCIOLOGICAL IMAGINATION

A Critical Assessment

Eri Fujieda

For sociology teachers, engaging novices with the sociological imagination is probably one of the most significant goals of teaching. As one of the social science disciplines, sociology aims to explain human behaviors by applying scientific methods. What distinguishes sociology from other social sciences is the assumption that social structures are critical to our understanding of human behavior. Social structures refer to the patterns of social relations that are rooted in history. Class, race, and gender are examples of social structures that shape the relationships, experiences, and identities of an individual. Actions of an individual or a group can also be explained in relation to social structures. This ability to interpret human behavior in relation to historically rooted social structures, which is coined as the sociological imagination (Mills, 1959), is central to sociology.

Experts in the discipline are capable of conceptualizing a topic in relation to social structures and investigating it using the scientific method. Those who are trained as sociologists value the sociological imagination, know the use of the scientific method in turning the sociological imagination into a valid body of knowledge, and articulate the relevance of sociological knowledge to real situations. In addition, they can also exchange the findings of their specialized research and contribute to the progress of the whole discipline, as well as to the promotion of human diversity and social justice. Due to the wide applicability of the sociological imagination, the discipline of sociology appears to be fragmented into many subfields.[1] For experts, however, the discipline is apparently founded on the sociological imagination.

Novices may not find the sociological imagination so evident. Their lives may be influenced by social structures, but they may not be aware of them. Rather, they may not be used to considering daily practices, observations, or experiences as something worth researching. To engage novices with the field of sociology, and to enable them to think like experts, some strategic consideration should be given to the pedagogy.

This chapter examines the pedagogy typically used in undergraduate sociology teaching, and critically reflects upon similarities and differences between disciplinary expectations and learning outcomes. Furthermore, I will suggest signature pedagogies that seem to effectively acculturate novices to the world of sociologists and enable them to think like sociologists. Invaluable to my endeavor are articles published in *Teaching Sociology*, a major outlet of pedagogy-related ideas and research for sociology teachers since 1973. Though it is obviously impossible to include all those contributions, this chapter aims to illuminate key issues relevant to the signature pedagogy of sociology.

An Overview of Traditional Pedagogy in Sociology

A typical sociology curriculum for the novice may be compared to a "Ferris wheel" (Eberts et al., 1990, p.2). Students who purchase the ticket to ride—that is, by completing the introductory course successfully—can get any seat on the "Ferris wheel" of sociology courses, however advanced (Berheide, 2005, p. 7). Though this observation originated almost two decades ago, the structure of the sociology curriculum has not changed much since then (Kain, 1999).

Students are typically first exposed to sociology through an introductory course, where development of the sociological perspective or the sociological imagination is emphasized as one of the main goals (Grauerholz & Gibson, 2006).[2] The dominant method of instruction employed in the introductory course is to focus on the coverage of a wide array of topics, and to encourage passive learning experiences. The standard introductory textbook covers many topics (e.g., demography, culture, socialization, social institutions, stratification, inequality) and addresses multiple concepts for each topic (Keith & Ender, 2004). Underlying this practice is the general belief that some coverage of all important topics and content is necessary to provide a general overview of the field (Androit, 2007). The surveys of the discipline are given in the introductory course, which tends to be large in class size. According to Howard and Zoeller (2007), although students may be asked at times to participate in discussion, they are expected to spend most of their class time passively absorbing the information presented by the instructor. Small-group activities, in-class writing assignments, video viewing, and online discussion occur, but less frequently. Students' learning is assessed by fairly conventional assessment tools, such as essays and exams.

The introductory course seems to play a gatekeeping role. Surviving the introductory course is a prerequisite for courses that seriously socialize students into the profession. Theory and research method courses are commonly required only for sociology majors. Other courses focus on specialized topics, such as social movements, social psychology, stratification, and specific social institutions (family, religion, state, etc.), and students are usually expected to acquire knowledge on each of these specific topics from standardized textbooks and the instructor's lecture. Students may have a chance to engage with some research activities in the research methods course, but they rarely get involved with anything more than the analysis of existing data. Other research activities, such as data collection or proposal writing, are relatively rare (Grauerholz & Gibson, 2006). They are also not necessarily required for the major (Kain, 1999). At the end of the sociology major, most students will have written a thesis and participated in internships, community-based service learning, and other individualized hands-on long-term research projects.

(Mis)conceptions about Sociology

What do students learn about sociology from the lecture-based, survey-oriented introductory course and their ride on the Ferris wheel assortment of courses? McKinney's (2005) face-to-face interview study of sociology majors found that students' interest in the sociology major is largely related to interpersonal influence; to the presence of diverse, relevant, and applicable content; and to situational factors. For them, a "successful" undergraduate career in sociology meant good study habits, interaction with faculty members, and efforts to relate the materials to their own observations or experiences. McKinney also reports that students are not necessarily able to demonstrate their deep understanding of the key disciplinary concept of the sociological imagination, even at the completion of the sociology major.

McKinney's research is instructive. It suggests that sociology instructors teach students to take in information provided by the instructor, interact with their superiors, and follow orders. Students do not have to achieve deep understanding of the discipline's core principles to think critically about the social world or to actively participate in and investigate into the social world (Leming, 1990; McKinney, 2005). Roberts (2002) also provided an intriguing observation about the irony of "good teachers." Well-organized, enthusiastic teachers can effectively encourage students to participate in the discussion, but these students do not necessarily become interested in thinking for themselves. The problem in the traditional method of instruction is thus the domination of the classroom by the teacher. Even when students participate under the traditional method of teaching, the classroom does not provide much space for them to articulate and reflect upon what they are taught and feed their own understanding back into the classroom dialogue.

It is plausible that students who are successful in sociology courses are the "good" students who have the cultural capital to be generally successful in college, and that students from less privileged backgrounds may not perform well (Isserles & Dalmage, 2000; McKinney & Reed, 2007). The reproduction of inequality, particularly due to the socioeconomic backgrounds of students, is exactly what sociologists intend to avoid. Although many factors may contribute to this ironic unintended outcome, the dominant method of teaching sociology is certainly part of the problem, and alternatives to this traditional pedagogy must be given serious consideration. Sociology is potentially a great tool for reframing the world and changing our responses to it, but when concepts are taught as mere "tools without a deeper understanding of context [they] will reproduce [the existing inequality] rather than effect change" (Isserles & Dalmage, 2000, p.164).

Besides these issues, passive learning experiences and the coverage model can generate certain misconceptions about the discipline, even among "good" students. This section considers three of such misconceptions that seem to influence students' progress in study-in-depth of sociology.

1. Sociology is an Ideological Opinion

Sociology courses ask students to think critically. In fact, critical thinking carries a particular meaning in the context of sociology. Grauerholz and Bouma-Holtrop (2003) reviewed other sociologists' conceptions of critical thinking and synthesized them into "critical sociological thinking," which refers to "the ability to use sociological knowledge and skills to reflect upon, question, and judge information while also demonstrating a sensitivity to and awareness of social and cultural contexts" (p. 487).

In the contemporary cultural context that values individualism as well as consumerism, however, critical sociological thinking can be misunderstood as a mere criticism of students' culture or society, or a manifestation of political bias (e.g., Martin, 2000; Netting, 1994; Thompson, 1996). Particularly, when taught with traditional methods, students may view the sociological knowledge that contradicts their culturally and historically embedded subjective knowledge as something they are forced to accept, rather than as the integral part of critical thinking. Sociology can be regarded as a knowledge that is biased and subjective.

Students see sociology as ideological particularly in courses that examine social class (e.g., Davis, 1992; Wills et al., 2005), race (e.g., Hunter & Nettles, 1999; Kubal, Meyler, Stone, & Mauney, 2003; Dundes & Spence, 2007), gender (e.g., Moore, 1997), and family (e.g., Magdol, 2003). These topics have provoked students' objection to the structural explanation of inequality and question the legitimacy of non-individualistic explanations. In addition, students have responded negatively to the notion that the instructor even has an ability to know the truth (Haddad & Lieberman, 2002). In some cases, students resist sociological knowledge because it suggests a certain class position (Isserles & Dalmage, 2000). The tone of despair and lack of hope when teachers describe structures of domination can also turn students against sociological knowledge (Moulder, 1997).

Although political-ideological contexts outside the classroom may account for some part of students' resistance, the effect of the common pedagogy in sociology is worth examining. In the traditional method of instruction, "common sense" is regarded as "myths" or a sign of "ignorance," and is something to be "debunked" or "remedied" by scientific sociological research based on facts and objectivity (Mathisen, 1989, p. 308). The instructor's role is then to expose students to sociological knowledge while encouraging them to disregard what they learn outside the classroom (Bengston & Hazzard, 1990). The traditionally structured authority in the classroom promotes this process. Students are implicitly asked to passively accept the knowledge communicated through textbooks and lectures. Students learn from this pedagogy the disparity between their own experiences in understanding of the social world, and the unquestionable moral authority assumed by the instructor, as well as by the textbook (Bengston & Hazzard, 1990; Hedley & Markowitz, 2001; Mathisen,1989).

The concentration of authority in the instructor and the textbook turns the classroom into the site of a war between positions and ideologies (Goldsmith, 2006). The classroom structure implies hierarchical social relations in knowledge and morality, in contrast to college cultures that encourage students to consider themselves consumers or clients to be served by the instructor. As consumers, students can invoke their rights to choose their own ideology against an ideology called "sociology." Their resistance to sociological knowledge is then a reflection of the classroom structure under the traditional method of teaching that denies their power to choose. As a consequence, students are not only unable to attain critical sociological thinking; they may also actively distance themselves from sociological knowledge.

2. Research Method is 'Just a Set of Techniques'

Kain (1999) argues that the sociological imagination, the hallmark of sociology, is demonstrated by sociological research, which "combines methodological tools with theoretical approaches to ask sociological questions" (p. 3). Professional socialization of undergraduate students then, means to provide research training that "involves systematic linkage between theory and method; only then are we talking about 'thinking sociologically'" (Kain, 1999, p.5). In addition, the research is also a social activity that requires social and communication skills, which are also important not only to sociologists, but to liberal arts students as well (Jenkins, 1995).

Currently students are taught research skills in a very fragmented way, without many opportunities to build the sociological imagination. For those who survived the introductory course, social theory, research methods, and specific methodological techniques are taught as separate, independent topics that students must master to earn a major in sociology. The emphasis on knowledge mastery makes the traditional method of instruction suitable, but students may not experience the process of synthesizing and integrating these different pieces into the sociological imagination. Furthermore, research methods are typically taught in one or two courses required for their major through the traditional mode of teaching (i.e., lectures, problem-solving assignments, and exams). In the introductory course, social research is usually treated as an autonomous topic (Keith & Ender, 2004), but not as one of the main learning outcomes (Grauerholz & Gibson, 2006; Markham, 1991). Grauerholz and Gibson (2006) reported that the majority of the courses include no research component.

The lack of hands-on research experience promotes an instrumental view of research. Howery and Rodriguez (2006) suggested that the curricular structure may make "students feel that research is disembodied from the rest of the curriculum" (p. 25). Students who are not mathematically inclined suffer anxiety in a quantitative research method course, for they see it as the site to learn a series of mathematically stipulated statistical techniques, rather than as a site to learn quantitative, analytical, and reasoning skills (Bridges, Gillmore, Pershing, & Bates, 1998; DeCesare, 2007). Research is thus (mis)conceived as an intellectual exercise to demonstrate the intellectual capability of an individual, rather than as a collective process of discovery.

3. Theory as a Fixed Set of Abstract Ideas

Well socialized professional sociologists know that theory is as central to the discipline as research methods. Although there is a debate on the role of theory in sociology (Lemert, 1991; Flint, 1993), theory is unquestionably an integral part of the discipline (Eberts et al., 1990). Although the understanding of past theories helps situate contemporary inquiry in a historical context, current research also fosters the further development of existing theory. Theory is also useful for critical thinking because it prevents "closed circle of thought, in which preconceptions are validated by translating them into sociological concepts and jargons" (Hale, 1995, p. 48). It further helps us consider moral and political implications of "participat[ing] in rapidly changing social, political, and economic institutions" (Johnson, 2001, p.163).

Despite the disciplinary importance of theory, it is not emphasized in the introductory course. In the 1990s, most of the introductory textbooks included theory in one of many chapters (Keith & Ender, 2004). Four or five major theoretical traditions are typically discussed in this chapter, making students aware of multiple perspectives within the discipline. When students pass this course, they can take an upper-division course designated for theory, which typically exposes students to numerous influential theorists. However, by the time students take the upper-division theory course, they are typically not interested in theory and may take the theory course reluctantly, fearful of the challenges of abstract thinking and difficult readings. According to Lowney (1998, p. 69), the theory section in the introductory course has often confused and discouraged students by the time they take the upper-division theory course. Being preconditioned, students come into the theory course, typically required for sociology majors, already feeling anxious. In this course, students typically read primary theoretical texts, but the abstract nature of writing, the need for logical thinking, the challenge of reading difficult texts, and the difficulty in relating theoretical points to life experiences are factors that make students avoid dealing with theory as long as they can (Lowney 1998; Silver & Perez, 1998). In addition, students may consider theory as a mere opinion expressed by people far removed from students' own concerns.

Students' reactions to theory may derive from the traditional pedagogy, which delivers theory as an arbitrary yet fixed set of abstract ideas, rather than as a "story" that each theorist constructed and told in a historically and culturally specific context (Rinehart, 1999). To students, the relevance of past theories to the contemporary context may not always be clear (Backman, 1992). Furthermore, students may not have sufficient academic skills necessary to engage these texts, such as verbal comprehension, critical thinking, and scientific reasoning (Johnson, 2001). This reaction can, however, change when students can learn theory from application and collaborative work. Applying theory as a "tool of analysis" (Bluth, 1975), particularly to daily events and experiences (Hale, 1995), helps students to engage with theory more deeply. Collaborative work to analyze, interpret, and reconstruct a theory enables students to become active learners who "move away from passive and sometimes hostile dependence on a remote authority figure toward assumption of the rights and responsibilities of citizenship in intellectual communities which they helped to create and which they can call their own"

(Rau & Heyl, 1990, p. 154, in Rinehart, 1999, p. 232). If theory were to be taught more substantively in the introductory course through a dialogic method of instruction, it could change students' perceptions about theory itself. Without these changes, however, theory will continue to stand like a disciplinary scarecrow.

SoTL and the "New" Signature Pedagogy

These misconceptions about the discipline can be regarded as symptoms of the problematic traditional method of instruction. They also reveal that the traditional method of instruction hinders "study-in-depth" of the discipline. Study-in-depth refers to "the capacity to master complexity, the abilities required to conduct independent work, and the achievement of critical sophistication through sequential learning experiences" (Wagenaar, 1993, p. 352). In the context of sociology, study-in-depth is interpreted as "the development of a coherent and mature understanding of sociology through sequential learning experiences that use both empirical and theoretical analysis to examine a wide range of topics. Study in depth . . . involves a process of intellectual development where students become increasingly independent and knowledgeable members of the community of discourse in sociology" (Berheide, 2005, p. 4).

To foster the study-in-depth in sociology, the significance of active, experiential, collaborative learning within and outside of the classroom has been emphasized (Eberts et al., 1990). This pedagogical emphasis has been translated into concrete pedagogical practices and innovations, and published as scholarship of teaching and learning (SoTL) articles in *Teaching Sociology*. As Howery (2002) and Weiss (2007) encapsulated, sociologists concerned with teaching and learning have been engaged in scholarly exchanges on undergraduate teaching since the 1970s.[3] Some of the scholarship has been the application of sociological theories to teaching and learning practices, but there have been many contributions on "best practices." In either case, asking critical questions, using empirical evidence, and employing multiple methods to create a measurement are common practices among sociologists who engage in SoTL (Howery, 2002). In addition, SoTL in sociology tends to pay special attention to human diversity, lived experience, and institutional context (Howery, 2002).

SoTL in sociology has provided evidence for and insight to alternative pedagogies. In particular, a number of sociology teachers have developed pedagogical strategies that aim at reflexive, out-of-class, and collaborative teaching and learning. These innovative pedagogies appear effective in shifting novices' attention away from misconceptions about the discipline and leading them on to the process of study-in-depth in sociology. This section considers how they can serve as plausible signature pedagogies in sociology.

1. Reflexive Incorporation of Students' "Common Sense"

In the traditional method of instruction, the knowledge students bring into the classroom is seen as an obstacle for students to learn expert knowledge, which creates resistance in some sociology courses. In response, innovative pedagogical strategies have emerged, many of which emphasize students' application of the sociological perspective to their unexamined but embodied knowledge about the world. When students are encouraged to value their "common sense," daily experiences, observations, and cultural dispositions as worthy of sociological analysis, they come to realize the usefulness of the sociological perspective, and engage with it much more deeply. In addition, approaching sociology from this angle helps students realize how integral theory and methods are to the sociological perspective.

Many sociology teachers have engaged students in sociology from this point of view. Pedagogical strategies for this purpose typically start with classroom activities that invoke students' culturally informed personal knowledge (or "pre-sociology knowledge") about the world. Then, teachers guide students to analyze the pre-sociology knowledge from a sociological perspective. Films (e.g., Volk & Beeman, 1998; Tan & Ko, 2004), TV programs (Misra, 2000), music (e.g., Ahlkvist, 2001; Albers & Back, 2003; Martinez, 1998), literature (e.g., Hall, 2000), poetry (e.g., Moran, 1999), comics (e.g., Hall & Lucal, 1999), cartoons (e.g., Scanlan & Feinberg, 2000), and historical narratives (e.g., Schumm et al., 2002) are all nontraditional materials that can be integrated into lectures so students can relate sociological knowledge to the world outside the classroom. Interactive experiential exercises (e.g., simulations, games, and experiments) also enable students to learn concepts and theories through bodily experiences, rather than verbal transmission (e.g., Auster, 2000; Corrado, Merenstein, Glasberg, & Peele, 2000; McCammon, 1999; Obach, 2000; O'Brien & Foley, 1999; Pence & Fields, 1999; Wybraniec & Wilmoth, 1999). Because these activities are also multisensory, students' engagement with these activities are also bodily and affective. At the same time, using nontraditional materials and conducting in-class exercises are "safer" ways for students to observe the transformation of their "reality" from non-sociological to sociological, and to cognitively and affectively learn the work of sociological knowledge. These activities provide students with an opportunity to model sociological thinking, without making it too personal. Students can still learn to take the sociological perspective at a more personal level and to think critically about their own values and beliefs in relation to the sociocultural contexts and social structures.

Students may be more challenged when they are asked to analyze, interpret, and present their own understanding and experiences from a sociological perspective. Students' critical assessment of "common sense" is employed to re-evaluate their relationships with the social world and identities (Bengston & Hazzard, 1990). Teaching students to analyze their own dispositions as "cultural capital" encourages students to evaluate their perceptions of their own capacities to affect the social world (Isserles & Dalmage, 2000). Goldsmith (2006) employed combined exploratory writing and problem-based learning to enable students to compare and contrast the (mis)conceptions about racial and ethnic relations. Through a well-structured series of individual and collaborative activities, students were able to recognize the impact of existing dominant ideologies on their common sense ideas about race and ethnicity and develop a sociological framework that they could apply to other cases. Persell (2004) instituted web-based structured discussions in a senior seminar on race and education as an alternative form of intellectual exchange that fosters students' higher level of learning (i.e., metacognition, integration, and synthesis). In all cases, students were encouraged to actively participate in the discourse of sociological concepts and methods, and became able to assess diverse opinions and social realities from a sociological perspective. Furthermore, these pedagogies enabled students to "unlearn" what they were socialized into and to replace it with the sociological perspective.

One cannot deny the presence of risk in asking students to examine their experiences and worldviews. In particular, angry emotional reactions can turn the classroom into an antagonistic rather than empathetic space, which can distract students from learning (Grauerholz & Copenhaver, 1994). Apathy and disengagement can lead to the devaluation of sociology as a discipline of "complaints" (Johnson, 2005). "Managing" students' emotions in a group setting can test teachers' abilities for emotional labor (Roberts &

Smith, 2002, p. 293). The instructor must take extra care in designing activities that promote questions and reflections on students' prior knowledge related to social issues that are inherently political and thus sensitive to many who live in the United States (Rosenbloom & Fetner, 2001).

These classroom activities significantly encourage novices to make a journey toward the study-in-depth of sociology. The realization that their worldview is socially constructed and the acquisition of sociological methods and concepts useful in coming to this conclusion are both significant for students to become independent members of the sociologist's community.

2. Involving Out-of-Class Social Situations

The traditional method of teaching assumes the classroom as the primary site of instruction, texts or other published documents as the main sources of teaching materials, and the instructor as the only agent who structures the environments for teaching and learning. This pedagogical structure has generated the misconceptions about sociology discussed above.

Recent SoTL research has begun to present substantial evidence that students achieve deeper understanding of sociology and professional socialization when they engage with out-of-class learning opportunities, such as volunteer work, internships, service learning, research with faculty, academic-based peer relationships, or involvement in campus organizations (McKinney, Medvedeva, Vacca & Malak, 2004). These activities can function as "the chance to apply what is learned to real life and/or to reinforce their learning of sociology," as well as the opportunity to increase students' ability to empathize with those who are socially different (McKinney, 2005, p. 374). In addition, when the sociology faculty or other sociologists are involved, out-of-class learning activities enable students to see sociology and sociologists in action and possibly contribute to the lowering of the barriers between the novice and the expert. Most importantly, out-of-class learning opportunities can counter common misconceptions about sociology.

Involving students in a research project is a laborious but rewarding method to create a link between classroom knowledge and the world outside the classroom, and is employed mainly in upper-division courses. Kain, Buchanan, and Marck (2001) and Singleton (2007), among others, incorporated a campus-related research project to the research methods course. A number of sociology instructors, including Potter, Caffrey, and Plante

(2003), Jakubowski and Burman (2004), Cunningham and Kingma-Kiekhofer (2004), Rajaram (2007), and Mobley (2007), engaged students with community-based action research projects. In all of these cases, students generally learned research from the researcher's point of view and realized that social research demands not only knowledge but also critical thinking skills, resources, persistence, and collaboration. Students also found sociological research to be intellectually stimulating, transformative, significant and valuable to the public, and personally and socially rewarding. Furthermore, these research-based, out-of-class learning opportunities help students enter a career in which they can apply knowledge and skills they have gained through the undergraduate sociology curriculum. These experiences together encourage students to think like a sociologist and promote students' active involvement with essential practices in sociology.

Although many of these case studies of out-of-class activities are from upper-division sociology courses, students in introductory courses can benefit from out-of-class activities when they are arranged appropriately. According to Wright's (2000) study of the impact of short-term, out-of-class, experiential learning projects for the introductory sociology course, novice students can indeed benefit from activities outside the classroom. The strategic selection and structuring of students' activities outside the classroom, and the allocation of sufficient time for critical sociological reflection are, however, critical to turn the out-of-class activity into a meaningful learning experience. Without such care, out-of-class learning opportunities could leave students with their experiences unprocessed, hardly effective to teaching or learning, and possibly boring and traumatizing. In addition, given the learning goals for the introductory course, choosing short-term out-of-class learning experiences, such as unobtrusive observations, field trips, and participant observation assignments at a site of the students' choice, can be a much more logical pedagogical strategy than creating fully pledged, long-term, out-of-class learning opportunities, which typically demand a heavy commitment of time and energy, and the potential sacrifice of in-class learning opportunities. Through these experiences, students realize the relevance of sociology to the "real" world they live in, while starting to decrease their dependency on stereotypes and other unexamined knowledge (Wright, 2000).

Study-abroad programs are out-of-class learning opportunities that have distinctive advantages as well as challenges. Students can achieve deeper understanding of sociological concepts and theories when they are surrounded by a totally new sociocultural environment. When abroad, students experience social marginality, which enables them to compare at least two societal contexts and to inductively understand the relevance of a theory or concept (Halsey, 1990). Finding relevance beyond the U.S. national borders also helps students to realize the cross-cultural value of disciplinary knowledge (cf. Armer, 1987), particularly when learning opportunities are structured based upon critical pedagogy (Fobes, 2005). In addition, students' awareness of global issues can deepen, and their civic engagement at the global level may increase (Lessor, Reeves, & Andrade, 1997).

Developing and implementing an effective study-abroad program takes institutional support, faculty development, collaboration across disciplines, detailed logistical planning, bureaucratic maneuvering, recruitment and training of students (including language), and dealing with unexpected events and problems (Fobes, 2005; Kain & D'Andrea, 1992; Lessor, Reeves, & Andrade, 1997; Wagenaar & Subedi, 1996). These challenges can make such learning opportunities difficult to facilitate, so it's important to ask if the pedagogical effect of students' experience overseas is substantively different from that of their experiences "at home." Can similar learning outcomes be achieved through other experiential learning activities, such as a cross-cultural "interview" project by using e-mail (Hare, 1999) or short-term field trips within the United States (Grant, Heirich, Martin, & Van Eck, 1981; Schmid & Buechler, 1991)? Although the significance of globalizing the sociology curriculum is unquestionable, pedagogical strategies for it are yet to be assessed in relation to the study-in-depth of sociology.

3. Collaborative Teaching and Learning

Students understand sociology as an arbitrary, sequenced set of courses because of the survey-type introductory course followed by the Ferris wheel curriculum. This prevents them from developing sociological competence and achieving study-in-depth in sociology (Wagenaar 1993; McKinney, Medvedeva, Vacca, & Malak, 2004). ASA has been addressing this issue in relation to the curricular structure at the department level (Eberts et al., 1990). These recommendations are generally not put into practice (Kain, 1999), in part due to the institutional contexts of higher education that discourage the serious discussion of teaching at the departmental and institutional level and prevent the employment of innovative, nontraditional methods of instruction and curriculum development (Wright et al., 2004; Kain, 2006).

Although the institutional context may negatively affect both pedagogical changes and the advancement of SoTL, Waltermaurer and Obach (2007) recently reported their attempt to collaborate across "core" sociology courses—that is, theory, research methods, and statistics courses. By applying the specific knowledge in each course to the same research project, students developed a deeper understanding of the materials covered in each course and cultivated the view that sociology is one coherent discipline, not a sum of many disparate fields. Students were able to link different parts of sociological knowledge through their participation in a common project. Teachers, on the other hand, had to shift their role from being the central authority in the classroom to becoming the facilitator of peer learning, and they went beyond the comfort zone of their specialized subfield.

This cross-course collaboration emerged from the necessity to create an institutional space for students to develop study-in-depth without changing the curriculum or other institutional contexts. It inadvertently disrupted the authoritarian and individualistic structure embedded in the traditional method of teaching while demonstrating to students the integrated nature of the discipline. Although logistical challenges are undeniably present, the merits of this innovative pedagogy are worth examining in the future.

Conclusion

Examining the commonly observed pedagogy in sociology and its consequences uncovers a number of issues that need to be addressed. Expert sociologists are very good at conceptualizing, researching, and analyzing reality as socially constructed and constructing an alternative reality logically deduced from the research results. The novice gets introduced to this discipline by learning concepts and facts relevant to specific subfields of sociology, developing specific skills in conducting research, and applying these skills in the relatively safe space, mostly in the classroom. Students learn mainly from standardized textbooks and interactive lectures, and less from other pedagogical strategies that may enhance their learning. Due to the institutional environment that justifies the large class size and provides faculty and the department with fewer resources and incentives to improve teaching quality, students have fewer opportunities to "do" sociology. Additionally, this method of instruction is not unrelated to commonly observed misconceptions about sociology. Students often believe sociological knowledge is an ideological opinion and regard theory and research methods as anxiety-causing "technical" knowledge. These misconceptions unfortunately prevent the novices from engaging with study-in-depth in sociology.

These problems with the traditional method of teaching are in fact central to the concerns addressed in numerous SoTL articles found in *Teaching Sociology.* These articles also provide examples of alternative pedagogies that may constitute signature pedagogies. Particularly prominent are the pedagogical innovations that enable students to examine knowledge, values, and perspectives they bring to the classroom. Various out-of-class activities are also employed to make sociology alive in "real" situations. Although it is important to acknowledge that the traditional method of instruction is embedded in the institutional context of higher education, these non-traditional pedagogies can more effectively promote study-in-depth in sociology.

To assess whether these pedagogical innovations can truly be signature pedagogies in sociology, however, more evidence must be collected through SoTL. For example, what are common attributes among these pedagogical innovations that apparently enable students to engage with study-in-depth? How do the backgrounds of students or the institutional context affect the effectiveness of these pedagogies? As Weiss (2007) maintained, SoTL in sociology is informed by the discipline's rich traditions, including theoretical concerns with social structures, the creative use of multiple methods, and moral and political interests in modern democratic social relations, and thus are capable of dealing with a broad range of questions in a creative manner. Formulating a signature pedagogy that will help students achieve a deeper understanding of the discipline will significantly contribute to the positive change in the teaching and learning of sociology.

References

Albers, B. D.,& Bach, R. (2003). Rockin' soc: Using popular music to introduce sociological concepts. *Teaching Sociology, 31*(2), 237–245.

Ahlkvist, J. A. (2001). Sound and vision: Using progressive rock to teach social theory. *Teaching Sociology, 29*(4), 471–482.

American Sociological Association (ASA). 1999. *Code of ethics and policies and procedures of the ASA committee on professional ethics.* New York: ASA.

Androit, A. L. (2007). A comparative analysis of existing standards for high school sociology curricula. *Teaching Sociology, 35*(1), 17–30.

Armer, J. M. (1987). Provincialism and internationalism in contemporary American sociology. *International Sociology, 2,* 315–324.

Association for American Colleges (AAC). (1985). *Integrity in the college curriculum.* Washington, DC: AAC.

Auster, C. J. (2000). Probability sampling and inferential statistics: An interactive exercise using M&M's. *Teaching Sociology, 28*(4), 379–385.

Backman, C. B. (1992). Life after death: An empirical project in the classical theory course. *Teaching Sociology, 20*(2), 104–113.

Bengston, W. F., & Hazzard, J. W. (1990). The assimilation of sociology into common sense: Some implications for teaching. *Teaching Sociology, 18*(1), 39–45.

Berheide, C. W. (2005). Searching for structure: Creating coherence in the sociology curriculum. *Teaching Sociology, 33*(1), 1–15.

Bluth, B. J. (1975). Teaching theory as a tool for analysis. *Teaching Sociology, 2*(2), 147–164.

Bridges, G. S., Gillmore, G. M., Pershing, J. L., & Bates, K. A. (1998). Teaching quantitative research methods: A quasi-experimental analysis. *Teaching Sociology, 26*(1), 14–28.

Corrado, M., Merenstein, B., Glasberg, D. S., & Peele, M. R. (2000). Playing at work: The intersection of race, class, and gender with power structures of work and production. *Teaching Sociology, 28*(1), 56–66.

Cunningham, D., & Kingma-Kiekhofer, C. (2004). Comparative collective community-based learning: The "Possibilities for Change in American Communities" program. *Teaching Sociology, 32*(3), 276–290.

Davis, N. J. (1992). Teaching about inequality: Student resistance, paralysis, and rage. *Teaching Sociology, 20*(3), 232–238.

DeCesare, M. (2007). Statistics anxiety among sociology majors: A first diagnosis and some treatment options. *Teaching Sociology, 35*(4), 360–367.

Dundes, L., & Spence, B. (2007). If Ida known: The speaker versus the speech in judging black dialect. *Teaching Sociology, 35*(1), 85–93.

Eberts, P., Howery, C. B., Berheide, C. W., Crittenden, K., Davis, R., Gamson, Z., & Wagenaar, T. C. (1990). *Liberal learning and the sociology major.* Washington, DC: AAC.

Flint, W. (1993). Ideological contradiction and the problem of closure in the sociology capstone course. *Teaching Sociology, 21*(3), 254–257.

Fobes, C. (2005). Taking a critical pedagogical look at travel-study abroad: "A Classroom with a View" in Cusco, Peru. *Teaching Sociology, 33*(2), 181–194.

Goldsmith, P. A. (2006). Learning to understand inequality and diversity: Getting students' past ideologies. *Teaching Sociology, 34*(3), 263–277.

Grant, L., Heirich, M., Martin, S. S., & Van Eck, E. (1981). The Detroit tours: Experiential learning within the framework of a large lecture course. *Teaching Sociology, 9*(1), 15–29.

Grauerholz, L., & Bouma-Holtrop, S. (2003). Exploring critical sociological thinking. *Teaching Sociology, 31*(4), 485–496.

Grauerholz, E., & Copenhaver, S. (1994). When the personal becomes problematic: The ethics of using experiential teaching methods. *Teaching Sociology, 22*(4), 319–327.

Grauerholz, L., & Gibson, G. (2006). Articulation of goals and means in sociology courses. *Teaching Sociology, 34*(1), 5–22.

Haddad, A T., & Lieberman, L. (2002). From student resistance to embracing the sociological imagination: Unmasking privilege, social conventions, and racism. *Teaching Sociology, 30*(3), 328–341.

Hale, S. (1995). First-year sociology: The importance of theory. *Teaching Sociology, 23*(1), 48–52.

Hall, K. J. (2000). Putting the pieces together: Using Jane Smiley's *A Thousand Acres* in sociology of families. *Teaching Sociology, 28*(4), 370–378.

Hall, K. J., & Lucal, B. (1999). Tapping into parallel universes: Using superhero comic books in sociology courses. *Teaching Sociology, 27*(1), 60–66.

Halsey, J. (1990). Teaching sociology, in an overseas program: The uses of marginality. *Teaching Sociology, 18*(2), 203–208.

Hare, S. C. (1999). Using e-mail to promote cross-cultural understanding of families. *Teaching Sociology, 27*(1), 67–73.

Hedley, M., & Markowitz, L. (2001). Avoiding moral dichotomies: Teaching controversial topics to resistant students. *Teaching Sociology, 29*(2), 195–208.

Howard, J., & Zoeller, A. (2007). The role of the introductory sociology course on students' perceptions of achievement of general education goals. *Teaching Sociology, 35*(3), 209–222.

Howery, C. B. (2002). The culture of teaching in sociology. In M. T. Taylor & S. P. Morreale (Ed.), *Disciplinary styles in the scholarship in teaching and learning: Exploring common ground* (pp. 143–159). Sterling, VA: Stylus Publishing.

Howery, C. B., and Rodriguez, H. (2006). Integrating data analysis: Working with sociology departments to address the quantitative literacy gap. *Teaching Sociology, 34*(1), 23–38.

Hunter, M. L., & Nettles, K. D. (1999). What about the white women? Racial politics in a women's studies classroom. *Teaching Sociology, 27*(4), 385–397.

Isserles, R., & Dalmage, H. (2000). Cultural capital as rules and resistance: Bringing it home in the introductory classroom. *Teaching Sociology, 28*(2), 160–165.

Jakubowski, L. M., & Burman, P. (2004). Teaching community development: A case study in community-based learning. *Teaching Sociology, 32*(2), 160–176.

Jenkins, R. (1995). Social skills, social research skills: Sociological skills, teaching reflexivity? *Teaching Sociology, 23*(1), 16–27.

Johnson, B. (2005). Overcoming "doom and gloom": Empowering students in courses on social problems, injustice, and inequality. *Teaching Sociology, 33*(1), 44–58.

Johnson, D. E. (2001). Teaching for mastery: Focus on social theory. *Teaching Sociology, 28*(2), 163–180.

Kain, E. L. (1999). Building the sociological imagination through a cumulative curriculum: Professional socialization in sociology. *Teaching Sociology, 27*(1), 1–16.

Kain, E. L. (2006). Bridging the gap between culture of teaching and culture of research. *Teaching Sociology, 34*(4), 325–340.

Kain, E. L., Buchanan, E., & Marck, B. (2001). Institutional research as a context for teaching methodological skills. *Teaching Sociology, 29*(1), 9–22.

Kain, E. L., & D'Andrea, V. (1992). Teaching sociology, in an international setting: Using London as a laboratory. *Teaching Sociology, 20*(1), 1–11.

Keith, B., & Ender, M. G. (2004). The sociological core: Conceptual patterns and idiosyncrasies in the structure and content of introductory sociology textbooks, 1940–2000. *Teaching Sociology, 32*(1), 19–36.

Kubal, T., Meyler, D., Stone, R. T., & Mauney, T. T. (2003). Teaching diversity and learning outcomes: Bringing lived experience into the classroom. *Teaching Sociology, 31*(4), 441–455.

Leming, M. (1990). Prioritizing sociological perspective over concepts. *Teaching Sociology, 18*(4), 533–535.

Lemert, C. (1991). The end of ideology, really. *Sociological Theory, 9*(2), 164–172.

Lessor, R., Reeves, M., & Andrade, E. (1997). Interdisciplinary team teaching on sustainable development in Costa Rica. *Teaching Sociology, 25*(2), 134–149.

Lowney, K. S. (1998). Reducing "theory anxiety" through puzzles. *Teaching Sociology, 26*(1), 69–73.

Magdol, L. (2003). Liberal values and a liberal education: The effect of a family sociology course on undergraduate students' family values. *Teaching Sociology, 31*(1), 95–109.

Markham, W. T. (1991). Research methods in the introductory course: To be or not to be? *Teaching Sociology, 19*(4), 464–471.

Martin, A. (2000). Telling into wholeness. *Teaching Sociology, 28*(1), 1–11.

Martinez, T. (1998). Race and popular culture: Teaching African American leadership styles through popular music. *Teaching Sociology, 26*(3), 207–214.

Mathisen, J. A. (1989). A further look at "common sense" in introductory sociology. *Teaching Sociology, 17*(3), 307–315.

McCammon, L. (1999). Introducing social stratification and inequality: An active learning technique. *Teaching Sociology, 27*(1), 44–54.

McKinney, K. (2005). Sociology senior majors' perceptions on learning sociology: A research note. *Teaching Sociology, 33*(4), 371–379.

McKinney, K., Medvedeva, M. A., Vacca, K., & Malak, J. (2004). Beyond the classroom: An exploratory study of out-of-class learning in sociology. *Teaching Sociology, 32*(1), 43–60.

McKinney, K., & Reed, L. (2007). Profile of an engaged sociology major. *Teaching Sociology, 35*(1), 77–84.

Mills, C. W. (1959). *The sociological imagination.* New York: Oxford University Press.

Misra, J. (2000). Integrating "the real world" into introduction to sociology: Making sociological concepts. *Teaching Sociology, 28*(4), 346–363.

Mobley, C. (2007). Breaking ground: Engaging undergraduates in social change through service learning. *Teaching Sociology, 35*(2), 125–137.

Moore, M. (1997). Student resistance to course content: Reactions to the gender of the messenger. *Teaching Sociology, 25*(2), 128–133.

Moran, T. P. (1999). Versifying your reading list: Using poetry to teach inequality. *Teaching Sociology, 27*(2), 110–125.

Moulder, F. V. (1997). Teaching about race and ethnicity: A message of despair or a message of hope? *Teaching Sociology, 25*(2), 120–127.

Netting, N. S. (1994). Can an individual change society? Empowering students in a context of social reality. *Teaching Sociology, 22*(2), 200–203.

Obach, B. K. (2000). Teaching about institutional discrimination and the controversies of affirmative action. *Teaching Sociology, 28*(1), 50–55.

O'Brien, E., & Foley, L. (1999). The dating game: An exercise illustrating the concepts of homogamy, heterogamy, hyperogamy, and hypogamy. *Teaching Sociology, 27*(2), 145–149.

Pence, D. J., & Fields, J. A. (1999). Teaching about race and ethnicity: Trying to uncover white privilege for a white audience. *Teaching Sociology, 27*(2), 150–158.

Persell, C. H. (2004). Using focused web-based discussions to enhance student engagement and deep understanding. *Teaching Sociology, 32*(1), 61–78.

Persell, C. H., Pfeiffer, K. M., & Syed, A. (2007). What should students understand after taking introduction to sociology? *Teaching Sociology, 35*(4), 300–314.

Potter, S. J., Caffrey, E. M., & Plante, E. G. (2003). Integrating service learning into the research methods course. *Teaching Sociology, 31*(1), 38–48.

Rajaram, S. S. (2007). An action-research project: Community lead poisoning prevention. *Teaching Sociology, 35*(2), 138–150.

Rau, W., & Heyl, B. S. (1990). Humanizing the college classroom: Collaborative learning and social organization among students. *Teaching Sociology, 18*(2), 141–155.

Rinehart, J. A. (1999). Turning theory into theorizing: Collaborative learning in a sociological theory course. *Teaching Sociology, 27*(3), 216–232.

Roberts, A., & Smith, K. I. (2002). Managing emotions in the college classroom: The cultural diversity course as an example. *Teaching Sociology, 30*(3), 291–301.

Roberts, K. A. (2002). Ironies of effective teaching: Deep structure learning and constructions of the classroom. *Teaching Sociology, 30*(1), 1–25.

Rosenbloom, S. R., & Fetner, T. (2001). Sharing secrets slowly: Issues of classroom self-disclosure raised by student sex workers. *Teaching Sociology, 29*(4), 439–453.

Scanlan, S. J., & Feinberg, S. L. (2000). The cartoon society: Using "The Simpsons" to teach and learn sociology. *Teaching Sociology, 28*(2), 127–139.

Schmid, T. J., & Buechler, S. M. (1991). Crossing boundaries: Sociology in the wilderness. *Teaching Sociology, 19*(1), 34–41.

Schumm, W. R., Webb, F. J., Castelo, C. S., Akagi, C. G., Jensen, E. J., Ditto, R. M., Spencer-Carver, E., & Brown, B. F. (2002). Enhancing learning in statistics classes though the use of concrete historical examples: The Space Shuttle *Challenger*, Pearl Harbor, and the *RMS Titanic*. *Teaching Sociology, 30*(3), 361–375.

Silver, I., & Perez, G. (1998). Teaching social theory through students' participant-observation. *Teaching Sociology, 26*(4), 347–353.

Singleton, R. A. (2007). The campus survey: Integrating pedagogy, scholarship, and evaluation. *Teaching Sociology, 35*(1), 48–61.

Sweet, S. (1998). Practicing radical pedagogy: Balancing ideals with institutional constraints. *Teaching Sociology, 26*(2), 100–111.

Tan, J., & Ko, Y. (2004). Using feature films to teach observation in undergraduate research methods. *Teaching Sociology, 32*(1), 109–118.

Thompson, J. (1996). "The between" of teaching sociology: Ways of knowing and teaching. *Teaching Sociology, 24*(3), 321–326.

Volk, R. W., & Beeman, M. (1998). Revisiting "The Eye of the Storm": The subtleties of gender bias. *Teaching Sociology, 26*(1), 38–48.

Wagenaar, T. C. (1991). Goals for the discipline? *Teaching Sociology, 19*(1), 92–95.

Wagenaar, T. C. (1993). Study in depth: Sociology versus other disciplines. *Teaching Sociology, 21*(4), 352–362.

Wagenaar, T. C., & Subedi, J. (1996). Internationalizing the curriculum: Study in Nepal. *Teaching Sociology, 24*(3), 272–283.

Waltermaurer, E., & Obach, B. (2007). Cross course collaboration in undergraduate programs. *Teaching Sociology, 35*(2), 151–160.

Weiss, G. L. (2007). A pedagogical boomerang: From Hans Mauksch to medicine to the teaching and learning of sociology. *Teaching Sociology, 35*(1), 1–16.

Wills, J. B., Brewster, Z. W., and Fulkerson, G. M. (2005). The stratification puzzle: An active-learning exercise in hard work and success. *Teaching Sociology, 33*(4), 389–395.

Wright, M. C. (2000). Getting more out of less: The benefits of short-term experiential learning in undergraduate sociology courses. *Teaching Sociology, 28*(2), 116–126.

Wright, M. C., Howery, C. B., Assar, N., McKinney, K., Kain, E. L., Glass, B., et al., (2004). Greedy institutions: The importance of institutional context for teaching in higher education. *Teaching Sociology, 32*(2), 144–159.

Wybraniec, J., & Wilmoth, J. (1999). Teaching students inferential statistics: A "tail" of three distributions. *Teaching Sociology, 27*(1), 74–80.

Notes

1. The Web site for the American Sociological Association (ASA) lists 44 sections as subfields (as of January 2008).

2. Other goals may include learning the course-specific concepts/theories/methods, the humanization of social relations (Sweet, 1998), and such liberal arts goals as written and oral communication skills and information and quantitative literacy (Wagenaar, 1991; McKinney, Medvedeva, Vacca, & Malak, 2004; Grauerholz & Gibson, 2006; Persell, Pfeiffer, & Syed, 2007).

3. According to Berheide (2005), when the ASA Project on Teaching Undergraduate Sociology started, its focus was on curriculum, teacher preparation and faculty development, and the institutional context of teaching. Little critical assessment was done on the impact of the faculty-driven curriculum and a laissez-faire decision-making process about students' learning among the faculty. It was in the mid-1980s that the centrality of students' learning began to penetrate the scholarship on teaching and learning in sociology.

SECTION FOUR

NATURAL SCIENCES AND MATHEMATICS

11

SIGNATURE PEDAGOGY IN AGRICULTURE

Animal and Dairy Sciences

Michel A. Wattiaux

Good teaching is hard to characterize, but Parker Palmer describes it as weaving a fabric of connectedness between the student, the teacher, and the subject matter (Palmer, 1998). Similarly, signature pedagogy (Shulman, 2005) is hard to characterize; but it reveals the patterns of an educational quilt that stitches together the various habits of mind of a discipline. In this chapter, I will describe pieces of the agricultural sciences teaching and learning quilt, beginning with an analysis of the enduring patterns within the discipline throughout the 20th century. This historical perspective allows us to identify the distinctive features, values, and manner of thinking of an agriculturalist. For the last 100 years, our graduating students have been not only specialists within a scientific discipline, but also individuals who have learned professional skills considered the core of successful farming: self-reliance, problem-solving, decision-making, and leadership. A short analysis of two distinct learning opportunities fairly unique to the agricultural disciplines—the judging contest and the capstone course—will help illustrate our signature pedagogy. Although the former epitomizes the predominant pedagogy of the 20th century, the latter embodies a vision more appropriate for the 21st century. In this vision, our classrooms provide genuine learning experiences in which instructors and students are fully engaged in decision making and real-world problem solving guided by sound scientific, business, and ethical principles.

A Historical Perspective

The unique historical identity of colleges, professional schools, and departments provides a context for the learning that occurs within a classroom. Higher education in agriculture has its roots in the land-grant colleges and experimental research stations created and supported by Acts of Congress passed in the late 19th and early 20th century. The welfare of our rapidly expanding nation depended in part on agriculture for economic growth and rural development. Scientific research, technological development, and the training and education of approximately six million farmers were important to the nation's food supply at the dawn of the 20th century (ERS, 2000). The mission of the agricultural sciences has always been to discover how to grow crops and manage farm animals in order to produce enough high quality food and fiber (e.g., wool) to satisfy the needs of an ever-growing population. For more than a century, agronomists and animal scientists have been unlocking the laws of nature that govern crop yield and animal (dairy, beef, and poultry) growth and development. Over the years we have seen astonishing successes of research, education, and community outreach in animal sciences (egg and meat production), dairy science (milk production), and closely related disciplines (agronomy, soil science, agricultural engineering, etc.). The collective impact of agricultural sciences on national prosperity has been undeniable. In the 1930s, one U.S. farmer produced food for 10 individuals, but in the 1990s, one farmer produced food for more than 100 (USDA, 2005).

The proper interplay among research, teaching, and extension activities has been essential to the success of land grant colleges; nevertheless some have argued that undergraduate teaching has been neglected since its inception. Fifty years ago, Washburn looked back at the first 50 years of recorded history in animal sciences and argued that "Teaching in general, however, has been treated as an orphan—being always considered secondary to research and other departmental activities" (Washburn, 1958, p. 1117). Nonetheless, early agricultural teachers had a broad view of their teaching mission. They saw higher education in agriculture as "a liberal education insofar as it liberalizes the mind, disciplines the conduct, refines manners, broadens aesthetic interests, and strengthens the capacity for happiness, efficiency, and social service" (Ruth, 1935, p. 158). Although practical hands-on courses such as evaluation of crops and livestock, for example, had been an integral part of the curriculum, instructors hoped to teach more science-based courses. Students' aptitudes, attitudes, and interpersonal skills were also recognized early as important components of an agricultural education (Rice, 1945). In essence, our teaching forefathers were training young men in a set of core values deemed necessary to the success of family farming, such as independent thinking, self-reliance, and decision making, or as Wentworth (1933) put it, "graduates who can create their own niches in the world" (p. 248).

The changing student population and the expanding career opportunities available to the graduates of four-year programs have substantially impacted the pedagogical landscape of agricultural sciences throughout the 20th century. The typical student of the first half of the 20th century was a male Caucasian who grew up on a farm and looked forward to returning to the farm or finding work as a public servant in an educational or governmental position after graduation (Washburn, 1958). In contrast, by the end of the century, women composed the majority of agricultural students, and one-third of dairy science majors (Kensinger & Muller, 2006) and two-thirds of the animal science majors had either no or limited farm background (Taylor & Kauffman, 1983). Since the early 1960s, it has been necessary to add flexibility to the curriculum in order to address the needs of this increasingly diverse student population and their changing career paths. Interestingly, the lack of first-hand agricultural experience in our current student population has provoked a resurgence in the demand for practical and hands-on courses (Kensinger & Muller, 2006). Today, students have innumerable options to choose from in preparing for futures that may include graduate school or veterinary school, careers in agricultural production (i.e., farming), sales and services, communication, marketing, finances, or business consulting with the allied industries (seed, feed, equipment, processing, etc.). Given the extent to which agricultural sciences prepare students for a farming-related profession, the discipline is not unlike the other professions, such as medicine and law, that have clear, well-established signature pedagogies on which Shulman based his article (Shulman, 2005).

Scholarship of Teaching and Learning in Agricultural Sciences

Not only were early agricultural educators aware of the value of inquiry in teaching and learning, but their analysis of the generally accepted attitude toward teaching is as true today as it was then. For example, as early as 1935, Ruth criticized the disparity in the way scientists engaged in research, compared to their mindset toward teaching: "Teachers of science accept in education what is done traditionally, although they experiment continually in their own fields in the hope of contributing to change" (pp. 154–155). The author, however, acknowledged that "participation in educational study by an agricultural college staff will probably never be as thorough and profitable as it might well be, because of the time that is required in reading and reflection outside the field of primary interest" (Ruth, 1935, p. 154). The lower status of teaching relative to research in many institutions has continued to frustrate committed educators since the early days. In 1931, King articulated the tension between teaching and research in stark language when he wrote, "A servant can not well serve two Masters" (p. 262). For his part, Helser (1933) was highly critical of instructors who "feel that the student is someone to be tolerated while investigation work is being done, papers prepared, speeches made and outside meetings attended" (p. 258). Unfortunately, many in the 1950s construed good teaching as merely sifting through research findings and incorporating the most important ones into courses (Davis, 1956). By then, the hands-on and practical courses (such as the judging courses) that characterized the pedagogy of the first part of the 20th century had been gradually superseded by lecture courses aimed at teaching scientific facts. As the original teaching mission was being lost, if not abandoned, some attempted to find conciliatory approaches. For example, Kauffman, Shrode, Sutherland, and Taylor (1984) saw scientific discoveries as exciting and liberating truths that enthusiastic instructors strongly desire to communicate clearly to students. Although laudable and still embraced by many today, this approach falls short of the original goals set forth by our forefathers in which students specialize in a discipline and gain a set of values and dispositions core to agricultural professions.

In the early 1980s, Taylor and Kauffman (1983) published a 75-year review of the teaching literature in animal sciences and put forth both groundbreaking and astounding conclusions. First, these authors concluded that educators of the 1980s were "reinventing the wheel" (p. 172), as what was considered new in teaching and learning had been registered in the literature more than five decades earlier. They also identified the "fine screens of reviewers" (p. 173) as the main reason for the paucity of teaching-related papers published between 1930 and 1980, and asked whether it would not have been unforgivable had the same review process prevented teaching-related publications of the earlier years.

In spite of the continued difficulty in publishing results of inquiries in one's own teaching in discipline-based journals, some dedicated educators have shared their cumulative years of experiences in the form of memoirs (Kauffman, Shrode, et al., 1984; Lasley, 1979; Simmons, 2004). As years of practices are reflected upon, those memoirs may constitute a form of important disciplinary history, if not a form of scholarship of its own right (Weimer, 2006). Remarkably, some have searched for "truth" in their teaching. Reflecting on his career, Simmons (2004) wrote, "Perhaps the one imperishable attitude, above all others, that has informed my practice as a teacher and learner has been my desire to recognize and hold fast to that which is genuine—to that which is 'real'" (p. 153). The sharing of such insights as well as more formal inquiries should be encouraged.

In addition to reflections and memoirs, existing scholarship in agricultural sciences focuses on curriculum assessment, including new course descriptions and other teaching improvement initiatives. Unfortunately, there are few formalized assessments of student learning or methodological tests of the effectiveness of teaching innovations. Most of this literature is published in two peer-reviewed journals: *The NACTA Journal*, published by the North American Colleges and Teachers of Agriculture (http://www.nactateachers.org/), and *The Journal of Natural Resources and Life Science Education*, published by a coalition of nine cooperating professional societies (http://www.jnrlse.org/about.html).

Disciplinary Values and Habits of Mind

Despite apparent changes in educational goals throughout its history and limited documentation of recorded scholarship, higher education in agricultural science has a unique pedagogy. Agricultural science programs are designed foremost to provide students with a learning environment in which they gain the knowledge, understanding, and leadership skills required to manage complex biological, economic, and social systems (i.e., a farm or any part of it), and thus make decisions and solve real-world problems. This superordinate goal was true throughout the 20th century and will remain true in the decades to come, in spite of the ever-growing career paths within the discipline. Indeed, regardless of one's college degree, the credibility of a professional in the agricultural world and closely allied industries is often dependent upon a deep-rooted and personal experience with the animals, the land, or the reality of daily life on a farm.

Farming was, is, and will remain a high-risk business. Farmers make decisions in the face of many uncertainties on a daily basis. They tend to be conservative individuals who take calculated risks. Not only are their livestock, crops, and markets unpredictable, but even the weather may have profound influences on their business. Thus, although the curriculum has emphasized efficiency and economical means of production since the early days (Kildee, 1925), our forefathers believed in a curriculum which would help students become decision makers and problem solvers. In 1935, Ruth wrote "Problem solving is the concrete expression of the purpose of education" (p. 162), but the author also stated that "Solving new situations by the judicious application of facts is not a natural habit" (p. 163). The emphasis on higher-level thinking skills (analysis, synthesis, and evaluation) as described by Bloom (1956) and the application of these skills in the professional training of students have been consistent educational goals throughout the past century in animal sciences (Grant, Field, Green, & Rollin, 2000), dairy science (Kensinger & Muller, 2006), and agronomy (Graveel & Vorst, 2007). Oral and written communication, leadership, and life-long learning skills have also been incorporated in most agricultural science curriculum throughout the country. These skills and dispositions characterize successful farmers, who often are not only role models but also leaders in their communities. Thus, the general goals of an undergraduate education in agricultural sciences have been fairly well defined since the early parts of the 20th century. How to reach these goals, however, has been matter of continual debate, tension, and frustration.

Teaching in Agricultural Sciences in the 20th Century

For any classroom instructor, the design of an environment conducive to deep understanding is an extremely complex process. Such environment must draw on the instructor's expertise in both content knowledge and pedagogical knowledge (i.e., the knowledge of how to teach). The union of content knowledge and pedagogical knowledge leads to pedagogical content knowledge (PCK), which has been recognized recently as a central element of scholarship of teaching (Paulsen, 2001) and as a point of differentiation between an excellent teacher and a scholar (Kreber, 2002). The need for PCK in agricultural sciences was expressed as early as in 1925, when McCampbell wrote, "Animal husbandry instructors as a whole are poor teachers. . . . They have had little or no training in the fundamentals underlying the science of teaching, and therefore do not know how to teach even though they may know well the subject matter they are called upon to present in the classroom" (McCampbell, 1925, p. 67).

Also, early animal science educators believed in the importance of students' attitudes in the teaching and learning process. Gay (1933) argued that masters of subject matter have failed as teachers in many instances in part because of their neglect of the learner: "Attitude of mind of the student is paramount to successful teaching and the first step essential to success on the part of the teacher is to create the proper attitude of mind in the student" (p. 254). Similarly, reflecting on his teaching career, Simmons (2004) acknowledged that "One of the largest errors of educators in agriculture is to presume that our students are 'blank slates' and have no prior conception or understanding of the subject matter" (p. 151). Even students with no direct agricultural background hold assumptions regarding the subject matter we teach. An ideal teaching and learning process will measure and address those preconceptions or misconceptions first.

Failure to account for students' beliefs and aspirations and overemphasis on content knowledge at the expense of PCK often translates into preoccupation for "what" to teach and ignoring "how" to teach. Agricultural science students should learn how to challenge their own knowledge, yet as pointed by Schillo (1997), teaching scientific facts in a teacher-centered classroom often amounts to indoctrination rather than education. Furthermore, teachers should differentiate between the organization of the knowledge as they communicate with disciplinary colleagues, and the organization of the knowledge in a class for the purpose of student learning. Educational scientists have provided evidence for the "expert blind spot" as an impediment to effective teaching. Teachers with advance subject-matter knowledge are blinded by their own use of powerful organizing principles and methods of analysis as guiding principles for their students' conceptual development. Instead, successful teachers rely on knowledge-scaffolding, which is central to the learning process of student novices (Nathan & Petrosino, 2003). This research demonstrates that teachers who are interested in helping students gain a deep understanding of a subject matter should deemphasize linear coverage and instead lead students toward making connections and thus gaining an increasingly sophisticated view of the issues of the discipline.

In 1971, Kauffman and colleagues highlighted the work of Bloom (1956) to argue that educational experience of animal science students should include the cognitive domain, the affective domain (interest, attitudes, and values), and the psychomotor domain (manipulations requiring neuromuscular coordination). Others have highlighted the linkage between emotions and cognition (Palmer, cited in Wattiaux, 2000). Teaching facts out of context rarely stimulates students' interest; therefore, individual research projects, individual and group laboratory projects, student travel and field trips, and intra- and inter-collegiate competitions have been proposed as means to engage students more fully in the learning process (Kauffman, Thompson, Anderson, & Smith, 1971). Today, this list can be expanded easily to include computer laboratories or discussions of case-studies, pre-assigned web postings, or other forms of content-rich multimedia material. Lasley (1979) suggested that students should be trained to ask questions rather than focus on answers. One could go a step further by challenging students to formulate hypotheses and evaluate evidences to support or reject answers to their own questions. Schillo (1997) advocates a teaching approach that engages animal science students in independent thinking and analytical skills about the scientific process itself. He argues that critical thinking skills can be achieved only if the uncertainty of scientific activity is acknowledged. These inquiry-based approaches can be time-consuming and difficult to manage in the classroom. Nevertheless, the habit of questioning and knowing how to evaluate scientific or other claims should be considered a critical aspect of any undergraduate degree in agricultural sciences.

In a recent study, Wattiaux and Crump (2006) described students' perception of the learning environment as the classroom instruction method transitioned from lecture to discussion of pre-assigned reading material. The Student Assessment of Learning Gains (SALG; Seymour, 1997) was modified and administered in three consecutive years, three weeks after the beginning of the semester and again at the end of the semester. These authors found that students who had a high interest in the subject matter perceived higher levels of learning gains with discussion and were strongly opposed to returning to a lecture mode of instruction. However, the opposite was true for students who had a lower interest in the subject matter. Although attempts to understand student motivation in our classes should be encouraged, there are limits to what could be and should be expected in terms of making a subject matter "interesting" to the students. Motivation is rooted in prior education, life events, socio-economic background, and a host of other factors determining the image of the self and potential for intellectual achievement (Dweck & Light, 1980). Nonetheless, instructors should be encouraged to incorporate multiple feedback mechanisms to monitor classroom dynamics. As each cohort of students is unique, the same class activity conducted for two consecutive semesters can lead to drastically different outcomes (Wattiaux & Crump, 2006). Used properly, formative assessments are powerful class management tools. They ought to be designed and used to improve the learning experience, to validate what appears to be working successfully, or to highlight what needs to be reconsidered. Classroom assessment techniques (Angelo & Cross, 1993), which can be used as formative assessment tools, are now available on numerous web sites (e.g., http://www.flaguide.org/cat/cat.php).

Unfortunately, our teaching methods have remained more structured around the limitations and constraints of the instructors rather than aligned with the discipline's genuine educational goals. In a recent Internet survey conducted among registrants of the annual joint meeting of the American Society of Animal Sciences (ASAS) and the American Dairy Science Association (ADSA), respondents were asked to choose one of the courses they had recently taught and to describe activities they used in their teaching. Results included 58 respondents from 38 institutions. The activities and their frequency were as follows: (a) lecturing, 100%; (b) discussion, 47%; (c) student presentations of class project, 41%; (d) individual or group activities (e.g., solving problem set), 64%; (e) computer lab, 21%; and (f) other, 12% (Wattiaux & Moore, unpublished). Although instructors appear to be using a variety of class activities to engage students more effectively, the heavy reliance on lecture may reflect a continued focus on delivering scientific facts.

Designing agricultural science classes to encourage critical thinking is challenging, and a review of the judging courses may be warranted. Judging has been omnipresent in the curricula of dairy science (Guthrie & Majeskie, 1997), animal sciences (Davis, Miller, Allen, & Dunn, 1991), agronomy (Elling, 1981), and soil science (Ponte & Carter, 2000) for most of the 20th century. These courses dominated the curricula in the early parts of the 20th century and thus had been a mainstay of agricultural education well before the science lecture course existed. Although they are now offered primarily as electives or extracurricular activities, they carry an important legacy. Judging provides students with the opportunity to compete individually or as a team to evaluate a series of specimens by identifying traits or characteristics deemed important, ideal, or most desirable by experts. For example, dairy cattle judging consists of ranking classes (i.e., groups) of four cows or heifers based on visual observation of body conformation relative to a breed-specific ideal (as agreed upon by a Breeders Association). Such an exercise demands not only the knowledge of the desirable traits, but also calls upon a higher level of knowledge to compare, evaluate, and judge the phenotypic value of an animal relative to another. After ranking the animals, contestants orally present the reasoning behind their classification to an expert judge. Winners are those who rank the animals correctly and demonstrate polished oral communication skills. Students who excel in these contests typically move on, under the tutelage of a coach, to regional and national intercollegiate contests. The ambivalence among educators in regard to the role and value of judging contests as an extracurricular activity was highlighted recently when Kensinger and Muller (2006) found that, despite the fact that dairy judging was the lowest-ranked of 16 skills or experiences deemed important by faculty, 80% of the institutions that responded to a survey had a dairy judging team. Judging contests have long been a recruitment tool (Washburn, 1958), and they remain a powerful way to generate interest in the profession prior to college (Schwanke, 1997).

Early authors deplored what they saw as an overemphasis of judging contests (Gay, 1938), but others have later recognized their value as a way to help students bridge their interest in practical, real-world experiences with a more fundamental understanding of their scientific discipline (Kauffman, Thompson, Anderson, & Smith, 1971). Although few studies have been conducted to evaluate the impact of competitive judging on learning critical life skills, some authors have attempted to investigate this question. For example, Guthrie and Majeskie (1997) have argued that judging contests contribute to critical thinking, self-discipline, situation analysis, decision making, verbal expression, and defense of decisions. Others have suggested that the sharpening of a variety of skills in contestants may contribute to recognition in their respective circles and successful careers (Elling, 1981). The long-term social networking is a definite benefit, but the competitive nature of the event and the restricted number of beneficiaries are two major limitations. Although they are still dear to many students and the farming community, judging contests have remained of limited benefit to a science-based education. Nevertheless, teaching and learning how to judge have served to nurture critical values and professional attitudes considered most desirable in the agricultural world throughout the 20th century, and the contests should be recognized as an important part of the history of agricultural sciences, even embodying some elements of a signature pedagogy for the discipline at the time.

A Vision for the Future: Toward a Signature Pedagogy of Agriculture

As the 21st century unfolds, higher education in agricultural sciences must be transformed profoundly to respond to the ever-increasing complexity of food production systems (Meyer, 1993) and an increasingly diverse student population (Gomes, 1998). Our classrooms ought to become microcosms of societal changes, and our students must be challenged to face problems in the same way as they will encounter them in the workforce. Today, curricula in colleges of agriculture and life sciences are being expanded far beyond agricultural production, to include biotechnology, animal welfare, environmental pollution, international trade, hunger and poverty, social justice, and other issues. It is no longer sufficient to teach only scientific facts and figures. We must help our students learn how the scientific method, as a human endeavor, can contribute to solving complex and global issues. To do so, our students must have first-hand opportunities to apply their nascent scientific expertise to real-world situations. Providing them with capstone experiences will be essential to our future pedagogy. As proposed here, a capstone experience is defined as an experiential learning opportunity whereby a student is called upon to apply critical scientific thinking to a real-world problem (Crunkilton, Cepica, & Fluker, 1997). However, properly structured independent studies, internships, service learning, summer research projects, study abroad, and other international programs can also provide students with a capstone experience.

This emerging signature pedagogy in 21st-century agricultural sciences faces a few challenges. For instance, neither the students nor the instructors may be aware of these opportunities (Wattiaux, 2006) and their full potential benefits. Additionally, many independent learning opportunities as currently configured are ill-conceived and do not result in a capstone experience for the student. For example, internships have been traditionally approached as opportunities for juniors and seniors to explore possible careers while gaining work experience. Instead, they should be viewed as an integral component of a student's educational experience (Kensinger & Muller, 2006). As another example, study abroad programs are often perceived as contributing to a student's personal growth and world vision, rather than a unique opportunity to gain expertise in academically important domains (Lukefahr, 1999; McKenna, 1991).

Despite the challenges, many traditional classroom courses have been designed to provide capstone experiences, and capstone courses are now prevalent among all disciplines of agriculture across the nation (Andreasen, 2004). They present students with opportunities to apply their knowledge of the subject matter learned in seemingly unconnected or disjointedly organized classes, and to integrate new information into their knowledge base to solve real-world problems. Typically, farms or businesses are partners in a capstone course. For example, in the current Farm Management Practicum course offered by the University of Wisconsin, Madison, dairy science program, students are placed in teams and called upon to act as consultants to a dairy farm. Students may travel to their assigned farm multiple times during a semester to discuss management issues with the owner or operator and to collect data and possibly samples for laboratory analysis. Back on campus, students complete a thorough analysis of multiple sources of information, including material learned in nutrition, breeding, reproduction, and other specialized courses, to identify current limitations in the management of the farm. By the end of the semester, students propose economically sound solutions to problems they have identified or changes to management that may be helpful to the business.

Carefully designed capstone courses that include experiential and contextualized learning are effective for calling upon students' higher levels of thinking. Andreasen and Trede (2000) have investigated the perceived benefits of a capstone course relative to other courses in the curriculum and cautioned that to be a truly summative educational experience for the student, the capstone course must be rooted in experiential learning, especially hands-on participation (Andreasen, 2004). Thus capstone courses provide students with the opportunity to create a coherent understanding of how to use science-based facts to improve the management of a complex system. Pedagogically, capstone courses have other undeniable educational benefits. First, they help diffuse the longstanding tension in the curriculum between the "how" (applied courses most desired by many students) and the "why" (science-based courses most desired by many faculty). Second, they help students confront their preconceptions or misconceptions of how science can be used to solve real-world problems. Third, they engage students in a discovery process that borrows heavily from the scientific method. Fourth, they create a learning environment in which neither the student nor the teacher has full control of the process, but both are committed to constructive and positive outcomes. Fifth, they convey credibility and validate the students' training as managers of complex systems. And sixth, they extend the boundaries of academia to the real world for every participating student. Interestingly, a consortia of agribusinesses has taken an interest in sponsoring a yearly dairy science capstone spin-off event organized as a three-day intercollegiate competition in which teams of students from around the country assess dairy farm management (Weber Nielsen, Domecq, Davis, Beede, Budine, & Martsolf, 2003).

The capstone course and other properly constructed capstone experiences provide unique opportunities for both the student and the teacher to appreciate the complexity of the real-world problems, to solve them with science-based knowledge, and to create a dynamic of common purpose. However, this learning environment should not be restricted to a one-semester course in the senior year: instructors should rethink the nature of the teaching and learning process, and in-class activities should be redesigned to provide students with capstone-like experiences. Similarly, entire curricula should be redesigned with the same goal in mind. The weaving of capstone-like experiences in class, out of class, and throughout the curriculum may provide a foundation for a long-term vision. However, for the time being, capstone courses exemplify a model of signature pedagogy for agricultural sciences education in the 21st century in part because the ways students learn in these courses model how they are expected to carry their college education into their future agricultural-related profession.

In Conclusion

The history of higher education in agricultural sciences is rooted in the spirit of independent, hard-working, innovative, and self-reliant settlers whose success depended on their ability to manage complex production systems. As scientific discoveries, technological advances, and the industrialization of agriculture proceeded at a mind-boggling pace throughout the 20th century, undergraduate programs have been reconsidered and redesigned to accommodate new career paths, new student demographics, and the changing role of agricultural education. However, the training of independent thinkers and leaders who can make decisions in the presence of numerous uncertainties does not always occur in higher education in agriculture, perhaps because these lofty goals were never enshrined in national standards or endorsed by any professional organization. Left to the discretion of faculty and individual instructors whose priorities are often elsewhere, decisions of what to teach and how to teach have been heavily teacher-centered and influenced by the desire for efficient "transfer" of scientific facts ("truth"). Unfortunately, trials and errors continue to trump systematic inquiry to improve student learning in our classes. The small minority of agricultural scientists who have engaged in the scholarship of teaching and learning are not only role models but also pioneers. In a sense, they emulate the fundamental values of their own teaching. These pioneers are independent, hard-working, innovative, and self-reliant individuals whose success as instructors depends on the ability to use a science-based approach to manage a complex system: the class they teach.

References

Andreasen, R. J. (2004). Integrating experiential learning into College of Agriculture capstone courses: Implications and applications for practitioners. *NACTA Journal, 48*(1), 52–57.

Andreasen, R. J., & Trede, L. D. (2000). Perceived benefits of an agricultural capstone course at Iowa State University. *NACTA Journal, 44*(1), 51–56.

Angelo, T. A., & Cross, K. P. (1993). *Classroom assessment techniques: A handbook for college teachers* (2nd ed.). San Francisco: Jossey-Bass.

Bloom, B. S. (1956). *Taxonomy of educational objectives. Handbook I: Cognitive domain.* New York: David McKay Co.

Crunkilton, J. R., Cepica, M. J., & Fluker, P. L. (1997). Portfolio of capstone courses in colleges of agriculture. USDA award# 94-38411-016. Washington, DC: U.S. Department of Agriculture.

Davis, G. W., Miller, M. F., Allen, D. M., & Dunn. K. L. (1991). An assessment of intercollegiate meat judging from 1926 to 1989. *NACTA Journal, 35*(4), 28–31.

Davis, H. P. (1956). Fifty years of progress in dairy production teaching. *Journal of Dairy Science, 39*(6), 795–799.

Dweck, C. S., & Light, B. G. (1980). Learned helplessness and intellectual achievement. In J. Garber & M. E. P. Seligman (Eds.), *Human helplessness.* New York: Academic Press.

Elling, L. J. (1981). The intercollegiate crops contest—1923–1978. *Journal of Agronomic Education, 10*, 5–13.

Economic Research Service (ERS). (2000). Growing a nation: The story of American agriculture. Retrieved April 2, 2008, from http://www.agclassroom.org/gan/timeline/index.htm

Gay, C. W. (1933). Effective methods of teaching animal husbandry. *The American Society of Animal Production, 1933*(1), 253–258.

Gay, C. W. (1938). The animal husbandry curriculum. *The American Society of Animal Production, 1938*(1), 169–175.

Gomes, W. R. (1998). Agricultural sciences and education in the 21st century. *Journal of Animal Sciences, 76*(12), 2991–2994.

Grant, P. M., Field, T. G., Green, R. D., & Rollin, B. E. (2000). The importance of comprehensive agricultural education in land-grant institutions: a historical perspective. *Journal of Animal Sciences, 78*(6), 1684–1689.

Graveel, J. G., & Vorst, J. J. (2007). Using alumni input as a reality check of agronomy teaching and advising. *Journal of Natural Resources and Life Sciences Education, 36*, 87–94.

Guthrie, L. D., & Majeskie, J. L. (1997). Dairy cattle judging teaches critical life skills. *Journal of Dairy Science, 80*(8), 1884–1887.

Helser, M. D. (1933). Effective methods of teaching animal husbandry. *The American Society of Animal Production, 1933*(1), 258–262.

Kauffman, R. G., Shrode, R. R., Sutherland, T. M., & Taylor, R. E. (1984). Philosophies of teaching and approaches to teaching. *Journal of Animal Sciences, 59*(2), 542–546.

Kauffman, R. G., Thompson, J. F., Anderson, D. B., & Smith, R. E. (1971). Improving the effectiveness of teaching animal science. *Journal of Animal Sciences, 32*(1), 161–164.

Kensinger, R. S., & Muller, L. D. (2006). Major advances in teaching dairy production. *Journal of Dairy Science, 89*(4), 1155–1162.

Kildee, H. H. (1925). Planning the animal husbandry curriculum. *The American Society of Animal Production, 1925*(1), 63–67.

King, F. G. (1931). Harmonizing teaching with research work. *The American Society of Animal Production, 1931*(1), 260–263.

Kreber, C. (2002). Teaching excellence, teaching expertise, and the scholarship of teaching. *Innovative Higher Education, 27*(1), 5–23.

Lasley, J. F. (1979). My successes and failures in teaching students on campus. *Journal of Animal Sciences*, 48(3), 711–714.

Lukefahr, S. D. (1999). Teaching international animal agriculture. *Journal of Animal Sciences, 77*(11), 3106–3113.

McCampbell, C. W. (1925). Teaching animal husbandry courses. *The American Society of Animal Production, 1925*(1), 67–70.

McKenna, J. R. (1991). Addition of an international option to an undergraduate agronomy program. *NACTA Journal, 35*(1), 14–17.

Meyer, J. H. (1993, May 14). The stalemate in food an agricultural research, teaching, and extension. Science *260*(5110), 881+1007.

Nathan, M. J., & Petrosino, A. (2003). Expert blind spot among preservice teachers. *American Educational Research Journal, 40*(4), 905–928.

Paulsen, M. B. (2001). The relation between research and the scholarship of teaching. *New Directions for Teaching and Learning, 86*, 19–30.

Ponte, K. J., & Carter, B. J. (2000). Evaluating and improving soil judging contests based on a selected proficiency level. *Journal of Natural Resources and Life Sciences Education, 29*, 8–14.

Rice, V. A. (1945). Evaluating the animal husbandry student. *Journal of Animal Sciences, 4*, 453–462.

Ruth, W. A. (1935). Suggested courses for students of animal husbandry. *The American Society of Animal Production, 1935*(1), 154–164.

Schillo, K. K. (1997). Teaching animal science: education or indoctrination? *Journal of Animal Sciences, 75*(4), 950–953.

Schwanke, C. A. (1997). Dairy youth programming: Where we've been, and where we go from here. *Journal of Dairy Science, 80*(8), 1880–1883.

Seymour, E. (1997). Student assessment of learning gain. Instrument description. Retrieved July 11, 2008, from http://www.salgsite.org

Shulman, L. S. (2005). Signature pedagogies in the professions. *Daedalus 134*(3), 52–59.

Simmons, S. R. (2004). "An imperishable attitude": A memoir of learning and teaching. *Journal of Natural Resources and Life Sciences Education, 33*, 147–154.

Taylor, R. E., & Kauffman, R. G. (1983). Teaching animal science: Changes and challenges. *Journal of Animal Sciences, 57*(Supplement 2), 171–196.

USDA. (2005). Trends in U.S. agriculture. Retrieved January 1, 2008, from http://www.nass.usda.gov/Publications/Trends/index.asp

Washburn, L. E. (1958). Fifty years of progress in teaching animal science. *Journal of Animal Sciences, 17*(4), 1101–1118.

Wattiaux, M. A. (2002) Parker Palmer's message on the art of good teaching. The Learning Link. University of Wisconsin Madison Teaching Academy. Retrieved January 1, 2008, from http://teachingacademy.wisc.edu/archive/LearningLink/LLArticles.html

Wattiaux, M. A. (2006). Preparing sophomores for independent learning experiences with a pre-capstone seminar. *NACTA Journal, 50*(3), 19–25.

Wattiaux, M. A., & Crump, P. (2006). Students' perception of a discussion-driven classroom environment in an upper-level ruminant nutrition course with small enrollment. *Journal of Dairy Science, 89*(1), 343–352.

Weber Nielsen, M. S., Domecq, J. J., Davis, L. E., Beede, D. K., Budine, M., & Martsolf, F. (2003). A partnership of universities and agri-business for an effective dairy herd management learning experience for undergraduates: The dairy challenge. *Journal of Dairy Science, 86*, 1029–1035.

Wentworth, E. N. (1933). Some general observations on the animal husbandry curriculum. *The American Society of Animal Production, 1933*(1), 245–249.

Weimer, M. (2006). Enhancing scholarly work on teaching and learning: Professional literature that makes a difference. San Francisco, CA: Jossey-Bass.

12

THE EVOLUTION OF SCIENTIFIC TEACHING WITHIN THE BIOLOGICAL SCIENCES

Angela Bauer-Dantoin

As scientists, biologists place the highest importance on accumulating empirical evidence to determine the validity of scientific assertions about the structure, function, history, and interactions of organisms. The methods whereby biologists acquire empirical evidence undergo close scrutiny within the scientific community (e.g., through discourse at professional scientific meetings and/or the peer review process required for publication in scientific journals), and only when the methods are deemed objective and reliable is the outcome of an experiment considered valid. Once validity has been established, evidence obtained from the experiment is then used to correct or substantiate our current knowledge base and guide future experimentation. This rigorous, evidence-driven method of inquiry is the hallmark of the scientific method, used by biologists and other scientists to continuously develop more useful and accurate models and experimental methods for understanding the world in which we live.

Many biologists are not only researchers but college or university educators as well. Given the scrutiny with which biologists choose their experimental approaches as researchers, one might assume that as educators, they are equally rigorous in selecting their pedagogical approaches. After all, the responsibilities of biologists as educators are considerable. Not only are they charged with the task of training future scientists to work in an era characterized by rapidly advancing technology and pressing biological issues (e.g., the threat of multidrug-resistant organisms, HIV and AIDS, world population growth), but they are also responsible for cultivating scientific literacy within the many non-majors in introductory and general education courses, in the hope that these students will make informed choices about significant biological issues (e.g., healthcare, the environment) later in life. Thus, given the profound societal implications of a well-trained workforce in the biological sciences and a biologically literate citizenry, it is of utmost importance that biologists choose teaching strategies and assess their impact on student learning with the same inquiry-driven, evidence-based approach that they employ as researchers.

The History of SoTL within the Biological Sciences

So, to what degree have biology instructors employed the scientific method in determining the most effective pedagogical approaches for promoting biological and scientific literacy? And to what extent have these pedagogical approaches and their impact on student learning been subject to peer review within the scientific community? A historical analysis of the literature reveals that the community of biology educators (botanists, zoologists, microbiologists, biochemists, molecular biologists, cell biologists, physiologists, and ecologists) has been disseminating information on teaching in peer-reviewed publications for decades. In fact, some of the earliest publications dedicated to biology and science education, most notably *American Biology Teacher*, *Bioscene*, *Journal of Biological Education*, and *Journal of College Science Teaching,* have been in publication since 1938, 1975, 1967, and 1971, respectively. But even though these journals have served as the earliest peer-reviewed venues for publishing information on undergraduate biology teaching (e.g., novel ideas for learning activities or laboratory exercises), historically they have not required that authors provide evidence of the effectiveness of their methods for promoting student learning. Thus, much of the content of these publications in their earlier stages of evolution was descriptive, with little evidence of outcomes (Allen & Tanner, 2005). In fact, it wasn't until the 1990s that a discernible shift in the content of the biology teaching literature took place, as more biologists began to take an evidence-based (SoTL) approach to investigating the effectiveness of their traditional pedagogies.

The evolution of the biology teaching literature into an evidence-based analysis of classroom and laboratory teaching methods accelerated in the

1990s after the scientific community issued repeated calls for the reform of science education (American Association for the Advancement of Science [AAAS], 1989, 1990; Boyer Commission, 1998; National Research Council, 1995, 1996; National Science Foundation, 1996; Project Kaleidoscope, 1991). The initial calls for reform came on the heels of studies conducted by the National Science Foundation (1989, 1990a and 1990b) and others (Green, 1989; Hilton & Lee, 1988) noting a number of disturbing trends in science education, including a steady decline in the number of freshmen interested in pursuing an undergraduate science major; a shift of approximately 50% of all science, mathematics, and engineering (SME) majors into other majors within the first two years at college; and low retention of women and minority students in SME majors, despite improved enrollment. Interestingly, studies seeking to explain attrition from SME majors (including biology) revealed that students switching to non-SME majors did *not* cite inadequate academic preparation or conceptual difficulties as reasons for leaving the sciences, as many had predicted; rather, the most frequently cited reason for leaving SME majors was the poor teaching and inapproachability of SME faculty (Seymour, 1992). In fact, complaints about poor teaching were the most commonly voiced concern of both students switching to non-SME majors and students still pursuing an SME major (Seymour, 1995).

These startling findings—combined with national reports on the continuing decline in scientific literacy among the general population within the United States (AAAS, 1989)—compelled a greater number of college and university biology educators to more closely scrutinize what was happening in their classrooms and instructional laboratories. Greater numbers of biology professors began to employ the scientific method for assessing the efficacy of their teaching approaches and to disseminate their findings at national scientific meetings and in peer-reviewed teaching publications. As a result, the nature of college-level biology teaching literature evolved in the 1990s. What had been a literature consisting primarily of descriptive summaries of teaching or laboratory methods evolved into evidence-driven analyses of the impact of these methods on student learning. In other words, a greater number of biology educators began to apply SoTL methods to examine their pedagogies and to disseminate their results to the broader community.

Consider the *Journal of College Science Teaching* (*JCST*) as an example of this evolution. In 1985 (approximately 5 years prior to the call issued for science education reform), a total of 40 articles on college science teaching were published in the "Classroom Reports" section of *JCST*. Of these 40 articles, only 5 (13%) assessed how the described course or curricular innovation impacted on student learning or attitudes toward science. This low percentage of articles qualifying as SoTL research during 1985 stands in stark contrast to the percentage observed in *JCST* 16 years after the call for reform: in the year 2006, virtually 100% of *JCST* articles describing a novel classroom approach provided assessment data demonstrating the impact of the approach on some aspect of student learning.

Not only did the content of preexisting biology and science teaching journals (like *JCST*) evolve as a result of the call for science education reform issued in the 1990s, but the biology teaching literature as a whole was transformed. What had previously been of interest only to science teaching organizations (i.e., scholarly investigations into teaching and learning) now became a priority within national societies of specific scientific disciplines and subdisciplines. As a result, biological societies began to sponsor peer-reviewed teaching publications devoted to pedagogical issues specific to their content areas. These journals, now much narrower in scope than the traditional science and biology teaching journals, include *Advances in Physiology Education* (1989), *Cell Biology Education* (2002), *Biochemistry and Molecular Biology Education* (2002), *Journal of Microbiology and Biology Education* (2000), and the *Journal of Undergraduate Neuroscience Education* (2002). Of note is the fact that many of these publications explicitly state in their *Instructions to Authors* that articles must include—in addition to a description of the new teaching innovation—assessment data demonstrating the impact of the approach on student learning. In other words, this "second generation" of college biology teaching journals is SoTL in nature, and most require that authors employ the scientific method to determine the validity of their pedagogical approaches. Journals such as *Cell Biology Education* even go so far as to state in their *Instructions to Authors* that "articles [lacking] an assessment component will be sent back to authors without review" (Cell Biology Education, 2007).

SoTL Themes within the Biological Sciences

Now that many biologists are scrutinizing their classroom approaches with the same rigor used to scrutinize their experimental approaches, what have we learned about student learning in college biology courses? And how have these findings impacted pedagogy within the biological sciences? An analysis of the past 20 years of SoTL research within the biological sciences reveals two prevalent themes, which will be explored throughout the remainder of this chapter. These themes are the benefits of active learning strategies for presenting material in biology courses and the value of inquiry-based (rather than "cookbook") laboratory exercises for engaging students in the scientific method.

The ensuing exploration of these two prevalent themes within the SoTL literature reveals the emergence of a signature pedagogy in the biological sciences that has been termed "scientific teaching." Scientific teaching mirrors science at its best: it actively engages students in a learning process that is experimental, rigorous, often collaborative, and based on evidence (Handelsman et al., 2004).

Active Learning Strategies in the Biology Classroom

The lecture-recitation model of teaching has been (and still is) the predominant method of instruction employed in college biology classrooms. This method of information transmission likely became the teaching method of choice in the biological sciences as a result of the significant descriptive component to teaching and learning the discipline (e.g., the appropriate use of anatomical terminology or phylogenetic nomenclature). But while traditional lectures are well suited for relaying information to be learned by rote memorization, many of the SoTL studies conducted since 1990 reveal that this approach is relatively ineffective at helping students develop a deep understanding of important biological concepts or acquire and hone critical thinking skills (Allen, 1997; Burrowes, 2003; Klionsky, 1998; Lord, 1997; Lord, 1999; Posner & Markstein, 1994). This is a major concern, because the latter skills are crucial for understanding and engaging in biology as a process and for developing the mindset of a biologist, who must be able to critically analyze data in order to solve problems.

These findings regarding the relative ineffectiveness of instructor-centric teaching strategies for teaching biology as a process (rather than a set of facts) echo those of studies conducted in other disciplines (Angelo, 1990; National Research Council, 2000; other chapters in this volume), particularly physics (Beichner & Saul, 2003; SCALE-UP, n.d.; Lattery, this volume). The standard lecture/note-taking format of teaching leads to passive learning and provides little opportunity for students to develop the flexibility, inquiry skills, and modes of higher-order thinking required of a biologist (Ahern-Rindell, 1999; Klionsky, 1998; Lord, 1994). Furthermore, this traditional method of teaching deductively (from the general to the particular) has been criticized by students for leaving little room to connect course content to the real world (Kardash & Wallace, 2001), because many instructors find that little time is left to discuss "real life" theoretical applications once the history and rationale of scientific theories have been presented. This failure to connect learning to life is a significant problem in the biology classroom, and it has caused some students to leave the sciences (Seymour & Hewitt, 1997).

Numerous SoTL studies conducted within the biological sciences demonstrate that significant learning gains are achieved—particularly those that foster the mindset of a biologist—when instructors replace, or at least supplement, uninterrupted lectures with active learning strategies (Allen, 1997; Burrowes, 2003; Klionsky, 1998; Lord, 1997; Lord, 1999; Posner & Markstein, 1994; Udovic, Morris, Dickman, Postlethwait, & Wetherwax, 2002). Active learning strategies can take on a variety of forms, from the simple (think-pair-share exercises, electronic audience responses systems) to the complex (problem-based learning, project-based learning, case studies). But in general, all have the common characteristic of actively engaging students in the learning process (usually through collaborative group work), as instructors serve as mentors or coaches, rather than founts of knowledge. Biology students educated in active learning classrooms learn to think like biologists: they are "skeptical of claims not supported by empirical evidence. They are good at, and get enjoyment from, solving problems. They know how to gather and organize data, critically analyze it, and draw conclusions from it" (Wood, 2003).

Many active learning strategies, particularly those that have gained favor in the biological sciences, require that instructors shift their pedagogical framework from a deductive to an inductive mode of teaching (Prince & Felder, 2007). Rather than teaching theories or general principles and then progressing to applications of those theories or principles (the deductive method of teaching typically employed in biology lectures), instructors who teach inductively facilitate learning by presenting students with problems or case studies to solve (typically in small groups), and relevant principles or theories are explored or discussed once students have established the need to know them.

Methods of inductive teaching are consistent with an educational philosophy known as constructivism, and thus are often interchangeably referred to as constructivist methods. Constructivism asserts that knowledge is not just received, but actively built. Whereas objectivist educators view knowledge as something to be imparted and thus favor lectures as their primary mode of instruction, constructivist educators believe that "new understandings are constructed by the learner as a result of new experiences" (Leonard, 2000) and thus favor active learning strategies. When engaged in constructivist activities, students "construct their own version of reality rather than simply absorbing versions presented by their teachers" (Felder & Prince, 2007). The psychological literature provides strong support for the idea that inductive/constructivist methods promote deeper learning (reviewed in National Research Council, 2000), as students seek to understand the deeper meaning of concepts in order to problem-solve, rather than simply memorizing them. Proponents of constructivist teaching within the biological sciences argue that its investigative nature fosters scientific thinking, because it encourages students to engage in a form of inquiry that more closely mimics the scientific method.

SoTL investigations of constructivist teaching in the biological sciences repeatedly confirm that this mode of instruction is more effective than traditional lectures not only for promoting overall academic achievement in a course (Allen, 1997; Caglayan, 1994; Freeman et al., 2007; Knight & Wood, 2005; Wilke, 2003; Wilke & Straits, 2001), but also for fostering the development of higher order thinking skills in biology students. Consider the findings of Lord (1997), who conducted one of the first studies examining the impact of constructivist teaching on specific types of learning within the undergraduate biology classroom. In this study, Lord compared the performance of students enrolled in two sections of an introductory biology class, one of which was taught in the traditional teacher-centered manner of lecture, and another taught in a student-centered constructivist format. In the constructivist format, content was addressed through collaborative learning activities in which students worked in small groups to complete an exercise (e.g., problem solving, concept mapping, case studies) designed by the instructor to address course material. Learning was assessed in both groups with the same evaluation instruments (four unit exams) that probed both lower and higher-level thinking skills (terminology recall questions vs. questions requiring interpretive, critical or projective understanding of the material). A comparison of average exam scores revealed that students who were taught via constructivist methods scored significantly higher on all four unit exams. Interestingly, differences in student performance were attributed to the development of higher-level thinking skills in the experimental group. While both sections received similar scores on recall questions, students who learned via constructivist methods achieved significantly higher scores on questions that required a deeper understanding of the material (e.g., interpretation or application questions). Other SoTL investigations of active learning strategies in biology courses have confirmed their positive impact on students' higher order thinking skills, including problem-solving abilities (Cortright, Collins, & DiCarlo, 2005; Giuliodori, Lujan, & DiCarlo, 2006) and experimental design skills (Wilke & Straits, 2001).

Studies regarding the effects of constructivist teaching on student learning indicate that the impact of the approach is proportional to the number of opportunities students have to engage in active learning. Using an approach similar to that of Lord (1997), Burrowes (2003) examined student learning in traditional lecture vs. constructivist introductory biology courses. Like Lord (1997), Burrowes observed significantly higher exam scores in students who learn within a constructivist context and found that this difference could be attributed specifically to students' performance on exam questions that probe higher order thinking skills. Burrowes made the additional observation that differences in exam scores between traditional vs. constructivist sections increase as the semester progresses. As students in constructivist-taught sections are provided with repeated opportunities to actively participate in specific aspects of the scientific process (interpreting graphs, applying concepts to resolve problems, drawing conclusions about data), they become more adept at thinking scientifically, and the gap between their exam scores and those of students taught via traditional lectures increases. Instructors using case studies in biology courses have observed the same correlation between extent of engagement in this active learning strategy and performance on problem-solving exam questions (Goran & Braude, 2007). These findings highlight the importance of regularly presenting biology students with active learning opportunities in order to maximally facilitate the development of higher order thinking skills and have significant implications for curricular design in our undergraduate biology programs.

Interestingly, comparisons of academic performance in traditional vs. constructivist biology courses find either no significant difference in students' acquisition of content knowledge in response to the two methods (Lord, 1997; McCormick & MacKinnon, 1999; Smith, Stewart, Shields, Hayes-Klosteridis, Robinson, & Yuan, 2005) or gains in acquisition of content knowledge when students are taught with a constructivist format (Wilke, 2003; Wilke & Straits, 2001). This is worth noting, because critics of active learning strategies often claim that the time required for their implementation in the classroom detracts from content coverage. Thus far the data are not consistent with this notion and instead indicate that learning to think scientifically in biology courses does not come at the expense of content knowledge acquisition. This is true for implementation of active learning strategies in both low (Cortright, Collins, & DiCarlo, 2005; Lord, 1999; McCormick & MacKinnon, 1999) and high enrollment courses in the biological sciences (Lord, 1997; Wilke & Straits, 2001).

Investigations into active learning strategies provide convincing evidence of their benefits for the development of higher order thinking skills in undergraduate biology students, which is paramount for developing the mindset of a researcher in the biological sciences. But what impact do student-centered approaches have on the affective components of learning? In other words, do students like these approaches, and if so, might they lead more students—and a greater diversity of students—to consider a career in the biological sciences? Overall, assessment of biology students' attitudes toward active learning reveals that the majority of students enjoy the approach (Bauer-Dantoin & Ritch, 2005; Kumar, 2005; Lord, 1997; Smith et al., 2005; Wilke & Straits, 2001). Specifically, students cite an appreciation for the real-world context that the strategies provide (Bauer-Dantoin, 2008; Lord, 1997; Smith et al., 2005), the opportunity to direct their own learning (Allen, 1997), and enhanced engagement with their peers, which they believe facilitates learning (Cortright, Collins, & DiCarlo, 2005; Giuliodori, Lujan, & DiCarlo, 2006). Moreover, students who learn biology via constructivist methods express a higher level of interest in biology than students who learn via traditional lectures (Burrowes, 2003), report greater confidence in their ability to "do science" (Cortright, Collins, & DiCarlo, 2005; Wilke, 2003), and exhibit increased engagement in research-oriented activities (Smith et al., 2005).

The affective benefits of student-centered learning strategies have significant implications for the retention of students in the biological sciences: if students enjoy their coursework, are more engaged with their peers, and feel more confident in their ability to participate in the scientific process, they are much more likely to envision a role for themselves in the scientific process and consider a career in the biological sciences. With this rationale in mind, biology educators have investigated whether the implementation of active learning strategies influences the retention of underrepresented groups (women and ethnic minorities) within undergraduate biology programs. Posner and Markstein (1994) found that minority students enrolled in introductory biology courses that utilize collaborative learning strategies receive significantly better grades than those enrolled in traditional lecture sections (average GPAs of 2.96 vs. 2.13, respectively). Furthermore, they found that minority students who participate in active learning strategies report an increase in self-confidence, and perceive the student-centered environment as being more supportive, both academically and emotionally. Most importantly, Posner and Markstein (1994) found that the incorporation of collaborative learning into introductory courses has a positive effect on minority student enrollment in subsequent courses within the biology curriculum (90% vs. 75% of minority students were retained from experimental vs. control sections, respectively). Similar academic gains by minority students (particularly females), as well as improved retention, have been observed in other undergraduate biology programs that have incorporated active learning strategies into their curriculum (Dirks & Cunningham, 2006; Handelsman, Miller, & Pfund, 2007; Hufford, 1991; Rosser, 1995). These findings are noteworthy in light of the fact that underrepresented groups (women and ethnic minorities) often feel alienated and disenfranchised in the traditional, competitive, fact-oriented science classroom (Handelsman et al., 2007; Seymour & Hewitt, 1997). Modification of courses to a student-centered format may be a small but transformative step that undergraduate biology programs can take to foster a more inclusive environment for women and minority students, who remain poorly represented in the sciences (National Science Foundation, 2004).

Both the cognitive gains and social benefits that students derive from the active learning classroom have been attributed in part to the social nature of this approach. Biology educators in particular place high value on the collaborative nature of active learning strategies because they believe it plays a significant role in fostering "the spirit of science" among students. As stated by Handelsman and colleagues (2007),

> Rarely is a new idea the product of a single mind. Scientists depend on each other to criticize ideas in seminars and reviews of manuscripts and research proposals. Participation in rigorous, open, scientific debate is one of the most stimulating aspects of being a scientist. Today, most high-impact scientific research is the product of interdisciplinary teams, and the success of these teams is entirely dependent on the ability of the members to work as a group. (pp. 23–24)

Thus, participation in small group activities gives biology students the opportunity to hone the collaborative skills that are vital for a successful career in the sciences. Most importantly, by working together, students discover and experience that science is an exciting, dynamic, challenging, and creative process, not simply a collection of facts.

Springer, Stanne, and Donovan (1999) conducted a meta-analysis of the effects of small group learning vs. traditional approaches in undergraduate science, mathematics, engineering, and technology (SMET) courses and found that collaborative learning with peers has profound effects. Students who learn in small groups generally demonstrate greater academic achievement, express more favorable attitudes toward learning, and persist in SMET courses and programs to a greater extent than their peers who were taught via traditional methods. In fact, the meta-analysis of Springer et al. (1999) revealed that small group work may reduce attrition in SMET courses and programs by as much as 22%. How or why collaborative work positively influences student performance and attitudes has not yet been established, but characteristics of the approach that may benefit students include enhanced social engagement with their peers, which is known to positively influence student satisfaction and academic achievement (Pascarella & Terenzini, 1991); the opportunity for immediate feedback from their peers, which is not available during traditional lectures (Giuliodori, Lujan, & DiCarlo, 2006); increased alertness due to the social nature of small group work (Goran & Braude, 2007); and enhanced mastery of material as students progress from learning biological concepts to articulating and teaching them to their peers (Cortright, Collins, & DiCarlo, 2005; Giuliodori, Lujan, & DiCarlo, 2006; Slavin, 1996).

Clearly, the wave of SoTL investigations induced by the initial calls for science education reform (American Association for the Advancement of Science [AAAS], 1989, 1990; Project Kaleidoscope, 1991) delineate measurable cognitive and affective gains in students who engage in active learning. As the wave of SoTL studies investigating the *how* of active learning approaches ebbs (i.e., how do active learning strategies influence student learning?), a new wave of SoTL studies investigating the *why* of this pedagogical framework swells. Why do students experience deeper learning with student-centered approaches? Why do these approaches enhance critical thinking skills and overall academic performance? And why do they instill confidence in students in their ability to "do science"? Biology educators who have investigated how student-centered strategies influence learning offer many explanations, several of which have been offered in this chapter (e.g., social engagement with peers during collaborative learning activities, enhanced alertness due to the social nature of group work, mastery of material as students articulate and teach concepts during group work). Another explanation, and a topic that is likely to be the focus of many future SoTL investigations in the biological sciences, invokes the metacognitive value of active learning strategies for students. When students engage in constructivist approaches (e.g., case studies, problem-based learning), they think about and take control of their own learning (Yuen & Hau, 2006). Constructivist approaches—compared to traditional lectures—offer students more opportunities to define their learning goals (what do I need to understand to solve this problem?) and to assess their progress (via interactions with peers and the instructor; Gallucci, 2006). Thus, constructivist approaches may encourage students to spend more time "thinking about their thinking." Certainly, direct instructor-centered metacognitive interventions (e.g., lessons on study strategies; Simpson & Rush, 2003; Zan, 2000) result in academic gains on the part of students. Future studies will be necessary in order to clarify whether the academic gains that biology students experience in response to student-centered learning strategies are due, at least in part, to the covert teaching of metacognitive skills.

Additional questions that remain unanswered regarding the benefits of active learning strategies in the biology classroom include the following: what is the appropriate balance between traditional lectures and active learning strategies in the biology classroom? Are active learning strategies more effective than traditional lectures for teaching all topics in biology, or only certain topics? Which active learning strategies are the most effective for helping students develop the mindset of a biological researcher? Do certain types of learners respond more readily to active learning strategies within the biology classroom? Are most biology instructors able to effectively direct active learning within their classrooms? What are the major roadblocks preventing biology instructors from adopting active learning techniques within their classrooms? These questions, and more, are likely to be the focus of future SoTL studies within the biological sciences.

Inquiry in the Undergraduate Biology Laboratory

Another prevalent theme within the biology teaching literature is the impact of open-ended, inquiry-based labs (vs. traditional "cookbook" labs) on the ability of students to think scientifically. Inquiry-based labs are defined as labs that require students to develop hypotheses, design and conduct experiments to test their hypothesis, and analyze and interpret their data. In other words, inquiry labs engage students fully in the scientific process, and provide them with the opportunity to experience the thrill of discovery. Inquiry-based labs stand in stark contrast to traditional "cookbook" labs, where students are told exactly how to perform the labs and at times are even informed of the "appropriate" outcome. Several facets of laboratory inquiry distinguish it from other methods of active learning (e.g., the engagement of students, both mentally and physically, in the process of science). Thus, the topic is more suitably addressed independently.

The earlier calls for science education reform (AAAS, 1989, 1990; Project Kaleidoscope, 1991) accelerated a discussion that had already begun among scientists regarding the efficacy of traditional laboratory instruction for teaching students science process skills (Leonard, 1989). The standard approach to instructional laboratories was (and unfortunately in many cases, still is today) to provide undergraduate students with a laboratory manual and expect them to replicate experiments conducted by thousands of students before them. While this approach exposes students to laboratory techniques that may later prove useful for a career in the sciences, it lacks the creativity and excitement that characterizes true scientific inquiry (Lord & Orkwiszewski, 2006; Luckie, Maleszewski, Loznak, & Krha, 2004) and may account in part for attrition of students in the sciences (Seymour & Hewitt, 1997), who report cookbook labs to be "boring and time consuming" (Luckie et al., 2004). As biology educators reconsidered approaches to laboratory instruction, the biology teaching literature in this area began to evolve. Journals and other literature that were previously dominated by descriptive articles of "canned" laboratory exercises gradually became infused with SoTL investigations into the impact of inquiry-based labs.

Much of the SoTL work on inquiry-based labs focuses on the affective gains conferred by this approach of instruction. A preponderance of studies demonstrates that the majority of students prefer inquiry labs to cookbook labs (FitzPatrick, 2004; Howard & Miskowski, 2005; Kolkhorst, Mason, DiPasquale, Patterson, & Buono, 2001; Lord & Orkwiszewski, 2006; Luckie et al., 2004). The aspects of inquiry in the undergraduate laboratory that excite students are the very characteristics that scientists would likely cite as the most enjoyable aspects of their profession: the excitement of discovery (Lord & Orkwiszewski, 2006), the creativity involved in experimental design (FitzPatrick, 2004), the freedom to explore exciting questions, and pride in ownership of novel ideas (Kolkhorst et al., 2001). Instructors frequently observe a higher level of energy and activity in inquiry labs compared to cookbook labs, indicating a higher level of student engagement with this type of instruction (Kolkhorst et al., 2001; FitzPatrick, 2004).

Students also experience cognitive gains in response to inquiry-based laboratory instruction. A side-by-side comparison of student performance in traditional vs. inquiry-based introductory biology labs reveals that students' scientific reasoning skills improve in response to inquiry labs (Benford & Lawson, 2001), but not traditional cookbook labs (Lord & Orkwiszewski, 2006). Additionally, inquiry-based labs foster greater retention of biology content than do traditional labs (Lord & Orkwiszewski, 2006; Luckie et al., 2004). Finally, as is the case for other active learning strategies, the impact of inquiry-based labs on higher-order thinking skills (e.g., analyzing and drawing conclusions from data) becomes more pronounced with repeated opportunities to engage in this form of learning (Howard & Miskowski, 2005). This last finding highlights the importance of infusing inquiry-based laboratory instruction throughout the undergraduate biology curriculum, giving students repeated opportunities to experience and enjoy the spirit of inquiry and ultimately develop the mindset of the biological researcher.

Several issues regarding the benefits that biology students derive from inquiry-based labs require further exploration. For example, are "guided inquiry" labs (in which the instructor provides some of the experimental framework—often in the form of a hypothesis—for the studies to be conducted) just as effective as true inquiry labs in promoting cognitive and affective gains in college biology students? Are inquiry labs that employ computer simulations or modules just as effective as wet labs in facilitating learning gains? What types of assessment are the most effective for providing students with feedback on their performance in inquiry-based labs? What is the optimal frequency for providing students with feedback on their performance during inquiry labs? Do inquiry labs (vs. cookbook labs) enhance the acquisition of scientific writing skills in biology students? Future SoTL studies will be needed in order to address these issues.

Finally, while the SoTL literature provides convincing evidence of the cognitive and affective benefits of inquiry-based laboratory instruction, those involved with science education reform have voiced concern over the reticence of science faculty—particularly at research universities—to reform their laboratory curricula (Handelsman et al., 2004). Thus, in order to promote change, science educators who have developed successful models of laboratory-based inquiry are now disseminating information about their approaches via the web (see Handelsman et al., 2004, for a list of Web sites). With increased awareness of the benefits of inquiry in undergraduate laboratories—as well as the benefits of other active learning strategies—biologists and other science educators intend to accelerate curricular reforms that help students "develop the habits of mind that drive science" (Handelsman et al., 2004). In other words, they hope to promote scientific teaching.

A Signature Pedagogy within the Biological Sciences

Given the values and practices (experimental, rigorous, evidence-driven inquiry) that biologists and other scientists hold nearest to their heart as they approach their work in the laboratory, it is not surprising that these same values and practices have emerged as the key characteristics of their signature pedagogy, scientific teaching. When biology educators engage in scientific teaching, they model—and indeed engage their students in—the same "habits of the mind, habits of the heart, and habits of the hand" (Shulman, 2005) that are valued within the scientific community. SoTL evidence overwhelmingly demonstrates that scientific teaching fosters the skills and mindset that not only allow students to succeed in their coursework, but to enjoy it as well. Thus, as more biology educators bring the rigor of the research lab into their classrooms, a positive result is inevitable:

a dynamic, rigorous, engaging curriculum that is infused with the thrill of discovery and that contributes a highly skilled, diverse group of graduates to the field.

References

Ahern-Rindell, A. J. (1999). Applying inquiry-based and cooperative group learning strategies to promote critical thinking. *Journal of College Science Teaching, 28*(3), 203–207.

Allen, D. (1997). Bringing problem-based learning to the introductory biology classroom. In A. P. McNeal, & C. D'Avanzo (Eds.). *Student-Active Science* (pp. 259–278). Orlando, FL: Harcourt Brace.

Allen, D. & Tanner, K. (2005). Approaches to biology teaching and learning: From a scholarly approach to teaching to the scholarship of teaching. *Cell Biology Education, 4*, 1–6.

American Association for the Advancement of Science (1989). *Science for all Americans: Project 2061*. New York: Oxford University Press.

American Association for the Advancement of Science (1990). *The liberal art of science: Agenda for action*. Washington, DC: American Association for the Advancement of Science.

Angelo, T. A. (1990). *Learning in the classroom (Phase I)*. A report from the Lawrence Hall of Science. Berkeley, CA: University of California.

Bauer-Dantoin, A. (2008). Using service learning in a course entitled biology of women to promote student engagement and awareness of community needs and resources. *Bioscene, 34*(1), 13–19.

Bauer-Dantoin, A., & Ritch, D. (2005). Moving beyond the "add and stir" approach to increasing diversity in the sciences: Design and implementation of a course entitled *Ethnic Minorities in Science*. *Journal of Women and Minorities in Science and Engineering, 11*(4), 329–343.

Beichner, R. J., & Saul, J. M. (2003). *Introduction to the SCALE-UP (Student-Centered Activities for Large Enrollment Undergraduate Programs) Project.* Retrieved January 4, 2008, from http://www.ncsu.edu/PER/Articles/Varenna_SCALEUP_Paper.pdf

Benford, R., & Lawson, A. E. (2001). Relationships between effective inquiry use and the development of scientific reasoning skills in college biology labs. *Report to the National Science Foundation*, Grant DUE 9453610.

Boyer Commission on Educating Undergraduates in the Research University (1998). *Reinventing undergraduate education: A blueprint for America's research universities*. Princeton, NJ: Carnegie Foundation for the Advancement of Teaching.

Burrowes, P. A. (2003). A student-centered approach to teaching general biology that really works: Lord's constructivist model put to a test. *The American Biology Teacher, 65*(7), 491–502.

Caglayan, S. (1994). Effectiveness of an active method in teaching physiology. *Advances in Physiology Education, 12*(1), S81–S86.

Cell Biology Education—Life Sciences Education (2007). *Instructions for Authors.* Retrieved December 31, 2007, from http://www.lifescied.org/misc/ifora.dtl

Cortright, R. N., Collins, H. L., & DiCarlo, S.E. (2005). Peer instruction enhanced meaningful learning: Ability to solve novel problems. *Advances in Physiology Education, 29,* 107–111.

Dirks, C., & Cunningham, M. (2006). Enhancing diversity in science: Is teaching science process skills the answer? *Cell Biology Education, 5,* 218–226.

Felder, R., & Prince, J. M. (2007). The case for inductive teaching. *ASEE Prism, 17*(2), 55.

FitzPatrick, K. A. (2004). An investigative laboratory course in human physiology using computer technology and collaborative writing. *Advances in Physiology Education, 28,* 112–119.

Freeman, S., O'Connor, E., Parks, J. W., Cunningham, M., Hurley, D., Haak, D., Dirks, C., & Wenderoth, M. P. (2007). Prescribed active learning increases performance in introductory biology. *Cell Biology Education, 6,* 132–139.

Gallucci, K. (2006). Learning concepts with cases. *Journal of College Science Teaching, 36*(2), 16–20.

Giuliodori, M. J., Lujan, H. L., & DiCarlo, S. E. (2006). Peer instruction enhanced student performance on qualitative problem-solving questions. *Advances in Physiology Education, 30,* 168–173.

Goran, D., & Braude, S. (2007). Social and cooperative learning in the solving of case histories. *The American Biology Teacher, 69*(2), 80–84.

Green, K. C. (1989). A profile of undergraduates in the sciences. *The American Scientist, 77,* 475–480.

Handelsman, J., Ebert-May, D., Beichner, R., Bruns, P., Chang, A., DeHaan, R., Gentile, J., Lauffer, S., Stewart, J., Tilghman, S. M., & Wood., W. B. (2004). Scientific teaching. *Science, 304,* 521–522.

Handelsman, J., Miller, S., & Pfund, C. (2007). *Scientific teaching.* New York: W. H. Freeman.

Hilton, T. L., & Lee, V. E. (1988). Student interest and persistence in science: Changes in the educational pipeline in the last decade. *Journal of Higher Education, 59,* 510–526.

Howard, D. R., & Miskowski, J. A. (2005). Using a module-based laboratory to incorporate inquiry into a large cell biology course. *Cell Biology Education, 4,* 249–260.

Hufford, T. (1991). Increasing academic performance in an introductory biology course. *Bioscience, 41*, 107–108.

Kardash, C., & Wallace, M. (2001). The perceptions of science classes survey: What undergraduate science reform efforts really need to address. *Journal of Educational Psychology, 93*(1), 199–210.

Klionsky, D. J. (1998). A cooperative learning approach to teaching introductory biology. *Journal of College Science Teaching, 7*(5), 334–338.

Knight, J. K., & Wood, W. B. (2005). Teaching more by lecturing less. *Cell Biology Education, 4*, 298–310.

Kolkhorst, F. W., Mason, C. L., DiPasquale, D. M., Patterson, P., & Buono, M. J. (2001). An inquiry-based learning model for an exercise physiology laboratory course. *Advances in Physiology Education, 25*(2), 45–50.

Kumar, A. (2005). Teaching systems biology: An active learning approach. *Cell Biology Education, 4*, 323–329.

Leonard, W. H. (1989). Ten years of research on investigative laboratory instruction strategies. *Journal of College Science Teaching, 19*, 304–306.

Leonard, W. H. (2000). How do college students best learn science? *Journal of College Science Teaching, 29(6)*, 385–388.

Lord, T. R. (1994). Using constructivism to enhance student learning in college biology. *Journal of College Science Teaching, 23*(6), 346–348.

Lord, T. R. (1997). A comparison between traditional and constructivist teaching in college biology. *Innovative Higher Education, 21*(3), 197–216.

Lord, T. R. (1999). A comparison between traditional and constructivist teaching in environmental science. *The Journal of Environmental Education, 30*(3), 22–28.

Lord, T., & Orkwiszewski, T. (2006). Moving from didactic to inquiry-based instruction. *The American Biology Teacher, 68(6)*, 342–345.

Luckie, D. B., Maleszewski, J. J., Loznak, S. D., & Krha, M. (2004). Infusion of collaborative inquiry throughout a biology curriculum increases student learning: A four-year study of "teams and streams". *Advances in Physiology Education, 28*(7), 199–209.

McCormick, B., & MacKinnon, C. (1999). *Evaluation of attitude, achievement, and classroom environment in a learner-centered introductory biology class.* Paper presented at the Annual Meeting of the National Association for Research in Science Teaching, Boston, MA.

National Research Council (1995). *National science education standards.* Washington, DC: National Academy Press.

National Research Council (1996). *From analysis to action: Undergraduate education in science, mathematics, engineering and technology.* Washington, DC: National Academy Press.

National Research Council (2000). *How people learn: Brain, mind, experience and school* (expanded ed.). Bransford, J. D., Brown, A. L., & Cocking, A. R. (Eds.). Washington, DC: National Academy Press.

National Science Foundation (1989). *Changing America: The new face of science and engineering.* Interim and Final Reports, The Task Force on Women, Minorities and the Handicapped in Science and Technology. Washington, DC: National Science Foundation.

National Science Foundation (1990a). *The state of academic science and engineering.* Directorate for Science, Technology and International Affairs, Division of Policy Research and Analysis. Washington, DC: NSF.

National Science Foundation (1990b). *Women and minorities in science and engineering.* Washington, DC: National Science Foundation.

National Science Foundation (1996). *Shaping the future: New expectations for undergraduate education in science, mathematics, engineering and technology.* Washington, DC: Report by the Advisory Committee to the National Science Foundation Directorate for Education and Human Resources.

National Science Foundation, Division of Science Resources Statistics (2004). *Women, minorities, and persons with disabilities in science and engineering.* Washington, DC: NSF 04–317.

Pascarella, E. T. & Terenzini, P. T. (1991). *How college affects students.* San Francisco: Jossey-Bass.

Posner, H. B., & Markstein, J. A. (1994). Cooperative learning in introductory cell and molecular biology. *Journal of College Science Teaching, 23*(4), 231–233.

Prince, M., & Felder, R. (2007). The many faces of inductive teaching and learning. *Journal of College Science Teaching, 26*(5), 14–20.

Project Kaleidoscope (1991). *What works: Building natural science communities.* Volume I. Washington, DC: The Independent College Offices.

Rosser, S. V. (1995). Reaching the majority: Retaining women in the pipeline. In Rosser, S. V. (Ed.), *Teaching the majority: Breaking the gender barrier in science, mathematics and engineering* (pp. 1–21). New York: Teachers College Press.

SCALE-UP (Student-Centered Activities for Large Enrollment University Physics). (n.d.). Retrieved January 3, 2008, from www.ncsu.edu/per/scaleup.html

Seymour, E. (1992). "The problem iceberg" in science, mathematics, and engineering education: Student explanations for high attrition rates. *Journal of College Science Teaching, 21*, 230–238.

Seymour, E. (1995). Revisiting the "problem iceberg": Science, mathematics and engineering students still chilled out. *Journal of College Science Teaching, 24*, 392–400.

Seymour, E., & Hewitt, N. (1997). *Talking about leaving: Why undergraduates leave science.* Boulder, CO: Westview.

Shulman, L. (2005). Signature pedagogies within the professions. *Daedalus, 134*, 52–59.

Simpson, M. L., & Rush, L. (2003). College students' beliefs, strategy employment, transfer, and academic performance: An examination across three academic disciplines. *Journal of Reading and Teaching, 33*(2), 146–156.

Slavin, R. E. (1996). *Education for all.* Exton, PA: Swets & Zeitlinger.

Smith, A. C., Stewart, R., Shields, P., Hayes-Klosteridis, J., Robinson, P., & Yuan, R. (2005). Introductory biology courses: A framework to support active learning in large enrollment introductory science courses. *Cell Biology Education, 4*, 143–156.

Springer, L., Stanne, M. E., & Donovan, S. S. (1999). Effects of small-group learning on undergraduates in science, mathematics, engineering and technology: A meta-analysis. *Review of Educational Research, 69*(1), 21–51.

Udovic, D., Morris, D., Dickman, J., Postlethwait, J., & Wetherwax, P. (2002). Workshop biology: Demonstrating the effectiveness of active learning in an introductory biology course. *Bioscience, 52*, 272–281.

Wilke, R. R. (2003). The effect of active learning on student characteristics in a human physiology course for non-majors. *Advances in Physiology Education, 27*(4), 207–223.

Wilke, R. R., & Straits, W. J. (2001). The effects of discovery learning in a lower-division biology course. *Advances in Physiology Education, 25*(2), 62–69.

Wood, W. B. (2003). Inquiry-based undergraduate teaching in the life sciences at large research universities: A perspective on the Boyer Commission Report. *Cell Biology Education, 2*, 112–116.

Yuen, K. M., & Hau, K. T. (2006). Constructivist teaching and teacher-centered teaching: A comparison of students' learning in a university course. *Innovations in Education and Teaching International, 43*(3), 279–290.

Zan, R. (2000). A metacognitive intervention in mathematics at university level. *International Journal of Education in Science and Technology, 31*(1), 143–150.

13

SIGNATURE PEDAGOGIES AND SoTL PRACTICES IN COMPUTER SCIENCE

Diane Christie

Computer science is a relatively new discipline that changes quickly, thus requiring educators to continually update their skills as well as their courses. Over the last decade, published papers in computer science education have also evolved. Previously, papers described someone's novel approach to a standard topic or proposed an innovative way of teaching, typically with anecdotal results. However, many recent papers now include more robust aspects of the scholarship of teaching and learning (SoTL), such as peer review and assessment, and have extended to topics such as course portfolios, active and cooperative learning, and teaching communities. This chapter reviews traditional pedagogies of computer science as well as recent trends, and discusses elements of what would constitute a signature pedagogy for computer science.

An Introduction to Computer Science

Computer science is the study of all aspects of computer systems and includes information that is both theoretical and practical. It encompasses both hardware and software, and has many sub-fields: computer programming, programming languages, graphics and visual computing, human-computer interactions, architecture and organization, operating systems, software engineering, computational science and numerical methods, algorithms and complexity, discrete structures, net-centric computing, intelligent systems, information management, and social and professional issues. When studying computer science, students take courses in many of these subfields. The typical course sequence begins with an introductory course in computer programming, but non-majors also take introductory computer science courses to fulfill general education requirements. This focus on programming in introductory courses arose from practical and historical factors: first, programming is an essential skill that must be mastered by anyone studying computer science, and secondly, the introductory course is used in other disciplines such as engineering as a skills course. Because majors other than computer science may require one or two courses in computer science, these students who never take upper-level courses in computer science may assume that what they learn in these introductory courses is what a computer scientist does.

However, introductory courses in the discipline are very different from upper-level courses and the work of computer scientists. Introductory courses in computer science have historically been taught as lecture courses in beginning programming. Many of these courses have a lab component, either a scheduled closed lab or an open lab time for the students to complete the assignments. Because collaborating would imply cheating, students are warned to do their own work. Students struggle with syntax along with problem solving in order to complete the assignments and succeed in the class. Most students' first impressions of a career in computer science are thus of an isolated programmer who worries about minute details of syntax to get the program to run. In contrast, upper-level classes require students to work together on projects. The main focus is on how to solve problems using various computer resources and techniques. Code reuse and collaboration among group members and sometimes between groups is encouraged. Students are expected to use any resources available to them to solve the problem. These classes are designed to get the students to start thinking and acting as professional computer scientists. The culture of the upper-level classroom is designed to give a preview of the culture of the field.

In practice, computer scientists work in teams, use all resources available to them, and collaborate with many people outside of their discipline to solve problems. Computers and computer software are used in every aspect of business and industry, from running the business operations in accounting, inventory, marketing, and sales to creating the product by controlling the manufacturing processes. Many manufactured products have electronic controls that must be programmed, and computer programs themselves are products in industries such as computer software and video games. Computer scientists find themselves working with people in many different areas of expertise, so the computer scientist must be able to collaborate, using ideas and suggestions from others to design the best solutions to the problem. Much time is spent on analysis of the problem and design of the solution. Programming is one activity included in the implementation of that solution, but it is not the only activity that the professional computer scientist performs. Because this is not at all the impression that introductory students get about careers in computer science, some departments try to address this problem through an introductory breadth-first course that gives students an overview of computer science. However, the popular programming-first approach is likely to remain dominant for the foreseeable future (Joint Task Force on Computing Curricula, 2001).

Traditional and Signature Pedagogies in Introductory Computer Science

Currently, even though the number of job openings continues to increase, computer science majors have seen a dramatic enrollment decline across the nation, a trend that is expected to continue (Vesgo, 2005). Two factors have tarnished the profession in the eyes of many outsiders: the dot.com bust and outsourcing (Avery, 2007). The industry downturn led to layoffs and the demise of many Internet start-ups early in the decade, and it caused many students who had viewed computer science as a route to quick wealth to pursue other majors. The growth of software industries overseas has convinced some students that there will be fewer jobs in North America that require computer science degrees. Many high school students, influenced by their parents and media reports, are seeking other majors to avoid professional downsizing later. A growing number of educators also point to the fact that, in most introductory courses, computer science basics are taught by creating programs that sort numbers or perform other tasks divorced from everyday life, tasks that don't capture the hearts or interest of students (Microsoft, 2005). These factors have sparked computer science educators who once focused solely on the content of the ever-changing courses to start looking at what might be the best methods of teaching that content. However, most computer science educators are not trained in education and are not familiar with educational research. Consequently, during this same time period, the growing SoTL movement has influenced the field of computer science. Because the introductory programming courses are the student's first exposure to computer science and will have a direct effect on retention, we are now seeing a change in the traditional pedagogy of computer science, and a signature pedagogy of computer science is emerging.

What does "teaching and learning programming" mean? Eckerdal and Berglund (2005) posed the question "What do you think learning means (involves) in this course?" to students in a beginning programming course. In the analysis of the student interview data, Eckerdal and Berglund proposed a five-level hierarchy: (1) learning to read and write a programming language; (2) learning a way of thinking aligned with a programming language; (3) gaining an understanding of computer programs as they appear in everyday life; (4) learning a way of thinking that enables problem solving; and (5) learning a skill that can be used outside of the programming class. They concluded that it is "of great importance that students see *learning to program as a way of thinking, which enables problem solving, and which is experienced as a 'method' of thinking.*" (p. 141, emphasis in original).

In fact, many educators feel that programming is an application of the problem-solving skills also learned in math and science courses, and thus should be a major goal in designing an introductory course. However, Palumbo's (1990) review of the literature connecting learning programming languages and problem-solving skills concluded that "the transfer of skills and expertise to a new problem-solving domain that is distinctly different in its stimulus features to the problem-solving domain where expertise had already been established" (p. 71) or "the transfer of general problem-solving strategies and procedures from one problem solving context to another" (p. 70) cannot be expected to happen in an introductory course because the time spent in practice is simply too limited. This conclusion points to a gap between what computer science educators want students to learn and the pedagogies they're using to teach.

There are many approaches to teaching introductory programming, such as explaining the mathematical foundations of programming, focusing on syntax and language, and teaching analysis and problem solving. A recent survey of the literature on teaching introductory programming (Pears et al., 2007) collected and classified important literature in computer science education research, including factors that are important when designing a new introductory course. The researchers concluded that, despite the large volume of literature relating to teaching introductory programming, there is little systematic evidence to support any particular approach, so this is a rich area for SoTL studies in computer science.

Historically, programming was taught by focusing on the structure and syntax of one of the common computer languages of the time. Until recently, most of these languages have been procedural, which means that the programming breaks down the program into a series of routines performed on the data. However, this has changed with the increasing popularity of object-oriented programming languages in which the object stores multiple pieces of related data and has methods (instructions that can operate on that data), making the object capable of receiving messages, processing data, and sending messages to other objects. Unlike procedural programming, which sees data and tasks as separate entities, object-oriented programming uses objects and their interactions to design programs. Object-oriented programming languages have existed for many years but did not become popular until the advent of C++, which was embraced by industry for large-scale development, demonstrating the usefulness of the object-oriented approach for commercial systems. (Currently, the most widely used programming languages in both industry and education are C, C++, and Java.) However, object-oriented and procedural concepts are not mutually exclusive: valuable design concepts of modularity and encapsulation have been taught in procedural programming classrooms for many years, and now these concepts are a cornerstone of object-oriented programming. However, object-oriented concepts allow us to relate data and instructions in a way that we couldn't before, and use design techniques that fundamentally augment the procedural suite of conceptual tools (Lewis, 2000).

Objects have thus spurred a change in how programming is taught. A great debate is raging on how to introduce both procedural and object-oriented concepts to the beginning programming student. Some computer scientists argue that we must teach the procedural programming paradigm before object-oriented programming (Burton & Bruhn, 2003). Others hold that objects must be introduced early in the curriculum (Nevison & Wells, 2003). In addition, there is no agreement on exactly when the object concept is best introduced, or what form the object introduction should take to best educate beginning students. "Objects early" and "objects first," terms now commonly used by computer science educators, convey the emerging pedagogy of using objects toward the beginning of the course to establish a solid conception of the field. These efforts involve assignments in which students write classes that define objects or use objects defined by preexisting classes. In addition to mastering the usual concepts and frustrating details of syntax, students must understand the additional concepts of objects and interactivity with Graphical User Interfaces (Cooper, Dann, & Pausch, 2003).

The objects-first method presents a mental challenge for the novice programmer who must grasp all of the concepts and skills almost concurrently. Many tools that support programming have complex features developed to meet professional programmers' needs, so other tools have been developed specifically with the beginning programmer in mind. An extensive taxonomy of programming environments for novices can be found in Kelleher and Pausch (2005). In response to the objects-first approach, a variety of visual/graphical software tools, such as BlueJ (Kolling & Rosenberg, 2001), Java Power Tools (Proulx, Raab, & Rasala, 2002), Karel J. Robot (Bergin, Stehlik, Roberts, & Pattis, 2005), and Alice (Dann, Cooper, & Pausch, 2006), have been developed. These tools help the beginner "see" what an object actually is in order to develop the student's intuition about objects. This approach works well for the students of today's classrooms. These students have grown up with technology and media integrated into their lives. They are accustomed to getting information through audio and video interaction. They prefer to learn by doing and seeing. As one element of the emerging signature pedagogy for computer science, a graphical approach to introducing objects in introductory computer science courses allows the students to grasp multiple concepts simultaneously by putting them into an audio/visual context that is familiar to the student.

In addition to the place of and methods for teaching objects in introductory programming courses, the pedagogies used to teach introductory courses affect students' understanding of the work of the computer scientist and thus their potential futures in the field. The traditional lecture, the staple of university teaching, is the most common teaching method found in an introductory computer science course. However, as declining enrollments have caused computer science departments to focus on attracting and retaining students of the "Nintendo generation," the traditional lecture is under scrutiny in its ability to engage students in the discipline. These 21st-century college students have a perception of technology that has been profoundly influenced by media such as MTV, video and computer games, video iPods, instant messaging, cell phones, text messaging, streaming video, wireless technology, and the internet as sources of instant information, as well as social networking sites such as Facebook. Executing the traditional first program that prints "Hello World" on the screen is not the interactive computing environment to which this generation responds. They expect interactivity and application to their world, so the typical lecture is no longer as effective for student learning. Students come into an introductory computer programming class expecting to learn to use the computer to create the same kind of media that they are surrounded by every day. What many students take away from the lectures is a large stack of notes that do not seem to relate to the world of computers that they live in. In their world, computers are exciting and can be used to do things that the students are interested in and care about, but in the introductory programming classes, the lectures are considered dull by this generation, and the assignments are tedious, so many students do not enroll in another computer science course.

Many strategies have come forth for engaging this new generation of students, and recently other methods have made inroads into the computer science curriculum. The SoTL movement's focus on student learning has also made instructors rethink the way they teach. In order to revive our curriculum and increase the number of students taking computer science courses, we need to leverage this generation's familiarity and interest in multimedia, computer and video games, and the digital world. Guzdial and Soloway (2002) introduced multimedia as a new strategy to teach introductory computer programming. Some courses use games for homework assignments and projects, and others integrate game material into both lab and lecture (Bayliss & Stout, 2006). Engaging students in the familiar application of computer and video games while they learn the principles of programming is a good way to foster learning, because students will spend more time on a task they find interesting. As a result, game development programs are emerging at universities and technical colleges across the nation as a way to attract students into computer science. Using applications of computer science rather than just learning about it actively engages students in doing computer science and should thus be a key element of the signature pedagogy.

Various active and cooperative learning techniques are also becoming more common in many computer science classrooms. Student participation and involvement in the learning process has been shown to be important, so educators are experimenting with strategies to promote these vital educational elements, which are also central to the work of the professional computer scientist. Interactive response systems use the Socratic method of questioning with technology, allowing the instructor to gather quantitative, real-time feedback information and adapt a lecture according to the feedback about students' comprehension difficulties (Lopez-Herejon & Schulman, 2004). Activity-based techniques also enhance learning in the traditional lecture by increasing student involvement and promoting assessment of outcomes by instructors (Pigford, 2001). Using laptops in the classroom (Campbell & Pargas, 2003) or desktop computers in a studio setting also help students learn by doing (Bruhn & Burton, 2003).

Cooperative or collaborative learning techniques are also becoming increasingly common. These techniques create a more supportive and less competitive atmosphere in the classroom, which has been shown to benefit women and minority students (Chase & Okie, 2000; Nelson, 1996; Yerion & Rinehart, 1995). Cooperative learning techniques also more precisely reflect what computer scientists do. Most cooperative learning efforts divide students into small groups to work on programming problems or laboratory exercises. Some instructors create teams of students and are careful to incorporate critical components of common task, small-group interactions, collaborative behavior, positive interdependence, individual and group accountability, and responsibility into the assignments (LeJeune, 2003). Students can also be assigned specific roles during the group exercises, which focus their attention on the most important concepts being learned (Beck, Chizhik, & McElroy, 2005).

Collaborative programming has also become a popular pedagogy in beginning computer science classes. Pair programming involves two students working together on a single computer. One student, in the role of the driver, does the typing. The other student, in the role of the navigator, checks for errors in the driver's work, such as typos and syntax errors. The students discuss their ideas for solving the problem and create strategies for implementing their solution. After a short period of time, the students change places so that both students become adept at both roles. Studies on pair programming show improved pass rates and retention in the major (McDowell, Werner, Bullock, & Fernald, 2003; Nagappan et al., 2003) and higher-quality programs (Williams & Upchurch, 2001), with no demonstratable disadvantages (McDowell, Hanks, & Werner, 2003). Team-based learning uses application-focused programming assignments in which students, divided into smaller groups, are responsible for completing a specific task that contributes to the realization of a pre-determined final product (Rankin, Lechner, & Gooch, 2007). Collaborative programming, also routinely used in upper-level courses, introduces the industry's culture into the beginning programming classroom. Industry's growth of extreme programming, or software development that uses customer feedback and emphasizes team work between managers, customers, and developers to deliver quality software that the customer needs when it is needed, has brought considerable attention to collaborative programming in the classroom (McDowell, Werner, Bullock, & Fernald, 2002). Collaborative programming is another key element in the emerging signature pedagogy for computer science.

SoTL in Computer Science

SoTL has only recently been mentioned in computer science publications. The Special Interest Group in Computer Science Education (SIGCSE) of the Association for Computing Machinery (ACM) provides opportunities for educators to communicate and disseminate ideas and practices about teaching in public forums. SIGCSE conferences and publications have long had articles with novel teaching approaches, innovative ideas, and examples of what teachers have done in their classes. Although early publications typically did not have specific evidence of student learning (Goldweber, Clark, Fincher, & Pears, 2004), more recent publications suggest education research in computer science is following a more quantitative approach (Lister et al., 2006). The ACM's *Journal on Educational Resources in Computing* announced in March 2007 that it will publish only articles that embody a scholarly approach to teaching and learning (McCartney & Tenenberg, 2007). Their view of scholarship is embodied by the characteristics that it must address a question or issue of significance, be linked to previous relevant research, use methods of investigation appropriate to the problem studied, have results that are important, and report the research honestly and carefully.

Scholarship and research in computer science education lead to innovations in educational practice and technologies for computer science educators, and ultimately to improvements in teaching and learning (Sheard & Carbone, 2004). However, the difficulty facing computing educators is the perception that educational research is not valued as highly as other fields of research, and SoTL is not well supported by universities in terms of allocation of resources and recognition for promotion. For example, the lack of support for SoTL in Australia prompted Sheard and Carbone to create an Australasian Computing Education Community. Their Web site is used to facilitate collaboration and provide new ways for educators to communicate and disseminate their ideas and practices, in support of scholarship and research in computer science education. In addition, some research universities realize the value of teaching methodology and research as a path to joining large research universities, and are creating teaching faculty positions (Dougherty, Horton, Garcia, & Rodger, 2004).

Another challenge in computer science SoTL work is that computer science faculty often lack knowledge of educational literature and experience in educational research methodology necessary for conducting research in this area. Formal education in the theory and methods of the profession, or practical training and experience in the actual work of teaching is rare, so educators have essentially no experience in what will be their daily tasks. Once they start teaching, "they almost always practice behind closed doors, isolated from the very community of professional colleagues with whom they might (but usually do not) share collective cultural knowledge about how to teach and how to become better teachers." (Tenenberg & Fincher, 2007, p. 514).

There are efforts to open classroom doors and critically examine teaching and learning. Course portfolios have been used to document and share knowledge about teaching and student learning in computer science classrooms, and to improve the quality of teaching computer science by establishing practices for the scholarship of teaching, making it public, peer-reviewed, and amenable for future use and development by other educators in the discipline. In a project called Disciplinary Commons, course portfolios were used to try to bridge the institutional divide (Tenenberg & Wang, 2005). In hopes of developing a discipline-specific pedagogical discourse, two instructors each created their own portfolios for the course they taught at their institution. They met weekly to critique of each other's work, discuss why courses were designed or enacted in the specific way, and foster a systematic examination and reflection upon evidence of student learning. The structure and content of portfolios included audience and purpose, course goals, content and structure, teaching method, student outcomes, and rationale. The instructors documented and shared best practices within the discipline.

An expanded version of this project consisted of two cohorts of computer science teachers, one group of 17 teaching introductory programming courses in the United Kingdom and another group of 10 teaching courses on the path for a baccalaureate degree in a computer science–related program in Washington state (Tenenberg & Fincher, 2007). Course portfolios and surveys of teacher participants discussing the value of the Disciplinary Commons allowed teachers to systematically reflect upon their practice, to exchange concrete ideas for teaching in their courses with other computer science educators in the discipline, to learn skills that apply directly to course and program evaluation, and to meet colleagues teaching computer science at other institutions.

In addition to the Australasian Computing Education Community and the Disciplinary Commons, other multi-institutional teaching communities in computer education exist in the United Kingdom, Sweden, and New Zealand (Fincher, Lister, Pears, Sheard, Tenenberg, & Young, 2006). These teaching communities engage, develop, support, and sustain a community of interested practitioners with the aim of improving teaching, learning, research, and development in this field. ACM's SIGCSE is probably the largest international organization that focuses exclusively on computer education. Through publications, conferences, and other events and activities, it provides a forum for problems common among educators working to develop, implement, or evaluate computing programs, curricula, and courses, as well as syllabi, laboratories, and other elements of teaching and pedagogy.

Many principles that apply to education in general are making their way to computer science education. Bloom's taxonomy of the cognitive domain and the structure of observed learning outcomes (SOLO) taxonomy are also now being discussed, and a computer science-specific learning taxonomy has been proposed (Fuller et al., 2007). Both Bloom's taxonomy and the SOLO taxonomy describe levels of increasing complexity in student understanding. The matrix taxonomy, which is a two-dimensional adaptation of Bloom's taxonomy, provides a more practicable framework for assessing learner capabilities in computer science, especially for learning programming.

The SoTL focus on teaching and learning practices has begun a shift in education from instructor-centered to student-centered teaching, a shift beginning in computer science as well. For example, Ben-Ari (1998) introduced constructivism to the community of computer science education researchers. He suggested that group assignments and closed labs are preferable to individual exercises because they facilitate the social interaction necessary for successful construction of knowledge by the student. It is evident that the emerging signature pedagogy for computer science will provide students with social interaction and focus on student learning.

The way computer science is taught is evolving, although we need to develop a higher profile for computer science education research and raise its importance in the computing community. Computer science education will make significant contributions to the quality of education for the million or more students globally who study it each year. This will have significant financial implications for the computing industry and for the economies of many countries. The computer science community is taking a closer look at what it means to be a computer scientist and how to update the educational system to better train students to think and work like computer scientists do—essentially, to develop a signature pedagogy of computer science. Recent research (Clear, 2006; Fincher & Petre, 2004; Pears, Seidman, Eney, Kinnunen, & Malmi, 2005; Seidman, Pears, Eney, Kinnunen, & Malmi, 2005) shows that computer science education research is incorporating the principles of SoTL, which will hopefully improve the teaching of computer science throughout the world. There is a distinct trend toward publishing research that shows evidence of student learning through assessment, and that contains more emphasis on systematic reflection on teaching and learning. This is evidenced in the course portfolios, active and cooperative learning strategies, and teaching communities discussed in this chapter.

There may be no one signature pedagogy for computer science at this time, but as computer science education continues to evolve and mature, the signature pedagogy will evolve. It is too early to predict the exact form of that pedagogy, but it will focus on student learning and increasing student engagement by using applications of computer science to incorporate digital media and social interaction through some form of collaborative programming, and it will be applicable to the rapidly changing technology with which our students are living and learning.

References

Avery, G. (2007, April 9). *Not adding up: schools faced with an enrollment drop in computer-science students.* Retrieved March 27, 2008, from dailycamera: http://www.dailycamera.com/news/2007/apr/09/not-adding-up/

Bayliss, J. D., & Stout, S. (2006). Games as a "flavor" of CS1. *Proceedings of the 37th Annual SIGCSE Technical Symposium on Computer Science Education,* 500–504.

Beck, L. L., Chizhik, A. W., & McElroy, A. C. (2005). Cooperative learning techniques in CS1: Design and experimental evaluation. *Proceedings of the 36th SIGCSE Technical Symposium on Computer Science Education*, 470–474.

Ben-Ari, M. (1998). Constuctivism in computer science education. *Proceedings of the 29th SIGCSE Technical Symposium on Computer Science Education*, 257–261.

Bergin, J., Stehlik, M., Roberts, J., & Pattis, R. (2005). *Karel J. Robot, a gentle introduction to the art of object oriented programming in Java.* Redwood City, CA: Dream Songs Press.

Bruhn, R., & Burton, P. (2003, December). An approach to teaching Java using computers. *ACM SIGCSE Bulletin, 35*(4), 94–99.

Burton, P. J., & Bruhn, R. E. (2003, June). Teaching programming in the OOP era. *SIGCSE Bulletin, 35*(2), 111–114.

Campbell, A. B., & Pargas, R. (2003). Laptops in the classroom. *Proceedings of the 34th Annual SIGCSE Technical Symposium on Computer Science Education,* 98–102.

Chase, J. D., & Okie, E. G. (2000, March). Combining cooperative learning and peer instruction in introductory computer science. *ACM SIGCSE Bulletin, 32*(1), 372–376.

Clear, T. (2006). Valuing computer science education research? *Proceedings of the 6th Baltic Sea Conference on Computing Education Research: Koli Calling 2006,* 8–18.

Cooper, S., Dann, W., & Pausch, R. (2003). Teaching objects-first in introductory computer science. *Proceedings of the 34th SIGCSE Technical Symposium on Computer Science Education,* 191–195.

Dann, W., Cooper, S., & Pausch, R. (2006). *Learning to program with Alice.* Upper Saddle River, NJ: Pearson Education.

Dougherty, J. P., Horton, T. B., Garcia, D. D., & Rodger, S. H. (2004). Panel on teaching faculty positions. *Proceedings of the 35th SIGCSE Technical Symposium on Computer Science Education*, 231–232.

Eckerdal, A., & Berglund, A. (2005). What does it take to learn "programming thinking"? *Proceedings of the First International Workshop on Computing Education Research*, 135–143.

Fincher, S., Lister, R., Pears, A., Sheard, J., Tenenberg, J., & Young, A. (2006). Multi-institutional teaching communities in computer education. *Proceedings of the 8th Australian Conference on Computing Education, 52*, 7–10.

Fincher, S., & Petre, M. (2004). *Computer science education research: The field and the endeavour.* London: Routledge Falmer, Taylor & Francis Group.

Fuller, U., Johnson, C. G., Ahoniemi, T., Cukierman, D., Hernan-Losada, I., Jackova, J., et al. (2007). Developing a computer science-specific learning taxonomy. *SIGCSE Bulletin, 39*(4), 152–170.

Goldweber, M., Clark, M., Fincher, S., & Pears, A. (2004). The relationship between CS education research and the SIGCSE community. *Proceedings of the 9th Annual SIGCSE Conference on Innovation and Technology in Computer Science Education*, 228–229.

Guzdial, M., & Soloway, E. (2002, April). Log on education: Teaching the Nintendo generation to program. *Communications of the ACM, 45*(4), 17–21.

Joint Task Force on Computing Curricula (2001). *Journal of Educational Resources in Computing (JERIC), 1*(3es), 22–34.

Kelleher, C., & Pausch, R. (2005). Lowering the barriers to programming: A taxonomy of programming environments and languages for novice programmers. *ACM Computing Surveys, 37*(2), 83–137.

Kolling, M., & Rosenberg, J. (2001). Guidelines for teaching object orientation with Java. *Proceedings of the 6th Annual Conference on Innovation and Technology in Computer Science Education*, 33–36.

LeJeune, N. (2003). Critical components for successful collaborative learning in CS1. *Journal of Computing Sciences in Colleges, 19*(1), 275–285.

Lewis, J. (2000). Myths about object-orientation and its pedagogy. *Proceeding of the Thirty-first SIGCSE Technical Symposium on Computer Science Education*, 245–249.

Lister, R., Berglund, A., Clear, T., Bergin, J., Garvin-Doxas, K., Hanks, B., et al. (2006). Research perspectives on the objects-early debate. *Working Group Reports on ITiCSI on Innovation and Technology in Computer Science Education*, 146–165. Bologna, Italy: ACM Press.

Lopez-Herejon, R., & Schulman, M. (2004). Using interactive technology in a short Java course: An experience report. *Proceedings of the 9th Annual SIGCSE Conference on Innovation and Technology in Computer Science Education*, 203–207.

McCartney, R., & Tenenberg, J. (2007). From the editors: A new vision for JERIC. *Journal on Educational Resources in Computing, 7*(1), 1–4.

McDowell, C., Hanks, B., & Werner, L. (2003). Experimenting with pair programming in the classroom. *8th Annual SIGCSE Conference on Innovation and Technology in Computer Science Education*, 60–64.

McDowell, C., Werner, L., Bullock, H., & Fernald, J. (2002). The effects of pair programming on performance in an introductory programming course. *33rd SIGCSE Technical Symposium on Computer Science Education*, 38–42.

McDowell, C., Werner, L., Bullock, H., & Fernald, J. (2003). The impact of pair programming on student performance and pursuit of computer science related majors. *International Conference on Software Engineering,* Portland, OR, pp. 602–607.

Microsoft. (2005, September 12). *More than fun and games: New computer science courses attract students with educational games.* Retrieved March 27, 2008, from Microsoft: http://www.microsoft.com/presspass/features/2005/sept05/09-12CSGames.mspx?pf=true

Nagappan, N., Williams, L., Ferzli, M., Wiebe, E., Yang, K., Miller, C., et al. (2003). Improving the CS1 experience with pair programming. *34th SIGCSE Technical Symposium on Computer Science Education*, 359–362.

Nelson, C. E. (1996). Student diversity requires different approaches to college teaching, even in math and science. *American Behavioral Scientist, 40,* 165–175.

Nevison, C., & Wells, B. (2003). Teaching objects early and design patterns in Java using case studies. *Proceedings of the 8th Annual Conference on Innovation and Technology in Computer Science Education*, 94–98.

Palumbo, D. (1990). Programming language/problem-solving research: A review of relevant issues. *Review of Educational Research, 60*(1), 65–89.

Pears, A., Seidman, S., Eney, C., Kinnunen, P., & Malmi, L. (2005). Constructing a core literature for computing education research. *ACM SIGCSE Bulletin, 37*(4), 152–161.

Pears, A., Seidman, S., Malmi, L., Mannila, L., Adams, E., Bennedsen, J., et al. (2007, December). A survey of literature on the teaching of introductory programming. *SIGCSE Bulletin, 39*(4), 204–223.

Pigford, D. V. (2001). Designing and implementing active learning in the computer science curriculum: An interactive tutorial. *Journal of Computing Sciences in Colleges, 17*(2), 199–204.

Proulx, V., Raab, R., & Rasala, R. (2002). Objects from the beginning—with GUIs. *Proceedings of the 7th Annual Conference on Innovation and Technology in Computer Science Education,* 65–69.

Rankin, Y., Lechner, T., & Gooch, B. (2007). Team-based pedagogy for CS102 using game design. *International Conference on Computer Graphics and Interactive Techniques.* San Diego, CA: ACM Press.

Seidman, S., Pears, A., Eney, C., Kinnunen, P., & Malmi, L. (2005). Maintaining a core literature of computing education research. *Koli Calling: 5th Annual Finnish/Baltic Sea Conference on Computer Science Education*, 170–173. Koli, Finland: Turku Center for Computer Science.

Sheard, J., & Carbone, A. (2004). From informal to formal: Creating the Austalasian computing education community. *Proceedings of the 6th Conference on Australasian Computing Education, 30*, 291–297.

Tenenberg, J., & Fincher, S. (2007). Opening the door of the computer science classroom: The disciplinary commons. *Proceedings of the 38th SIGCSE Technical Symposium on Computer Science Education*, 514–518.

Tenenberg, J., & Wang, Q. (2005). Using course portfolios to create a disciplinary commons across institutions. *Journal of Computing Sciences in Colleges, 21*(1), 142–149.

Vesgo, J. (2005, May). Interest in CS as a major drops among incoming freshmen. *Computing Research News, 17*(3), 17.

Williams, L., & Upchurch, R. (2001). In support of student pair programming, *32nd SIGCSE Technical Symposium on Computer Science Education*. 327–331.

Yerion, K. A., & Rinehart, J. A. (1995, December). Guidelines for collaborative learning in computer science. *ACM SIGCSE Bulletin, 27*(4), pp. 29–34.

14

MATHEMATICAL REASONING

Challenging Students' Beliefs about Mathematics

Kathryn Ernie, Rebecca LeDocq,
Sherrie Serros, and Simei Tong

Yes, mathematics has two faces; it is the rigorous science of Euclid, but it is also something else. Mathematics presented in the Euclidean way appears as a systematic, deductive science; but mathematics in the making appears as an experimental, inductive science. Both aspects are as old as the science of mathematics itself. But the second aspect is new in one respect; mathematics "in statu nascendi," in the process of being invented, has never before been presented in quite this manner to the student. (Polya, vii)

The teaching scholar and mathematician George Polya made this statement about the nature of mathematics in his preface to the first printing to his landmark work *How to Solve It: A New Aspect of Mathematical Method* in 1945. Initially, Polya presents what mathematicians do as rigorous formal reasoning leading to the creation and proof of new theorems. When most people think about mathematicians, perhaps they think of the Elements of Euclid, the Pythagorean Theorem, Goldbach's Conjecture, or, more recently making headlines in the media, Fermat's Last Theorem. Each of these conjures up visions of great mathematicians laboring over manuscripts by candlelight to create and prove conjectures and theorems. Certainly, this development and extension of the theoretical base of mathematics is one important avenue for a mathematician's work.

Yet Polya also presents another side of the work of mathematicians, perhaps one that most of our students have not considered: the mathematician who experiments and uses knowledge and inductive reasoning to solve new problems. Thanks to the media, most people are generally aware of global positioning systems, fractals, chaos theory, and perhaps the Mandelbrot set, but many do not realize that these are the work of mathematicians who actively apply mathematics and create algorithms and models to solve problems. Today, the nature of mathematicians' work and what they can accomplish has changed in a world of ever-increasing speed, memory capacity, and technology. Mathematicians solve a wide range of problems, from the theoretical (finding the next [largest] prime number of a specific type or the solution of the four-color problem) to the interdisciplinary (creating and analyzing models to understand and predict global warming, wildlife populations, or the spread of AIDS).

Polya, perhaps the most well known mathematics teaching scholar of the twentieth century and the inspiration for many undergraduate mathematics SoTL projects, was dedicated to finding ways to help undergraduates solve problems. Whether inductive, deductive, adaptive, analogous, or plausible, mathematical reasoning provides students with approaches that use their mathematical knowledge in the process of solving problems. Through reasoning, students can extend their own understanding, make new discoveries, and explain how they solve problems. Polya's work shows educators how to develop questions that allow students to internalize the reasoning process behind problem solving, and it also offers a wide variety of heuristics useful in problem solving. In addition, his work describes the overall phases or structure of this reasoning process and focuses our attention on non-routine problems where problem solving takes place. This attention to process in the teaching of mathematics is a major departure from the traditional pedagogy of undergraduate mathematics in the twentieth century. The traditional way of teaching first-year students was to lecture on facts, concepts, and principles as a way of imparting mathematical content. In this model, the instructor briefly summarized the results of homework practice exercises and presented the new content, imbedded with procedures that the students followed in exercises similar to the ones presented in class. This teacher-centered pedagogy led to students engaging in watch-learn-practice (Stonewater, 2005).

Understandably, then, first-year students entered undergraduate mathematics courses expecting a teacher-centered classroom in which learning involved completing hundreds of problems as homework exercises. This experience has shaped students' views of mathematics, which in turn has "shape[d] their behavior in ways that have extraordinarily powerful (and often negative) consequences" (Schoenfeld, 1992, p. 359). The common student beliefs about mathematics, as Schoenfeld (1992) describes in his summary of Lampert's review of the research, include the following:

- Mathematics problems have exactly one answer, and there is only one correct way to obtain that answer.
- Memorization of isolated facts and processes will allow students to solve problems in just a few minutes.
- Mathematics is an individual activity.
- The mathematics learned is unrelated to students' lives and the real world.

The lecture method, which focuses on facts, concepts, and procedures as knowledge to be memorized, contributed to these well-documented misconceptions of mathematics. As Lithner (2003, p. 54) states, "The data suggest that many of the counterproductive behaviors we see in students are learned as unintended by-products of their mathematics instruction. A very strong classroom emphasis on performance—on memorizing constructions and practicing them until they can be performed with a very high degree of accuracy—ultimately results in the students losing sight of the rational reasons for the correctness of those constructions." However, the pedagogy of undergraduate mathematics started changing radically during the 1980s and was paralleled by the reform of school mathematics initiated by the National Council of Teachers of Mathematics (NCTM). This new pedagogy challenged the student's role as a passive listener who memorized facts and worked only on assigned problems. These new pedagogies attempt to alter students' belief systems about mathematics. In this chapter we will describe the ways that traditional mathematics pedagogy reinforces these disciplinary misconceptions, and we will outline the relevant research on emerging signature pedagogies of mathematics.

Conventional Mathematics Teaching: One Right Way

In the traditional pedagogy of first-year undergraduate mathematics during most of the twentieth century, instructors lectured on facts and theorems that they carefully wrote on the chalkboard, and then presented solutions to related practice items. Students memorized the key facts, reviewed the brief section from their mathematics textbook, and then completed the even-numbered problems using the same procedure presented by the instructor. (Answers to the odd-numbered exercises were included at the end of the text for additional practice.) Students assumed there was a procedure they could memorize for any specific problem, and their goal was to memorize them all.

Unfortunately, without a focus on meaning and reasoning, a majority of students were unsuccessful. In fact, 50 years ago, at least 60% of first-year students failed calculus. This statistic "signals that something is fundamentally wrong with the way that we teach calculus, and perhaps with the way we teach undergraduate mathematics overall," noted Gavosto, Krantz, and McCallum in their review of the impetus for the pedagogical reform movement (1999, p. xiv). Concerns about the lack of student success in undergraduate mathematics, particularly in calculus, as well as concerns about the state of mathematics education and its importance with respect to our competitiveness in the global market and advances in technology, led to the 1986 Tulane Conference, which was organized "to examine the state of modern mathematics teaching" (p. xiv) and which marked the beginning of the reform movement in undergraduate mathematics teaching. Gavosto, Krantz, and McCallum characterize this reform as a focus on geometric insights (visualization), concepts instead of simply calculations, innovative uses of technology, and the use of Socratic dialogue and discovery.

Calculus reform led the way in revolutionizing the teaching of undergraduate mathematics. In a 1995 national survey of undergraduate mathematics by the Conference Board of the Mathematical Sciences (CBMS), 40% of calculus instructors reported using computer assignments and other reform instructional strategies (Loftsgaarden, Rung, & Watkins, 1997). In the CBMS 2005 survey, more than 50% of calculus instructors at four-year colleges and 80% of calculus instructors at two-year colleges reported using technology such as graphing calculators and other reform pedagogies (Lutzer, Rodli, Kirkman, & Maxwell, 2007). According to Herzig and Kung (2003) in their review of Ross (1996), "Most reform efforts involve complex sets of classroom changes" including "the use of calculators and computers, multiple representations of mathematical concepts, student projects, and communicating about mathematics, and group work" (Herzig & Kung, 2003, p. 30).

During this reform calculus movement of the late 1980s through the 1990s, the scholarship of teaching and learning in mathematics used both qualitative and quantitative methods (observations, interviews, case studies, surveys, group problem solving, and pre/post testing on student learning) to focus on improving first-year undergraduate courses. Meel's (1998) review of research on technology-integrated reform calculus found most of the early studies to be comparative in nature, based on post testing or final exam grades, comparing students in a traditional calculus class with students in a refocused calculus course (Bookman & Friedman, 1994; Judson, 1989; Keller, 1994; Melin-Conejeros, 1993; Park, 1993; Schrock, 1989). These comparative studies indicated that students in reform calculus courses integrating computer algebra systems, and software where multiple representations are investigated, "performed significantly or minimally better than students in traditional courses on conceptual test items and did so without compromising computational proficiency" (Meel, 1998, p. 166). Meel noted that more recent studies have moved away from "comparative studies based on comparing final grades to the examination of conceptual, procedural, and problem-solving differences between students" (Meel, 1998, p. 165). Meel also reviewed several noncomparative studies in his analysis. Crocker (1992) used questionnaires, observations, and interviews to examine problem solving and students' conceptual development, and Ellison (1994) used qualitative case studies to focus on the evolution of student concept images (Meel, 1998).

As calculus reform began to be firmly rooted in undergraduate institutions, an emerging signature pedagogy developed that includes teaching students to use multiple representations to reason about interesting and challenging real-world problems in a student-centered environment (Tong, Burke, & Bennett, 2006). The focus on multiple representations of mathematical ideas to solve problems led to a process called "The Rule of Three" in the early reform calculus movement. Symbolic, graphical, and numerical representations of the same mathematical idea were used to teach mathematics, with special attention paid to the connections between all three ways of knowing (Simundza, 2006). Polya's focus on multiple representations in problem solving was a definite contribution to this aspect of the reform movement. The Rule of Three—numeric (tabular), graphical (visual), and symbolic/algebraic (formula)—incorporates the heuristics of focusing on simpler versions of a problem, creating models and diagrams of the problem in the simpler version, collecting data from these diagrams and placing the data into a table or into a graphical representation, and finding a formula based on the data.

Not only do students use multiple methods to study a mathematics problem, but they also have multiple ways of studying mathematical objects or concepts. Learning multiple ways to represent problems and sharing strategies for specific problems builds experience that is foundational to further mathematical work. Reasoning through a problem using different approaches or hearing their peers explain solutions using different representations than their own directly challenges students' misconception that there is just one technique or one solution to a mathematical problem (Ernie, 2007). The Rule of Three was then expanded to The Rule of Four by adding increased attention to student communication, both written and verbal (Simundza, 2006).

This pedagogy continues to morph as new technologies become available. For example, in the past five years teachers have started using Internet laboratory applications in which students vary parameters in a systematic way as the computer displays the effects on the characteristics of mathematical phenomena. In computer laboratory settings, students reason about mathematical objects such as polynomial functions, and create and answer their own questions about these objects. Using visual data generated dynamically, students develop their own conjectures and experiment to provide evidence to support their reasoning. The increasing development of dynamic environments where students physically control attributes of mathematical objects "plays a role in meaning building" (Kieren, 2007, p. 731). For instance, students can use animation to observe changes in a graph, or change the length of a pendulum to observe changes in the frequency. Simundza recommends adding this way of directly experiencing mathematics to The Rule of Four, forming a new Rule of Five for undergraduate mathematics pedagogy (Simundza, 2006).

This emerging signature pedagogy encourages dynamic and active learning that engages students in *doing* mathematics rather than hearing about mathematics. Because these two contrasting pedagogies are still present in the first-year classroom, we must ask questions about what students are learning. First, to what degree does mathematical understanding and reasoning occur in the traditional "lecture–memorization–test" model (Uhl & Davis, 1999, p. 67), and to what degree does mathematical reasoning and understanding occur in the emerging dynamic environment of "visualization–trial–error–speculation–explanation" (Uhl & Davis, 1999, p. 70)? Additionally, how do multiple representations, cooperative learning, technology, and real-world problems affect learning and attitudes about mathematics? Darken, Wynegar, and Kuhn (2000), in their survey of research on undergraduate mathematics education, conclude that most studies of calculus reform methods suggest there is a positive effect on learning and attitudes, but caution that more well-designed studies are warranted. In this section we outlined how the traditional pedagogy's focus on a single approach to solving problems has evolved into one that focuses on multiple representations. In this next section we will explore how the pedagogy evolved further to address the belief that problem solving is a quick task.

Two-Minute Problems

A common misconception among students at all levels is that solving mathematical problems requires memorization of formulas and application of known procedures, not deep understanding. Consequently, students also believe that solutions to mathematical problems should never take more than a few minutes. When faced with a non-routine problem, they won't struggle with the problem very long before simply giving up. Many of these students also expect teacher-centered classrooms where they listen as the teacher produces perfected solutions to routine problems. The students later mimic the teacher's process on homework and examinations. Traditional mathematics textbooks reinforced this belief. They were designed to encourage students to memorize formulas and mimic solution techniques, to work alone, and to do numerous drill exercises. Although procedural skills and memorized facts are necessary to do mathematics, continued progress in the subject is dependent on conceptual understanding: Successful undergraduate (Brown & Rodd, 2004; Povey & Angier, 2004) and graduate (Carlson, 1999) mathematics majors share the tendency to persevere or take their time when solving challenging problems.

This misconception about process and time-on-task has been documented in a variety of studies. Muis (2004) summarized 33 research studies on student-held beliefs about mathematics. Although only eight of those studies involved undergraduate students and none addressed changing beliefs through instructional strategies, the evidence from Muis's analysis of the research is quite clear: Elementary, secondary, and tertiary students all assume that mathematics is done quickly from known facts and processes. Furthermore, these beliefs are influenced by the common instructional strategies that affect student learning choices, performance, and motivation. In a study of more than 400 students, Schommer, Crouse, and Rhodes (1992) demonstrated that this belief in knowledge as a collection of isolated facts was negatively associated with both comprehension and student self-determination of learning. They found that "students who believed that knowing isolated facts was adequate to understand the material assumed that they had understood the text when their test performance indicated that they did not" (p. 441).

Eley and Meyer (2004) developed the Mathematics Study Process Inventory (MSPI) to target processes and activities used by students to study mathematics, from rote memorization to metacognitive strategies. Through their analysis of more than 400 students, the MSPI revealed that the scale associated with the use of non-purposeful approaches, such as giving up quickly or blind substitution of values into formulae, was a factor in distinguishing between borderline failing students as well as between good and superior students, as measured by semester grades. In a similar study of student beliefs, gender, and achievement in remedial mathematics courses, Stage and Kloosterman (1995) also found that most students felt doing mathematics consisted of following specific procedures. Tellingly, the women in the study who did not hold this belief were the most successful in the course, and contrary to what most university instructors believe, no relationship was found between female students' ability, beliefs, or achievement and their high school preparation. Because remedial courses serve as gatekeepers for a large population of students, replication of these results would help highlight the need to transform student beliefs about mathematics.

A component of any signature pedagogy in mathematics must include instructional and assessment techniques that address conceptual knowledge and promote perseverance in problem-solving situations. SoTL research in mathematics aimed at developing signature pedagogies must address how instructional strategies, classroom environment, and assessment tools can alter the belief that mathematics consists of isolated facts used to solve problems quickly, and more SoTL work is also needed to focus on the relationships between these beliefs, student study habits, student self-determination of comprehension, student success, and teaching strategies. Boaler's work (2002) at the secondary level connects nontraditional classroom environments to the development of perseverance and a positive disposition toward mathematical problem solving, but at the undergraduate level, there is a need to use existing inventories and previous research to analyze how instructional, environmental, and evaluative changes can improve study strategies and comprehension, and restructure beliefs about what it means to do mathematics.

A Lonely Task

In the past, it was not uncommon for students to sit in mathematics classrooms at desks arranged neatly in rows facing the "all-knowing" professor at the front of the room. Class time consisted of the professor lecturing and the students taking notes. Interaction between the professor and the students was minimal, and interaction between students was practically forbidden. Students were graded on their individually completed homework, quizzes, and exams. With this history, it is no wonder that many students commonly think that mathematics is a "solitary activity," one in which they struggle alone to understand and solve the assigned problems. With such a strongly held misconception, it is perhaps not surprising that many people develop math anxiety and even an active dislike for mathematics. However, although many mathematics classrooms today may still be set up with rows of desks facing the front of the room, this is where the similarity to the old classroom typically ends.

Most working mathematicians would certainly disagree with the idea of mathematics as a solitary activity. Nonacademic mathematicians are more likely to work on projects in groups than alone. Even in the academic setting, collaboration in mathematical research is routine. Professors often discuss teaching and learning issues with their colleagues. Communication and interaction between professors and their colleagues, between professors and their students, and between students in mathematics classes is now a common and essential aspect of mathematics education.

Increased use of cooperative learning techniques in mathematics education is one hallmark of the new mathematics classroom and of the emerging signature pedagogy. It is well-documented that cooperative learning in the classroom has many benefits (Johnson, Johnson, & Stanne, 2000; Slavin, 1990, 1991). The college mathematics classroom is no exception. Research on cooperative learning in undergraduate mathematics tends to be guided by two basic sets of research questions. First, much of the research deals with the effects of cooperative learning on student achievement, persistence, and attitudes (Springer, Stanne, & Donovan, 1999). The second set of research considers the effectiveness of specific cooperative learning techniques (Rogers, Reynolds, Davidson, & Thomas, 2001; Slavin, 1990, 1991).

Though there is substantial research on cooperative learning at the presecondary levels, the first meta-analysis of research on cooperative learning in mathematics and related disciplines at the postsecondary level was published in 1999 (Springer et al., 1999). In this study, the authors found that "various forms of small-group learning are effective in promoting greater academic achievement, more favorable attitudes towards learning, and increased persistence through SMET (science, mathematics, engineering and technology) courses and programs" (Springer et al., 1999, p. 21). Particularly large effects were seen "on the academic achievement of members of underrepresented groups and the learning-related attitudes of women and preservice teachers" (p. 42). In addition, the analysis suggests that "greater time spent working in groups leads to more favorable attitudes among students in general" and "even minimal group work can have positive effects on student achievement" (p. 42). Schwartz (1992) indicates that use of cooperative learning techniques is one way to help increase liberal arts students' interest in mathematics. Cooperative learning in mathematics is the subject of an entire volume of the *Journal of Research in Mathematics Education* (vol. 22, no. 5, 1991), and cooperative learning in college mathematics specifically is the subject of a 2001 book in the Mathematical Association of America Notes Series (Rogers et al., 2001). In response to the wealth of research on the utility of collaboration in the mathematics classroom, as well as the actual work of disciplinary practitioners, the American Mathematical Association of Two-Year Colleges (AMATYC) includes this emphasis on cooperative learning as a basic guiding principle in their recent standards document: "Mathematics content and instruction should include opportunities for students to engage in inquiry, problem solving, modeling, and collaborative learning, using appropriate technology" (AMATYC, 2006, p. 10).

The second set of research on cooperative learning focuses on the effectiveness of specific techniques. In their meta-analysis of cooperative learning techniques, Johnson, Johnson, and Stanne (2000) review 164 studies investigating eight different cooperative learning techniques. For example, Davidson (1990) wrote a handbook for teachers on cooperative learning strategies that use small groups in mathematics teaching and learning. He also included an extensive list of resources for teachers on the topic of cooperative learning in the classroom.

The emphasis and research on cooperative learning in mathematics has led to the development of another important area of research in mathematics education: communication and writing in the language of mathematics. In order to work in groups, students must be able to talk about their ideas and explain them in ways that others can understand. They must use appropriate vocabulary, be able to reason, and defend their reasoning when others in the group fail to understand or are disbelieving. Davidson (1990) reports that both teachers and students cite this communication as one of the many positive effects of the use of cooperative learning in the classroom. Students learn to communicate in the language of mathematics as well as cooperate with others. The push for writing across the curriculum has also contributed to the growth of writing in mathematics.

A component of any signature pedagogy in mathematics must include instructional techniques that involve collaborative work, both inside and outside of the classroom. Much of the development of mathematics throughout history has been the result of collaboration. This well-established practice of collaboration in mathematical research has moved into the classroom, and the research shows that the students and the discipline are better off as a result.

In a Vacuum

In addition to pedagogy that misinformed students about the processes of doing mathematics, the content of traditional mathematics textbooks has contributed to significant disciplinary misconceptions that can be corrected with an emerging signature pedagogy. Mathematics textbooks reflect the history of teaching and learning in mathematics, and they record the development and struggles involved in advancing students' learning and understanding of mathematics. They can foster a student's interest and understanding of mathematics, or they can stifle it. The content and the way it's presented, then, are critical.

One of the key debates in textbook authoring is which approach to reasoning should be used to present the mathematical content. There are two standard types of reasoning: deductive and inductive. The distinction between the two is often described in a beginning course in mathematical proof. Smith, Eggen, and St. Andre (2006) in their widely used textbook *A Transition to Advanced Mathematics* describe inductive reasoning as the kind typically used by the natural or social scientist. Such a scientist "generally makes observations of particular cases or phenomena and seeks a general theory that describes or explains the observations" (Smith et al., 2006, p. 1). This type of reasoning is certainly used by mathematicians, but the authors assert that "the characteristic thinking of mathematicians . . . is deductive reasoning, in which one uses logic to draw conclusions based on statements accepted as true" (Smith et al., 2006, p. 1). In other words, the observations come as special cases of a theory that has been proven true using the rules of logic.

Following this assumption about the primary role of deductive reasoning in mathematics, many traditional textbooks use a deductive approach in presenting content. Each section begins with the definition of a new concept, followed by a couple of examples to help students become familiar with the terms. Theorems relating to the concept are then given, followed by their proofs. These may then be followed by more examples to help students digest the results of the theorem. With such a presentation, it is probably no surprise that the exercises in the text tend to be primarily skills-based questions meant to provide practice in using the definitions and applying the theorems. In addition to focusing on acquiring these rote skills, the deductive design of traditional textbooks omitted illustrations of how the content applied to real world situations. Students thus saw no connections between the mathematics they were being taught and the world that they lived in. On the contrary, most mathematicians would argue that mathematical reasoning is not only relevant but easily expressed in content relevant to students' lives.

This traditional textbook presentation misses the motivation for the development of the mathematical concepts and hence could hardly be expected to raise students' interests and get them excited about learning. Lynn Arthur Steen, in his *Twenty Questions about Mathematical Reasoning*, discusses the need for caution:

> Context can affect learning in two opposing ways: generally, it enhances motivation and long-term learning, but it can also limit the utility of what is learned. Knowledge often becomes context-bound when it is taught in just one context. Anyone who has ever taught mathematics has heard complaints from teachers in other subjects that students don't appear to know any of the mathematics they were supposed to have learned in mathematics class. (Steen, 1999, p. 278)

The almost exclusive presentation of deductive mathematics in these traditional textbooks limits students' ability to understand the utility of mathematics. This narrow focus on deductive reasoning leaves the impression of mathematics as divorced from the real world. In addition, this deductive presentation that focuses on rote skills acquisition, combined with students' preexisting lack of motivation, is more likely to engender a dislike of the content of the specific course and of mathematics in general. It is also likely to cause anxiety for students who struggle with understanding material presented in a vacuum.

Because the change in mathematics textbooks followed as a consequence of the reform, and because many instructors use the text as their primary resource, some of the problems resulting partially from the textbooks persisted, delaying the classroom effects of the reform movement, including the signature pedagogy emerging from the reforms. Most introductory-level mathematics textbooks today, however, address the common misconceptions head on and attempt to dispel rather than support and perpetuate them. Although the traditional mathematics textbook presented content deductively, a new breed of textbooks has started using inductive reasoning, along with the standard deductive approach, including using real life examples or historical background to promote the introduction of new mathematical concepts. Deductive reasoning is then employed to give a logical confirmation of results involving the mathematical concept. In this approach, making conjectures is a natural consequence of the inductive development.

One example of this new breed of textbook is Burger and Starbird's *The Heart of Mathematics: An Invitation to Effective Thinking* (2005). This text is widely used in introductory college mathematics courses, which are the only mathematics courses many college students will take. In the note describing the cover of the text, the authors state that:

> The dodecahedron reflects how mathematics allows us to see and understand our world with greater clarity. The images of urban settings, sky, and beyond remind us that mathematics is all around and can be found in everyday activities. We hope that students using this book will recognize the power of mathematics in their world. (p. iv)

They also describe their goal as offering students "the genuine ideas and modes of thinking that attract all of us to mathematics" (p. ix). Through a cursory review of the text, one can note the significant differences in the approach as compared to traditional mathematics textbooks. The book has been widely acclaimed by reviewers, instructors, and students (Cohen, 2001). Another popular textbook for liberal arts mathematics courses is *For All Practical Purposes: Mathematical Literacy in Today's World* which was written by the Consortium for Mathematics and its Applications or COMAP (2006). This text, which is in its seventh edition, also places mathematical problems within a real-world context to make mathematics more meaningful and thus more understandable for students. As part of the preface to the student, the authors state that mathematics "is important in explaining the way the world works. It is important because knowing it can make your life easier. . . . In school, you spent a great deal of time learning the tools of mathematics . . . in a sense, you've learned to hammer nails and saw wood. Now we're going to build houses" (COMAP, 2006, p. xiii).

After more than a decade of debate and reform, the methodology of mathematics textbooks has greatly improved. It is now common to include examples and exercises with real-life connections as well as the typical skill-based exercises. Historical background is given as a way to put material in context. Most textbooks now contain problems that ask students to explain their reasoning in writing using appropriate mathematical language, and many contain projects to encourage students to explore the new concepts and their applications. Although these problems can be used as assignments for individual students, most are actually intended as group projects. Although textbooks will continue to change as new and better ways of presenting the content are found, it seems clear that the major changes in the recent past have been, in large part, a result of the reform in mathematics education. The change in textbooks, in turn, has informed and served as an impetus for further improvement in the approaches to the teaching and learning of mathematics.

Conclusion

Much of the research presented in this chapter, as well as the chapter itself, calls for additional research in teaching and learning mathematics. As noted by Selden (2005), the expert-novice paradigm allows us to recognize differences in students' conceptual difficulties with particular topics and in how they process mathematical practices, as well as in how affective beliefs, attitudes, and emotions influence learning. Each of these realms relate to student mathematical reasoning and pose opportunities for future SoTL work in the development of signature pedagogies in mathematics. Absent from the research is the establishment of any link between instructor beliefs and instructional strategy choice. Additionally, SoTL research is needed that replicates works cited in this chapter and extends the current research by looking for associations between changing beliefs and instructional strategies. Finally, for systemic impact, it is necessary that the results of past and current research be available to the larger mathematical community.

Avenues for this continued scholarship are as varied as the research presented in this chapter. Both quantitative and qualitative studies are needed for SoTL projects to capture the different factors that can dispel myths and promote mathematical reasoning. Descriptive, qualitative work that corroborates anecdotal evidence may suggest links between pedagogy and learning. Selden (2002), in looking to unify mathematicians and mathematics educators to improve undergraduate education, describes examples from medical research and neuropsychology wherein substantive information is based on very small samples. She identifies areas where mathematics education research has identified topics of difficulty and calls for the scholarly documentation of course development, including content, pedagogy, and the conjectures that led to the links between the two. This type of detailed documentation may form a foundation for SoTL projects in undergraduate mathematics.

Despite the call for further SoTL, there is indeed a rich history of mathematicians and mathematics educators' involvement in SoTL projects. A recent history of the transformation from a cognitive study of the learning of mathematics at the post-secondary level to a sociocultural and anthropological one is documented by Artigue, Batanero, and Kent (2007). In other realms of research that support SoTL work, there has been considerable examination of many topics, including gender issues related to mathematics (Hyde, Fennema, & Lamon, 1990) and the development and implications of the calculus reform movement. Holton (2001) provides a review of many international SoTL projects, including the action-process-object-schema development of mathematical concepts and the impact of technology in the learning and teaching of mathematics. Numerous professional organizations support the scholarship of the teaching and learning of mathematics, including the following:

- The Association of Mathematics Teacher Educators (AMTE)
- The Conference Board of the Mathematical Sciences
- The International Group for the Psychology of Mathematics Education (PME)
- National Council of Teachers of Mathematics
- Research Council on Mathematics Learning (RCLM)
- The Special Interest Group of the Mathematical Association of America on Research in Undergraduate Mathematics Education (RUME)

One of the difficulties in defining a signature pedagogy for the first-year undergraduate mathematics course is the diversity of courses developed in various branches of mathematics, and the diversity of students and faculty. First-year students choose from a wide range of mathematics offerings, perhaps more so than in any other discipline: a liberal arts overview of mathematics, an algebra modeling class, a business mathematics course, a course in statistics, or courses on quantitative literacy, trigonometry, finite mathematics, or calculus. The selection of a first mathematics course depends on students' program interests, background in mathematics, and perhaps even scheduling. This first, and perhaps only, mathematics course they take as college students has the potential to address misconceptions and to engage students in ways of mathematics knowing, thinking, and reasoning.

Despite this difficulty in identifying a single signature pedagogy, specific pedagogical practices have emerged as a consequence of SoTL research, resulting in recommendations for classroom experiences that will educate students to view mathematics as a discipline in which (a) problems of interest to them are posed, (b) solutions are generated collaboratively, (c) conceptual reasoning is required, and (d) multiple approaches and solutions are encouraged. When these components are present in the pedagogy of a course, students will begin to think as mathematicians, thus developing signature characteristics of the profession.

Continued scholarly investigation of teaching and learning in mathematics depends on the interaction of mathematicians and mathematics educators. As these groups unite to improve the teaching and learning of mathematics, both disciplines will benefit. Improved education at the tertiary level can lead to an increase in the number of students pursuing STEM careers and an understanding of the ever-changing relationships between the communities of learners and educators. Through the development and implementation of new pedagogies in undergraduate mathematics, perhaps students at all levels can begin to engage in what Boaler (2002, p. 119) describes as the "disciplinary dance"—what we understand to be a signature dance of mathematicians.

References

American Mathematical Association of Two-Year Colleges. (2006). Beyond crossroads. Retrieved December 22, 2007, from http://www.beyondcrossroads.com/

Artigue, M., Batanero, C., & Kent, P. (2007). Mathematics thinking and learning at post-secondary level. In F. K. Lester (Ed.), *Second handbook of research on mathematics teaching and learning a project of the National Council of Teachers of Mathematics* (pp. 1011–1049). Charlotte, NC: Information Age Publishing.

Boaler, J. (2002). The development of disciplinary relationships: Knowledge, practice and identity in mathematics classrooms. *Proceedings of the 26th Conference of the International Group for the Psychology of Mathematics Education, 2,* 113–120.

Bookman, J., & Friedman, C. P. (1994). A comparison of the problem solving performance of students in lab based and traditional calculus. In E. Dubinsky, A. H. Schoenfeld, & J. Kaput (Eds.), *Research in collegiate mathematics education I. CBMS issues in mathematics education,* (4) (pp. 101–116). Providence, RI: American Mathematical Society.

Brown, M., & Rodd, M. (2004). Successful undergraduate mathematicians: A study of students in two universities. *Proceedings of the 28th Conference of the International Group for the Psychology of Mathematics Education, 4,* 97–104.

Burger, E. B., & Starbird, M. (2005). *The heart of mathematics: An invitation to effective thinking* (2nd ed.). Emeryville, CA: Key College Publishing.

Carlson, M. P. (1999). The mathematical behavior of six successful mathematics graduate students: Influences leading to mathematical success. *Educational Studies in Mathematics 40*(3), 237–258.

Cohen, M. D. (2001). Review of the heart of mathematics: An invitation to effective thinking. *American Mathematical Monthly 108*(6), 573–577.

Consortium for Mathematics and its Applications. (2006). *For all practical purposes: Mathematical literacy in today's world* (7th ed.). New York: W.H. Freeman.

Crocker, D. A. (1992). *A qualitative study of interactions, concept development and problem solving in a calculus class immersed in the computer algebra system Mathematica,* Dissertation Abstracts International 58(8), 2850A.

Darken, B., Wynegar, R., & Kuhn, S. (2000). Evaluating calculus reform: A reform and a longitudinal study. In E. Dubinsky, A. H. Schoenfeld, & J. Kaput (Eds.),

Research in Collegiate Mathematics Education IV. CBMS Issues in Mathematics Education (8) (pp. 16–41). Providence, RI: American Mathematical Society.

Davidson, N. (Ed.). (1990). *Cooperative learning in mathematics: A handbook for teachers.* Menlo Park, CA: Addison-Wesley.

Eley, M. G., & Meyer, J. H. F. (2004). Modeling the influences on learning outcomes of study processes in university mathematics. *Higher Education, 47*, 437–454.

Ellison, M. J. (1994). *The effects of computer and calculator graphics on students' ability to mentally construct calculus concepts.* Dissertation Abstracts International 54(11) 4020A.

Ernie, K. T. (2007). Choices, representations, and strategies used in solving problems by elementary education students in their first mathematics content course. *2007 Joint Meeting of the American Mathematical Society and the Mathematical Association of America.* January, 6, 2007.

Gavosto, E. A., Krantz, S. G., & McCallum, W. (1999). Preface. *Contemporary Issues in Mathematics Education 36* (pp. xiii–xv). Mathematical Sciences Research Institute. New York: Cambridge University Press.

Herzig, A., & Kung, D. T. (2003). Cooperative learning in calculus reform: What have we learned? In A. Selden, E. Dubinsky, G. Harel, & F. Hitt (Eds.), *Research in Collegiate Mathematics Education V. CBMS Issues in Mathematics Education* (12) (pp. 30–55). Providence, RI: American Mathematical Society.

Holton, D. (Ed.) (2001). *The teaching and learning of mathematics at university level: An ICMI study.* New ICMI Study Series (7). Dordrecht: Kluwer Academic.

Hyde, J. S., Fennema, E., & Lamon, S. J. (1990). Gender differences in mathematics performance: A meta-analysis. *Psychological Bulletin, 107*(2), pp. 139–155.

Johnson, D. W., Johnson, R. T., & Stanne, M. B. (2000) *Cooperative learning methods: A meta-analysis.* Retrieved December 22, 2007, from http://www.co-operation.org/pages/cl-methods.html

Judson, P. T. (1989). *Effects of modified sequencing of skills and applications in introductory calculus.* Dissertation Abstracts International 49 1397A.

Keller, B. A. (1994). *Symbol sense and its development in two computer algebra system environments.* Dissertation Abstracts International 54(11) 5704B.

Kieren, C. (2007). Learning and teaching algebra at the middle school through college levels: Building meaning for symbols and their manipulation. In F. K. Lester (Ed.), *Second handbook of research on mathematics teaching and learning: A project of the National Council of Teachers of Mathematics* (pp. 707–762). Charlotte, NC: Information Age.

Lithner, J. (2003). Students' mathematical reasoning in university textbook exercises. *Educational Studies in Mathematics, 52*, 29–55.

Loftsgaarden, D. O., Rung, D. C., & Watkins, A. E. (Eds.). (1997). *Statistical abstract of undergraduate programs in the Mathematical Sciences in the United States: Fall 1995 CBMS Survey*. Providence, RI: American Mathematical Society.

Lutzer, D. J., Rodli, S. B., Kirkman, E. E., & Maxwell, J. W. (Eds.) (2007). *Statistical abstract of undergraduate programs in the mathematical sciences in the United States: Fall 2005 CBMS survey*. Providence, RI: American Mathematical Society.

Meel, D. (1998). Honors students' calculus understandings: Comparing calculus & Mathematica and traditional calculus students. In A. H. Schoenfeld, J. Kaput, & E. Dubinsky (Eds.), *Research in Collegiate Mathematics Education III. CBMS Issues in Mathematics Education* (7) (pp. 163–215). Providence, RI: American Mathematical Society.

Melin-Conejeros, J. (1993). *The effect of using a computer algebra system in a mathematics laboratory on the achievement and attitude of calculus students*. Dissertation Abstracts International 53(7) 2283A.

Muis, K. R. (2004). Personal epistemology and mathematics: A critical review and synthesis of research. *Review of Educational Research, 74*(3), 317–377.

Park, K. (1993). *A comparative study of the traditional calculus course vs. the Calculus & Mathematica course*. Dissertation Abstracts International 54(1) 119A.

Polya, G. (1945). *How to solve it: A new aspect of mathematical method*. Princeton, NJ: Princeton University Press.

Povey, H., & Angier, C. (2004). Some undergraduates' experiences of learning mathematics. *Proceedings of the 28th Conference of the International Group for the Psychology of Mathematics Education, 4*, 57–64.

Rogers, E. C., Reynolds, B. E., Davidson, N. A., & Thomas, A. (Eds.). (2001). *Cooperative learning in undergraduate mathematics: Issues that matter and strategies that work. MAA Notes 55*. Washington, DC: Mathematical Association of America.

Schoenfeld, A. H. (1992). Learning to think mathematically: Problem solving, metacognition, and sense making in mathematics. In D. A. Grouws (Ed.) *Handbook of research on mathematics teaching and learning* (pp. 334–370). New York: Simon & Schuster.

Schommer, M., Crouse, A., & Rhodes, N. (1992). Epistemological beliefs and mathematical text comprehension: Believing it is simple does not make it so. *Journal of Educational Psychology, 84*(4), 435–443.

Schrock, C. S. (1989). *Calculus and computing: An exploratory study to examine the effectiveness of using a computer algebra system to develop increased conceptual understanding in a first-semester course*. Dissertation Abstracts International 50(7) 1926A.

Schwartz, R. (1992). Revitalizing liberal arts mathematics. *Mathematics and Computer Education, 26*(3), 272–277.

Selden, A. (2002). Two research traditions separated by a common subject: Mathematics and mathematics education. Tennessee Technological University, Technical report No. 2002–2.

Selden, A. (2005). New development and trends in tertiary mathematics education: Or, more of the same? *International Journal of Mathematical Education in Science and Technology, 36*(2–3), 131–147.

Simundza, G. (2006). The fifth rule: Direct experience of mathematics. In N. B. Hastings (Ed.), *A fresh start for collegiate mathematics: Rethinking the courses below calculus. MAA Notes 69* (pp. 320–327). Washington, DC: The Mathematical Association of America.

Slavin, R. (1990). Research on cooperative learning: Consensus and controversy. *Educational Leadership, 47,* 52–54.

Slavin, R. (1991). Synthesis of research of cooperative learning. *Educational Leadership, 48,* 71–82.

Smith D., Eggen, M., & St. Andre, R. (2006) *A transition to advanced mathematics.* (6th ed.). Pacific Grove, CA: Brooks/Cole.

Springer, L., Stanne, M. E., & Donovan, S. S. (1999). Effects of small group learning on undergraduates in science, mathematics, engineering, and technology: A meta-analysis. *Review of Educational Research, 69*(1), 21–51.

Stage, F. K., & Kloosterman, P. (1995). Gender beliefs and achievement in remedial college-level mathematics. *Journal of Higher Education, 66*(3), 294–311.

Steen, L. A. (1999). Twenty questions about mathematical reasoning. In L. Stiff & F. Curio (Eds.), *Developing mathematical reasoning in grades K-12 1999 yearbook* (pp. 270–285). Reston, VA: National Council of Teachers of Mathematics.

Stonewater, J. K. (2005). Inquiry teaching and learning: The best math class study. *School Science and Mathematics, 105*(1), 36–47.

Tong, S., Burke, M., & Bennett, C. (2006). Evidence, impact and momentum. 2006 CASTL Colloquium on Scholarship of Teaching and Learning, April 2006, Madison, WI.

Uhl, J., & Davis, W. (1999). Is the mathematics we do the mathematics we teach? In E. A. Gavosto, S. G. Krantz, & W. McCallum (Eds.), *Contemporary Issues in Mathematics Education 36* (pp. 67–74). Mathematical Sciences Research Institute. New York: Cambridge University Press.

15

SIGNATURE PEDAGOGIES IN INTRODUCTORY PHYSICS

Mark J. Lattery

This chapter describes signature pedagogies in the first-year undergraduate physics course. If signature pedagogies "disclose important information about the personality of a disciplinary field—its values, knowledge, and manner of thinking" (Calder, 2006), then it is natural to ask, What exactly is the *personality* of the field of physics? What are its values and manner of thinking? And what impact do traditional and signature pedagogies have on student learning in introductory physics? In raising these questions, I have two goals in mind: to re-examine how we teach physics in view of the nature of the discipline, and more broadly, to highlight the Scholarship of Teaching and Learning (SoTL) as a means to improve higher education.

In the first two sections, I describe the character of the physics discipline, including its goals, methods of training, and distinctive ways of knowing. Then I define and compare traditional and signature pedagogies in physics. Special attention is given to features that reflect, or do not reflect, the nature of the discipline. I conclude with five examples of signature pedagogies.

The Physics Discipline

Physics is the study of particles and their interactions. All phenomena are explained in terms of just four interactions: gravitational, electromagnetic, weak (radioactive), and strong (nuclear) forces.[1] As such, physics provides the essential foundation for all of chemistry, and therefore all of biology.[2]

When one thinks of physics, many things come to mind: prisms, inclined planes, pulleys, magnets, x-rays, atoms, $E=mc^2$, quantum mechanics, or tricky word problems. However, the main goal of physics is a single, unified "theory of everything" to describe the Universe *at the most fundamental level.* The search for such a theory has led to a surprising number of questions about the nature of space, time, matter, and measurement. The answers to these questions are quite strange and unexpected.

Physics is also the basis for modern technology, although this is not generally understood. Unlike Edison's invention of the light bulb (or rather stories about the invention), we do *not* get cell phones, HDTVs, computers, microwaves, space shuttles, and so on by random trial-and-error. To create new technology, one must have a deep understanding of physics—especially detailed mathematical descriptions of how extremely tiny, quick things move. It is no exaggeration to say that without physics, modern technology would not exist, so preparing physicists is critical to the quality of modern life.

Physics departments have two main responsibilities: to train physicists and to teach (even filter for) students with an aptitude for engineering, medicine, and other science-related fields. The list of science-related careers is growing, so the former role is becoming a smaller portion of our teaching activities (Redish, 2003). In other words, the number of physics courses for non-majors is rising. Often these courses become "pilot sites" for innovative methods of physics teaching.

The preparation of a physicist can be divided into three stages: (1) undergraduate school (4–5 years), (2) graduate school culminating in a doctorate degree (5–8 years), and (3) postdoctoral work—comparable to a medical residency (1–3 years). The core subject areas in physics are classical mechanics, electricity and magnetism, and quantum mechanics, though other physics topics are taught as well. The physics curriculum is spiraled, which means that students study the same subject over and over again, at successively higher levels of difficulty. For example, most physics students study classical mechanics for the first time in high school, again as college freshmen, and again as juniors or seniors. In graduate school, they study it yet again. At each level, the fundamentals are rehearsed. At higher levels, the three core subjects become fully integrated, and the philosophical aspects of the field begin to emerge. The concepts of spiraling and integration are, of course, well developed in education (e.g. Bruner, 1960), and they work extremely well in preparing students to become physicists.

In addition to coursework, all physics students are encouraged to assist with faculty research. Such experiences can be paid or volunteer and occur in a one-on-one mentoring relationship or in a research group. Participation with faculty in research exposes students to numerous dimensions of "doing" science: computer-based data collection and analysis, scientific modeling, construction and maintenance of physics apparatus, literature reviews, presentation of research at conferences, and paper writing. By the second or third year of graduate school, these research experiences replace coursework as the dominant mode of learning. The professor-student mentor relationship is especially important at this level.[3] Students are generally expected to achieve first-authorship on a published scientific paper before they defend their Ph.D. thesis.

How Physicists Think: A Personal View

By-and-large, physicists are philosophical objectivists. They believe in an external reality, they see their efforts as a "search for the truth," and they believe they can make non-culturally embedded observations about nature. Halloun (2004) summed up this position thusly:

> In the absence of human intervention, physical systems exist, interact, and evolve, producing certain phenomena in the universe, all independently of human existence and activity. Humans can eventually come to realize the existence of such systems and phenomena, and develop about them ideas of variable degrees of viability. (p. 14)

This point of view contrasts strongly with the dominant philosophy of the humanities, which embraces an increasingly relativist/constructivist view of knowledge. The philosophical rift between the hard sciences and the humanities is skillfully described by C. P. Snow (1993).

The chief intellectual activity of physics is the construction and evaluation of scientific models, or idealized representations of the real world (Hestenes, 1987; Nersessian 1995). Common representations include equations, diagrams, graphs, charts, computer algorithms, and written descriptions. An oft-used example of a model is the Ptolemaic system of astronomy (second century) in which each planet (except Earth) rests on perimeter of a rotating disk that, in turn, circles Earth. The power of a model is measured by the precision and reliability with which it predicts the future.[4] Currently, the most powerful model in physics (indeed, in all of science) is the Standard Model of Interactions.[5] Physicists revere experimental data as the definitive judge of their models.

Physics involves storytelling—not stories about the history of physics, or its many heroes, but fanciful stories about the natural world. Stories are told of balls that drop down holes that penetrate the Earth, cats in boxes that are simultaneously alive and dead, tiny demons that open and close trap doors in cooling tanks, identical twins that age at different rates, and the more conventional, blocks on frictionless inclined planes. Such stories are found throughout the physics curriculum (Helm & Gilbert, 1985a, 1985b). Some stories begin as fantasy and end as reality. Newton devised an unbelievable story about an object that was projected horizontally from the top of a pyramid, with such force, that the object actually circled the Earth and returned to the thrower. Highly exaggerated stories are used by physicists to evaluate and reject models. At times, this activity avoids the need to conduct an actual experiment (Lattery, 2001a). Physics storytelling is *not* just entertainment; scientific progress depends on them (Matthews, 1994; Kuhn, 1964).[6]

Physics depends on collaboration and dialogue. Models are generally constructed by research groups, not by individuals, and because face-to-face communication is essential, physicists engage in continuous verbal jousts at conferences and in closed research meetings. These debates carry over into scientific journals and books.[7]

Physicists value conceptual knowledge. Conceptual knowledge refers to a qualitative (non-mathematical) understanding of how the world works. A student may be able to solve an equation or perform a calculation, but they may not understand when a particular idea should be invoked, or the type of solution to expect. Such competencies require an intuitive or "gut-level" understanding of content, which may or may not accompany a mastery of mathematics (Camp & Clement, 1994). Physicists also value a unified understanding of nature. They seek to organize all phenomena around just a few scientific models (Hestenes, 1987). Physicists strongly desire their models of the world to be simple and elegant. Ironically, they celebrate the failure of their very best models, a signal that more work needs to be done!

Like other academic disciplines, the field of physics also values intellectual honesty, clarity, perseverance, thoroughness, creativity, and an ability to solve problems from multiple perspectives. The attitudes, values, and dispositions of the field are exemplified by such icons as Galileo Galilee, Isaac Newton, Michael Faraday, Niels Bohr, Albert Einstein, and Richard Feynman.

Traditional and Signature Pedagogies in Introductory Physics

Lectures and confirmation labs constitute the traditional, or default, pedagogies in introductory physics (Redish, 2003). For large classes (N > 50), lectures typically meet three times per week. Students sit in rows and columns of seats facing the instructor—the focus of the attention. As the instructor writes on the chalkboard, students take notes. For most students, the lecture is a non-interactive, passive experience. The goal of the instructor is to "cover the material" and the goal of the student is to "get everything down so I can study it later." In conjunction with the traditional lecture, students participate in confirmation labs (usually once per week). As the name suggests, the purpose of this experience is to verify formulas presented in lecture or the textbook. Students follow a procedure or "recipe" from a laboratory manual; secondary goals might include laboratory skills or evaluation of experimental errors. These activities may or may not be coordinated with the lecture material. Education researchers have lamented the traditional format for decades (McDermott, 2001), and as I describe later, research shows that traditional pedagogies are relatively ineffective.

In contrast to traditional pedagogies, signature pedagogies engage students in the types of activities and styles of thinking that experts in the discipline value (Shulman, 2005). In this case, they encourage students to "think and act like a physicist." A review of current signature pedagogies (described in the following section) reveals three key characteristics:

- Engagement in scientific model development and evaluation
- Emphasis on the conceptual understanding of the content
- Employment of peer discussion and collaboration

These three characteristics (the three Es) imply a higher level of student participation than often expected in a traditional course. Using signature pedagogies, students may be asked to make a prediction, explain an idea to a peer, solve a problem, or defend an idea in front of the entire class. The focus of the instruction is on the student, not the instructor. In a traditional classroom, the instructor is the "sage on the stage," but in signature pedagogies, the instructor is the "guide on the side." The emphasis is not on how well instructors organize and present content, but rather how students think and make sense of the material.

In some cases, traditional distinctions between course contexts—lecture, recitation, or laboratory—blur. In so-called 'studio courses,' such as Workshop Physics at Dickinson College, PA, the lecture, laboratory, and recitation sections are rolled into one (Laws, 1991). Students meet in the same location for all class sessions. In the same classroom period, students work through an activity guide in groups, discuss conceptual problems, carry out short laboratory activities with the aid of a computer, and occasionally listen to a mini-lecture. The physical classroom environment encourages student interaction. Instead of a theater seating arrangement, students face each other in clusters of three or four, with a shared computer station. These clusters line the perimeter of the classroom so the instructor can easily monitor student progress and guide learning.

Examples of Signature Pedagogies

The following are five examples of signature pedagogies in introductory physics. They are by no means the only, or necessarily the best examples, yet they highlight a wide range of methods that expose students to the nature of the discipline.[8]

Modeling Method

One effective way to get students to "think and act like a physicist" is the Modeling Method of Physics Instruction (ASU, 2008; U.S. Department of Education, 2002; Wells, Hestenes, & Swackhamer, 1995). As the name suggests, this method engages students in the formation, development, and revision of scientific models. Rather than presenting physics equations at the outset of a lesson (a deductive approach), the Modeling Method guides students to uncover the equations in a lab setting (an inductive approach). The goal of these activities are not numerical answers to be checked at the back of the textbook, but rather models to help students organize their understanding of physics.

An example of the Modeling Method is the *Force and Motion* unit of Workshop Physical Science, a studio course (Lattery, 2001b; Lattery, 2008).

The purpose of the unit is to expose students to the scientific thinking process and teach Newton's second law. To reach these objectives, students are asked to model the motion of a fan cart. A fan cart is a small rolling cart with an electric fan unit on the top. In the "simplest experiment," also called the one-way trip, the fan cart is placed at rest and the fan is turned on. The spinning fan propels air to the rear of the cart; this "rocket action" accelerates the cart forward from rest (similar to, but more controlled than, air let out of a balloon.)

The motion of the fan cart can be measured with an ultrasonic motion detector and a computer. The results are displayed in real time, as a speed-time graph on a computer screen. Students investigate the fan-cart motion in a variety of cases: two fans attached to the body, carts with different masses, fans that propel air at various angles, fans that turn on and off during the motion, and so on.

For each experiment, students engage in processes of model building and revision. Students express their models in terms of force diagrams, position- and speed-graphs, motion maps, and in writing—all skills developed earlier in the course. Students discuss their models with group members, and perform experiments to check their results. Then, students report their results on a whiteboard for large group discussions. The peer interactions are similar to what one sees at a scientific conference (MacIsaac, 2008; Schmitt & Lattery, 2004). Eventually, students come to consensus on the relation of force and motion for this "simplest experiment."

For the one-way trip activities, the instructor restricts the investigation in two ways: (1) the fan cart always starts from rest (it is never pushed), and (2) the fan cart always moves in one-direction (no stopping and turning around). This sets up the culminating modeling activity: the two-way trip of the fan cart. For the two-way trip, the cart is placed at rest on the track, the fan is turned on, and then the fan cart is pushed in a direction opposite the fan thrust. For reasons beyond the scope of this chapter, students abandon essential correct models of force and motion (for the one-way trip) for pre-Newtonian models (for the two-way trip) (Lattery, 2008). This produces significant cognitive conflict within the students, and a lively debate.

Next, students are placed in pairs to write a scientific paper on the two-way trip. The paper must (1) articulate a model of the two-way trip in diagrams, graphs, and writing, and (2) attempt to square this model with their model of the one-way trip. Student papers are exchanged, pairs receive (anonymous) peer feedback, and pairs submit a rebuttal to a peer review—a process similar to the peer review process of a scientific journal. Students are jarred by the range of views offered and the interactions can become heated.

The project ends with a large group discussion in which the students air and defend their final ideas publicly. The strengths and weaknesses of each model are evaluated using empirical, logical, and (even) metaphysical considerations. The instructor guides the entire process. The accepted scientific view (the Newtonian view) eventually surfaces.

According to a recent evaluation of this method of instruction (Lattery, 2007), these modeling activities lead to significant learning gains on the Force Concept Inventory (FCI) (Hestenes, Wells, & Swackhamer, 1992). Additionally, students learn that "doing physics" means comparing multiple, competing scientific models—a point rarely, if ever, made in a traditional course. Students also learn the value of conceptual knowledge (inferences are built from the qualitative motion of the cart), unification (students grapple with inconsistent rules of force and motion for the one- and two-way trips), thought experiments ("What would happen if the track were infinitely long?"), and peer discourse.

Peer Instruction

While the above example seems best suited to smaller classes, signature pedagogies can also be implemented in large-enrollment lecture courses. Harvard University's *Peer Instruction* program is a noteworthy example (Mazur, 1997). The instruction begins with a short (5–7 minute) lecture, and to check their understanding, students take a ConcepTest based on questions culled from years of research on student learning difficulties. Students individually record their answers using a hand-held electronic clicker, and the collective response of the class (and answer-choice distribution) is projected on a large screen at the front of the room. This approach can be implemented with ClassTalk™ or Personal Response System™ (PRS), although students can also use flashcards to present their answers (for other implementations, see Beuckman, Rebello, & Zollman, 2007; Reay, Bao, Li, Warnakulasooriya, & Baugh, 2005).

Next, the instructor asks the students turn to their nearest neighbor to "prove that they are right." A brief, lively scientific discussion ensues as students exchange ideas and articulate and defend themselves just as scientists would. Following this discussion, students again enter their answers into the PRS. As a wrap-up, the instructor discloses the "correct answer" and provides direct instruction. The entire process takes about 15 minutes.

Mazur discovered that the percentage of correct student answers on the ConcepTest increased noticeably after just two minutes of peer discussion. Further, Crouch & Mazur (2001) report that student learning gains on the FCI are more than two times larger for peer instruction than for traditional courses.

The success of peer instruction is not surprising. Peer instruction cultivates disciplinary habits of mind by engaging students in activities that characterize the discipline. Students sketch graphs, solve conceptual problems, defend a view or position, and model physical systems with diagrams. Throughout the instruction, significant value is placed on peer-to-peer discussion and conceptual understanding, not on the coverage of topics (Meltzer & Manivannan, 2002).[9]

Interactive Lecture Demonstrations

Another alternative to the traditional lecture is the Interactive Lecture Demonstration (ILD). Here, the instructor describes a demonstration to be carried out, and then performs the experiment without collecting data. Students write down their predictions and share their ideas with a neighbor. Once verbal consensus is reached, written predictions are revised. Then, the instructor performs the experiment with the aid of computer-based probes and detectors. Real-time graphs (e.g., position, temperature, pressure, force, current, and voltage) are projected onto a large projection screen.[10] Students discuss the observations, and write down the results. The instructor facilitates a large group discussion, pointing out key concepts and principles, and discussing real-life applications. The proper interpretation of the data is not taken for granted; instead, it is the basis of a conversation between the students that leads to better understanding. This approach reflects the fundamental spirit of dialogue within the discipline.

The order and content of the ILD steps were carefully researched to optimize student learning (Sokoloff & Thornton, 1997). An example ILD is to join two rolling carts with a metal wire, such as a twist tie. Each end of the wire is attached to a force probe connected to the cart. Forces between the carts are measured for a variety of situations. The students are stunned to learn that the forces on the two probes are equal in magnitude, despite the motion of the system and relative mass of the carts. SoTL studies show that ILDs enhance student learning in mechanics, and in recent studies (Sokoloff & Thornton, 2001), student performance on the Force Motion Conceptual Evaluation test yielded normalized learning gains more than twice that of traditional courses.

Tutorials in Introductory Physics

Signature pedagogies have also been implemented in small- to medium-sized recitation sessions (N < 20) that provide an opportunity for students to review concepts, ask questions, and solve problems. These sessions are usually offered once a week, and are run by graduate TAs. Unfortunately, recitation sessions often degenerate into passive lectures (Redish, 2003, p. 144). To avoid this problem, the University of Washington has developed an alternative to the traditional recitation section, called Tutorials in Introductory Physics (McDermott & Shaffer, 2002). In this approach, students work through conceptual worksheets in three- to four-member groups. Most activities are done with paper and pencil, though occasionally a few simple laboratory items (e.g., batteries and bulbs) are needed. As the students work, one or more TAs wander around the classroom, engaging students in Socratic dialogue (Morse, 1994).

The University of Maryland independently researched the instructional effectiveness of Tutorials by examining student performance on paper and pencil tests for sixteen (16) university courses (Redish, Saul, & Steinberg, 1997). Treatment groups were taught with Tutorials, and control groups were taught with traditional recitations. Treatment groups showed 50%+ improvement over the control group.[11]

Tutorials are effective for two reasons. First, the activities are designed to address common student difficulties highlighted in physics education research. Standard textbook problems often do not promote a conceptual understanding. In fact, Kim and Pak (2001) found that student misconceptions persisted after solving over 1500 standard textbook problems. Second, high value is placed on student communication. Students actively discuss the problems with peers, and engage in Socratic dialogue with the instructor or graduate TAs. Koenig, Endorf, and Brown (2007) demonstrate that the use of Socratic dialogue to check answers is a crucial factor to the success of the method. Such experiences prepare students to think and interact like professional physicists.

Real-Time Physics

Sokoloff & Thornton (1997) developed Real-Time Physics (RTP) laboratories to replace traditional laboratory. Unlike traditional labs, RTPs are inductive; i.e., student learning begins with the phenomena and proceeds to the principles. Rather than confirming an equation already presented in lecture, the students build an understanding of physics one step at a time (Redish, 2003, p. 162).

Similar to ILDs, RTPs rely on a computer-based data collection analysis system, so students spend less time collecting data, and more time interpreting data. Students work in small groups through a carefully researched set of questions and activities. As students take measurements and discuss questions, an instructor or TA answers questions and sparks discussion. RTPs have been shown to produce significant student learning gains relative to traditional instruction (Wittmann, 2001). The largest learning gains are obtained by combining ILDs in lectures with RTPs in laboratories.

Conclusion

The physics education research (PER) literature is vast. For excellent reviews, see Gabel (1994) and McDermott & Redish (1999). Useful summaries are also found on the Web sites of major Physics Education Research groups, such as the University of Maryland and University of Washington. The literature explores a wide range of topics, including alternative student conceptions and epistemologies, problem solving, group learning, assessment, classroom technology, social and affective dimensions of learning, gender issues, and science teacher education.

The broad conclusion of SoTL studies in physics is that students in courses that use signature pedagogies outperform those in traditional courses. Specific and compelling evidence for this claim is given by Hake (1998). In a study of over 6,000 students in introductory physics, Hake found that students in courses that employ signature pedagogies (called "interactive engagement courses") achieved learning gains roughly two times larger than those in traditional courses, as measured by performance on the FCI.

The interpretation of this data has been discussed extensively in the literature (see Henderson, 2002, and references therein). Most concerns about the validity and reliability of the FCI have been addressed. The Hake study and other research suggest that traditional methods do not serve students well (McDermott, 1990; Redish, 2003). One source of the problem is student inactivity. Specifically, students fail to acquire the intellectual habits and skills of a physicist because they are not asked to perform like one. Looking in on a traditional classroom, one may wonder, as Zollman's (1996) eight-year-old daughter did, "Do they just sit there?"

SoTL studies suggest that when "who we are" as a discipline shows up in the classroom, the results for student learning are positive. Implications for undergraduate liberal education are evident: We should re-examine current methods of instruction in light of the nature of the discipline, and continue to evaluate new and existing methods of instruction using SoTL research.

References

Arizona State University (ASU). (2008). Modeling instruction program. Retrieved January 10, 2008, from http://modeling.asu.edu/

Beuckman, J., Rebello, S., & Zollman, D. (2007). Impact of a classroom interaction system on student learning. *Proceedings of the 2006 Physics Education Research Conference, 888*, 129–132.

Bruner, J. (1960). *The process of education.* Cambridge: Harvard University Press.

Calder, L. (2006). Uncoverage: Toward a signature pedagogy for the history survey. *Journal of American History, 92*(4), 1358–1370.

Camp, C., & Clement, J. (1994). *Preconceptions in mechanics.* Dubuque: Kendall/Hunt.

Crouch, C., & Mazur, E. (2001). Peer instruction: Ten years of experience and results. *American Journal of Physics, 69*, 970–977.

Gabel, D. (1994). *Handbook of research on science teaching and learning.* New York: Macmillan.

Halloun, I. (2004). Modeling theory of science education. Dordrecht: Kluwer.

Hake, R. (1998). Interactive-engagement vs. traditional methods: A six thousand student survey of mechanics test data for introductory physics courses. *American Journal of Physics, 66,* 64–74.

Helm, H., & Gilbert, J. (1985a). Thought experiments and physics education—part 1, *Physics Education, 20,* 124–131.

Helm, H., & Gilbert, J. (1985b). Thought experiments and physics education—part 2, *Physics Education, 20,* 211–217.

Henderson, C. (2002). Common concerns about the Force Concept Inventory. *The Physics Teacher, 40,* 542–547.

Hestenes, D. (1987). Toward a modeling theory of physics instruction. *American Journal of Physics, 55,* 440–454.

Hestenes, D., Wells, M., & Swackhamer, G. (1992). Force concept inventory. *The Physics Teacher, 30,* 141–153.

Kuhn, T. (1964). A function for thought experiments. Reprinted in T. Kuhn, *The Essential Tension.* Chicago: University of Chicago Press.

Jacobs, D. (2008). An alternative approach to general chemistry: Addressing the needs of at-risk students with cooperative learning strategies. Retrieved March 1, 2008, from http://gallery.carnegiefoundation.org/djacobs

Landis, C., Ellis, A., Lisensky, G., Lorenz, J., Meeker, K., & Wamser, C. (2001). *Chemistry ConcepTests: A pathway to interactive classrooms.* New York: Prentice Hall.

Lattery, M. (2001a). Thoughts experiments in physics education: A simple and practical example. *Science & Education, 10*(2), 485–492.

Lattery, M. (2001b). Student-directed projects: A full-immersion experience of science. *The Physics Teacher, 39*(3), 166–171.

Lattery, M. (2007). *Wisconsin Teaching Scholar final report: Research on student model formation and development.* University of Wisconsin Oshkosh (unpublished).

Lattery, M. (2008). The long decay model of one-dimensional projectile motion. *Science & Education, 17*(7), 779–798.

Laws, P. (1991). Calculus-based physics without lectures. *Physics Today, 12,* 24–31.

MacIsaac, D. (2008). Whiteboarding in the classroom. Retrieved January 10, 2008, from http://physicsed.buffalostate.edu/AZTEC/BP_WB/index.html

Matthews, M. (1994). *Science teaching: The role of history and philosophy of science.* New York: Routledge.

Mazur, P. (1997). *Peer instruction: A user's manual.* Upper Saddle River, NJ: Prentice Hall.

Meltzer, D., & Manivannan, K. (2002), Transforming the lecture-hall environment: The fully interactive physics lecture. *American Journal of Physics, 70,* 639–654.

McDermott, L. (1990). Millikan Lecture 1990: What we teach and what is learned: Closing the gap. *American Journal of Physics, 59,* 301–315.

McDermott, L. (2001). Oersted Medal Lecture 2001: Physics education research—The key to student learning. *American Journal of Physics, 69*(11), 1127–1137.

McDermott, L., & Redish, E. (1999). Resource letter on physics education research. *American Journal of Physics., 67*(9), 755–767.

McDermott, L., & Shaffer, P. (2002). *Tutorials in introductory physics.* Upper Saddle River, NJ: Prentice Hall.

Morse, R. (1994). The classic method of Mrs. Socrates. *The Physics Teacher, 32,* 276–277.

Nersessian, P. (1995). Should physicists preach what they practice? Constructive modeling in doing and learning physics. *Science & Education 4*(3), 203–226.

Reay, N. W., Bao, L., Li, P., Warnakulasooriya, R., & Baugh, G. (2005). Toward the effective use of voting machines in physics lectures. *American Journal of Physics, 73,* 554.

Redish, E., Saul, J., & Steinberg, R. (1997). On the effectiveness of active-engagement microcomputer-based laboratories. *American Journal of Physics, 65,* 45–54.

Redish, E. (2003). *Teaching physics with the physics suite.* New York: Wiley.

Schmitt, J., & Lattery, M. (2004). *Facilitation discourse in the physics classroom.* NCREL Annual Conference, March 11, 2004. Retrieved July 2, 2008, from http://planck.phys.uwosh.edu/lattery/_docs/art_mm_fac.pdf

Shulman, L. (2005). Signature pedagogies in the professions. *Daedalus, 134,* 52–59.

Smith, T., & Wittmann, M. (2007). On teaching Newton's third law: Comparing three methods for teaching Newton's third law. *Physical Review Special Topics Physics Education Research, 3,* 020105.

Sokoloff, D., & Thornton, R. (1997). Using interactive lecture demonstrations to create an active learning environment. *The Physics Teacher, 35,* 340–347.

Sokoloff, D., & Thornton, R. (2001). *Interactive Lecture Demonstrations.* New York: Wiley.

Snow, C. (1993/1959). *Two Cultures.* Cambridge: Cambridge University Press.

U.S. Department of Education (2002). Promising and exemplary program in science (1-2001). Retrieved from http://www.ed.gov/offices/OERI/ORAD/KAD/expert_panel/math-science.html

Wells, M., Hestenes, D., & Swackhamer, G. (1995). A modeling method for high school physics instruction. *American Journal of Physics*, 64, 114–119.

Wittmann, M. (2001). Real-time physics dissemination project: Evaluation at test sites. Talk presented at U. of Oregon, October 23, 1999. Retrieved 2003 from http://perlnet.umephy.maine.edu/research/RTPevaluation1.pdf.

Zollman, D. (1996). Do they just sit there? Reflections on helping students to learning physics. *American Journal of Physics, 64,* 114–119.

Notes

1. Recent research in cosmology suggests that this list is incomplete.

2. As Ernest Rutherford (discoverer of the nuclear atom) once put it, "All science is either physics or stamp collecting."

3. My graduate research advisor and I spent hours discussing physics and the details of our research together; twice we ate Thanksgiving dinner together!

4. By this measure, the Ptolemaic model is exceedingly powerful.

5. The Standard Model describes the phenomena of electromagnetism, radioactivity, and nuclear interactions.

6. Einstein's various stories about trains in a lightning storm are nice examples of story telling. His stories helped the physics community come to grips with relativity. The power of *storytelling* strongly connects physics with the humanities.

7. It is an interesting fact that many early papers in physics were written as dialogue between characters in a play (e.g., Sagredo and Simplicio in the *Two Sciences*).

8. For greater detail (except the very first example), see Redish (2003).

9. Similar approaches have been studied in introductory chemistry (e.g. Landis, Ellis, Lisensky, Lorenz, Meeker, & Wamser, 2001; Jacobs, 2008).

10. By "real-time," we mean that there is no noticeable time delay between the measured event and the display of the data.

11. Smith and Wittmann (2007) compare three tutorials designed to improve student understanding of Newton's third law: (1) *Tutorials in Introductory Physics* (University of Washington), (2) *Activity-Based Tutorials* (University of Maryland), and (3) *Open Source Tutorials*.

ABOUT THE AUTHORS

Denise Bartell is an associate professor in human development at the University of Wisconsin–Green Bay. She has a Ph.D. in human development and family sciences from the University of Texas at Austin. Her primary areas of research are mate selection in young adults and the influence of college experiences on development in young adulthood.

Angela Bauer-Dantoin is chair of the Human Biology Program and an associate professor of human biology, biology and women's studies at the University of Wisconsin–Green Bay. She holds a bachelor's degree in psychology and neuroscience from Lawrence University (1988) and a Ph.D. in neuroscience from Northwestern University (1992). She joined the faculty at UW–Green Bay in 1997, after conducting postdoctoral studies in molecular endocrinology at Harvard Medical School and Northwestern Medical School. Currently, Dr. Bauer-Dantoin teaches undergraduate courses at UW–Green Bay in the areas of reproductive biology, endocrinology, women's health, and diversity issues in the sciences. In addition to directing an undergraduate research program investigating the impact of hormone mimics on the function of a variety of endocrine systems, Dr. Bauer-Dantoin is active in the field of SoTL. Foci of her current SoTL studies include the benefits of active learning strategies in science courses for majors vs. non-majors, and the impact of diversity courses in the sciences on students' attitudes toward race and their awareness of racial dynamics.

Nancy L. Chick is an associate professor of English at the University of Wisconsin–Barron County, where she teaches literature, composition, and women's studies. She is also the director of the University of Wisconsin's Wisconsin Teaching Scholars Program and member of the board of directors for the International Society for the Scholarship of Teaching and Learning (ISSOTL), as well as the editor of *The International Commons*, the ISSOTL newsletter. She has published literary scholarship on various multicultural women writers; pedagogical articles on engaging affective learning through poetry, feminist pedagogy, and teaching diversity through literature; and SoTL on literary complexity, misconceptions in literary studies, and diversity learning. She is currently writing a book that expands this book's chapter on signature pedagogies in literary studies.

Diane Christie teaches computer science and serves as the program director of the Applied Math and Computer Science (AMCS) Program at the University of Wisconsin–Stout. She has published lab manuals and student solution manuals for several introductory text books. She is active in the scholarship of teaching and learning movement and has published her research in the *Teaching Professor* and on the Web. Prior to her career in academia, Diane worked in research and development at Cray Research, Inc. She received her Ph.D. from the University of Minnesota.

Gary Don is an associate professor of music theory in the Department of Music and Theatre Arts at the University of Wisconsin–Eau Claire. He holds a Ph.D. in music theory from the University of Washington, where he taught theory and aural skills. He has also taught at Skidmore College. His research interests include music theory pedagogy, Goethe's influence on music theorists of the 19th and 20th centuries, overtone structures in the music of Debussy, and modality in the music of Prokofiev. He has presented papers on these topics at the West Coast Conference of Theory and Analysis, Music Theory Midwest, the Great Lakes Chapter and national conferences of the College Music Society, and at national meetings of the Society for Music Theory. He has published articles in *Computer Music Journal, In Theory Only, Perspectives of New Music*, and *Music Theory Spectrum.*

Kathryn Ernie, professor of mathematics at the University of Wisconsin–River Falls, received her Ph.D. from the University of Minnesota in 1979. A major focus of her research is the integration of technology in the teaching of mathematics. Kathryn was instrumental in the establishment of a technology-enhanced mathematics education classroom, the incorporation of computer lab sessions into calculus and mathematics courses for future elementary and middle school teachers, and the development of culturally relevant teaching materials for the curriculum. Kathryn has been recognized with two distinguished teaching awards by the College of Arts and Sciences. Her current research focuses on the study of multiple representations on conceptual understanding and generalization. This research was presented at the first contributed paper session on SoTL in Undergraduate Mathematics at the Joint Conference of the MAA and the AMS in 2007. Currently, Kathryn is coordinator of the university's SoTL Project Infusing K–12 Exemplars in Pre-service Content Courses.

Eri Fujieda is assistant professor of sociology at the University of Wisconsin–Superior, where she teaches a wide range of sociology courses. She has a doctorate in sociology from the University of Illinois at Urbana-Champaign, and her areas of research include the political economy of globalization, the impact of global processes on gender and race relations, and transnational feminist pedagogy. Her engagement with SoTL became deeper when, as a 2006–07 Wisconsin Teaching Fellow, she investigated the pedagogical value of an interview-analysis assignment in an introductory sociology course.

Christa Garvey, oboist, joined the University of Wisconsin–Eau Claire, where she teaches applied oboe, chamber music, and aural skills, in the fall of 2003. She is an active performer and a member of the Wisconsin Woodwind Quintet, Sonora Reed Trio, and the Eau Claire Chamber Orchestra. She previously served on the faculty of the Metropolitan State College of Denver and was a Visiting Lecturer of Oboe and Musicology at the Lionel Hampton School of Music at the University of Idaho. Dr. Garvey has performed with the Colorado Symphony Orchestra, the Colorado Ballet Orchestra, the Cheyenne, WY Symphony, the Colorado MahlerFest Orchestra, the Boulder Bach Festival, and the Aspen Music Festival. Dr. Garvey holds a Doctor of Musical Arts degree in Oboe Performance and Pedagogy from the University of Colorado at Boulder. While at CU, she was the College of Music winner for a campus-wide Creative Work Award for a dissertation project, developed an oboe method book, and received grant funding for research in the Czech Republic to study the manuscript scores and correspondence of Bohuslav Martinu. Her undergraduate degree was received from Indiana University, Bloomington.

Helen R. Klebesadel earned an M.F.A. in visual art from UW–Madison in 1989, where she also studied and taught women's studies. Like other visual artists in the academy, her primary research is her visual art. She considers her painting to be her "research in women's studies." She is best known for richly detailed narrative watercolor paintings that explore environmental and women-centered themes. Klebesadel periodically curates exhibitions that explore diverse voices and issues in contemporary art. Helen has taught courses and workshops on creativity, studio art, and the contemporary women's art movement for two decades. Klebesadel's experiences informed the writing of a chapter entitled "Re-Framing Studio Art Critique and Practice," which she contributed to the recently published book *New Museum Theory: An Introduction*. An associate professor, she taught studio art and gender studies at Lawrence University for a decade before leaving in 2000 to accept the position of director of the University of Wisconsin System's Women's Studies Consortium. Her art and prose have been published in *Frontiers, Feminist Studies,* and *CALYX*. She is a past national president of the Women's Caucus for Art. Helen Klebesadel's artwork can be seen at http://Klebesadel.com.

Cary Komoto received his Ph.D., M.A., and B.S. in geography at the University of Minnesota. He is a professor of geography at the University of Wisconsin–Barron County and for the University of Wisconsin Colleges Online Program. He joined the faculty at UW–Barron County in 1991. He teaches a wide range of geography courses from Introduction to Cultural Geography to Physical Geography. Since 1998 he has taught physical geography for the UW Colleges Online Program. Currently he is the chair of the UW Colleges Geography and Geology Department and also serves as the chair of all UW Colleges academic department chairs.

Lisa Kornetsky is director of the Office of Professional and Instructional Development (OPID) for the University of Wisconsin System. Her work is directed at meeting the professional development needs for faculty and instructional staff at 15 institutions and 26 campuses. OPID administers a series of programs focused on student learning, the scholarship of teaching, and faculty roles and rewards. In this position, Lisa has given numerous workshops and presentations to statewide audiences, and has written and presented on faculty development in Wisconsin to National and International audiences. Lisa received her B.A. from Hampshire College and her M.F.A. in theater from the University of Massachusetts, Amherst. Prior to her move to the UW System administration, she was associate professor of dramatic arts at the University of Wisconsin–Parkside, where she also served as department chair. Like other theater faculty, her scholarly activity has been her creative activity. She has directed at UW–Parkside, the Piccolo-Spoleto festival, and the Edinburgh Theatre Festival, and she is a founding member of the Upstart Theatre in Racine, Wisconsin. She will be returning to her faculty role in the fall of 2008 to resume her career as a teacher/director, where she is very excited to explore SoTL in performance.

Mark Lattery is an associate professor of physics at the University of Wisconsin–Oshkosh. He holds a Ph.D. in experimental high-energy physics from the University of Minnesota. His current areas of research interest include physics education and the history of physics. Lattery is particularly interested in connections between the history of physics and student learning with respect to scientific modeling. He is director of the Modeling Dynamics Program (funded by the Spencer Foundation) and the recent president of the Wisconsin Association of Physics Teachers. In 2006, Lattery was named as a UW-System Wisconsin Teaching Fellow (2006–2007).

Rebecca LeDocq received her Ph.D. in 1991 from the University of Iowa. Since then, she has been a member of the Mathematics Department at the University of Wisconsin–La Crosse, where she is currently an associate professor. In addition to publishing papers on her research in commutative ring theory, Rebecca has been actively involved in faculty governance, and has played an integral part in the creation of a writing-in-the-major program within her department. In recent years, she has been involved in research and projects focusing on the use of new technologies to enhance student learning, faculty development issues involving technology, and pre-service teacher education. Her current interests include the development of the Technological Pedagogical Content Knowledge (TPACK) of pre-service teachers.

Rebecca Meacham is the author of the award-winning story collection *Let's Do* (UNT Press, 2004). She has published numerous short stories, book reviews, and encyclopedia entries, as well as scholarly articles on race in the college classroom and on African American writers. She received her M.F.A. in fiction from Bowling Green State University and her doctorate from the University of Cincinnati. She is an associate professor of English, humanistic studies, and women's studies at the University of Wisconsin–Green Bay, where she teaches courses in creative writing, American fiction, women's memoir, and ethnic American literature.

Blaine F. Peden is a professor in the Department of Psychology at the University of Wisconsin–Eau Claire. He completed a baccalaureate degree at Fresno State College and a doctoral degree at Indiana University. He has taught research methods since 1975. He performs collaborative research with undergraduates presented at professional conferences. Early interests and publications included topics in animal learning and behavior such as autoshaping, learned performance in open and closed economies, and foraging. More recent interests and publications include teaching and learning about research methods, critical thinking, group matching, virtual research ethics, online courses, scientific writing, teaching with technology, and the scholarship of teaching and learning.

Mitra Sadeghpour, soprano, is associate professor of music and theatre arts at the University of Wisconsin–Eau Claire, where she teaches applied voice, directs the opera program, and is coordinator of the voice and choral area. An active performer and scholar, her research has ranged from SOTL projects on practice habits of college voice students and creating a learner-centered environment in opera workshop to lecture-performances on women's roles in contemporary American opera and an in-depth analysis and semi-staging of Libby Larsen's song cycle, "Try Me, Good King: Last Words of the Wives of Henry VIII." She has recently stage directed the operas *Dido and Aeneas*, *The Merry Widow*, *Suor Angelica and Gianni Schicchi*, and *Cinderella*. Dr. Sadeghpour is an active member of the National Association of Teachers of Singing (NATS) and National Opera Association (NOA); she has presented poster sessions and panel discussions at NATS, NOA, and ISSOTL conferences, and has participated in the NATS Intern program. She holds bachelor's degrees from Luther College in music and theater, and she completed the Master of Music and the Doctor of Music degrees at the Indiana University Jacobs School of

Music, where her dissertation examined the English songs of French composer Charles Gounod.

Sherrie Serros, professor of mathematics at the University of Wisconsin–Eau Claire, received her Ph.D. in 1986 from the University of Wisconsin–Milwaukee. Since that time she has been actively involved in gender issues in mathematics and served as a Distinguished Visiting Professor of Women and Science in an NSF-sponsored program of the UW System. Sherrie served as the director of the Teaching Excellence Center at UW–Platteville and has given numerous professional development presentations for faculty at the state and national level. In recent years, her interests have focused on pre-service and in-service teacher education in both Kentucky and Wisconsin. Her current specific interests include the development of communication skills for pre-service teachers and the use of new technologies to enhance learning.

Joel Sipress is a professor of history at the University of Wisconsin–Superior. He received his Ph.D. in U.S. history from the University of North Carolina at Chapel Hill. His research interests include the social and political history of the American South. He is currently researching the resistance of the Wisconsin Ojibwe to the policy of Indian Removal. His involvement in the scholarship of teaching and learning began as a participant in the Wisconsin Teaching Fellows Program, during which explored the difficulties students have understanding the relationship between assertions and evidence in historical discourse.

Dr. Simei Tong is an associate professor of mathematics at University of Wisconsin–Eau Claire. Her research area includes functional analysis, convex geometry, and applied mathematics. She published papers on Lp spaces in Banach space theory of functional analysis. In recent years she has been working on topics in analytic methods in convex geometry and applied mathematics such as optimal solutions of transportation models in emergency evacuations. Simei is passionate about scholarship of teaching and learning (SoTL) in mathematics. She is inspired by many ideas and practical methods in pursuing high quality of student learning in mathematics. She has involved in SoTL activities for many years and she also led a group of 14 colleagues from her mathematics department to do an SoTL project in three different areas: cooperative learning in introduction-level math courses, transition to abstract mathematics learning, and technology in mathematics learning. She was asked to present the project result at the National Mathematical Joint Meetings in 2008.

Kristin M. Vespia is an assistant professor of human development, psychology, and women's studies at the University of Wisconsin–Green Bay. She holds a Ph.D. in counseling psychology from the University of Iowa, and she currently teaches courses on counseling theory, multicultural counseling, and psychological testing. She is a 2007–08 Wisconsin Teaching Fellow who has presented and published work in the areas of faculty development and the scholarship of teaching and learning. She is particularly interested in the ways in which education might influence the development of multicultural competence. She has also published articles or book chapters related to counselor training and supervision, college student mental health services, and the ways in which culture can inform our understanding of topics such as vocational psychology and mental illness.

David J. Voelker (Ph.D., University of North Carolina at Chapel Hill, 2003) teaches history and humanities at the University of Wisconsin–Green Bay. In 2006–07, he participated in the Wisconsin Teaching Fellows program of the University of Wisconsin System. His scholarship of teaching and learning focuses on encouraging and assessing historical thinking in large introductory courses. He also writes on the history of politics and religion in the early American republic.

Michel Wattiaux (pronounced "Watt-ee-oh") is an associate professor in the Department of Dairy Science at the University of Wisconsin–Madison with a 70% teaching and 30% research appointment. He earned an M.S. in animal sciences from the Université Catholique de Louvain, Belgium (1983) and a Ph.D. in dairy science from the University of Wisconsin–Madison (1990). Michel's disciplinary research focuses on improvement of dairy farm management in a way that fosters the social, economical and environmental soundness of production systems. Michel has gained an international reputation as an educator and received the 2002 International Dairy Production Award of the American Dairy Science Association for a series of technical dairy books published in six languages. As an assistant professor Michel engaged in the scholarship of teaching and learning, he created five new courses and published his research on students' perception of classroom learning environment. In addition, Michel was a Wisconsin Teaching Fellow and he chaired the UW–Madison Teaching Academy. In 2006, he was promoted and tenured on the basis of excellence in teaching. The same year Michel was the recipient of the UW-Madison Chancellor's Distinguished Teaching Award. In 2008, he received the Jung Teaching Award of the UW–Madison College of Agriculture and Life Sciences. Currently, Michel teaches five courses and co-teaches College Classroom: Teaching in Science and Engineering, which introduces graduate students to teaching and learning issues.

Carmen R. Wilson VanVoorhis is professor of psychology at the University of Wisconsin–La Crosse. She earned an M.A. and Ph.D. in counseling psychology from Iowa State University and began teaching at UW–La Crosse in 1996. She teaches a wide variety of courses including Abnormal Psychology, Child and Adolescent Psychopathology, Counseling Theories and Methods, Empathic Listening, Research Methods, and Psychological Measurement. Her most recent research interests in the scholarship of teaching and learning include the value of active learning exercises in statistics courses, the relationship between the wording of short-answer test questions and student performance, and reflection activities to maximize the study abroad experience. Carmen has also participated in several Lesson Studies, a process developed in primary schools in Japan where a team of instructors develops, delivers, observes, and evaluates a single lesson in a particular course.

INDEX